Women and Redemption

# Women and Redemption

## A Theological History

Rosemary Radford Ruether

FORTRESS PRESS
MINNEAPOLIS

WOMEN AND REDEMPTION
A Theological History



Book and cover design by Joseph Bonyata.

Author Photo: EPS Studios, Evanston

---

Library of Congress Cataloging-in-Publication Data

Ruether, Rosemary Radford
Women and Redemption : a theological history / Rosemary Radford Ruether
p. cm.
Includes bibliographical references.
ISBN 0-8006-2947-7 (hardcover : alk. paper). — ISBN 0-8006-2945-0 (pbk. : alk. paper)
1. Woman (Christian theology)—History of doctrines.
2. Redemption—History of Doctrines. 3. Feminist theology.
I. Title
BT704.R835 1998
230'082—dc21 98–11783
CIP

---

The paper used in this publication meets the minimum requirements of American National Standards for Information Sciences—Permanence of Paper for Printed Library Materials, ANSI Z329.48-1984.

---

Manufactured in the U.S.A. AF1-2945 (paper) AF1-2947 (hardcover)

02 01 00 99 98 1 2 3 4 5 6 7 8 9 10

*This book is dedicated to my sister,*
*Rebecca Radford Fleming,*
*friend and teacher of Scripture*

# Contents


List of Illustrations ix

Acknowledgments xi

Introduction 1

1. In Christ No More Male and Female? The Question of Gender and Redemption in the New Testament 13
   - Gender Equality in the First Jesus Movement 14
   - From Reassembled Jesus Movement to Early Hellenistic Mission 21
   - Jewish and Early Christian Readings of Genesis 24
   - Redemption and Gender in Conflict in Pauline Churches 30
   - Gender and Redemption in Two Forms of Pauline Churches 38

2. Gender and Redemption in the Patristic Era: Conflicting Perspectives 45
   - Trajectories of Early Christianity 45
   - Gender and Redemption in Some Second-Century Christianities 51
   - Two Late Patristic Syntheses: Gregory of Nyssa and Augustine 62

3. Male Scholastics and Women Mystics in Medieval Theology 79
   - Hildegard of Bingen 81
   - Thomas Aquinas 92
   - Mechthild of Magdeburg 97
   - Julian of Norwich 104

4. MALE REFORMERS, FEMINIST HUMANISTS, AND QUAKERS IN THE REFORMATION 113
Gender in the Theological Anthropology of Luther and Calvin 117
Renaissance Feminism and the Debate about Women 127
Women in Radical Protestantism 135

5. SHAKERS AND FEMINIST ABOLITIONISTS IN NINETEENTH-CENTURY NORTH AMERICA 147
The Shaker Tradition: From England to North America 148
Abolitionist Feminists 160

6. FEMINIST THEOLOGIES IN TWENTIETH-CENTURY WESTERN EUROPE 179
Feminist Theology and German Protestantism 179
Feminist Theology and Catholicism 190
Kari Elisabeth Børresen 190
Catharina Halkes 193
Mary Grey 198
European Feminist Theology in the 1990s 202

7. FEMINIST, WOMANIST, AND MUJERISTA THEOLOGIES IN TWENTIETH-CENTURY NORTH AMERICA 209
Letty Russell 211
Mary Daly 215
Rosemary Ruether 221
Carter Heyward 224
Delores Williams 229
Ada María Isasi-Díaz 234

8. FEMINIST THEOLOGIES IN LATIN AMERICA, AFRICA, AND ASIA 241
Feminist Theology in Latin America 245
African Feminist Theology 254
Asian Feminist Theologies 262

CONCLUSIONS 273
NOTES 283
INDEX 359

# List of Illustrations

1. *Orante.* Scenes from the life of a deceased woman in the chamber of the "Velatio." Early Christian fresco, second half of the third century, C.E. Catacomb of Priscilla, Rome, Italy. Scala/Art Resource, N.Y.

2. Icon of Saint Macrina, the Cappadocian ascetic, architect of a female monastic community, and ascetic inspiration to her brothers Gregory and Basil.

3. Hildegard of Bingen receiving her revelations. Manuscript illumination by Hildegard of Bingen. Copyright © Beltz Verlag, Weinheim und Basel, Programm Beltz & Gelberg.

4. Quaker Woman Preacher, from print after painting by Egbert van Heemskerk. From *VisionaryWomen: Ecstatic Prophecy in Seventeenth-Century England,* Phyllis Mack. Copyright © The Regents of the University of California.

5. Statue of Lucretia Mott, Susan B. Anthony, and Elizabeth Cady Stanton by Adelaide Johnson, donated to the U.S. Congress by the Women's Party in 1921 to celebrate the victory of women's suffrage. The inscription hails the victory as "one of the great bloodless revolutions of all time that liberated more people than any other without killing a single person." Copyright © *Chicago Tribune.*

6. *Christa,* Edwina Sandys. Copyright © Edwina Sandys, 1974; Bronze (54" x 40" x 8").

7. *Creation,* Sergio Velasquez. Nicaraguan Cultural Center.

8. *Kwan In.* Painting used by Chung Hyun Kyung in her multimedia presentation for the WCC assembly in Canberra to illustrate her image of the Holy Spirit.

# Acknowledgments

THIS BOOK REPRESENTS OVER THIRTY YEARS OF research and teaching across the fields of patristics, medieval and Reformation historical theology, nineteenth-century American religious thought, and twentieth-century feminist theologies in Western Europe, the United States, Latin America, Asia, and Africa. It has also benefited from many trips to Western Europe, Latin America, Asia, and Africa to dialogue with feminist theologians of these areas. Many colleagues have read parts of this manuscript in the areas of their expertise and provided helpful feedback. I wish to thank particularly Antoinette Wire, Diane Tracey, Kari Børresen, Mary Grey, Dorothee Soelle, Catharina Halkes, Herta Leistner, Letty Russell, Carter Heyward, Delores Williams, Ada María Isasi-Díaz, María Pilar Aquino, and Kathleen O'Brien Wicker. I thank Garrett-Evangelical Theological Seminary, which supported the sabbatical leave to work on this book, and the Religion Department of the University of Bristol and Claremont Theological School, where I wrote parts of this book as a visiting scholar.

# Introduction

ARE WOMEN REDEEMED BY CHRIST? Central to Christianity is the claim that "in Christ there is no more male and female," but what does this mean in the Christian tradition? An equal opportunity for happiness with God in life after death? Liberation from sexist oppression in society? If women are equally redeemed by Christ, why has the Christian church continually reinforced sexism in society and in the church? These are some of the questions this study seeks to answer.

Answers to these questions have changed in Christian history. These changes are relative to the way women are defined in creation or "original nature" and in the "fall" or the consequences of sin. Were women created equal or subordinate in God's original intention for creation? Are women more, less, or equally culpable for sin? Are women the primary sinners or the primary ones who have been sinned against? Changing answers to these questions alter how redemption is defined in relation to women.

In this study of women and redemption I trace historically these changing paradigms of gender, male and female, in relation to the Christian claim of a universal and inclusive redemption in Christ. The story necessarily begins with Jesus, because "something happened" in his ministry that suggested to some early Christians that gender relations had been changed by redemption. This does not mean that there was some pristine moment when all women and men were equal and exercised an equal ministry in the earliest Christian church. But some women exercised leadership and prophetic teaching in some early Christian churches, and this was supported by some men in these Christian communities as an expression of their faith in a "new humanity" that overcomes gender hierarchy.

But these practices and ideas sparked controversy and opposition. Some early Christians formulated fuller theological justifications of these changes, while others sought to refute these theories and repress such practices to shore up continued patriarchal relations as normative for the Christian church and family. The New Testament literature, as well as early noncanonical gospels, reflects this struggle in early Christianity over the significance of redemption in Christ for gender relations in the church and in society.

The canonical envelope of the New Testament[1] obscures the conflict by seeking to impose the decisive answer that women were created second, sinned first, and are to keep silence in church, to be saved by subordination and childbearing; but alternative views and practices on women's roles continued. Successive generations of Christian theologians have addressed this question anew. This process continues in conflicting views of gender in the church, family, and society between feminist and patriarchal Christians today. This book seeks to provide a historical framework for evaluating this conflict over the fundamental meaning of the Christian gospel for gender relations.

The first paradigm by which some early Christians sought to justify the dissolution of gender hierarchy in redemption drew on Hellenistic Jewish speculations about the original creation of the human by God in pregendered spiritual unity. The Gen. 1:27b text that defined humanity as created "male and female" was thus seen as a second stage of creation, one that expressed a fall into sin and death, necessitating sexual dimorphism, sex, and reproduction. Redemption reversed this later fallen stage of creation, returning to the original unity in which there is "no more male and female." Some early Christians defined a theology of baptism in which this restoration to pregendered unity happens when the baptized are incorporated into a redeemed humanity "in Christ."

Other early Christian leaders, however, notably Saint Paul, rejected this theology of "baptismal realized eschatology" and insisted that marriage and traditional gender relations are to continue in the Christian community even after baptism. Although the new humanity in Christ has been assumed spiritually, physically, and morally, we are still "in sin." Some expressions of women's leadership were accepted by Paul but in a framework that muted any challenge to traditional relations in the family. The full realization of redemption in Christ, in which gender hierarchy will be dissolved and there will be "no more marrying and giving in marriage," was reserved by Paul for an eschatological completion of redemption that is imminent but still future.

Paul's argument against a theology of baptismal realized eschatology in which gender hierarchy is dissolved here and now was reinforced in the post-Pauline tradition recorded in the New Testament. Here traditional patriarchal relations, which mandated that wives are to obey their husbands, slaves their masters, and children their parents, were shored up. This early Christian argument for continued patriarchy in the church culminated in the theology of creation and fall in 1 Timothy, which claims that women's original subordination in creation has been redoubled as punishment for their primacy in sin. Only by strict adherence to this double subordination of creation and fall can women be saved.

But this argument in Timothy was itself posed over against communities of radical Christians who continued an alternative early Christian view that gender hierarchy is already dissolved in redemption. Christian conversion means entering into a new status of spiritual equality, expressed in renunciation of marriage and sexuality for the virginal state. The spiritual state restored in Christ not only anticipates the heavenly redeemed state in which there will be no more marrying and giving in marriage; it also is expressed here and now in the empowering of women to leave subordination in the family, to travel as itinerant preachers, to prophesy and heal as charismatic leaders of the church.

The repression of several variant theories and practices of eschatological equality in Christ by those churchmen who emerged as definers of Christian orthodoxy was expressed in two major versions in the Greek and Latin Christian worlds. The Eastern or Greek Orthodox view is found in the theology of spirituality of the fourth-century church father, Gregory of Nyssa. This is based on a theory of prefallen spiritual unity of humanity before the fall into gender dimorphism. The fall brought the mortal body, sin, and death, and so necessitated sexual dimorphism, sex, and reproduction as the remedy for mortality. But with Christ this era of the fallen mortal body is coming to a close and humanity can return through celibacy to its original pregendered virginal state. Women too can participate as equals in this ascent to spiritual unity and communion with God, but as women they can exercise no external social authority in society or the church.

Saint Augustine in the late fourth and early fifth centuries enunciated the version of orthodox theology that would remain normative for the Latin West through the Reformation. Augustine accepted the development that had taken place in some Eastern church fathers whereby the human soul in women as well as in men was made in the image of God in a nongendered spiritual form. Thus woman's soul possesses the same potential for redemption as that of man. But, for Augustine, male and female bodies, sex, and reproduction did not come about through the fall but were part of God's original design for creation. Qua female, woman was created subordinate to man for the purposes of sex and procreation.

This subordination of women to men as husband and wife in marriage and reproduction was intended by God from the beginning. Although sexual dimorphism, sex, reproduction, and female subordination were part of the original order of creation, these things have been worsened through sin. In the fall humanity lost its original spiritual union with God, which brought a fall into mortality, a corruption of sex into lust, and the bondage of the will by which humans are unable to obey God of their own free will.

Due to the fall, women's subordination has been worsened into coercive servitude, which women must accept as their special punishment for sin. This continues even for Christian virginal women in the church, although, when the created order is dissolved in a future heavenly world beyond sin and death, this subordination in creation, worsened as punishment for sin, will be overcome. Then women will be spiritually equal with men according to their inner virtues.

This Augustinian view was accepted with slight variations by the Latin theological tradition found in Thomas Aquinas and was continued in the Reformation theologies of Martin Luther and John Calvin. Some medieval woman theologians and mystics, however, began to change the symbolic meaning of female gender in relation to God and Christ. For the classical Christian tradition found in Augustine and Aquinas, maleness and spirituality are equated. Women as women cannot be made in the image of God or represent Christ because God and Christ are male, and maleness represents rationality, spirituality, and the divine. So women can be included in the image of God restored in Christ only in a sex-neutered form.

Some medieval women mystics began to shift gender symbolism for God and Christ to include femaleness, thereby changing the assumptions that femaleness as such cannot be theomorphic or christomorphic. They drew on metaphors for God from the Wisdom tradition, which personified God as female, particularly in divine roles of self-manifestation as the "second person" of God through which the world is created, sustained, and redeemed.[2] As creator and redeemer God can be imaged as sophiological and so as female-like. Also Christ in his incarnation takes on the vulnerable body. Women as representatives of the vulnerable body thus can be seen as Christlike in relation to Christ's incarnation and suffering.

This inclusion of female metaphors for God and Christ began to shift the assumptions that women as women are not Godlike and Christlike. But these developments, which culminated in the thought of the fourteenth-century English mystic Julian of Norwich, did not change gender relations of office in church or society. Their spirituality continued to be linked with celibacy and spiritual ascent by which women or men may anticipate the heavenly state in which there is no more marrying or giving in marriage.

The next major paradigm shift was begun by a feminist humanist in the sixteenth century and developed by the Quakers in the seventeenth century, although it would not become a movement for social transformation until modern feminist theology in the nineteenth and twentieth centuries. Agrippa von Nettesheim, in his treatise on *Female Preeminence* (1509), enunciated several major components of an incipient feminist paradigm. He argued that women were created equally in the image of God with men in regard to their spiritual souls. But he drew on the Wisdom tradition of medieval mysticism and rediscovered Jewish Kabbalism[3] to argue that, as female, women were superior to men, reflecting the Wisdom nature of God and so more attuned to life and virtue.

Agrippa argued further that the domination of men over women is neither

God's original design for creation nor punishment for female priority in sin, but rather reflects the propensity of men to injustice and tyranny. Christ restored women to equality and gave them equal leadership in the church, but men refused to accept this and have distorted the message of Christ to justify the continued subordination of women in the church and in society. For Agrippa women's full equality in public life, including political leadership, simply reflects what is due women according to their nature. This has been reaffirmed by Christ but prevented by tyrannical men who have denied women education and participation in cultural and political life and socialized women to accept this situation by training them from childhood to be submissive.

Nothing as strong as Agrippa's view would be published, as far as I know, until the advent of modern feminism with writers such as Mary Wollstonecraft at the end of the eighteenth century.[4] But Quakers and some English feminist humanists in the seventeenth century picked up some aspects of his view. The Quakers particularly took over the idea that an original equality of men and women in creation was, through sin, turned into usurpation of power of some over others. Male domination thus is a manifestation of sin. Equality of men and women has been restored in Christ, who mandated that women as much as men should be prophetic evangelists of the gospel. Those who would silence women in church are the "seed of Satan" who continue the fallen state of humanity that has not yet received the "inner light" of the redemptive Spirit.

The Quakers translated their theology of original and restored gender equality into a participation of women in missionary work, preaching, and ministry in Quaker meetings. But they did not inaugurate a struggle for women's equality in public society, because their sectarian view of the non-Quaker realm as an expression of the fallen world disposed them to withdraw from, rather than participate in, public political life.

This sectarian stance was challenged, however, in nineteenth-century America by several abolitionist feminists, particularly Sarah and Angelina Grimké and Lucretia Mott, who united the Quaker theology of creation restored in the Spirit with American democratic thought. These foremothers of American feminism not only inaugurated the struggle for women's civil rights in American society that would be carried on by their younger colleagues, Susan B. Anthony and Elizabeth Cady Stanton, to the beginning of the twentieth century, but they also did so on biblical and theological grounds.

For the Grimké sisters and Lucretia Mott, humans—male and female—were created to stand side by side as equals in all respects—mentally, morally, and socially. The domination of men over women is in no way God's original plan for creation or the fruit of female sin but rather reflects the propensity to domination that was and continues to be the primary expression of sin. All forms of human injustice and violence—subordination of women, the enslavement of blacks to whites, and war—flow from this basic sinful tendency to domination of some over others. This has been expressed primarily by powerful white males, although white women have too often collaborated with this sin by acquiescing in their own oppression or in that of others, such as enslaved blacks, and by cheering on the drums of war.

Redemption for these nineteenth-century American feminists meant not only the restoration of women to interpersonal equality with men but also the transformation of social and legal systems that have denied women's rights, perpetuated slavery, and waged war. Redemption is realized, not primarily in an otherworldly escape from the body and the finite world, but by transforming the world and society into personal and social relations of justice and peace between all humans. This is the true message of Christ and the gospel. The churches have betrayed Christ by preaching a theology of female silencing and subordination.

The understanding of creation, sin, and redemption begun by these nineteenth-century feminists was reinvented and developed by the new wave of feminist theology that began in Western Europe and in North America in the 1960s after more than half a century of eclipse. Contemporary Christian feminist theology builds on certain basic assumptions. One of these is rejection of any theological or sociobiological justifications of women's subordination as due to some combination of (1) natural inferiority, (2) a divine mandate that women be subordinate in the order of creation, and (3) punishment for their priority in sin. Women's full and equal humanity with men and their right to equal access to education, professions, and political participation in society are assumed.

The classical justifications of women's subordination as due to natural inferiority, subordination in the order of creation, and punishment for sin are assumed to be false ideologies constructed to justify injustice. The domination of men over women is sinful, and patriarchy is a sinful social system. Far from reflecting the true will of God and the nature of women, such theological constructions subvert God's creation and distort human nature. Feminist theology is about the deconstruction of these ideological justifications of male domination and the vindication of women's equality as the true will of God, human nature, and Christ's redemptive intention.

Redemption in modern feminism follows a modern Western cultural shift from otherworldly to this-worldly hope. Redemption is not primarily about being reconciled with a God from whom our human nature has become totally severed due to sin, rejecting our bodies and finitude, and ascending to communion with a spiritual world that will be our heavenly home after death. Rather, redemption is about reclaiming an original goodness that is still available as our true selves, although obscured by false ideologies and social structures that have justified domination of some and subordination of others.

Redemption puts us back in touch with a full biophilic relationality of humans with their bodies and one another and rebuilds social relations that can incarnate love and justice. Thus redemption is about the transformation of self and society into good, life-giving relations, rather than an escape from the body and the world into eternal life. Otherworldly eschatology is usually not explicitly denied, but it is put aside.[5]

Modern feminist theologies in North America and Western Europe are engaged in an in-depth exploration of the many aspects of this reenvisioned understanding of nature, sin, and redemption. This involves detailed critique of how the false ideologies that sacralized patriarchy have been constructed in different historical branches of Christian theology. It involves dismantling these theological justifications of patriarchy and the enunciation of alternative views of God, humanity—male and female—relations to the body, nature, and society that envision egalitarian mutuality as the true meaning of original and redeemed creation and reconciliation with God.

These explorations leave open many disputed questions. One of these is the relation of human nature to maleness and femaleness. Feminist theology and feminist theory have struggled with how to reconcile a one-nature and a two-nature anthropology of gender.[6] A one-nature anthropology, rooted in the Christian theology of an original asexual image of God given to all humans in creation, assumes one generic human "nature" possessed by all humans equally. This has been an important theory for vindicating women's essential equality with men. But the problem with the one-nature anthropology is that it is implicitly androcentric. Essential human nature is identified with qualities, such as reason and moral will, linked with males. Women are included in this "essential human nature" only by negation of their femaleness.

Two-nature anthropology is based on male and female difference as essential. Modern secular complementarity is also rooted in sophiological and mariological notions of good femininity. It assumed an equal value and even superiority of the "feminine" qualities of altruistic love and service in a way that enforces women's passive receptivity to male agency. Maleness continued to be identified with reason and moral will, complemented by female intuitive and altruistic qualities. While exalting women as more virtuous than men, this anthropological model also excludes women from being active agents in society.

In the twentieth century this anthropology has been adopted by the Catholic hierarchy to argue for women's exclusion from voting and political office and then from ordained ministry. Once women won the vote in most Western societies, Catholic leaders conceded participation in public life to women in secular society as an expression of their equality in the creational image of God, although still preferring to divide male and female roles between public and domestic life. But they denied women's capacity to image and represent Christ in the redemptive and sacramental order. Christlikeness and Mary-likeness are split to exalt women's spiritual receptivity but to deny them sacramental agency as representatives of Christ.[7]

Feminism has sought to transcend this conflict between an androcentric one-nature anthropology and a complementary two-nature anthropology. Feminists have sought to define an enlarged understanding of the human that unites all human qualities in a transformed whole and to define journeys of growth into wholeness for women and men by which each can reclaim those lost parts of themselves that have been assigned to the other sex. But questions of how women are different (better?) from men, while at the same time being *equal* and possessing the *same* humanness as a basis for equal rights in society, continue to plague feminist anthropology.

In the last two decades of the twentieth century, however, this feminist discussion of what a wholistic humanness in mutual relation would mean for transformed women and men in a good society has been challenged by postmodernist thought and by the rise of new voices of women from nonwhite and non-Christian cultures. Postmodernist thought has rejected the whole concept of universals, not only of different profiles of essential maleness and essential femaleness but even the idea of an essential humanness. All such notions of an essential self and universal human values are declared to be social constructions that veil the universalizing of dominant cultural groups of men and women. We have to recognize infinite particularity. There is no generic "woman's experience" that can be used as a basis of feminist critique of patriarchy or sisterhood of women.[8]

The emergence of new voices of women in religion from African American, Hispanic American, Asian American communities, as well as from Asia, Africa, and Latin America, has also challenged the tendencies of some earlier feminist theology done by white women to ignore their ethnic and class contexts. These women of "color" in America and from the "Third World" have been engaged in defining feminist theology from their own historical cultural contexts. But by and large these women are not interested in an endless emphasis on *difference* that ends in impenetrable particularity, but rather in establishing their own distinct contexts in order to construct new and more authentic ways of reaching across these differences toward solidarity in struggle against systems of oppression that are global.

In the last three chapters of this book I will chart the emergence of feminist theologies of the twentieth century in Western Europe, North America, and the Third World. As feminist theologies begin to emerge from Hispanic and African American women in the United States and from women in Asia, Africa, and Latin America, there is increasing emphasis on the plurality of cultural and social contexts for doing women's theological reflection. I will show the new emphases in theology that emerge from this plurality of contextualizations. I will ask how Latin American, African, and Asian feminists are defining their distinctive approaches in order to envision a more authentic basis for solidarity among women, and between men and women, to rebuild more life-sustaining societies in their own lands and between nations on a threatened Earth.

1. *Orante*. Scenes from the life of a deceased woman in the chamber of the "Velatio." Early Christian fresco, second half of the third century, c.e. Catacomb of Priscilla, Rome, Italy. Scala/Art Resource, N.Y.

## Chapter 1

# In Christ No More Male and Female?

## The Question of Gender and Redemption in the New Testament

IN THIS CHAPTER I LAY THE FOUNDATION for exploration of the relationship between redemption and the dissolution of gender hierarchy in Christianity, looking at the first century of its development. The focus of this chapter will be the key text found in Paul's Letter to the Galatians:

> As many of you as were baptized into Christ have clothed yourselves with Christ. There is no longer Jew or Greek; there is no longer slave or free; there is no longer male and female; for all of you are one in Christ Jesus. (Gal. 3:27-28)

The text appears as an interpretation of the transformation that takes place in baptism as the believer enters into a new community that identifies itself collectively as living a redeemed new life "in Christ."

How did this text arise to interpret what the redeemed life in Christ means? What did this text mean in the context of the early Christian movement? How did this text reshape social relationships specifically between men and women? How was the meaning of this text reinterpreted as the early Christian movement developed? To answer these questions with any precision would require a large volume. New Testament scholarship is intensive and its bibliography immense. For purposes of laying the basis for a study of the ongoing interpretation of the relation between redemption and gender hierarchy in later Christian centuries up to the present, all that can be attempted in this chapter is a very basic outline. In this outline I will present what seems to me the most likely story, distilled from current scholarship, of how this text developed in the context of the early Christian mission and how it was reshaped and reinterpreted to express conflicting visions of gender transformation in baptismal regeneration.

## Gender Equality in the First Jesus Movement

The New Testament, together with some extracanonical gospels that record the first Jesus movement, does not lend itself to any definitive reconstruction of Jesus' own teachings. The Gospels have not only gone through a multilayered redaction process in the context of the first century of the Christian movement, but they also are intended to proclaim a message of redemption ever reinterpreted in the context of the believing community, not to give "objective" historical information about Jesus.

Although the debates about which sayings are from Jesus himself and express his own understanding and teaching will probably never be resolved with certainty, reconstructions that have emerged from intensive scholarly discussion[1] give, in my opinion, a likely picture of the main characteristics of the Jesus movement in Jesus' own time. I summarize these characteristics here primarily with a view to explaining why, in the next stage of the Jesus movement after Jesus' death, it might appear to Christians in mission that gender dissolution was a central meaning of the new life in Christ effected through baptism.

Although baptism quickly emerged after Jesus' death as the central Christian rite of initiation into the new life in Christ, Jesus never baptized anyone. Rather, he himself was baptized by a figure known in Christian tradition as John the Baptist. It is generally agreed that both John the Baptist and Jesus were located within a Palestinian Judaism engaged in intensive religious and social struggle against the political, military, and cultural colonization that had been imposed on the Jewish people in Palestine by the Hellenistic empires from the third century B.C.E., and then by Rome in 60 B.C.E.[2]

This struggle took external form in efforts to rebel against the colonizing power or else to negotiate with it to allow adequate cultural and religious self-determination to Jews. These were complemented by internal movements of religious renewal either to expel or to adapt to the effects of Greco-Roman cultural colonization. Although temple Judaism with its priestly caste and rituals was official Judaism, the Jewish communities within Palestine and in the Diaspora exhibited a volatile range of religio-political responses to this dilemma, ranging from guerrilla uprisings against the occupying empire to philosophical adaptations of Greek philosophy to interpret Torah observance and temple worship.

A major expression of this struggle against colonization for religious Jews was an intensified development of messianic hope. God would not long allow his people to languish under the power of pagan empires (interpreted theologically as the power of Satan) but would intervene through human and angelic representatives to deliver (redeem) his people from bondage. Since Jewish religious thought interpreted such adversity not simply as innocent victimization but also as punishment for infidelity on the part of Israel itself, this messianic advent must also entail some conversion on the part of Jews. There must be an internal spiritual renewal, a return to faithfulness to God, which would either help evoke coming redemption or prepare Jews for it.[3]

From the time of the Maccabean revolt against the Hellenistic empire in 165 B.C.E. until the Jewish wars of 66–73 C.E. and 133–36 C.E., Palestinian Judaism saw waves of messianic prophets and movements of renewal across a broad spectrum of ways of interpreting this combined call for internal conversion and preparation for God's delivery from colonial occupation. Although the time of John the Baptist and Jesus did not yet experience the full-scale guerrilla warfare that would arise in the next generation, there was continuous turmoil in their day, both fed by and expressing messianic hope.

This turmoil took a variety of forms. There were spontaneous and more organized nonviolent street protests against Roman insults to Jewish religious sensibilities. There were popular bandits, such as Judas the Galilean, who in 6 C.E. organized a revolutionary resistance group. There were scribes and visionaries in rabbinic schools, including groups such as the Essenes, who searched the Scriptures and reworked new commentaries on them to interpret God's hand at work in history and advise how Jews should behave here and now to promote deliverance. There were itinerant wonderworkers who showed people how God was already at work in their midst through miracles that brought rain and healed the sick.[4]

These ways of envisioning and acting out hopes for deliverance also opened up internal socioreligious tensions within the Jewish community: between the temple priesthood and independent schools of scribes and teachers; between constructions of religious righteousness through intense observance of the Torah and the poor and uneducated unable to follow such a path (the *am ha'aretz* or people of the land); between the politically, religiously, and economically privileged and the disprivileged in these many forms. Deliverance from colonial power and internal repentance and renewal suggested to some a social revolution to overcome these patterns of discrimination that divided Jews from each other.

John the Baptist was one representative of the type of popular prophet who, in the third decade of the first century C.E., announced God's coming wrath and judgment, not only against Rome but also against the internal elites in control of the Jerusalem temple. He gathered into the desert those seeking redemption from both external and internal colonization and offered them a baptism that would seal their decision to repent of their sins and prepare themselves for the "wrath to come," in which God would sweep away God's enemies, including the corrupt temple priesthood, and gather the repentant into a renewed, liberated Israel.[5] Jesus was first a disciple of this John, seeking from him the baptism of repentance of sins in preparation for the coming reign.

Jesus was at this time a young man of artisan class from the Galilean village of Nazareth. He had brothers and sisters and, as the "son of Mary," may have been seen as illegitimate.[6] As a religious seeker, he was attracted first by John's apocalyptic message of repentance. But sometime thereafter he broke with the perspective taught by John, inspired by a vision in which he saw "Satan fall from heaven like a flash of lightning" (Luke 10:18).[7] This vision convinced Jesus that those seeking the reign of God did not simply have to wait, fasting in sackcloth, for its coming, but that Satan's power was already broken. The power of God's reign was already "in our midst." Although not yet fully manifest, its presence could be experienced now in miraculous signs of exorcism and healing. Fasting and mourning could give way to feasting and rejoicing.

The distinctive character of the message of Jesus, as he began to preach and to "perform" it in actions for those who "heard him gladly," was the experience of the reign of God already present both in signs and wonders and in celebratory meals that broke down the divisions in Jewish society between the "pure" and the "impure." These divisions between the "pure" and the "impure" had been constructed in the organization of the temple and had been applied in daily life by rabbinic teachers in matters of daily associations, particularly bodily contact through sex and food.[8] The majority of Jews only partly observed these divisions, but that only confirmed their status in the eyes of the strict observers as members of the "impure," to be both avoided and condemned as deserving of God's disregard.[9]

Such divisions between the pure and the impure marginalized many classes of people. First of all, they marginalized all women within the Jewish people itself as being of secondary status in relation to both temple holiness and rabbinic study by their very nature as women, and as causes of ritual pollution on a regular basis through their sexual functions of childbirth and menstruation.[10] The religious laws also marginalized the vast majority of poor and uneducated Jews who did not know how to and could not observe the minute regulations of purity.

These laws also marginalized the sick, the lame, the blind, the deformed, lepers, and persons with various kinds of skin ailments and bodily fluxes, such as the woman "with a flow of blood" (Mark 5:25-34; Matt. 9:20-22; Luke 8:43-48). Such persons were seen as in a permanent state of impurity. They were categorized as sinners, for such ailments were regarded as caused by sin, either their own or that of their parents. The laws also marginalized vast numbers of people who made their living by means regarded as polluting and sinful, among them tax collectors, prostitutes, servants, slaves (who by definition could not keep the laws of purity), swineherders, seamen, and peddlers of fruit and garlic.[11]

Finally, the laws of purity divided Jew from gentile, idolaters from those worshiping the God of Israel, the ultimate division between the holy and the unholy. One can say that the outer limit of the division between holiness and unholiness was the division between Jew and gentile, Israel and the "nations," while the inner and most intimate division between the holy and the unholy divided male from female.[12] Not only social relations but also time and space were regulated to divide holy from unholy, the Sabbath from ordinary days, the Holy of Holies in the temple in Jerusalem from its various levels of inner and outer courts.[13]

Jesus' message that God's coming reign was not to be prepared for simply by repentance (usually construed as redoubled effort to observe these separations), but was already present in our midst in anticipatory "signs," was understood by the first Jesus movement, presumably by Jesus himself as its initiator, as the joyful good news that these separations had been overcome in an overflowing graciousness of God. A new family, a new community of Israel, was arising as these divisions fell, brought together by God's forgiving goodness. This new people included all those previously marginalized within Israel, and perhaps the occasional gentile as well (although the Jesus movement was not yet constructed as a mission to the gentiles, but as a renewal movement within Israel). All these would be collectively referred to by the Jesus movement simply as "the poor," a group whose deprivation was of many kinds, but united in their "unholy" status vis-à-vis "the righteous."[14]

It was to these many kinds of "poor" that the Jesus movement announced its glad tidings of "good news to the poor," the setting at liberty of "the oppressed" (Luke 4:18). The liberation that Jesus expressed was not that of a military uprising, a political campaign, or a strategy for economic or social change, but an immediately experienced liberation of the blind, the lame, lepers, those with bodily fluxes, those possessed by demons that caused madness and "fits," all those healed and restored to mental and physical health; also the "sinners," the prostitutes, tax collectors, and various impoverished people, all affirmed as God's beloved children.

All these previously hopeless ones, including women in every category—widows, prostitutes, those given to fits caused by demons, the bleeding and the bent over, even perhaps a Samaritan or a Canaanite—not only received healing, forgiveness, and hope but gathered in a joyful banquet in which, by sharing with each other their small provisions, they created abundance together, so that twelve baskets were required to gather up all that remained after the feast (Mark 6:43; Matt. 14:20; Luke 9:17).

Such feasting together of the "unholy," together with a popular rabbi and his disciples, and an occasional Pharisee, observing no separation of clean and unclean persons, no careful distinction of holy and profane times was scandalous, a sure evidence for the "righteous" that Jesus was himself an agent of Satan, given his power by Beelzebul (Mark 3:22; Matt. 12:24; Luke 11:15). But for those who "heard him gladly" he was their "rabbi," a true prophet in Israel, an envoy of God's wisdom, perhaps even the messiah himself. In him, and in the community he generated through his teachings and acts, the abundance and goodness of the reign of God were already tasted.

In addition to healing stories, often involving women as both the healed and the believing "poor" who "heard him gladly," two other patterns of thought express the early Jesus movement's experience of the messianic community. One was the understanding of themselves as a "new family" that supersedes the old patriarchal family. The other was the announcement of iconoclastic reversals of social-sacral relationships.

The sayings about the Jesus community as the true family juxtapose the traditional kinship group, represented by Jesus' own mother and brothers, who are presented as "coming to get him," with the community of his followers who are identified as his true relatives, as "my brother and sister and mother" (Mark 3:31-35; Matt. 12:46-50; Luke 8:19-21). It is a new family made up of those who have together experienced newness of life, freed from a condition of marginalization, but one in which the father is conspicuously absent (like Jesus' own family?). Perhaps Jesus' understanding of God as *Abba*, as loving, gracious father, takes the place of the human father in this new family.[15]

This new family is not to duplicate patriarchal relationships. Those who wish to be "great" are not to "lord" it over each other "like the gentiles" (Roman imperialists?), but should be like "servants" to each other, and like "little children" who lack power and trust entirely to the goodness of those who love them. They are to "call no one your father on earth, for you have one Father—the one in heaven" (God as *Abba*) and to "call no man teacher, for you have one teacher," Jesus (Mark 9:34-36; Matt. 23:8-12).

In the iconoclastic reversal sayings, the reign is likened to unlikely small things, such as a mustard seed (a weed for peasant farmers) that grows into a sheltering bush (Mark 4:30-32; Matt. 13:31-32; Luke 13:18-19); like a leaven that a woman sows in a measure of flour that leavens the whole (Matt. 13:33; Luke 13:20-21), reversing the holiness of unleavened bread; like an old woman sweeping her floor to search for a lost coin (Luke 5:8-10) or a shepherd who uncharacteristically leaves his ninety-nine sheep to search for the one that is lost (Matt. 18:10-14; Luke 15:3-7). Entering the reign of God reverses the patterns of righteousness. The last shall be first; the tax collectors and the harlots will go into the reign of God before the chief priests and elders (Matt. 21:31).

These then are some of the characteristics of the movement gathered around Jesus in the experience of a reign of God already dawning. In this experience the poor, the maimed, the sinners, those on the fringes of the people of Israel, including women in all categories, are gathered together in a new community of equals from below. They share their limited provisions to create an abundance for all. It was believed that this reign, experienced in its beginnings in "signs," will soon be completed in a worldwide display of divine power that will sweep away evil within and beyond Israel and create a new world in which "God's will be done on earth, as it is in heaven." Thus the eschatology of the Jesus movement was neither apocalyptic nor simply sapiental (i.e., an immanental communing in the Wisdom that sustains creation), but a synthesis of the two in a future-present.[16]

Toward the end of the third decade C.E. Jesus became convinced that this time of fulfillment of the Kingdom was at hand. Gathering together his core followers, men and women, he went "up" to Jerusalem to be present for this great day. During his visit to Jerusalem he engaged in performative acts—a triumphal entrance into Jerusalem (Mark 11:1-10; Matt. 21:1-9; Luke 19:28-38) and a cleansing of the temple (Mark 11:15-19; Matt. 21:12-13; Luke 19:47-48) that convinced both the Roman authorities and some part of the temple elite that he was a dangerous troublemaker, one of those messianic prophets who arose from the hinterlands from time to time to stir up hopes among the Jewish masses for liberation from both external and internal authorities.[17]

Jesus was seized by the Roman authorities, who dealt him the usual death reserved for those seen as revolutionary agitators: crucifixion.[18] He was nailed to a cross on a hill of execution outside Jerusalem to die an agonizing death for all to see. The intention was to terrorize all his followers and would-be followers with the fate they too would meet if they continued his movement, and thus send them slinking back to their humble villages in terrorized silence.

Initially this act of political terrorism by execution of the leader worked. Most of Jesus' followers scattered and fled back to Galilee. But a few of them, perhaps prominent among them some of his women disciples,[19] became convinced that he was not dead but alive. He had risen from the dead and was present with them "in the Spirit." The presence of the reign they had experienced with Jesus continued to be available through his risen presence in their midst, empowering them to live the New Creation here and now.

We gain a tantalizing glimpse of what this process of reassembling of the followers of Jesus might have looked like from the perspective of the powerful in the words preserved in Josephus, the major historian who wrote of this period of Jewish history leading to the Jewish Wars:

> About this time there lived Jesus, a wise man. . . . For he was one who wrought surprising feats and was a teacher of such people as accept the truth gladly. . . . When Pilate, upon hearing him accused by men of the highest standing amongst us, had condemned him to be crucified, those who had in the first place come to love him did not give up their affection for him. . . . And the tribe of Christians, so called after him, has still to this day not disappeared.[20]

## From Reassembled Jesus Movement to Early Hellenistic Mission

Scholars suggest that Jesus' teachings on breaking down social discrimination and anticipating status reversal in relation to the reign of God conveyed a liberating message to women, who were particularly affected by these forms of marginalization. It is likely that women played an important role among Jesus' followers, both in the companies of traveling missionaries and in providing places and resources for table fellowship. Many parables and stories affirm poor and marginalized but believing women, over against various religious and social authorities. Women disciples probably played a key role as the first witnesses to the resurrection.

As the Jesus movement spread into major cities in the Diaspora, such as Antioch and Alexandria, first as a party within Judaism and then beginning to differentiate itself as a distinct community, some women played important roles as members of missionary teams and as local leaders, prophets, and teachers. This was not unprecedented in this period. The first century C.E. saw significant numbers of economically independent women appear as priestesses and patrons of religious cults in the Hellenistic world, in both pagan and Jewish communities. Epitaphs for women who are called "Elders," "head of the Council of Elders," and "head of the Synagogue" appear in various Hellenistic cities in the Roman period.[21]

The social and economic basis for this relative autonomy and affluence of some women was the burgeoning manufacturing and trade economy of the first-century Roman empire. The old Greek and Roman aristocracy despised manual labor and commerce. For them political and military leadership, together with supervision of agricultural estates run by slaves, were roles for "gentlemen." This left wide avenues for upward mobility for ambitious slaves, freedmen, and middle-class provincials, who could move into leadership both in the imperial bureaucracy (the household of Caesar) and in manufacturing and trade. Some women in these groups were able to take advantage of these economic opportunities.

Although women never gained citizen rights (the vote, political office) in ancient cities, legal changes in Roman law allowed daughters to retain autonomous control over their own inheritance in marriage.[22] Some Hellenistic cities, notably Alexandria, had traditions that gave relative legal autonomy to women.[23] Although women were married in their teens, often to men who were in their thirties or older, and were generally not given the opportunity for higher education, those who survived childbirth might become propertied widows while still in early middle age. They could consolidate their independence as widows if they did not remarry. Religious views that affirmed celibacy as a means to higher spiritual life could strengthen the hand of such economically independent widows.

Women as slaves suffered arbitrary physical and sexual abuse, and yet a skilled slave woman artisan in a wealthy household had opportunities to buy her freedom and set herself up as head of a workshop with her former master or mistress as patron. Since slaves could not legally marry, such a freedwoman might find herself independent of husband or children (even though she might have had children who remained with a former master or mistress). It is among these classes of independent widows and freedwomen, with their modest economic wealth through manufacturing and trade, that we find the kind of women who became prominent in the early Christian movement.[24]

The shaping of a Hellenistic Christian mission to the gentiles began among Greek-speaking Jews with ties to cities in the Diaspora before Paul became a prominent leader in it in the mid-40s to early 60s C.E. Sometime prior to Paul's leadership in the Hellenistic mission, there probably had been two stages in the development of a baptismal theology of gender change. The first stage identified transformation into the new creation in Christ as overcoming and reversing the sexual dimorphism that arose in God's creation of the human, "male and female" (Gen. 1:27b). The second stage of development extended this formula to three pairs of social hierarchies: "No more Jew or Greek, no more slave or free, no more male and female." This is the triadic form that Paul received as already known to him and repeated in Gal. 3:28.

There is good reason to think that "no more male and female" was the original form of this baptismal formula and the other two pairs were added later, in the context of a Hellenistic mission that mingled Jews and Greeks, slaves and free (and freed persons) in their fellowship. The "no more male *and* female" has a different form from the ethnic and class pairs: Jew *or* Greek, slave *or* free. Also male and female denote the biological rather than the social pair (man and woman), and this echoes Gen. 1:27b. It is clearly intended as a commentary on and eschatological reversal of the development of the biological pair in creation.

Second, several noncanonical gospels speak of redemption in terms of this biological pair only, without the other two pairs, and thus very likely go back to an original form of the formula in which the biological pair stood alone. In the *Gospel of the Egyptians*, Jesus replies to Salome's question about when redemption will happen with the statement, "When you tread on the garment of shame, and when the two become one, the male with the female, neither male nor female."[25]

A Corinthian sermon from the early second century quotes the dominical saying: "For the Lord himself, when asked by someone when his Kingdom would come, said, 'when the two are one, and the outside as the inside, and the male with the female, neither male nor female.'"[26] The *Gospel of Thomas* has a similar saying:

> Jesus said to them, "When you make the two one and you make the inside as the outside, and the outside as the inside, and the above as the below, and when you make the male with the female into a single one, so that the male will not be male and the female not be female . . . then you shall enter the Kingdom."[27]

What did this idea that the dissolution of sexual dimorphism was central to the coming of the reign of God mean, and how did it arise? We should not see in the early Christian movement of Jesus' day or in the first generation after his death a "discipleship of equals," if we imagine by such a phrase either a programmatic theory or a general practice of social equality between men and women.[28] Rather we should probably think in terms of a much more ad hoc situation in which some talented, energetic women, in some cases from life situations of economic means that allowed them to live independently, were able to participate in traveling teams of evangelists, to host local Christian fellowships, and to engage in catechesis and public prayer in Christian groups.

This opening to women's participation was facilitated by a movement type of sociology that did not yet have fixed leadership structures in a group that represented mostly working-class people with some but not great class stratification.[29] Their place of assembly was the home (hence lacking differentiation of public and private space).[30] Women's participation was also validated theologically by teachings that suggested the overcoming of various socioreligious status hierarchies in the reign of God already dawning in the community of believers. Dissolving these status hierarchies (clean-unclean, poor-rich, Jew-gentile, righteous-sinner) gave an opening to women to claim their equality, perhaps even priority, in the reign, but it did not speak specifically of gender.

## Jewish and Early Christian Readings of Genesis

Yet there must have been enough of an anomaly of active independent women in such communities to suggest to some early Christian exegetes the need to thematize the meaning of the new humanity in redemption specifically in terms of gender. These exegetes turned to the interpretations of cosmic anthropology available in Hellenistic Jewish philosophy. A brief excursus on Gen. 1:27 and its interpretation in contemporary Judaism will elucidate these cosmic anthropologies available for early Christians to interpret the relation of gender and redemption.

Gen. 1:27 says, "So God created man in his own image, in the image of God he created him; male and female he created them." In the thought of the original priestly authors, the first phrase on God's creation of Adam in God's image and the second phrase, "male and female he created them," are not in apposition to each other but are differentiated. The creation of Adam in God's image is that of a single male-identified generic human who exercises God's dominion over the other creatures. This exercise of God's dominion as God's human representative is the essential meaning of the term "image of God" in this text; that is, it does not mean a physical similarity to God or a participation in the being of God.

The second phrase, "male and female he created them," designated the biological pair (not the social pair, man and woman). According to Phyllis Bird, maleness and femaleness are not identified with the image, but differentiated from it. This points to the biological dimorphism that characterizes the human pair as like the other animal pairs, and as differentiated for the purpose of procreation; both aspects are unlike God.[31] The male generic Adam, read inclusively as meaning all humans of both genders, suggests to modern Christians that all humans of both genders are "in the image of God" and presumably participate equally in dominion over creation, read today ecologically as "stewardship" or care of creation under God.[32]

I believe, however, that this inclusive reading was far from the intention of the original writers. In an androcentric, patriarchal culture and social system, the male head of household exercised dominion over both the dependent persons of the family (women, children, slaves) and over his nonhuman property, as a collective person; that is, representing both himself and those under him. Today one can barely begin to imagine women exercising dominion "equally" with men in the context of a modern economic and political system of individualism in which each (adult) person is presumed to represent him- or herself. In our modern context the earlier family as a collective structure, with the paterfamilias as both the public individual and the collective representative of the family, has been (partly) dissolved.[33]

But no such individualism, allowing women to stand as political equals, was thinkable in antiquity. Thus, the generic Adam of Gen. 1:27a who was created to exercise God's dominion as God's image is an androcentric patriarchal construct in which Adam, like the paterfamilias, is a collective person who exercises sovereignty for himself, and for and as the whole family.[34]

The creation of Adam in Gen. 1:27 (and 5:1-2) was supplemented by the priestly authors with an older folk story (Genesis 2–3) in which God first created "a man" from the soil of the earth and made him a living being by breathing into his nostrils the breath of life. God then planted a garden with every tree, and a river in four branches to water it, and put "the man" into the garden to till it. God then formed the birds and animals to be the man's helpers and brought them to him to name them. But because none of these animals could be a helping partner to him, God caused the man to fall asleep and made a woman out of man's rib to be a helper as partner.

This story of the creation of the man, and then the woman from his rib, is even more explicitly androcentric than Gen. 1:27. Although Eve is a member of the same flesh (species) as Adam and hence able to be a partner with him in a way the animals are not, this is hardly an egalitarian partnership, as some modern exegetes have argued.[35] The man is both a male individual and the physical source of the woman. She is not denigrated as evil, but neither is she a free-standing person in a companionship of social equals. His priority and her derivative origin from him locate her as both an extension of him and a partner to aid him in procreation and family life. She is "of him" and "for him" in a way that disallows the possibility that she can be "for herself," as he is for himself.

In Genesis 3 this woman is described as initiating the disobedience to God's command not to eat of the tree of the knowledge of good and evil, in response to the "crafty" promptings of the serpent. To prevent man from seizing the fruit of the tree of life and hence becoming immortal, in addition to knowing good and evil, God curses the serpent and the man and woman, inflicting pain in childbearing and male domination on the woman, and hard toil in agricultural labor on the man. God then expels the man and woman from Eden to live out the effects of this worsened existence.

These two stories of the creation of humans, male and female, or man and woman, as well as the expulsion from Eden, posed many problems for Jewish exegetes in the two centuries before and during the beginnings of Christianity. Was the female of Genesis 1:27 the same as that of Genesis 2–3, or an earlier figure more equal to Adam than the woman created from his rib? Did the derivative nature of Eve's creation from Adam, as well as her priority in sin, suggest that she was morally inferior, ever tending to lead the man astray if he again makes the mistake of "listening to the voice of your wife" (Gen. 3:17)?

The history of exegesis of these texts in early Judaism is extensive.[36] Some Jewish commentaries assume the shared image of God in both men and women, while others move to a subordinationist and a misogynist reading of these texts. I will discuss here the second type as background to Paul's assumption (in 1 Cor. 11:7) that the male is the image of God while the female is a secondary reflection of that image. For example, the *Wisdom of Ben Sirach*

(c. 190 B.C.E.) says, "From a woman did sin originate and because of her we all must die . . . if she goes not as thou would have her (i.e., according to your hand), cut her off from thy flesh" (i.e., divorce her) (25:24,26).[37]

The *Books of Adam and Eve*, compiled in the first century C.E., gather together a wealth of early Jewish midrashim on Genesis 1–4. In these writings Adam is exalted as a glorious being superior to the angels in his status as God's image. The angels fell because they resented this high status of Adam and God's commandment that they "worship the image of God as the Lord God hath commanded" (14:1).

Adam's sin consists in his foolish decision to listen to his wife and accept her advice, when he should have commanded her. Eve, by contrast, continually abases herself before Adam for their now miserable condition, for which she takes full responsibility. She suggests that he banish her and let her die. She even walks away to die, weeping and mourning, but when Adam realizes (six months later) that she was pregnant and has borne a child, he kindly chooses to go get her and take care of her and her son, Cain (the son of the devil, not of Adam).[38] This birth is followed shortly by that of a second son, Abel, then by Seth, and then by thirty sons and thirty daughters.

After a long life, in which Eve continually acknowledges her fault in causing the evils that have befallen humans, Adam dies. The repentant angels arrive in a glorious chariot and fall down and worship Adam, as they were originally commanded to do by God, crying out to God that Adam is indeed God's image (33:5).[39] In this text, being "image of God" is an exalted status of Adam as a male, not shared by Eve, who is the source of all Adam's troubles, even though he is too kind to actually desert her as she deserves.

From the second century B.C.E. to the first century C.E., as Palestinian Judaism entered heightened conflict with the Hellenistic and Roman empires, a pessimistic worldview developed that saw the whole creation as having been taken over by evil cosmic powers. These cosmic powers were identified with apostate angels whom God *allows* to rule, subjugating the world to oppression, although in due time God will intervene to liberate humanity (Israel) from their evil sway.

To explain the origins of these evil powers, some exegetes used the story of the "sons of God" who took daughters of men for their wives, producing giants (Nephilim), at a time of worsening human wickedness that led to the flood

(Gen. 6:1-4), and combined it with the story of Eve's responsibility for the expulsion from paradise. These offspring of the angels and the daughters of men were interpreted as being the evil cosmic powers that presently govern human affairs. Women played a special role in causing these evil powers, because it was precisely women's sexual seductiveness, heightened by cosmetics on their faces and adornments of their hair, that caused this fall.[40]

The author of the *Testimony of Reuben* (c. 109–106 B.C.E.) sternly advises his male Jewish readers to "command your wives and your daughters that they adorn not their heads and faces to deceive the mind; because every woman who uses these wiles has been reserved for eternal punishment. For thus they allured the Watchers who were before the flood." The author then makes clear that forbidding women facial and hair adornment is not enough. Only the strictest separation of men from women, so they have as little opportunity to gaze on each other as possible, will suffice to prevent the sin of lust, the chief cause of every evil, from breaking out. Lust is caused by the very nature of women, who "are overcome by the spirit of fornication more than men." "Evil are women, my sons, and since they have no power or strength over men, they use wiles by outward attraction, that they may draw him to themselves."[41]

These expressions of early Jewish exegesis reserved the term "image of God" only for Adam (men), they emphasized the need not to repeat Adam's sin by heeding a wife's advice and suggested that women's sexual seductiveness was the prime cause of cosmic evil and human fallenness. These interpretations were circulating in Jewish exegetical circles at the time of early Christianity. Yet one should not conclude that Jewish women's status had worsened in that period compared to the era of the priestly authors of Genesis.

Rather, we should assume that the lesser need in the earlier period to add explicitly subordinationist and misogynist interpretations meant that patriarchal relations were relatively unchallenged then. In the two centuries surrounding Christian beginnings, however, Jewry in Palestine and the Diaspora were experiencing a breakdown of a more insulated society, unleashing opportunities for Jewish women to take part in activities for which they are memorialized in epitaphs as "Elders" and "Mothers of the synagogue" by grateful members of their communities. As gender relations loosened, intensive debates about gender relations took place, with commentary on Genesis 1–6 as one locus classicus for such debate.[42]

Particularly in Alexandria, home to one of the most prominent communities of Hellenistic Jews, exegetes elaborated a commentary on Genesis 1–3 influenced by Platonic mystical philosophy. Philo, our primary source for this Hellenistic Jewish exegesis, explains the original image of God and the advent of evil through women by a three-stage interpretation of human creation. The original Adam, formed according to the image of God, was wholly spiritual, "perceptible only to the intellect, incorporeal, neither male nor female, imperishable by nature."

Only secondarily does God form the earthly Adam out of clay, into which God then breathes the divine spirit. This earthly Adam is made up of two parts, the corporeal part that is mortal, and the spirit that is immortal, partaking of the divine Logos, the original Spiritual Adam. This Adam of body and soul was happy and lived an exalted and immortal life as the image of the cosmos, as long as he was single. His downfall was the creation of his wife. With the creation of Eve came sex, "which is the beginning of iniquities and transgressions, and it is owing to this that men have exchanged their previously immortal and happy existence for one that is mortal and full of misfortune."[43]

The very creation of Eve, then, for Philo, is the fall of Adam, the separation from him of that mortal part pertaining to the body that was previously kept from asserting its evil power by being under the control of the immortal soul. With the separation of Eve out of Adam, the mortalness of the body asserts its power over the immortal soul, dragging the man down to sin and death. Philo sees a remedy for this fall: Men can reject marriage and sexual activity and return to their original celibate state, recovering their spiritual wholeness and union with the immortal part of themselves that partakes of the divine nature.

Although women represent the fall of the immortal soul under the sway of the moral body, causing sin and death, they too can choose celibacy, and thus paradoxically reclaim virginal wholeness in communion with God. In "The Therapeutae," Philo describes a Jewish double monastery in which both men and women live celibate lives, spending six days contemplating the Scriptures and the seventh day in holy Sabbath celebration.[44]

These Hellenistic Jewish readings of Genesis 1–3 most probably lie behind the development of the early Christian baptismal theology as gender transformation into a redeemed state in which there is "no more male and female." While this baptismal theology affirmed women's spiritual equality, it did so in terms that were wholly negative toward women as female sexual bodies. Women (and men) regained their spiritual wholeness and immortality only by returning to a celibate state prior to sexual bimorphism. (This need not mean they cease to have bodies, but that the mortal and sinful proclivities of their bodies would be controlled by being united to the divine Spirit they share with the Logos of God.)[45]

This understanding of return to spiritual wholeness is androcentric in form (not androgynous; that is, no more male and female; not both male and female). Women are called to construct their spiritual identity as "putting off the works of the female" (i.e., sex and reproduction) and becoming spiritually "male."[46] Redeemed life is perfected spiritual masculinity. Women can become "perfect," whole, and spiritual, only by rejecting everything about themselves that, both culturally and biologically, was identified as specifically female.

## Redemption and Gender in Conflict in Pauline Churches

We have suggested that Paul did not originate the baptismal theology of overcoming gender bimorphism (no more male and female), and also did not add the religio-ethnic and class pairs to this theology (no more Jew or Greek, no more slave or free). This addition was probably pre-Pauline, but in the context of a Hellenistic Christian mission closely associated with the one Paul joined, one that combined membership of slaves, free people and freedmen, Greek and Jews, and active women. The triadic formula also suggests the reversal of social patterns of discrimination in Greek and Jewish culture that prized the superiority of one's ethnicity, as well as maleness and free status, at the expense of women, slaves, and "barbarians" (in the case of Greek men), and women, slaves, or "uneducated boors," and gentiles (in the case of Jewish men).[47]

The addition of these pairs focuses baptismal theology more on the social consequences of "oneness in Christ." Women as well as men, gentiles as well as Jews, slaves and free people, all share the same community and the same table fellowship, they speak in prayer and prophecy, they teach proselytes and evangelize on a somewhat equal basis. What does this mean for women's subordination to their fathers and husbands? What does this mean for the subservience of slaves to their masters and mistresses?

The baptismal formula of "no more male and female" suggested an ontological change in which baptismal regeneration returned men and women to a prefallen spiritual wholeness before sexual bimorphism. For Philo this was expressed sexually by celibacy, and socially by retirement to a monastic community of religious contemplatives. This was not the social setting of early Christianity that used this formula. When slave and free, Jew and Greek are added, this suggests overcoming the religious and ethnic-cultural privilege and superiority claimed by both Greeks and Jews (in different terms), and also the sociopolitical and legal power of the paterfamilias over wives, daughters, and slaves in the household.

I believe that Paul did not create this baptismal formula, either in its single paired form or its triadic form, because he did not actually promote either an ontological return to prefallen wholeness or its implications of social equality of women with men, slaves with masters, that would allow either women or slaves to throw off their subordination to the paterfamilias of the household.[48] He includes this text in Gal. 3:28 because he was not focused on either of these implications: ontological or social. The part of the formula that concerned him in Gal. 3:28 was the religio-ethnic pair, Jew-Greek; or, as he puts it in Gal. 5:6: "For in Christ Jesus neither circumcision nor uncircumcision counts for anything; the only thing that counts is faith working through love."

Only when a conflict arose with the church in Corinth, which had a strong constituency that endorsed this baptismal theology in both its ontic and social meanings, did Paul take heed of these gender implications and begin to formulate his own theology of redemption to differentiate his view from theirs. In the process he reformulated the baptismal formula itself so that it lost both its ontic gender implications and its social implications for both women and slaves in the patriarchal household.

The city of Corinth had been destroyed by the Romans in 146 B.C.E. and refounded by Caesar in 44 B.C.E. as a Roman colony and settled with Italian freedmen. In 50 C.E., when Paul arrived there, Corinth was a booming center of commerce where Italians, Greeks, and Orientals mingled, as well as many Jews.[49] Paul evangelized in Corinth and the region of Achaia for about eighteen months. During that time Apollos, a Jewish Christian originally from Alexandria, arrived. Acts describes Apollos as "an eloquent man, well-versed in the scriptures . . . with burning enthusiasm" for the "things concerning Jesus."

Originally a follower of a version of Christianity from disciples of John the Baptist, Apollos was further instructed by Priscilla and Aquila in Ephesus and then encouraged to come to Corinth (Acts 18:24-27).[50]

Paul left Corinth for Ephesus in 51. In 54 he wrote a letter to the Corinthians to reestablish his authority there and to refute many ideas and practices with which he disagreed. Many Christians of Corinth had come to espouse a theology and practice of realized eschatology associated with Apollos. For these Corinthians the new life in Christ, begun in baptism, overcame the old world of sin and brought the believer into a present experience of resurrected life. This new life in Christ was experienced particularly in Spirit-filled assemblies in which all members, women and men, could participate in spontaneous testimonies of prayer and prophecy that combined "intelligible" and ecstatic forms of speech or "tongues."

The church at Corinth was made up of lower- to middle-status urban people who ranged from household slaves to some local officials, but most were artisans and small merchants. Among them were significant numbers of independent women. The Jewish Christian evangelist couple Priscilla and Aquila lived in Corinth while Paul was there. They were tent-making artisans with extensive trade connections, moving easily from Rome to Corinth to Ephesus.[51] The household of Chloe was apparently headed by the woman of that name and had slave and freedmen members who traveled readily from Corinth to Ephesus, most probably through trade connections.[52] Paul also speaks of a Phoebe as deacon of Cenchreae, the port city near Corinth, who was a leader (*prostasis*) for many, including Paul himself (Rom. 16:1-2).[53]

These women belonged to those who were Paul's supporters in Corinth. We can assume many more women were prominent but followers of other factions, particularly that of Apollos.[54] Paul does not name these women, although they were among the central targets of his various proscriptions. The Corinthian women, and presumably men who shared their views, believed the new life in Christ in some way overcame gender differences. Since gender difference was dissolved through celibacy, many of these women were either withdrawing from sexual relations in marriage or not marrying at all (or not remarrying if they were widows). Particularly when possessed by the Spirit, praying and prophesying in the Christian assembly, they discarded the head coverings traditionally worn by married women in public, thereby testifying to their liberation from female subordination, having become "like men"; that is, with uncovered heads.[55]

These Corinthians also seem to have believed that in the New Creation, which they had already experienced, the power of demons or fallen angels was overcome. Therefore they no longer needed to observe strict divisions between their table fellowship and that found in the temples of the city where meat sacrificed to idols was shared, nor worry about buying and eating such meat sold in marketplaces. They could disregard worry about ritual pollution from contact with idols, since such evil cosmic powers no longer existed. They practiced an open fellowship, allowing the unconverted to attend their assemblies and even to speak. They also allowed a man to attend who was living with his father's wife.

In short, the Corinthian opponents of Paul practiced what Mary Douglas has called "weak grid and semi-weak group";[56] that is, dissolution of gender and other status hierarchies within their community, and open boundaries between themselves and the world around them. These practices were not arbitrary but reflected a theological belief that the evil powers that lay behind a world divided by gender, social status, and clean and unclean spheres had already been overcome in the new life in Christ.

Paul finds these practices, as well as the underlying theology that justifies them, highly threatening and sets out to change them on a number of fronts. In the process he seeks to shore up both internal status hierarchy (gender and leadership class) and external boundaries between Christian and pagan, the moral and the immoral. Paul begins (1 Corinthians 1–4) by shoring up his own apostolic authority, claiming that he seeks to overcome factions in the church (particularly between himself and Apollos). He praises Corinthian opponents for the many spiritual gifts of speech and knowledge they have already received from Christ. He then speaks of his own weaknesses and sufferings, laying out a theology of the cross by contrast to which the Corinthian belief that they already possess transcendent wisdom is identified with a worldly foolishness of those who are still "infants in Christ," not yet ready for "solid food."[57]

Having brought the Corinthians down to their proper place as infantile beginners in the faith, not those already possessed of the fullness of redemptive life, knowledge, and power, Paul brandishes his paternal power over them as their "father in the gospel," even threatening to "come to you with a stick," if they fail to heed his admonitions (4:21). He then addresses a number of disciplinary issues that he sees as exemplifying their ignorant assumptions, which they have foolishly taken for spiritual wisdom.

The first issue is the case of a man living with his father's wife (5:1). Since women were married in their early teens, often to much older men, a grown son of a previous marriage might well be of an age similar to that of his father's young wife. Paul sees this as a shocking case of incest, but if the wife divorced her elderly husband or was widowed and then married the son, it may not have seemed so to the Corinthians.[58] The fact that this is the only real case of immorality that Paul mentions specifically suggests that he may be exaggerating the issue of sexual immorality; i.e., there is no reason to think the Corinthians were "gnostic sexual libertines".[59] The key is Paul's insistence on reassertion of strict boundaries between the pure and the impure. Even one case of immorality allowed in their midst could corrupt the whole body of the community, like a bit of yeast that can permeate an entire batch of dough. The Corinthians are to have no association with such a person, but "drive out the wicked person from among you" (5:13).

Paul goes on to rebuke the Corinthians for taking their legal disputes to the ordinary courts. His objection is not simply to the fact that they have disputes, but that they submit such disputes to pagans—the "unrighteous"—rather than "taking them before the saints."[60] The issue again is one of boundaries. "The unrighteous" and the "saints" are to be strictly separated. Those who are to "judge the angels" should not allow themselves to be judged by unbelievers. Paul denounces the Corinthians' assumption that they are not contaminated by such contacts with the "impure"; that because the evil powers are already conquered, therefore "all things are lawful"; he uses the analogy of the whole body being corrupted by contact with a prostitute. We should not assume, however, that the Corinthian church is filled with people who frequent prostitutes. That this section follows the one about lawsuits suggests that, for Paul, any contact with unbelievers or the immoral is construed as analogous to "fornication."[61] Like the "yeast of corruption," one bit of contact corrupts the whole batch.

Paul then addresses the issue of some Corinthians desisting from marital relations (1 Corinthians 7). He approaches the issue cautiously since he himself is celibate and espouses a version of the belief that withdrawal from sex anticipates the reign of God. But he is distressed by the widespread adoption of this lifestyle by the Corinthians, both because he does not believe they are really capable of celibacy and fears they (the males) will fall into immorality, and also because he recognizes that celibacy is a prime basis for the Corinthian women's assertion of their transcendence of sexual subordination.[62] Although his insistence that each spouse has authority over the body of the other appears egalitarian, in the context of the first-century Corinthian church this principle in effect denied what the women sought to gain by celibacy: having authority over their own bodies.[63]

Paul advises that almost everyone should marry and maintain sexual relations. The married may by mutual agreement abstain briefly for a time of prayer, but they should "come together again," lest they fall into the worst case, lust. Paul has a more difficult case with widows and virgins, but here too he advises that although "it is well for them to remain unmarried as I am" (7:8), if they cannot repress their sexual feeling they should marry. Nor need the believing wife or husband separate from the unbelieving spouse if they consent to live together, although Paul consents to the separation of such a couple if the unbeliever initiates it.

Paul's argument grows more confused as he discusses virgins—the never-married who have resolved to remain virgin in preparation for the coming reign of God. Paul acknowledges that they should remain virgins if they are able to do so without being distressed by sexual feelings. This includes those already engaged, where one of the partners wants to remain unmarried.[64] His argument moves to a theology of "eschatological reservation." Although the time of final crisis is approaching in which all the separations between the married and the unmarried, slave and free, Jew and Greek, will be overcome, the time is not yet here. So no one should "jump the gun," anticipating the transformation to come by changing their status of circumcision or uncircumcision, seeking freedom if they are a slave, or withdrawing from marriage if they are married.

To remain in one's present condition is Paul's basic advice (7:17-24); in other words, do not anticipate a transformation of sociobiological conditions that will happen in the redemptive future but is not yet here. Paul clearly has the triadic baptismal formula of Jew-Greek, slave-free, male-female in mind here. He is saying that these changes will happen only in a still-future reign. They have *not* happened in baptism; the baptized are not authorized to begin such changes now.

Paul then turns to a series of issues having to do with the liturgical assembly. He addresses the questions of Christians eating foods that have been consecrated in pagan temples (including using such foods in the fellowship meal); disorderly eating in which some do not wait for all the others to begin; women praying and prophesying with uncovered heads; and disorderly prayer where many offer testimony at the same time.[65]

Again Paul is in a dilemma, for he concedes some of the theological reasons why the Corinthians do these things and has taught such principles himself; for example, "that no idol in the world really exists, and that there is no God but one" (8:4). He cautions against eating foods consecrated in temples as a concession to the "weaker" brothers who think idols exist and are scandalized by such transgression of the boundaries between the holy and the unholy. But soon he sounds as though idols really do exist and are dangerous demonic powers. To bring such foods into the Lord's Supper is to pollute it; "You cannot partake of the table of the Lord and the table of demons" (10:21).

Paul then moves to an insistence that women should cover their heads when they pray and prophesy (1 Corinthians 11). He opens this section with an assertion of a hierarchical theology of "orders of creation"; God as head of Christ, Christ as head of the male, and the male as head of the female. This counters what was probably the Corinthians' belief in an original spiritual unity of male and female joined to the divine Logos, a unity that has been restored in Christ through baptism. For Paul, not only is the order of creation one of God-Christ-male-female, but this hierarchy has not been changed for the baptized.[66] Therefore the women have no right to discard their head coverings in prayer. Far from the fallen angelic powers having already been overcome, so that Christians pray with angels, the angels are still fallen powers. Women should continue to have "authority" on their heads, for this not only signifies their subjugation to the authority of male over female but also points to the dangerous role the uncovered female head played in seducing the angels and generating demonic powers.[67]

Paul then turns to disorderly eating and disorderly prayer. The Corinthians should practice an ordered fellowship meal in which the eucharistic elements of the Lord's Supper are clearly separated from ordinary eating. By strengthening the lines between regular eating and the Lord's Supper, Paul relegated ordinary eating to private meals in the home apart from the church assembly. This also separated women's food preparation in the private home, rather than having women come early to the place of liturgical assembly to prepare food that was both a fellowship meal and the Lord's Supper.[68]

Paul then insists that orderly, intelligible speech and interpretation should be separated from speaking in tongues. Only a few should speak in each form, and in sequence. But if there is no one to interpret a tongue, "let them be silent in church and speak to themselves and to God" (14:28). The statement that absolutizes this silencing for women as a group, "Women should be silent in the churches. For they are not permitted to speak, but should be subordinate, as the law also says" (14:34), is probably not from Paul himself. But the editor of Paul's letters who added this gloss was not entirely wrong in thinking that he was merely spelling out Paul's intentions.[69]

In a culture where women were mostly uneducated and banned from the exercise of public rhetoric but were allowed ecstatic, Spirit-possessed speech, women felt able to participate in Christian assemblies in spontaneous, ecstatic testimony, mingling with tongues. This was further mandated by a belief that women's status had already been raised to equality with men in the New Creation. If both this form of speech and its theological validation, signaled by the uncovered head, were rescinded, most women would not have felt empowered to speak. The priority for ordered, explanatory speech would also have prioritized an educated male elite and silenced those without these skills.

Paul seeks to counter the argument that since all Christians are members of the body of Christ, all should participate in the same way in prayer, prophecy, healing, speaking in tongues, various forms of leadership, and assistance (12:12-31). He argues that although all Christians—Jew and Greek, slave and free (significantly, male and female are dropped here)—are baptized into the one body of the church, this body is hierarchically ordered. As in the physical body, all parts are indispensable but have different functions that are not to be confused. Indeed those that are weaker are indispensable, and those that are thought less honorable are treated with greater respect by being clothed. Paul has in mind here women, who are seen as like the genitalia of the body, "weaker" but indispensable, thought to be "inferior" and "less respectable," but which one "honors" by covering them.[70]

The letter culminates with Paul's theology of resurrection. It is not that the Corinthians do not believe in the resurrection, but they do not believe in Paul's understanding of it. They think the resurrection has already begun, and they experience it already in their transformed lives. Paul corrects this by a separation of salvation history into distinct stages that are not to be blurred.[71] First, there is Jesus' resurrection, followed by a series of male witnesses to the resurrection (culminating in Paul), who authorize apostolic mission. The resurrection appearances to women, found in all four canonical Gospels as well as in extracanonical gospels, are significantly missing here.[72]

The present life of Christians is one of receiving the message in faith while continuing to struggle against the power of sin in their bodies, signifying the active demonic powers still in charge of the cosmos. Only in the future will there be a third stage of redemption in which Christ conquers the demonic powers, and finally death itself, and "hands over the kingdom to God the Father" (1 Cor. 15:24). Only then will sin and death be conquered; only then will the divisions between male and female be nullified. Here and now, however, such divisions and hierarchical orderings are still in place, and the Corinthians are not to anticipate such changes as if they had already happened, as if they already sojourn in the new creation where there is "no male and female."

## Gender and Redemption in Two Forms of Pauline Churches

The reception of Paul's efforts to reimpose his authority and correct the Corinthians' patterns of Christian life and thought caused great dissension between factions and anger toward him by those of different views, although later communications and visits by Paul and his representatives may have smoothed this over.[73] Paul's interventions probably did not change the theology or practices of those most committed to an alternative viewpoint. But the confrontation between Paul and his Corinthian opponents should be seen as a key turning point in early Christian development.

In the generation after Paul those who claimed to speak for him became increasingly divided. One line of Pauline tradition moved toward patriarchalization in which equality in Christ is spiritualized and combined with continued social subordination of women and slaves. A second viewpoint continued to mandate a spiritual equality for women, signaled by celibacy, a break with subordination to the patriarchal family, and freedom to engage in itinerant preaching and teaching. The first line of Pauline tradition became "orthodox" and entered a canonized New Testament collection, while the second line was relegated to the fringes and transmuted into various forms.

We see the first line of patriarchalizing Paulinism in the post-Pauline letters of Colossians and Ephesians.[74] Colossians contains one of the strongest New Testament statements of a baptismal theology of (almost) realized eschatology. The author continually claims that the baptized have already been rescued "from the power of darkness and transferred . . . into the kingdom of his beloved Son" (1:13), have conquered the demonic powers and elemental spirits of the universe, and come "to fullness in him, who is the head of every ruler and authority" (2:10). Already in baptism they have passed through death and been "raised with him through faith in the power of God, who raised him from the dead" (2:12).

This already realized life in the New Creation liberates them from the old regulations in regard to food, drink, and festivals. The Christian can ignore the old taboos that said, "Don't handle, don't taste, don't touch." Having "stripped off the old self with its practices" and being clothed in a "new self . . . renewed in knowledge according to the image of the creator," the old social divisions are no more. "There is no longer Greek and Jew, circumcised and uncircumcised, barbarian, Scythian, slave and free; but Christ is all and in all!" (3:9-11).

But again, as in 1 Cor. 12:13, the male-female pair is omitted. Moreover, the author construes this overcoming of social divisions as a coexistence in diversity of spiritual equals in the one Christian community, but does so in a way that does not change the hierarchical relations of the patriarchal family. Thus he moves to the statements, "Wives, be subject to your husbands"; "Children, obey your parents in everything, for this is your acceptable duty in the Lord," and "Slaves, obey your earthly masters in everything, not only while being watched and in order to please them, but wholeheartedly, fearing the Lord" (3:18, 20, 22).

The commands for submission by the three subjugated groups in the patriarchal family—the wives, the children, the slaves—is balanced by commands to the paterfamilias as husband, father, and master to be kind, forebearing, just, and fair to his wife, children, and slaves. Thus the earlier subversive vision of equality in Christ has been transmuted here into "love patriarchalism," in which patriarchal power is softened by the call to kindliness toward subordinates, but the subordinates are to internalize their submission to their earthly "Lord" as their Christian duty.[75]

Ephesians contains a further Christianizing of the patriarchal family. Not only are wives, children, and slaves again called to submit to the paterfamilias, but the relation of the husband to the wife is assimilated into a theology of the church, in which the husband is compared to Christ, the head of the church, and the wife to the church, his body. "Just as the church is subject to Christ, so also wives ought to be [subject] in everything, to their husbands" (5:24).

The force and repetition of these strictures in successive New Testament books (see also 1 Peter 2:18—3:8),[76] addressed to wives, children, and slaves and calling them to submit to the patriarchal head of the household, testifies, however, to a different reality. Women continued to reject the role of wife, and young people and slaves flouted their fathers and masters to adopt a religion other than that of the head of household (itself a subversion of familial and political order).[77] And they continued to see this new religion as liberating them from subordination to these traditional authorities.

This continued conflict between two visions of Christianity is expressed most directly in 1 Timothy, an epistle attributed to Paul but written sometime in the first half of the second century. In this epistle women are not only called to submit to their husbands, but this is related specifically to a prohibition against women teaching in church or having authority over a man: "she is to keep silent" (2:12b). The silencing of women as teachers and leaders in the church is then related to the stories of the creation and fall of Adam and Eve in Genesis 2–3: "For Adam was formed first, then Eve; and Adam was not deceived, but the woman was deceived and became a transgressor" (2:13-14). This exegesis reflects the view we have seen in rabbinic commentary that tended to lessen Adam's fault while heaping most of the blame on Eve.

This silencing of women, in view of women's secondary place in creation and primacy in sin, is then related specifically to marriage: "Yet she will be saved through childbearing" (2:15). The epistle denounces the views of Christian teachers who "forbid marriage and demand abstinence from foods" as "the hypocrisy of liars whose consciences are seared with a hot iron" (4:2-3). The church is further assimilated into the patriarchal household by making the qualities of a good paterfamilias—"manag[ing] his household well, keeping his children submissive and respectful in every way" (3:4)—the chief qualifications for the choice of bishop.

The gender and generational hierarchy of the patriarchal family is now the pattern for the Christian church. The bishop is to be like the paterfamilias. Deacons are to be like good adult sons of the paterfamilias, themselves "manag[ing] their children and households well" (3:12). Women who serve as deacons are to be like frugal housewives, "serious, not slanderers . . . temperate, and faithful in all things" (3:11). Younger men and women are to honor older men as fathers, older women as mothers, younger men as brothers, and younger women as sisters (5:1-2).

The church of 1 Timothy continues to have a female ministry, but it is now relegated to a separate service to women. There is a group of widows who serve the church, but this is to be limited to elderly women over sixty years of age who have no living relatives to support them (5:3-9). With these strictures the author seeks to cut off some groups of celibate women ministers who exist in his church: women who are younger, who have chosen not to marry or remarry, who have relatives who could support them, but who have left their families and live together as a household of women.

Such younger women, who are not "true widows" (that is, have never married, are insufficiently elderly, quiescent, and destitute) yet claim the office of widow, are eyed with suspicion as "gadding about from house to house; and they are not merely idle, but also gossips and busybodies, saying what they should not say . . . some have already turned away to follow Satan" (5:13,15). It is particularly such women ministers, whose chief office is to visit other women and to catechize them in their households, that the author probably has in mind when he warns Christian teachers to "have nothing to do with profane myths and old wives' tales."[78]

Prominent among the "profane myths and old wives tales" against which the author writes is an alternative form of Christianity. This alternative Christianity was probably one that also claimed the authority of Paul, but taught views opposite to those endorsed in 1 Timothy. Its primary promulgators were probably communities of celibate women teachers who prepared other women for baptism. This Pauline Christianity is found in *The Acts of Paul and Thecla*, which can be dated as a written text to the late second century but probably existed in oral forms at the time of the writing of 1 Timothy. It, like 1 Timothy, comes from Asia Minor. First Timothy very likely was written to refute the kind of Christianity reflected in *The Acts of Paul and Thecla*.[79]

In the *Acts of Paul and Thecla*, [80] Paul arrives in Iconia to preach and converts a beautiful young virgin, Thecla, who is betrothed to a man named Thamyris. Thecla immediately expresses her new Christian identity by rejecting her marriage to Thamyris. He and her mother, Theocleia, complain to the governor against Paul's influence on women and Thecla's rejection of marriage. The governor orders her to be brought to the theater to be burned at the stake, but a hailstorm extinguishes the flames and Thecla is saved.

Thecla then cuts her hair, adopts male dress, and follows Paul to Antioch, asking him to baptize her. Paul hesitates, believing that she is not yet ready to resist the temptations of the world (i.e., the temptation to marry). While they are traveling, a Syrian named Alexander falls in love with Thecla and tries to seduce her, but she rejects his advances, tearing his cloak and ripping off the golden crown that signified his honors. He too leads Thecla to the governor, who throws her to the wild beasts in the arena. But now the women of the city, including Queen Tryphaena, support her. Even a female lion defends her against a bear and then a male lion.

A panoply of wild beasts are now unleashed against Thecla, but she stands with hands upraised in prayer and then throws herself into a tank of water, baptizing herself. A cloud of fire surrounds and covers the naked Thecla, killing the seals in the tank. The governor and Alexander now recognize that Thecla is too powerful for them. The governor orders her clothing to be brought and releases her into the arms of Tryphaena and the rejoicing women. Thecla instructs the entire household of Tryphaena in the faith. Thecla, again dressed in men's clothes, then leaves with a retinue of male and female followers to find Paul, who is teaching in Myra of Lycia. When she announces that she has received baptism, he affirms all she has done and then sends her on her way to "teach the word of God" in Iconium.[81]

Such a form of Christianity not only taught that women converts should reject marriage, thereby attaining the male status of freedom to travel, teach, and baptize, but did so in a way that claimed the authority of Paul (while making women themselves the main dramatis personae). If these are the sort of "old wives' tales" the author of 1 Timothy has in mind, and the communities of teaching "widows" are the likely promulgators of such a women-affirming Christianity, we can better understand the adversaries against whom he complains. These adversaries were not in some other church, but taught and ministered out of the very houses of widows that his own church supported; these he sought to limit and control.

2. Icon of Saint Macrina, the Cappadocian ascetic, architect of a female monastic community, and ascetic inspiration to her brothers Gregory and Basil.

Chapter Two

# Gender and Redemption in the Patristic Era

## Conflicting Perspectives

### Trajectories of Early Christianity

AS WE HAVE SEEN IN THE FIRST CHAPTER ON FIRST AND early second-century Christianity, the Christian movement from its beginnings was diverse and syncretistic. The Jesus movement in the lifetime of its founder, as well as in the several decades between his death and the Jewish wars of 66–73 C.E., drew into itself individuals and groups shaped by the existing diversity of Palestinian and Diaspora Judaism, particularly of the more dissident types (i.e., non-Sadducean). This included everything from scribal and Pharisaic Jews to those from the Baptist, Zealot, and Essene movements, apocalyptic speculation, and Hellenistic Jewish philosophical and sapiental mysticism.[1]

Nor should one assume that these were clearly differentiated options. Rather, these perspectives met and mingled in the Jewish communities of the eastern Mediterranean, and many formative leaders were drawn from restless and mobile "seekers" who had sampled a range of non-Jewish, as well as Jewish, schools of thought and forms of salvation "on offer" in such cities. In Jesus' lifetime the movement was held together by the charisma of his person, but immediately after his death it moved in a variety of directions—geographically, culturally, and theologically.

One group in Jerusalem, clustered around James, the brother of the Lord, developed a form of Pharisaic Jewish Christianity, while another, identified with "the Hellenists," moved across the Jewish-gentile divide. Some, influenced by philosophical Judaism, identified Jesus with Wisdom or Logos of cosmological mysticism, while others elaborated a Christian apocalyptic parallel to the Jewish militants anticipating the final showdown with "Satan" in the form of the Roman empire. The Pauline trajectory, which dissolved the Jewish-gentile divide and moved along a Greek-speaking path from Antioch to Ephesus, Macedonia, and Achaia, shaping much of the writings that became the canonical New Testament, was paralleled by other trajectories just as powerful in their time, such as an Aramaic-speaking Christianity, shaped by the Essene movement, that evangelized within the Jewish communities from eastern Syria to Persia.[2]

Nor did these options remain confined to fixed regions. A formative leader, shaped in the strict asceticism of Essenic Syriac Christianity, or the cosmological speculation of Alexandria, in turn influenced by Jewish, Christian, and pagan educational and salvific quests, might show up in Rome in the mid-second century with new synthesis of thought and practice regarded as startlingly deviant by some Christian groups there, but this individual saw his ideas as building solidly on the "tradition" as he knew it. Moreover, those evangelized by this teacher could themselves form an evangelizing movement, based on house church or study group gatherings, that spread rapidly across urban centers, both within existing Christian communities and gathering new converts from Jews and pagans.

Within this creative diversity of Christianity of the first and second centuries we can map a certain range of options, options that were not yet hardened into fixed alternatives theologically or organizationally. One range of options, present from the beginning of the Jesus movement, ran along a sapiental-apocalyptic arc. Sapiental thought connected Jesus with Wisdom or Logos, drawing into itself a wealth of primatalogical and cosmological thought from Jewish-Hellenistic mystical philosophy. Here the focus was on the beginning, the original cosmic paradise as it was first created and intended by God, and the restoration of the state of an unfallen Adam in that paradisial condition.[3]

Apocalyptic thought, by contrast, spoke of the messiah and the coming reign of God in an imminent future against an evil political society and cosmos ruled by fallen angelic powers. Jesus is proclaimed the Messiah (Christ) who has fought the decisive battle against these evil powers, has delivered his followers from their grip in a hidden way, and will soon return to complete this emancipation in its fully manifest form.

From the mid to late first century, these two forms of thought were mingling, creating the basis for Christologies that understand Jesus as Christ (Messiah, the end-time deliverer) as the paradigmatic manifestation of Wisdom or Logos through whom the cosmos was created in the beginning, the ground of the existing cosmos and true identity of the human soul.[4] Although the sapiental and apocalyptic perspectives merge early in Christianity, the emphasis can nevertheless fall across a large range of possibilities, from one end in a stress primarily on an internal transformation of the inner self that refers back to the true nature of the soul and the cosmos, rooted from the beginning in Wisdom, to the other end in an expectation of a future soon to be revealed in the dismantling of the present world order.

Although all Christians understand salvation as including the "outer" as well as the "inner" dimensions of overcoming evil, the emphasis can also range from inner transformation—overcoming the split between soul and God, and between spirit, soul, and body in the individual—to vehement protest against political and economic evils, represented by the political tyranny of the empire and the injust possessions of the rich and powerful against the poor and oppressed.[5]

All Christians also understand that the basic principle of salvific transformation has been already given to them in some sense in baptism, but how complete this transformation is or can be within this present life and "world" also varies. It is a mistake to regard any Christian group as having a totally realized eschatology, in the sense of imagining that all inner and outer evil have vanished. A certain tension between the salvation already present in Christ and given or imputed to the believer in baptism and continuing existing evil, sin, and death is an undeniable "fact" of experience.

Yet, within this basic tension a great range of options exists. For some, redemption is "almost" entirely present. The coming reign of God is "secretly" already "here" and/or the original Wisdom through which the world was created and which upholds the world and soul as its true foundations can be experienced here and now simply by shifting one's perspective. As The *Gospel of*

*Thomas* (a mid-to-late first-century sapiental Christianity) puts it: "Split wood and I am there; lift the stone and you will find me."[6] Death, poverty, ignorance exist, but they are unimportant delusions that can be overcome by transformative insight into what truly *is*.

For others, the Christian, although claimed by the salvific power in baptism, is still actually under the powers of evil that define the overwhelming tendencies of his or her bodily and psychic disposition. The proper stance of the Christian then is one of penitential discipline, awaiting a deliverance that is still distant temporally and/or ontologically. The first view tends to favor an egalitarian inner authority of each believer, while the second distrusts such dispersed inner authority in favor of a privileged charismatic leader or clerical caste who knows what must be thought and done, even if they themselves are not "perfect."

The extent to which salvation is seen as already here and in the "possession" of believers also determines how radically the believer and believing community feel they can "act out" changes in personal and social lifestyle that reflect what this transformation is understood to signify. What these changes are also depends on how evil is identified. If evil is seen primarily as a fall into the mortal body, sexual differentiation and procreation, then those who believe themselves already saved feel empowered to discard social expressions of gender difference and cease sexual intercourse and procreation. If the focus is on a body controlled not only by sexual passions but also by hunger, then not only sexual abstinence becomes important, but also fasting or avoidance of "hot foods," that is, red meat and wine. If to this is added a protest against wealth, then the discarding or sharing of possessions and homeless itinerancy without visible means of support come into play.

Some insist that the "fullness of the times" are still distant and that penitential discipline and moral formation are demanded; they usually object to any such "jumping the gun" by which believers act out personal and social transformation that departs from established social patterns. Such radical transformations, while perhaps still affirmed ultimately—after death and/or after the final cosmic transformation beyond history—are inappropriate "now." Inner transformation may be related to a gradual process of growth, but in a way that allows the external social patterns of the believing community to be accommodated to existing political tyranny; extremes of wealth and poverty; relations of patriarchal domination of old over young, masters over slaves, and men over women, clerical elites of office or learning over laity.

In addition to differences between how realized or unrealized the hoped-for redemption is now, there is also a range of views on how deeply split the person and cosmos are between good and evil. The fault line may run between a wrong attitude vis-à-vis the whole self, soul and body, or between soul and body, or between an inner spiritual part of the soul (spirit) and the psyche and body. These differences in where the fault line runs may also be reflected in how one sees the lines of the split between God and the good creation and an evil self and fallen creation in society and the cosmos.

On one end of the spectrum, the whole creation may be seen as basically good, body and soul, but distorted by wrong moral and spiritual perceptions. Or the creation may be seen as originally good, but disobedience caused a "fall" that creates forms of the body and the physical world that are evil; that is, a mortal body, split between sexual differences, requiring sexual procreation. At the other end of the spectrum, the entire material and psychic world that can be experienced by touch and sight may be seen, not only as fallen from an original good creation, but actually created by fallen evil powers. The true self and paradisial world are radically transcendent to this visible embodied one. The body and psyche that spring from fallen powers are not redeemable, but must be discarded in order to escape back to a radically "other" spiritual world "above"; here, alone, true union with the divine can be found.

This more radical or anticosmic option is usually identified with "Gnosticism," seen as heretical vis-à-vis an "orthodox" Christianity that affirms the ultimate goodness of the body and of the visible creation, as originating from the same God through whom it is now being redeemed in Christ. But the term "gnostic," like "heretical" and "orthodox," is slippery, often amounting to little more than a term of abuse of others and affirmation of one's own views. In this period orthodox and gnostic share many common presuppositions foreign to today. The orthodox also generally saw corporeality, sexuality, and mortality as evils not intended by God, but the result of human disobedience, when humans were tempted by fallen angels. More radical dualists attributed these evil characteristics to demonic powers who then entrapped fallen spirits in human psychosomatic "encasements."

The more radically dualistic position is more pessimistic about the world and the body as essentially evil. Yet those who hold this view are also often more radical about disaffiliating themselves from gender, class, and clerical hierarchies, which they see as expressions of demonic powers and not the true spiritual "world" of authentic divinity and immortal life. Those who have a more moderate view of the cosmic split are more likely to see such social and ecclesiastical hierarchies as part of the original "order of creation," or else as a necessary set of arrangements decreed by God to accommodate and exercise control over a fallen world. Thus obedience to such social patterns, not jettisoning of them, is called for by Christian conversion.

Christianity from its beginning to the end of the second century (with continuing repercussions up to the present) represents all of these different options in a variety of expressions. Moreover, those forms that stress a more realized eschatology, inner authority, and the right to act out expressions of redemption here and now—by discarding home, family, possessions, and marks of social differentiation between men and women—had wide play and were the predominant church in some places, although other Christianities that stressed continuing sin, the need for external authority, and accommodation to existing family and sociopolitical forms were not lacking from the early beginnings.

The general trend of Christian development from the late second century into the fifth century, however, is for the second tendency to gradually win out, reshaping Christian memory to make it appear to have been the sole original form of the Christian movement and making the other varieties of Christianity appear secondary deviations (heresies) from an original norm. The "myth of orthodoxy" begins to be shaped by leaders such as Tertullian and Irenaeus in the late second century, as they identify this emerging patriarchal and clerical Christianity with the original "apostolic" faith passed down through an established succession of leaders (bishops) from the apostles who possess the original faith, preserved in the teachings, Scriptures, and practices of the churches led by these apostolic successors.[7]

A canonical New Testament begins to be shaped that privileges second-century writings reflecting this view and that interprets earlier writings in its own terms and cuts off writings that reflect other perspectives. Christians of other views are cut off from these Christian assemblies and forced to meet in separate gatherings that are increasingly marginalized as "orthodoxy" wins social predominance. With the Constantinian establishment of the mid- to late fourth century, which creates a politically established Christianity patronized by the empire and incorporated into its political bureaucracy, it becomes possible to persecute and repress other varieties of Christianity, thus leaving clerical patriarchal Christianity as the empowered norm.

Since the records of these alternatives survive only in fragments, often reported through the eyes of their enemies, it takes considerable imagination to think ourselves back into a Christianity of the mid-second century. We can only dimly glimpse a time when a great variety of Christianities, some experimenting boldly with the personal and social changes and theological interpretations of redemption, not only competed as equals with emerging clerical and patriarchal forms, but in many places were the predominant forms of Christianity. These, just as much as those who won as the "orthodox," saw themselves as building on ancient traditions going back to Jesus and the first generation of his followers.

Within the compass of this chapter I can only point briefly to some of the expressions of these Christianities of the second century and the range of options for the relation of gender and redemption that are suggested in them. I will then go on to focus on two forms of the "orthodox" synthesis that merged in the late fourth and early fifth centuries: namely, Gregory of Nyssa in the Greek-speaking East and Augustine in the Latin West. What happened to the theories and practices of new gender relations in these "orthodox" syntheses?

## Gender and Redemption in Some Second-Century Christianities

One second-century Christian movement that seems to have been condemned largely because of its renewal of archaic forms of prophetic, apocalyptic Christianity and the prominence of women in its leadership is Montanism. The movement of New Prophecy began in the mid-second century in Phrygia, a rural area of Asia Minor, led by three prophets, a man and two women: Montanus, Maximilla, and Priscilla. It quickly spread throughout the major Christian communities in Asia, North Africa, and Gaul, and was found even in Rome. The very description of the "new prophecy" as beginning in this period, however, reflects the perspective of its enemies. It saw itself as the continuation of apostolic Christianity, in confrontation with those Christians who had deviated from the ancient tradition of direct inspiration of the Holy Spirit.[8]

The major characteristics of the "new prophecy" reflect first-century Christian patterns. It assumes that normative Christian leadership comes from prophets, both male and female, who are possessed by the Paraclete sent by Christ and speak in the name of the Risen Lord. Thus Maximilla declares, "Hear not me but Christ." [9] As apocalypticists they regard themselves as living in the last days of history, awaiting the imminent advent of the New Jerusalem. Like Syriac Christians, they image the Paraclete (as ongoing presence of the Risen Christ) in female form, a pattern that reflects an identification of Wisdom with the Spirit, as well as traditions of female deities. Thus Priscilla says: "Under the appearance of a woman, clothed in a shining robe, Christ came to me and revealed to me that this place is sacred (Pepuza, the holy city for the Montanists) and that it is here that Jerusalem will descend from heaven." [10]

As those who believed themselves to be preparing for the end, Montanists practiced continence and fasting, discarding marriage relations, procreation, and possessions and taking on the role of itinerant prophet-preachers. Those who took such preparatory steps were backed by communities of householders who provided them with support. This system of support for the radicals seems to have been well organized, since their opponents speak angrily of their reception of gifts and the providing of financial support for preachers.[11]

Yet despite these provisions for support, the new prophecy lived in readiness, not only for the end, but also for martyrdom. The imperial power was seen as the historical representation of Satan's sway over the present world, and they expected to engage in combat to the death with it, thereby completing their union with Christ: "Do not wish to die in bed, in failure or in languishing fevers, but rather in martyrdom, in order that he may be glorified who suffered for you" (Montanus).[12] They saw themselves as the last prophetic dispensation before the culmination of history: "After me there will no longer be any prophet, but the end of all" (Maximilla). Maximilla also defends herself against the charge that she is a false prophet: "I am pursued as a wolf far from the sheep. I am not a wolf: I am Word, Spirit and Power."[13]

The condemnation of the new prophecy took place gradually in the late second and early third centuries by representatives of an emerging episcopal leadership that saw such charismatics as threatening. Yet many major church leaders of the day, such as Irenaeus in Lyons, defended them, seeing them as representatives of an old and familiar Christianity.[14] The acerbic leader of North African Christianity, Tertullian, joined their ranks shortly after the beginning of the third century, deploring the loss of direct inspiration of the Spirit in a domesticated church.[15]

The account of the North African martyrs who died in 203 C.E. preserved in the *Martyrdom of Perpetua and Felicitas*, probably by Tertullian himself,[16] reflects the spirit of the new prophecy. The central figure is the well-born woman Perpetua, a wife recently delivered of a child. Her slave woman, Felicitas, is pregnant and delivers a child in prison. Despite separation of social class the two woman are equals as Christians. The core of this document seems to have been a journal account written by Perpetua herself in which she recounts her visions and preparation for martyrdom.

Characteristic of this account is the repudiation of family responsibilities and paternal authority by this young woman in favor of her higher calling to martyrdom. Her father comes repeatedly to prison to beg her to relent, but she refuses. In her visions she sees the paradise that awaits them as martyrs in a bucolic scene in which a white-haired shepherd gives her milk to drink, an image that reflects the practice of giving milk to the newly baptized. Her spiritual powers also allow her to deliver through prayer the soul of her brother who died without baptism. In her vision of her victorious combat with an Egyptian gladiator, Perpetua becomes male, indicating that she has transcended the female condition. In the final combat with wild beasts, Perpetua not only fearlessly supports her male and female companions, but she can be killed only when she herself "steered the erring hand of the novice gladiator to her own throat."

Another expression of radical Christianity that challenged second-century church leaders was Marcionism. A convert from the Jewish community of Pontus, Marcion saw himself as renewing the teachings of Paul, which he believed had fallen into disregard and distortion in late-first-century Christianity. Marcion shaped his renewed Pauline theology and evangelized in Asia Minor between 110 and 150 C.E. Churches reflecting his views were already widely accepted in Asia when Justin wrote his *Apology* in 150.[17]

The core of Marcion's teachings was a radical interpretation of Paul's dualism of law and gospel. For Marcion the creator of this world, the giver of the law, is the author of an oppressive universe, under whose sway his creatures suffer social divisions, war, punitive violence, and death. Far beyond and unknown to this cosmic creator is the God of love revealed in Jesus. Marcion does not derive this Cosmocrator from the Higher God of Love nor regard redeemed humans as having a "spark" of this God encased in the lower trappings made by the creator. Rather, the gift of redeeming grace from the God revealed in Christ is a pure act of gratuitous mercy given to strangers whose natural destiny is defined by law and death. Through this act of grace received in faith (not gnosis), those who receive this good news receive "adoption" as reborn children of the loving God who breaks down enmity and gives immortal life.[18]

This reborn life is manifest in a radical departure from all the rules and social divisions of the "order of creation" that express the Creator God. This includes rejection of marriage and procreation. Marcionite churches, in common with others of the Syriac tradition, connected baptism with the vow of celibacy.[19] Baptism was seen as the seal of those who had escaped from the death-dealing grip of the World-Creator. Marcion saw redemption as breaking down all the divisions that separated humans as strangers from one another: Jews from gentiles, men from women, masters from slaves, even lepers and menstruating women from those who see such "polluted ones" as untouchable.[20]

The community of those redeemed from the laws of the World-God are joined in a radical discipleship of equals, including gender equality. That the Marcionite churches permitted women to exorcise, heal through laying on of hands, and to baptize is widely attested by their opponents.[21] Thus one can assume that these churches saw restrictions on women's public ministry as part of those laws of the oppressive Demiurgos that had been dissolved in the community of the redeemed. Although Marcion's radical Paulinism was vehemently rejected by the leaders of emerging orthodoxy, such a theology and practice found wide acceptance in the back country of Asia Minor and Syria. There, this seems to have been the predominant form of Christianity perhaps as late as the sixth century.[22]

Valentinianism is another variant of radical egalitarian Christianity of the second century. Valentinius was an Egyptian Christian, educated in Alexandria, who taught at Rome in 138–166 C.E. Initially his followers participated in the regular Christian assemblies, expounding their esoteric interpretation of Christian Scriptures and sacraments in their study groups, which included women and men.[23] Valentinius generated a wide following in many Christian centers, with disciples who became teachers and expounders of their own developments of this school of theology, such as Ptolemaeus and Marcus, Heracleon and Theodotus.[24]

The Valentinian school interpreted the Adamic fall and redemption in Christ through a story of cosmic devolution from and reintegration into a higher divine world. The higher divine world, or Pleroma, is described as evolving through a process of unions of cosmic male and female principles. The primal pair consists of Depth and Silence, from which came forth the second pair, Mind and Truth, and then two more pairs, Logos and Life, Human and Church. Ten and then twelve more Aeons came forth, making up a Pleroma of thirty, the last of these being Sophia or Wisdom.

Sophia is the cosmic Eve in the Valentinian system. It is she who seeks to "know the Father" in a way that violates the ordered hierarchy of the Pleroma and causes a disruption in it, resulting in chaotic forces: ignorance, grief, fear, and shock. These chaotic forces become the basis for the generation of a fallen cosmos. The Valentinians elaborate various versions of how the higher "eons" separate Sophia from her fallen passions, restoring her to the Pleroma, but the passions, together with "sparks" of true being, remain. From these passions the "powers" come into being, shaping a lower cosmos that mimics the Pleroma but is rooted in ignorance and falsehood. Sparks of true being are trapped in the psychic and somatic expressions of this lower cosmos.[25]

Valentinians reinterpret the Genesis 2–3 story of Adam and Eve. In their reading the cosmic authorities try to create Adam, but lack the power to make him rise from the ground until the Higher Spirit comes down and gives him a living soul. The creation of Eve from the side of Adam represents the separation of the spiritual principle from what remains as the merely psychic Adam. The authorities try to entrap this primal pair in the lower world of ignorance by forbidding them the fruit of the tree of knowledge, but the Higher Spiritual Principle appears to Eve as a snake and instructs her in the true spiritual world and the demonic character of the cosmic authorities.

After Eve eats the fruit of knowledge and shares it with Adam, they recognize "their nakedness of the Spiritual Principle." The jealous authorities expel the primal pair from the garden to prevent them from taking the next step of cosmic liberation (the tree of life). By throwing them into a life of toil, the "rulers" hope to prevent humans from "the opportunity of being devoted to the Holy Spirit." But the promise is given of the "true Man" to come, who "will anoint them with the Unction of life eternal" and free them from blindness and death, "which is of the Authorities."[26]

In the Valentinian *Gospel of Philip*, Christian baptism is interpreted as reuniting the psychic with the spiritual self, thereby overcoming ignorance and death.[27] Even though ignorance and death are "from the Authorities," Adam would not have died if Eve had not been separated from him. Baptism and anointing culminate in the sacrament of the bridal chamber, expressed in the holy kiss between communicants; this represents the reuniting of the male and female or psychic and spiritual principles of the self: "When Eve was still in Adam death did not exist. When she was separated from him death came into being. If he again becomes complete and attains his former self, death will be no more." Or, in another version of this idea:

> If the woman has not separated from the man, she would not die with the man. His separation became the beginning of death. Because of this Christ came to repair the separation which was from the beginning and again unite the two, and to give life to those who died because of separation. But the woman is united to her husband in the bridal chamber. Indeed those who have been united in the bridal chamber will no longer be separated.[28]

This Valentinian version of the new humanity in Christ, in which male and female are reunited, is striking because it is the female (Eve) who represents the spiritual power, separated from the psychic (Adam), who apart from her cannot live. It is the female spiritual principle who communicates with the higher divine world, mediated by Sophia, while the male by himself has affinity with the oppressive powers. Thus the female (spirit) is needed to lift the male (soul) to the higher world beyond ignorance and death.[29]

Presumably Valentinians understood actual men and women to have both principles, but in a form in which the union of the two had been lost. Thus both men and women attain a living wholeness in the sacrament of the bridal chamber. Since actual marriage and procreation both mimic this higher union and express the fall of male and female into separation and death, those who are reunited in androgynous wholeness also transcend actual sexual union. Thus for Valentinians a celibate redeemed group, male and female, minister to and help those who still exist on the fallen level of actual marriage to rise to this higher state: "In the Kingdom of Heaven the free will minister to the slaves: the children of the bridal chamber will minister to the children of the marriage."[30]

Valentinians not only saw women as participating equally in the community of the redeemed, but often presented women as having the deeper spiritual insight into the gospel needed to correct the lesser understanding of men. Thus in the *Gospel of Mary*, an early third-century writing,[31] the Risen Christ instructs his disciples and departs, after having told them to trust their inward insights and not to lay down any external laws and constraints. The male disciples grieve, wondering how they will have the courage to preach the gospel to the gentiles who will surely kill them as they have killed Christ. Mary (Magdalene) stands up and puts them back in touch with the good that they have experienced in Christ.

Peter turns to Mary, asking her to expound the gospel: "the Savior loved you more than the rest of the women," for she understands hidden teachings that Christ did not teach the male disciples. Mary describes a vision of the delivery of the soul from the lower powers of ignorance. Andrew then challenges this as "strange ideas." Peter joins this challenge, asking why the Savior would have preferred to teach a woman truths that he did not teach the males. Levi rebukes Peter's egoism:

> Peter, you have always been hot-tempered. Now I see you contending against the woman like the adversaries. But if the Savior made her worthy, who are you indeed to reject her? Surely the Savior knew her very well. That is why he loved her more than us.[32]

In this remarkable dialogue, Valentinian Christians not only defended woman's apostolic authority, in the person of Mary Magdalene, against those (Petrine) Christians who reject women's ministry and elaborate new "laws and rules," but even suggested that the ability to attain redemptive humanity depends on being able to hear from women spiritual insight into the true meaning of Christ's teaching. Rather than contending against women's teachings, the true Christian should "be ashamed, put on the perfect humanity, separate as he commanded us and preach the gospel, not laying down any other rule or other law beyond what the Savior said." The disciples then "began to go forth to proclaim and to preach."[33] Here the Valentinians claim that their views, in their rule-free and egalitarian form, are the true original apostolic teaching.

In the late second and early third centuries, major theological teachers—Tertullian in North Africa, Irenaeus in Gaul, Clement and Origen in Alexandria, among others—arise to defend a contrary view of apostolic teaching against the Marcionite and Valentinian constructions. Their writings come down to us as "orthodoxy," marginalizing their opponents whose writings survive only in fragments.

Common to all these orthodox thinkers is the basic affirmation that creation and redemption are in positive continuity. The God who created the world is the same God through which it is being redeemed. The Logos of creation is the same Logos revealed in Christ. The systems of Marcion and Valentinius that set a higher divinity against the creator are rejected as blasphemy. But within this basic affirmation of the oneness of God as creator and redeemer, there is a range of views on the body, sexuality, and the goodness of continued procreation.

Irenaeus represents a powerful vision of creation and redemption as one continuous process. The Logos and Spirit are the "two hands" by which God created the world and continues to sustain it, revealing in the human and natural body the sacramental presence of the divine. This same Logos and Spirit are manifest in Christ and are now guiding a process by which the entire created world is being led into communion with God. For Irenaeus this redemptive process will take place as a paradisial creation where the physical universe itself flowers in peace and harmony, and then a transformation by which the physical universe is immortalized and made spiritual and everlasting. The immortal and spiritual are thus not set against the body but connected through a process of ever fuller union of the bodily physical world with its creator, sustainer, and redeemer.[34]

Tertullian also insists that the body and physical world are created by God, but for him there is a deep tension between the bodily passions, expressed in lusts for sex and food, and the spiritual self that seeks communion with the divine Spirit.[35] By stern disciplining of these lower passions through continence and fasting, the soul is attuned to the Spirit. Sex and marriage have their place, but they are for the young, to discipline their sexual urges in faithful monogamous marriage. But the Christian should confine "his" intercourse to the minimum and gradually renounce it altogether. For Tertullian, like Paul, sex and prayer are incompatible. One abstains from sex in order to pray. To pray continually, one gives up sex completely. One marriage is enough. Once widowed, the Christian should remain continent.[36]

This emergence of continent older Christians, men and women, however, in no way alters the firm patriarchal ordering of the household, society, or church. Women are the "Devil's gateway." From women's sexual seductiveness sin and death entered the world.[37] Even virgins are to remain fully veiled to confess their subordinate and guilty status in the economy of fall and redemption.[38] Although as a Montanist the older Tertullian could affirm prophetesses who revealed the spiritual world in trances, even these women are not to violate the proper decorum of dress or humble subordination to male authority in the family and the church.[39]

In Clement of Alexandria, who presided over a Christian study circle in this cosmopolitan city in the late second century, we have the opposite of every kind of countercultural radicalism. For Clement all truth is ultimately one, whether from the Hebrew, the Greeks, or the gospel, for God is one, manifested through that Logos through which the world was created, which is present in every human soul and revealed in its fullness in Christ. All human quests for truth have partial truths that find their unity and completeness in Christ as divine Reason.[40]

All humans are created in the divine image and are to grow into the divine likeness by cultivating rational control over the passions and philosophical wisdom united to faith. Marriage is not to be despised, nor good food, but all is to be used in moderation for their proper purposes, procreation and nourishment of the body, while overcoming all forms of irrational passions in which the desire for pleasure overcomes the rational mind. Clement envisions the marriage relation as a companionship of men and women in virtuous living and mutual care for each other, in which sex is used sparingly as a purposive act to create children.[41]

For Clement the image of God, as the created expression of the divine Reason, is gender-neutral, present in all humans. Women have no less capacity than men to cultivate their image of God into the divine likeness through the same route of spiritual knowledge and control over the passions.[42] But this gender-neutral equality before God changes nothing of the pattern of the patriarchal family of classical moralists, with the husband presiding as sober patriarch and the wife dedicating herself to her domestic work, appearing in public as little as possible, cultivating her soul with prayer and virtue, and not adorning her external appearance "beyond the proper limit."[43]

In Origen, the brilliant scriptural exegete who followed Clement as a Christian teacher in Alexandria, we find both a more daring speculative mind and more radical ascetic temperament. He is said to have castrated himself in his youth to adhere literally to the words of Christ to become a eunuch for the reign of God and to put aside sexual temptation forever.[44] For Origen sexual continence is not a state to grow into by gradual discipline through marriage into old age, but a virginal purity to be aspired to as soon and as completely as possible.[45]

Origen's ascetic ethic is an integral expression of his theological cosmology, as he outlines it in his treatise *On First Principles*. In the beginning is God, the eternal intellectual One from which proceed from all eternity the Logos or Mind as a perfect intellectual manifestation of God and the Spirit as the power of holiness.[46] A spiritual creation also arises from all eternity, consisting of a certain limited number of intellectual beings or *logikai* who dwelt in blessed communion with God the Father through the Logos and the power of the Spirit.

At a certain point these intellectual spirits chose to separate themselves from God. Depending on how far they distanced themselves spiritually from their source, their bodies, which once shone with celestial splendor, took on various visible forms, either shining like the planetary spheres, or gross and material as human bodies, or dark as demonic powers. For Origen matter is a nature "admitting of all possible transformations" and its degree of physicality and mortality is the measure of its closeness or distance from the divine.[47]

God in merciful providence organized a cosmos around the various levels of the fallen intellects through which these spirits can reascend a ladder of spiritual stages of knowledge. The demonic powers ever seek to pull the fallen intellects down further, while angels, prophets, and ultimately the soul of Christ, as the one unfallen Spirit, enter the lower world to aid spirits to ascend back to their original heavenly state.

For Origen, gender, like the material body, is an excresence that represents particular states of fallenness. Originally spirits were without either visible bodies or gender, being created images of the divine Logos. It is this intellectual spirit that is referred to in Genesis as "image of God." "Male and female" referred to the union of spirit and soul in this original spiritual creation.[48] Only when the spirit falls and the soul increasingly grows cold, as it loses its union with the higher Spirit, taking on the appearance of physical bodies, do the distinctions of bodily gender manifest themselves.

But for Origen such distinctions are ephemeral, to be denied by seeking reunion with one's inner spirit and growing ever upward to a return to the spiritual state. By choosing and appropriating communion with God as one's own free choice, the intellect grows from received image into the likeness of God, regaining the immortal celestial body as resurrected spiritual body. The virgin who from youth chooses to remain sexually pure and uncorrupt anticipates this resurrected body of restored communion with God.

Since gender and body are mere ephemeral appearances of the fallen body to be negated by the virginal life and spiritual ascent, women as much as men are called to make that same ascent to become once again pure intellects in which soul is united to spirit in union with God. But for Origen this in no way empowers female virgins in the flesh to claim special public roles in the Christian assembly. In his commentary on 1 Cor. 14:34-35 Origen assails the Montanist women who claim the right to speak as inspired prophets.

If the Spirit ever speaks through women, such prophecies are to be spoken in private to be conveyed to the assembly by men. Likewise, insofar as women may teach, they may teach only younger women, instructing them to be silent and submissive. Whether married or virgin, no matter how holy she may be or how admirable the things she might have to say, a woman must never speak in the public assembly.[49] Thus, for Origen, gender hierarchy as men over women in the body, and as spirit over soul in the spiritual realm, remains an unalterable part of the cosmic ontology.

## Two Late Patristic Syntheses: Gregory of Nyssa and Augustine

In the first and second centuries of Christian history the renunciation of marriage was linked with a countercultural ethic that suggested a departure from gender and class hierarchies, rejection of worldly power and wealth, and the unleashing of a new community of equals. The author of 1 Timothy firmly countered such radicalism by an insistence on marriage and the patriarchal order of the family as normative for the church. Yet even for the orthodox of the second century, celibacy and anticipation of redemption were deeply connected, reconciled in various ways with marriage and patriarchal order. With Origen we see the beginning of a new synthesis of radical asceticism and the virginal life to be embraced even in youth, but patriarchal order remains.

In the late third and fourth centuries monastic life arose as the new vehicle for ascetic life.[50] A married priesthood stood over against the new virtuosos of the spiritual life who anticipated the heavenly world by celibacy, fasting, and praying unceasingly, living in the body as if they had none. Only gradually, with a new generation of ascetic intellectuals who also became bishops, such as Basil the Great and Augustine, did episcopacy and monastic life begin to merge. It would be many centuries, however, before celibacy was mandated for the ordained in the Latin church, while the Greek church reconciled the dichotomy by allowing priests to marry but choosing its bishops from among the monastic clergy.[51]

In the fourth and fifth centuries these shifting relations between asceticism, monasticism, and the clergy were still fluid. This period also saw a remarkable flowering of female ascetics drawn from the provincial and Roman nobility who shaped their version of the monastic life based on their own family networks and estates. At a time when clerical control over monasticism in general and female monasticism in particular had not yet hardened, these women appear remarkably as self-starters, making their own decisions to resist the demands of their families for marriage (or more often for remarriage) and shaping their own forms of monastic life for themselves and other women.

One such woman was Marcella, scion of the highest Roman nobility, who adopted the ascetic life as a young widow in her late teens after only seven months of marriage.[52] She was influenced by the first appearance of the monastic ideal, represented by stories of monks like Saint Anthony in Egypt, brought to Rome by exiles such as Athanasius in the 340s. Marcella gathered an ascetic circle of women of high rank who turned their own palaces into monastic retreats. There they not only shunned marriage and the pleasures of the table, but became eager students of Scripture under tutors such as Jerome.

Marcella continued to live as an ascetic in Rome into the first decade of the fifth century, dying from physical abuse brought on by the Gothic sacking of the city. Several others from this Roman female ascetic circle would depart from the capital city in the 370s and 380s to make the "grand tour" of the Egyptian hermits in the Nitrian desert, then founding monastic communities in the holy land.

One of these was Melania the Elder, of the powerful Valerii clan, left a widow with three children in 364 at the age of twenty-two. She adopted the ascetic life when two of her children died. Drawn into the ascetic circle of Marcella, Melania devoted herself to mortification and good works. In 372 she departed for the East, toured the monastic communities of Egypt, and eventually settled in Jerusalem. Joined by Rufinus, the translator of Origen into Latin, she founded a community for men and another for women on the Mount of Olives, as well as a hospice for pilgrims.[53] This monastic establishment would be inherited by her granddaughter, Melania the Younger, and her husband

Pinium, who fled from the Gothic advance in 410 and eventually made their way (having adopted a vow of celibacy) to Jerusalem about 418 C.E.[54]

Another such member of Marcella's circle was Paula, also left a widow with five children in her thirties. Together with her daughter Eustochium, she departed for the East about 385 C.E., together with Jerome. In Bethlehem she founded three monastic communities for women and one for men. When she died in 404 this establishment would be inherited by her daughter, Eustochium, and later by her granddaughter, Paula, the child of her son Toxotius, who had been sent by her parents to grow up in the Bethlehem monastery. In the lives of these wealthy ascetic women, family lineage, wealth, and power mingle with their apparent renunciation, as they use their wealth to found monasteries and do works of charity, then hand over their foundations to female descendants.[55]

Another ascetic circle knit together by family ties was that of Macrina, together with her mother and brothers, in fourth-century Cappadocia. Descended on both maternal and paternal sides from Christian martyrs of the late third century, Macrina was the eldest daughter of nine children whose father was a member of the landed aristocracy. In his *Life of Macrina*, her devoted brother Gregory describes her as a prodigy of holiness from childhood.[56] Even as she was being born, her destined saintliness was revealed to her mother in a vision in which she was given the secret name of Thecla, prototype of Christian women ascetics who had risen above the female condition.

Betrothed at the age of twelve to an upright young lawyer who died before the marriage could be consummated, Macrina refused a second engagement and resolved to live the virginal life at home as the helper of her mother. When her mother, Emmelda, was left a widow, Macrina became "father, teacher, attendant, mother, the counselor of every good" to her brother Peter, born posthumously.[57] As the other sisters married, Macrina increasingly shaped the family estates into a monastic community together with her mother, who gave up her former luxuries to live on the same level of simplicity with women who had been her former servants. Macrina's brother Peter took his place as the head of a male monastery, while she presided over the female community.

Macrina is credited with being the prime mover in the monastic vocation of her brother Naucratius, who died in a hunting accident after living for five years as a hermit, and also for her famous brothers, Basil and Gregory. Basil, who was sent to acquire advanced rhetorical education in Athens in preparation for a brilliant political career, is described by Gregory as returning from his studies "enormously puffed up with pride over his rhetorical abilities, despising all worthy people and exalting himself in self-importance above the illustrious men of the province." But Macrina soon converted him to the life of humility and asceticism (called by the Cappadocians "the philosophical life"):

> She drew him with such speed to the goal of philosophy that he renounced worldly renown . . . (and) deserted to the laborious life of manual labor to prepare himself by complete poverty and unfettered life directed toward virtue.[58]

For Gregory, who was married in his twenties,[59] Macrina was both the model of Christian ascetic holiness and his tutor in the path of spiritual ascent to union with God. Gregory was appointed a bishop by his brother Basil, who in the 370s became the powerful bishop of Cappadocian Caesaria and leader of the Neo-Nicene party against imperial Arianism. When Basil died in 379, Gregory hastened to visit his sister Macrina, whom he had not seen for eight years, only to find that she was on her deathbed.

Even though her body was failing, Gregory described Macrina as the transfigured self whose holy discourse led him from his doubts and questions about the nature of redemption to a vision of the destiny of soul and the resurrected body. Even in death Macrina's sanctity and virginal purity transformed her into the icon of the redeemed soul awaiting the resurrected body: "Even in the dark, the body glowed, the divine power adding grace to her body that, as in the vision of my dream, rays seemed to be shining from her loveliness." Sanctity also gave the holy one healing power, as well as deep understanding of spiritual truths. Thus Macrina is described as healing her own body from cancer by prayer and also healing the diseased eye of a child, as well as having other powers, such as casting out devils and prophesying future events.[60]

While it is not easy to get back to the real woman behind these hagiographic descriptions, what is evident is that Gregory credits Macrina as being the font of the ascetic life and architect of monastic community for his family, as well as his own mentor in the "philosophical life." In his ascetic and doctrinal treatises Gregory would eventually go beyond his own brother Basil in shaping the mystical theology that would underlie Eastern monasticism, drawing on deep veins of Christian and philosophical thought from Origen, Philo, and Plato.

In his treatise on *The Making of the Human*, Gregory lays out the theological anthropology that underlies his understanding of redemption.[61] Like Philo and Origen, Nyssa understands the term "image of God" of Gen. 1:27 as being a purely spiritual, intellectual being, brought forth by God at the beginning as the created reflection of the divine Logos. This intellectual being was incorporeal and immortal, lacking mortal body and gender. Yet God also gave this intellectual being free choice and anticipated that it would choose disobedience. Thus gender dualism as male and female was "added" by God from the beginning, not as an expression of the divine image itself, but as a nondivine and alien characteristic in anticipation of the fall.

As these originally created immortal "minds" chose separation from God, their created substance took on fallen bodies, or "coats of skin," characterized by sexual differentiation and mortality.[62] Marriage, sexual intercourse, and procreation then came about, both as the expression of bodies fallen into corruptibility and as the remedy for mortality, through the production of children. If this fall into sin and death had not occurred, there would have been a multiplication of incorporeal spirits up to the "full number" intended by God, but without sexual generation, through some "angelic means." But the fall into mortality meant that this full number of souls is created in the course of a temporal historical process at the same time that bodies are conceived through sexual procreation.[63]

Marriage, sexual reproduction, and birth, for Gregory, are not evils, but a remedy for death and the means for the production of embodied souls that fulfills God's intention, although by a "lower" means mixed with the evils of physical death and temptation toward those sinful lusts that ensnare the soul in spiritual death. Christians should not despise marriage and procreation as goods through which new human lives destined for redemption are produced. Like Clement, Gregory imagines that the disciplined Christian married couple, like his own parents—and presumably like his own experience of marriage with his beloved partner, Theosebeia—could soberly engage in the sexual act for the sake of procreation, while maintaining a spirit fixed on God. Chastity, in the sense of a purified spirit and well-disciplined body freed from lust, is not incompatible with the moderate "use" of the marital act, in Gregory's view.

Gregory, however, finds such discipline rare. Most "weak" persons cannot risk the sexual act without being ensnared in the pleasures that arise from its exercise. He advises persons to flee to the life of celibacy as refuge and fortress against the insistent demands of bodily pleasure.[64] Gregory is clear that sexual pleasure is not the only danger of marriage. For him even the virtuous married life—in which there is true affection and companionship between the spouses, good fortune, and healthy offspring—is still shadowed by mortality. All its goods are hedged about with the threat of temporality. The youthful wife may die in childbirth or the child may die. The wife lives in anxiety of widowhood. Marriage means the demands of family ties, honor, power, and property, all ephemeral goods soon to perish.

Thus to flee to virginity is also to flee from the engulfing threat of mortal goods to those immortal goods of the spirit that cannot perish. As marriage and procreation were the mortal remedy for mortality, so virginity is the ultimate escape from the cycle of birth and death into that incorruptible world in which there is no more birth and death, but immortal life. It is also the surest means to free the soul from those demands of the body that tie us to sin and corruptibility. Yet mere abstinence from sex is not itself virginity. It is only an instrument of the virginal life that must find its inward expression in a soul purified of desires and fixed on union with God. Nor does Gregory endorse an extreme asceticism that weakens the body with self-tortures and excessive fasting, practices that he recognizes as creating an obsession with the body by way of its negation. Rather he envisions a moderate ascetic regime for a healthy, well-balanced body that can put as few obstacles as possible in the way of the spirit's flight to communion with God.[65]

The goal of virginity is to see God. Virginity is a means to restore the self to its original nature as image of God that can grow through voluntary obedience into the "likeness of God," the increasing approximation of the divine nature. Through virginity, as the renunciation of all ensnarements of the soul by bodily lusts and its increasing purification in union with God, the human being, while still in the mortal body, approximates the redeemed life that will be completed through the joining of the soul to the resurrected body.

In Nyssa's dialogue with Macrina, recorded in his *On the Soul and the Resurrection,* his sister speaks as the voice of wisdom who leads him through a dialogical process toward increasing understanding of the mysteries of the soul, how it is knit together with the mortal body, separated from it at death and yet to be united with the transformed body in the resurrection.[66] This journey of the soul and resurrected body stands revealed as one continuous process in which the divine image of the original creation is restored to its primal glory before its fall into sin and death that caused its body to take on the "coats of sin" of corruptible process.

In the resurrection the body will be united with the soul as its good created vehicle, no longer as fleshly antagonist. It sheds those mortal properties or "coats of skin" that appeared with and as an expression of sin, finitude, and death. Thus Macrina tells Gregory:

> I here equate the word "skin" with the aspects of the animal nature with which we clothe ourselves when we become accustomed to sin. Among these are sexual intercourse, conception, child-bearing, sordidness, the nursing and nurturing of children, elimination, the process of growing up, the prime of life, growing old, disease and death. If that skin no longer envelopes us, how can those things connected with it continue to exist in us? . . . For what does being fat or thin, ill or healthy, or anything else coincident with the changing nature of our bodies have to do with the anticipated existence so different from the fluid and transitory course of this life?[67]

Once freed from the mortal body, the soul, united with its "spiritual body," can soar aloft to become ever more transformed into an approximation of the divine nature, going on from glory to glory in a process of growth no longer shadowed by mortality, but now imitating that infinite possibility of the eternal. Moreover, Macrina assures her brother, this transformation will eventually include all fallen spirits. Those who made more spiritual progress while in the mortal body will grow more quickly, while those who remained more tied to sin and death will undergo a longer purgation after death. But eventually God will be all in all, with the whole Pleroma of redeemed creation: "None of the beauties we now see, not only in humans, but in plants and animals, will be destroyed in the life to come."[68]

In this redemptive reascent to their divine source, women in their spiritual capacities stand as equals to men. Gregory does not envision women taking public leadership roles as priests or bishops, but in an imperial Christianity the episcopacy had come to look suspiciously like another political power role.[69] The exemplary Christian is the ascetic virtuoso of the "philosophic life." Here women are not only fully equal with men as fellow travelers, but, in the person of a holy sister like Macrina, can be both model and teacher for their weaker brothers.

In Augustine, the young North African rhetor who in 379 was just beginning his quest for fame and fortune as Gregory of Nyssa conducted his discourses on the soul and the resurrection with his dying sister, we find a different temperament and a different relation to women in the family and in sexual experience. Out of this temperament and experience Augustine would shape a markedly different construction of gender relations and the Christian story of creation, fall, and redemption. While the various stages of Gregory's development from youth to marriage to episcopacy to asceticism remained within the embrace of his prosperous and pious provincial family network, Augustine, also a provincial but of more modest means, was defined in the first half of his life by the struggle to transcend his social origins.

Augustine had a very different relation to his parents and siblings. He patently disliked his pagan father, whose harsh, prideful, and libidinous character reflected all that Augustine wanted to shun in himself. Although he would embrace his mother's Catholic Christianity on a higher level at the end of a long search for truth, in his youth her church represented to him a naive religiosity unworthy of his intellectual acumen.[70] Yet Augustine was defined by both parents to be the family's rising star. His father dug deep into his pockets to invest in his education as the bright son who was to rise through his wits from home town to provincial capital to Rome. It was hoped this ascent would culminate in a marriage and career that would carry Augustine into the circles of the imperial nobility.

This educational and career trajectory also meant that Augustine was not to consider the containment of his youthful sexual urges through legal marriage to a girl of his home town. Instead, he settled at eighteen for thirteen years of monogamous concubinage with a girl he loved but whose social origins precluded marriage. She bore him a son in the first year of this relationship.[71] In that same year, as he pursued his higher education in Carthage, he also became a Manichean, seeking in this ascetic Persian sect deeper insights into the nature of good and evil that he contemptuously assumed could not be found in his mother's simple faith.[72]

In 384 at the age of thirty, Augustine had moved far toward his chosen goals. His brilliance as rhetor and teacher had brought him into the imperial circles in Rome and then Milan. He was engaged to marry a twelve-year-old heiress of a Milanese Catholic family. The pagan nobility appreciated him both for his intellectual gifts and for his heterodoxy, which put him outside of the church of their Catholic rivals. His mother sent his concubine packing back to North Africa vowing fidelity to their relationship. Augustine turned to a short-term mistress while he waited for his bride to come of age. In such a marriage there was no question of intellectual companionship, but only another stepping stone in his "brilliant career."[73]

By this time, however, Augustine also began to listen to the sermons of Ambrose, bishop of Milan, who combined the most sophisticated philosophical education with membership in a ranking senatorial family. Ambrose introduced Augustine to allegorical interpretation of Scripture, which allowed him to see that his intellectual sophistication need not be offended at the barbarous world of the Christian Bible. Ambrose also promoted a stern asceticism, demanded above all of the clergy, in which sexual continence and service to the church were closely linked.

Augustine began to struggle to commit himself to the Catholic faith in baptism, a decision that for him was virtually identical with renunciation of sexual relations, including jettisoning of his advantageous marriage. His feelings of deep impotency as he sought to use intellectual decision to master his unruly will, "bent on these lower things," was to come to define the very center of his understanding of the fallen self. Only through a direct intervention of divine grace, which broke his self-will and gave him the power of obedience to the divine will, did Augustine see himself as able to make the leap of conversion and sexual renunciation.[74]

The theological implications of this conversion experience would only gradually reshape Augustine's still Platonic theology. In the first stage of his appropriation of his new Catholic Christian identity, he retired with like-minded friends, as well as his teenage son and his mother, Monica, for a season of philosophical discourse. He then returned to North Africa with the intention of founding and living in a monastic community. Called by the bishop to preach, then to the ordained priesthood and finally to the episcopacy in Hippo, by 395 Augustine had assumed the role of leading bishop for the Catholic community of North Africa. This role would shape the second half of his life until his death in 431.

His mother, Monica, who had been the only female religious mentor in his life (although on nowhere near the same level as Macrina in relation to Gregory), was dead.[75] There do not seem to have been female ascetic intellectuals on a par with a Marcella, Paula, or Melania the Elder in Augustine's circles in the North African church, although Melania the Younger and her husband, Pinian, would sojourn there for some years between 410 and 418. But for Augustine the adoption of celibacy did not open up the possibility of spiritual friendship with ascetic women, unlike his contemporaries Jerome and Rufinus. Sexual lust, though repressed, was, for Augustine, never really conquered, and he imposed on himself and his clergy strict rules that forbade meeting alone with any woman, even a relative.[76]

Augustine's mature theological anthropology would be hammered out in a series of controversies with enemies: first, his old confreres, the Manicheans; then the Donatists, who represented the popular North African church that, for a hundred years, had claimed to be the true church of the martyrs against the Catholic church as the church of the empire;[77] and finally the Pelagians, who challenged Augustine's construction of original sin, the bondage of the will, grace, and predestination, and his peculiar interpretation of sexual lust.

In an effort to clarify his own understanding of human nature, gender, sex, and sin, Augustine would return again and again to Genesis 1–3. Augustine dealt with these passages first in his *Two Books on Genesis against the Manichees* in 388–89, and then in an attempted commentary on Genesis in 393, which he never completed, breaking off his exegesis right before Gen. 1:27 on maleness and femaleness.[78] He returned to these passages in the final three books of the *Confessions,* and then in a monumental work in twelve books, *On Genesis Literally Interpreted,* which he worked at from 404 to 420.[79] He also dealt with the first chapters of Genesis in books 11–14 of *The City of God,* written by 417–18, and he attempted final clarifications of his teachings on sex and sin in the writings of his old age against the Pelagian-leaning bishop, Julian of Eclanum.[80] His reflections on these themes are also scattered in his treatises on marriage, virginity, adulterous marriages, and marriage and concupiscence.[81]

In his early writing on Genesis against the Manicheans Augustine followed the Origenist tradition in seeing humans as created first as an incorporeal unity. The image of God refers, not to the physical body, but to the "interior man" or intellect through which humans rule the lower creation and contemplate eternal things. Male and female originally meant the union of spirit and soul, with the male part of the inner self ruling over the female. Together this unitary human would have reproduced angelically, creating "spiritual offspring of intelligible and immortal joys." Only after sin did physical sexual differentiation and "carnal fecundity" appear.[82]

In his later writings Augustine moved away from this Platonic approach, insisting that Adam and Eve were created from the beginning with real physical and sexually differentiated bodies. Gender differentiation, sexual intercourse, and physical offspring were part of God's original created design, not simply characteristics that appeared after sin and as a remedy for mortality.[83]

God first created the (nongendered) idea of the human, the intellectual "image of God" found in all humans, male and female. But in the actual production of the human, the male was created first and then the female from his side to indicate the relation of superiority and subordination by which the genders are to relate to each other in the social order. For Augustine, gender hierarchy is a part of original nature; it did not appear only after the fall.[84]

In paradise Adam and Eve would not have died, not because their bodies were not physical, but because their bodies would have been so united with their intellect in union with God that the body would have been prevented from dying. Adam and Eve were intended by God to have sexual intercourse and produce physical offspring through which the full number of the human community would have been generated over time. But Adam would have sown his seed in Eve without lust as a rational act fully under the control of his mind, as a farmer sows seed in a field. Moreover, Eve would have remained virginal in intercourse and parturition, never losing her bodily "integrity," a notion that suggests something less than a corporeal process of sex and birth.[85]

But this lust-free generation never actually happened, because the creation of Eve was followed straightway by the fall. Although Adam and Eve were created with the ability to obey God and hence not to sin, they used their free will to disobey God. The serpent, who represents the enticement to disobedience to God and preference for selfish desires, approached Eve first, because as a woman she had less rationality and understanding and was closer to the "lower soul," hence was easily deceived. Following 1 Timothy 2:14, Augustine claims that Adam was not deceived. He knew better, but consented to go along with Eve as an act of kindly companionship lest she be left alone outside paradise.[86]

Although Eve's delusion began the fall, Adam's consent (representing the intellect), was the decisive act, for a person does not sin unless the mind consents to the temptation. Both Adam and Eve are equally culpable but in different ways. Adam's particular sin lay in losing male rank by obeying his wife (his lower self) rather than making his wife obey him as her "head."[87] Despite Augustine's theoretical view that both men and women have intellects (the image of God), when referred to as a couple, men and women as male and female are seen as representing the relation of mind and body, intellect and passions, as dominant and subordinate, superior and inferior.

Woman here is seen as the lower part of a collective image of God represented by the male. Interpreting Paul's view in 1 Cor. 7:11 that woman is not made in the image of God, Augustine declares that:

> separately in her quality as a helpmeet, which regards the woman alone, then she is not the image of God, but, as regards the man alone, he is the image of God as fully and completely as when the woman too is joined with him in one.[88]

Here we seen the ambivalence of Augustine's view of the image of God in woman, for although she has it, as nongendered intellect, she does not "represent it" as woman.

Through the fall the human race lost both its original immortality and freedom of the will. It was plunged into sin and death manifested in profound dislocation of mind, will, and desire. No longer did the sexual parts move in calm obedience to the mind, but rather the fallen (male) body experienced a war "between the law in the members that wars against the law of the mind." In sexual attraction and intercourse the male experiences uncontrollable "concupiscence" that manifests this basic discord between mind and body that both appeared with and expresses the fallen condition. Since no sexual act can be carried out without concupiscent ejaculation, this for Augustine meant that every sexual act is both sinful and is the means for transmitting the original sin of Adam to all his descendants.

For Augustine fallen humans had departed decisively from their original created state, but in a very different way from that imagined by Origen or Nyssa. The mortal body did not appear with sin, but rather was released into death when humans lost their union with God. Humans also lost their original free will. No longer are they able to obey God as a free act, but rather they are entrapped in their own egoism and desires for self-will. Only divine acts of grace beyond present human nature can break this bondage of the will and force the divided self to obey God rather than self.[89]

For Augustine God foresaw from all eternity that humans would sin and so also elected a certain limited number of humans who would receive the grace to obey and persevere in obedience. Most humans, despite their illusion of free moral acts, are governed by the selfish will and will be damned eternally along with the fallen angels. Here Augustine departs from the theological patterns of the Greek fathers that made human free choice—first as the choice to turn away from God and then as the choice to turn back to God—the pivot of the story of human fall and redemption.[90]

For thinkers like Irenaeus, Clement, Origen, and Nyssa, God acted graciously in sending the prophets and then Christ to redeem us. But the human, even in sin, remains essentially the image of God. Humans both can and must act through free moral choice to restore the image and grow into the likeness of God. Since this image of God and its potential to grow into the likeness of God are present in all humans, redemption is potentially universal. Some, like Origen, saw it as embracing all intellectual spirits—angelic, human, and demonic. Redemption also was understood to embrace the whole cosmos.

Augustine's doctrines of bondage of the will, limited election, and double predestination (some to salvation and the rest to damnation) broke this accepted tradition in which the actualization of human freedom to become the true self as image and likeness of God was the heart of the Christian message.[91] Augustine's view of fall and original sin not only limited salvation to a predestined few, but substituted for the vision of moral freedom a divine coercion outside and against our present natures. Pelagius and his followers saw themselves as defending this long Christian tradition of moral freedom to choose to love God as our true natures, rejecting what they saw as Augustine's pessimistic determinism, which they suspected as being a remnant of Manicheanism.[92]

Not only was Augustine's God seen as an arbitrary tyrant who acted coercively from outside the human condition rather than from within its natural capacities for goodness, but also Augustine's view of the fall justified social hierarchy and coercive relations of men over women, masters over slaves, state over subjects. Augustine argued that the rule of men over women was a part of the original created nature, but the fall came about through female subversion of this right relation. Thus in fallen society men are justified in acting coercively to force their wives to obey them, and women should submit to this coercion as their duty, even if at times it is unjust or excessive.[93]

Although Augustine believed that in paradise there would have been no other relations of domination by which one male would dominate another male, in the fall sinful self-will causes social disorder. Thus various relations of force—slavery, coercion of children by parents, coercion of recalcitrant peasants by landlords, repression of rebels by the state—are all justified to keep the peace and to prevent worse evils of lawlessness.[94] This view of the necessity of coercive power relations to keep order in sinful society would be used by Augustine to justify the use of the coercive arm of the state to compel Christian dissidents and sectarians (such as the Donatists) to submit to the rule of the Catholic church.[95] Augustine is the father of the Inquisition, applying his views of original sin to rationalize coercive use of state power to force dissenting Christians to submit to church authority.[96]

In turning to the question of marriage, Augustine argues that the production of children was the original purpose of the creation of the male-female pair in paradise, for if it was primarily a matter of companionship, another male would have been a better companion than the female.[97] The good of procreation remains after sin, even though the sexual act can no longer be conducted without sin. Yet this sin is allowed and forgiven if the couple engage in it only for reproduction or even for the secondary good of remaining faithful and avoiding illicit sex with others. But any sexual act, even in marriage, undertaken only for pleasure, impeding procreation, is wholly sinful and equivalent to fornication.[98]

Although marriage and sex for procreation remain a natural good, they have now been transcended in the new order of redemption in Christ. The full number of humans desired by God has already been produced, and so God no longer commands humans to "increase and multiply."[99] The higher way of life more in keeping with redemption is virginity.[100] Failing that, Christians can embrace chaste widowhood or continence within marriage. Augustine responds to those who denigrate all sex, even in marriage, and those who put marriage and virginity on an equal level, by insisting that marriage is a good of nature, but continence is a better good that points toward the higher life of grace.

Although true virginity is ultimately an inward submission of the self to God and not simply a physical condition of abstinence from sex, nevertheless Augustine believes that true virgins (who are virgins both inwardly and outwardly) will receive a higher status in heaven than those who have followed the lower path of virtuous marriage. Better a humble wife than a proud virgin, to be sure. But those who are "intact" in soul and body are, for Augustine, mysteriously holy in a way that is not attainable by those who have lost this quality through sexual "indulgence," even if contained within virtuous marriage.[101]

For Augustine redemption is not simply a restoration of the original state of nature, but also a transcendence of it. The first humans were able not to sin and not to die, but the redeemed humans at the resurrection will be raised beyond the mortal body and the possibility of the choice of sin into a union with God defined, not by our choice of God but by God's sovereign choice of us (the elect few). In the resurrection women will rise as women just as men will rise as men, but in such a way that their sexual parts related to procreation "will be fitted to glory rather than to shame."[102]

Based on their equality in the image of God, those women who have lived the spiritual life in God's grace will shine as gloriously as men. There will be no gender or other social hierarchy in heaven (although apparently there will be a hierarchy of spiritual merit). But here on earth the hierarchy of men over women remains the order of creation, to be coercively enforced in the fallen condition. This is the regime to which all women, even virgins, should submit.

Salvation does not liberate women from male domination here on earth, but teaches them to redouble their submission to their earthly lords, both to repent of the original subversion of this gender order by their wayward mother Eve and to anticipate that heavenly state in which redeeming grace empowers us to submit our wills to the will of God. Before God all Christians are as women.

3. Hildegard of Bingen receiving her revelations. Manuscript illumination by Hildegard of Bingen. Copyright © Beltz Verlag, Weinheim und Basel, Programm Beltz & Gelberg

Chapter Three

# Male Scholastics and Women Mystics in Medieval Theology

THE NEW TESTAMENT AND PATRISTIC MESSAGE of the inclusion of women in the image of God redeemed in Christ, however androcentrically conceived and in dichotomous tension with women's subjugation in creation and fallenness, activated women as agents in seeking and acting on this offer of redemption. One discerns this presence of the female subject behind many New Testament and patristic male authors, either when men seek to contain and limit this female agency or when they appeal to women's particular interests; that is, promotion of asceticism to women as freeing them from the trials of male domination and childbearing.[1] But one seldom hears the voices of these women directly.

A few scraps remain of women's own words: some oracular cries from the Montanist prophets; something from the prison diary of the martyr Perpetua; the Christian story cast into the schoolbook form of lines from Virgil by the fourth-century Roman matron Proba; a holy land travelog by the late-fourth-century nun Egeria; some letters, poems and a martyr's life by the fifth-century empress Eudocia; and a few other letters, poems, epitaphs, and inscriptions.[2] But mostly we must try to discern the contours of female lives and thought through the eyes of their male friends. We can assume that Macrina thought about the Christian life much as her brother Gregory describes, but we can never know how key points might be nuanced by her woman's perspective.

Of the great ascetic foundresses of the fourth and fifth centuries, Macrina, Marcella, the Paulas and Melanias Elder and Younger, we have scarcely a line, even though we know from their male friends that they pursued studies of Scripture and of the church fathers and wrote extensively in the form of letters of inquiry on exegetical points, as well as interventions in doctrinal and church disputes.[3] The reasons for this lack of preservation of writings of the church mothers are not hard to find. The lack reflects the limits imposed upon their authority by their brothers, the church fathers.

Women may be equal in holiness and ultimately in heaven. A woman may even be learned, so much so that priests seek out her counseling on points of Scripture, theology, and the spiritual life, as Gregory of Nyssa bowed to his sister as his mentor. But women may not teach publicly. Women's words of counsel and inspiration are to remain private. They are excluded from the public teaching of the church. Ergo, however much their memory and even their relics are venerated as saints, their writings are not preserved as official tradition.[4]

This situation of women's lack of public teaching authority in the church continued in the Middle Ages and was renewed in the Reformation. Indeed it has only begun to be overcome in the late twentieth century. But for various reasons its implications for the lack of preservation of women's writings began to change. Starting in the tenth century with the plays of Hrotsvit of Gandersheim, growing in the eleventh century and becoming a mighty stream in the twelfth to fifteenth centuries, we find more and more women's writings. These women write in a variety of genres, not just letters and saint's lives, but plays, theological treatises, guides to the spiritual life and, above all, accounts of their mystical experiences, the latter becoming women's particular genre of theological writing.

More and more women began to commit their thoughts to paper, often with the aid of a male scribe, and these writings were preserved. The reasons reflect the institutions of female religious life. There women learned elements of literacy in Latin and the vernacular. There they had libraries and scriptoria (which included painting and illumination) where their thoughts could be not only written down but preserved, copied, and sent to other readers. There through continual liturgical prayer, women might gain an extensive knowledge of Scripture and some theology, and could also express themselves in poems and plays to be put to music and performed liturgically in their communities—again to be written down, copied, circulated to other communities.

There remained from the New Testament legacy an important exception to women's lack of public teaching authority in Christianity, an exception that women used to gain a public voice in the medieval church. Although women could not be priests, they could be prophets.[5] God might speak directly to a woman, conveying an urgent message to the church and society of her time. Women might experience God in revelatory disclosures that could direct others on the path of holiness. In these roles as direct vehicles of God's presence and voice, women both denounced evils and pointed to the way of restored life with God.

Women's revelatory experiences were not self-validating. They had to be validated by male ecclesiastical authority—a personal counselor, an abbot, a bishop, even the Pope, the higher the rank the better. Visionary women who failed to gain such male support (or male support of sufficiently high rank and influence) could hardly gain a voice. When male authorities were divided on women's prophetic authenticity, which authorities won determined whether a woman and her writings were circulated and preserved or suppressed or even burned at the stake along with her body. When a woman claimed revelations, the critical question was from whence came these communications, God or the devil? Was she therefore a prophet or a witch? And, as in the case of Joan of Arc, which men had the power to make the crucial decision?[6]

## Hildegard of Bingen

In the twelfth century, Hildegard of Bingen was the most notable example of a woman who received such validation from the highest authorities of church and state. Thus she was able to exercise her extraordinary creative powers to the fullest extent, within the limits of the roles available to her of abbess and prophet. Hildegard's long life of eighty-one years covered most of the twelfth century, 1098–1179. Born as the tenth child to a noble family, well connected to political and church leaders, in Bermersheim bei Alzey in Rhine-Hessen, she was given to the church as a tithe at the age of eight, being entrusted to the care of Jutta of Sponheim, a noblewoman, whose hermitage was attached to the male Benedictine monastery of Saint Disibod. There Hildegard gained a thorough grounding in the Latin Bible, particularly through the monastic office.

Although she claims that both her mentor, Jutta, and she herself remained "unlearned," it is evident from her subtle and masterful but idiosyncratic Latin that she was able to explore a range of authorities on theology and natural history of her time. But she remained largely self-taught both in developing her distinctive exposition of the orthodox Christian worldview and in her use of imagery, music, and language. Hildegard regarded her language as itself revelatory and issued stern warnings against any editor who might revise it, beyond grammatical corrections. She also developed a secret language, based on Latin, which was used as a mystical form of communication in her community.[7]

In her *Life*, written at her dictation when she was in her mid-seventies, Hildegard recounts that from earliest childhood she had luminous visionary experiences, a second sight into hidden realities that took place while she retained ordinary consciousness. These visions were vividly pictorial, although also interpreted to her in Latin, in such a form that both the vision and its meaning were clearly imprinted on her memory.[8] These visions were accompanied by debilitating illnesses "that threatened to bring me to death's door."[9] When she realized as a small child that others did not see as she saw, she learned to keep silent about such experiences, communicating them privately to her mentor, Jutta. In her fortieth year the pain of suppressing these visions became so great that she divulged them to Volmar, the monastery provost, who encouraged her to write them down.[10]

The hermitage with Jutta and Hildegard attracted many other women members and grew into a well-endowed cloister, attached to the male community of Saint Disibod. When Jutta died in 1136 Hildegard was elected its head. It was in 1141, when Hildegard was forty-two years old, that she received visions of fiery light that gave her an infused knowledge of the Scriptures, Old and New Testaments, accompanied by a heavenly voice commanding her to "say and write what you see and hear."[11] With the editorial assistance of Volmar and her favorite nun of her community, Richardis von Stade, Hildegard began to dictate these visions, together with the exegesis of their meaning that came to her through the heavenly voice.

Over the next ten years, 1141–51, her first major book, *Scivias*, took shape. Eventually each vision in its visual form would be painted, probably at Hildegard's dictation, by women who did the illuminations in the monastery scriptoria.[12] Thus we have each of the twenty-six visions in the *Scivias* in three forms: described in words, in a painting in vivid colors, and interpreted by the heavenly voice. These twenty-six visions, divided into three books, comprise a comprehensive theological cosmology, a summa theologica that touches on the entire range of topics of salvation history from beginning to end.[13]

In the *Scivias* we are led through complex pictorial images, which are then exegeted: God's creation of the world; Lucifer's fall; Adam and Eve's fall from paradise; the incarnation of the Word who created the world taking human flesh in the womb of the Virgin Mary to heal the breach opened up between God and humans; the course of salvation history from Adam's fall, Noah, Abraham, and Moses, the patriarchs and prophets, then the apostles and martyrs of early Christianity; to the building of the church in her own day, with the struggles between faithful and unfaithful Christians, to the anticipation of the final conflicts with the Antichrist, the judgment and transformation of creation into its eschatological form, culminating in heaven and hell beyond the present temporal order.

Although Hildegard receives and exegetes this story seriatim in visions and discourses that begin with creation, go on through salvation history and end with eschatology, there is a sense both in the *Scivias* and in its redoing in her final great work (written in her late seventies), *The Book of Divine Works*, that this salvational drama is present in her mind as a unified whole, all simultaneously here and now, from the perspective of God who stands outside time, a simultaneity that Hildegard partially shares as one caught up in vision to the divine viewpoint. Again and again in her letters she will sketch this whole drama in a few powerful strokes: Lucifer's fall, the paradisial and then fallen condition of Adam, Christ taking on human flesh in the virgin's womb, the final conflict between God and Satan, all brought to bear on the present condition of the church as both the community of redemption and devil-ridden in its human weakness and strife.[14]

Modern interpreters of Hildegard have been particularly struck by her habitual method of affirming her prophetic authority as a vehicle of God, while simultaneously discounting herself as a "poor little female figure" *(paupercula feminea forma)*,[15] physically weak, unlearned, without status as fallen Eve. From a modern and feminist perspective that sees self-affirmation as crucial to women's well-being, this constant dichotomy between Hildegard's diminishment as a woman and God's authority seems either internalized self-hatred or a rhetorical trick or perhaps some of both. But this puzzle reflects modern anthropological views that disappear once the assumptions of Hildegard and her context are taken seriously.

We should recognize at least four levels of meaning that dictate this dichotomy between Hildegard as "poor little female figure" and the divine that speaks through her as prophet. First, as indicated above, this was the only way a woman could gain a public voice in medieval Christianity. As one under subjugation in creation and domination in the fall, a woman could not publicly teach theologically or exercise authority in her own name, but only as one whose subjugation had been overridden by a God who used her as a vehicle of revelation to raise her beyond both her female condition and the human condition in general. As prophet a woman has authority not in her own name, but as one used by God despite her "weakness." Thus in utilizing this contrast between her feminine weakness and the revelatory voice of God that speaks through her, Hildegard simply accepts and conforms to the view of her church, which negates her as a woman only to allow her to speak with the highest and most thunderous authority possible as voice of God.

Once validated as a true prophet, however, Hildegard could and did speak with precisely such a thunderous voice to the greatest men of her day. And this voice of divine authority was generally accepted by these men, despite the conflicts some had with her. Many sought her out humbly, asking for her prayers, her insights about the future, whether God had told her anything about them, about the fate of souls in the next life, and about cures for the infertile and the demon-possessed. Once the authenticity of her divine voice was accepted, her female "weakness" was not so much an impediment as a marvel, a continual affirmation of the scriptural principles that "the Spirit blows where it will" (John 3:8) and "God chose what is weak in the world to shame the strong" (1 Cor. 1:27).[16]

Second, for Hildegard this self-negation corresponds to the human condition generally. All humans are "ashes of ashes, filth of filth,"[17] both in the created body apart from God's vivifying power and as fallen into captivity to this identity as "ashes and slime" in sin. Humans, male or female, cannot expect to speak truth or live in a holy manner unless they empty themselves and allow God to use them as a vehicle of grace. In her letter to the younger woman mystic Elisabeth of Schönau, Hildegard makes clear that not only women, but all true Christian visionaries who hope to impart God's word to their fellow humans, can do so only if they empty themselves of any self-will. Not only she but the greatest prophets and apostles of Scripture, such as Paul, could be true vessels of God's word only to the extent that they acknowledged and made themselves "nothing," so God could be all in all in and through them.

Hildegard shows that this is the original and essential way all creation remains united with God, while the crux of fallenness is the assertion of self against God's life-giving presence:

> I am but a poor creature and a fragile vessel; yet what I speak to you comes not from me but from the clear light. Human beings are vessels God has made and filled with the Spirit so that the divine work might come to perfection in them. . . . It was through the divine word alone that everything came into existence perfect. The grasses, the woods, the trees came forth. The sun too and the moon and the stars went to their appointed places to perform their service. . . . It was only humans themselves who did not know their creator. For although God bestowed great knowledge on humans, they raised themselves up in their hearts and turned away from God . . . But God endowed some persons with insight so that humankind should not completely fall into derision.[18]

Hildegard alludes to Abel, to the Hebrew seers, and finally to the coming of Christ as the mending of this relation to God. But in her own day there had been a steady decline of the human grasp of this life-giving presence. It was, as Hildegard calls it, a "womanish time" (a time of lack of virtue), and so God was lifting up new prophets, even women, to be divine instruments. To be true instruments, persons such as herself and Elizabeth had to avoid the devilish temptations to claim such authority as their own, rather than making themselves humble vehicles of God:

> Those who long to bring God's words to completion must always remember that, because they are human, they are vessels of clay and so should continually focus on what they are and what they will be. . . . They themselves only announce the mysteries like a trumpet that which indeed allows the sound but is not itself the source that produces the note.[19]

On a third level, Hildegard accepts this dichotomy between her weakness and the divine authority that speaks in her because it corresponds to her personal experience of herself. Hildegard knows herself to be physically assailed by continual illness, of inadequate learning, marginal as a woman in her church and society, and yet empowered by extraordinary energy that even in old age can make her feel like a young girl.[20] She has visionary knowledge that can see the whole cosmos and world history from end to end in a glance; she is endowed with gifts in music, language, sciences, and with enormous willpower to contend with the greatest powers of church and state in her day. While we might say both voices and energies are Hildegard's, she herself could explain the duality in her experience, and assure that the second voice was accepted by her society, only by assuming that the first was herself, while the second was God acting in her.

On a fourth level, subordinate to the first three, Hildegard wields the contrast between her littleness and the divine voice rhetorically, as a power tool by which she not only sets forth her visions but also contends with adversaries in her church and society and responds to humble requests from petitioners who seek her prayers and advice. Nor is she above using this duality ironically, as a put-down to the great men of her day who assume that their maleness, combined with high class and ecclesiastical status, automatically makes them the voice of God.

Hildegard's last great struggle at the end of her life was against the prelates of Mainz, who imposed an inderdict on her community because she refused to exhume the body of a man buried in her monastic cemetery who they claimed (and she denied) had died excommunicate. Hildegard threatened the prelates with divine judgment, contrasting their own exemplification of "womanish times" with her divinely given authority as God's *bellatrix* (female warrior):

> And I heard a voice saying thus: Who created Heaven? God. Who opens heaven to the faithful? God. Who is like Him? No one. And so, O men of faith, let none of you resist Him or oppose Him, lest He fall on you in His might and you have no helper to protect you from His judgment. This time is a womanish time, because the dispensation of God's justice is weak. But the strength of God's justice is exerting itself, a female warrior battling against injustice, so that it might fall defeated.[21]

All Hildegard's writings from her forties to her seventies, following her vision of the voice that commanded her to "say and write what you see and hear," show absolute confidence in this voice as God speaking through her. Her success in having this voice authenticated by the highest ecclesiastical authorities provided an essential condition for her ability to wield it in her society. After confiding her visions privately to Jutta and Volmar, she wrote to the greatest monk of her day, Bernard of Clairvaux, in 1146, several years into the writing of her *Scivias*, to seek his approbation of her visionary authority. Bernard's reply to this appeal, from one who was at that time an unknown nun, was perfunctory but affirmative, urging her to "recognize this gift as a grace" and to respond to it eagerly but also humbly.[22]

In 1146–47, by a lucky stroke of fortune, Pope Eugenius III, a Cistercian and disciple of Bernard, was meeting in synod in Trier. Volmar had told his abbot, Kuno, of Hildegard's visions; Kuno informed Heinrich, archbishop of Mainz. Heinrich mentioned this to the pope, who dispatched two legates for a copy of the incomplete *Scivias*. Bernard intervened to affirm Hildegard's authenticity to Pope Eugenius, who was impressed and read parts of the text before the assembled prelates. He then wrote a letter to Hildegard giving her his apostolic approbation.[23]

So, by a fortuitous chain of male ecclesiastical approval, Hildegard was able to gain the highest validation in the church. She also gained protection over her monastery by then-emperor Frederick Barbarossa. Despite her later denunciations of him, this protection held firm throughout her life.[24] Hildegard's divine voice was thus credentialed by the highest authorities of her time. She would maintain this authority, despite private doubts by some, through several crucial battles with church authorities, in which she did not spare her denunciations of the corruption she saw in the lives of great prelates and princes.

In at least one of these conflicts, when Hildegard claimed divine mandate to move her community to a new site at Rupertsberg, freeing it from dependence on Saint Disibod, she reports that some questioned her authority and even her sanity:

> Many people said, "What's all this—so many hidden truths revealed to this foolish, unlearned woman, when there are many brave and wise men around? Surely this will come to nothing!" For many people wondered whether my revelation stemmed from

> God, or from the parchedness of aerial spirits that often seduced human beings.[25]

Hildegard's theological anthropology of gender in creation, fall, and redemption is not easy to sort out with precision, for she was an imagistic thinker, not a philosophical systematician. But the general pattern of her thought can be summarized. First, she herself and all women, in relation to God as God's creation, are simply and completely *homo*, fully and completely equivalent to men as expressions of the image and likeness of God. Characteristically, when God speaks to her, as when she speaks to others (mostly men) in the voice of God, she is referred to simply a "O man" *(O homo)*. God does not address her as woman, even in affectionate terms, such as daughter, handmaiden, or the like, but simply as a human person.[26]

For Hildegard the original Adamic nature was dual, being made from "wet mud" *(limosa terra)* and filled with God's vivifying spirit, which Hildegard calls *veriditas* or "greening power," a term she uses for the whole cosmos as filled with God's life-giving power.[27] As originally filled by the Spirit, Adam was glorious, endowed with divine knowledge and harmony that expressed itself in a beautiful singing voice (a distinctively Hildegardian touch).[28] Eve shared in this same nature, while as woman she was also created to be mother to their joint offspring.

In the original paradisial state Adam and Eve would have made love virginally. Lust would have been absent, but there would have been the sweetest pleasure, communicated in a nongenital embrace and "sweat" passed between their sleeping bodies. Eve would have given birth, not through her vagina but through her side, as she herself had been born from Adam's side, and thus would have remained virgin in impregnation and parturition. This original virginal impregnation and birth were restored in Christ's birth from Mary and are represented in the church born from the side of Christ.[29]

Adam lost the fullness of this vivifying power, however, by seeking to grasp his own self-will rather than making himself simply an instrument of God's indwelling Spirit, although this life-giving Spirit remains the true life principle of humans. For Hildegard, the primary cause is not human, male or female, but the jealousy of the devil. Prior to the creation of humans, God created the angels. But part of the angelic hosts, led by Lucifer, tried to seize God's glory and fell from heaven, becoming the source of all diabolic plotting against divine life. Unlike humans, Lucifer fell utterly, losing all capacity for goodness and becoming wholly evil.[30]

God then created humans from clay and filled them with life. God planned that this new creature would replace the fallen angels. The devil, utterly antagonistic to Adam and his offspring (which Eve carried in her body like stars), plotted to deceive the couple. He hated Adam's sweet singing voice and the harmonious life of paradise, and so the devil sought to destroy it, to get humans into his power by deceiving them. The devil came to Eve because, in her innocence, she was more susceptible to being misled and also because Adam would accept her suggestion out of his love for her. But Hildegard sees these aspects in the primal misstep as modifying its gravity. Adam and Eve are more childish and victimized than evil. They do not fall wholly, as does Lucifer, and thus can be reclaimed by God. In a striking image, Hildegard pictures Adam as turning from God by *failing* to pluck the flower of obedience to God and so losing the indwelling spirit.[31]

Once fallen and ejected from paradise, Adam and Eve have lost their original harmoniousness, and their knowledge of God is dimmed. Their sexuality is corrupted into lust, although Hildegard sees this as more a male than a female characteristic. Women, she believes, are naturally averse to the sexual act and only experience some sexual lust after they have been introduced to it by men.[32] Most of all, the fallen world is one buffeted by the constant attacks of the devil, who seeks to get God's human creature wholly in his power. But God from the beginning sends vehicles of divine grace, starting with Abel and Noah.

Hildegard's view of human nature is more that of the "two tendencies" than an Augustinian loss of free will. The vices, agents of the devil, seek to pull humans one way, while the sweet voices of the virtues (typically presented as feminine)[33] recall humans to their true glory. God's project of restoration of humans culminates in the birth of Christ, who takes human flesh from the Virgin Mary and thus restores that original form of humanity in which human flesh is a perfectly receptive instrument of the divine Spirit. All Christians share this restored human nature through rebirth in the womb of mother church and through feeding on the sacrament of Christ's eucharistic body.

Hildegard's view of woman as woman, in relation to man as male, is double-sided. Physically and socially she accepts gender hierarchy as the created order, although she also hints that men use the claim that women are punished for Eve's sin to unjustly oppress them.[34] But women as women are assumed to be physically weaker than men and in need of their protection. Also, for Hildegard, the biological complementarity of the male as sower of the seed and women as nurturer of it dictates a hierarchical social order that demands that women as wives obey their husbands.[35]

This difference in male and female roles is continued in the church in the exclusion of women as priests. These "natural" male and female social roles, parallel to males as begetters and women as conceivers, should not be confused by cross-dressing or by women taking on male roles.[36] In a similar way Hildegard accepts class hierarchy in her society and sees this as a reflection of natural hierarchy, the hierarchy of the angels, as well as the difference between species of animals. She bristles in defense of her own practice of admitting only women of noble birth to her monastery, when this is challenged by another abbess.[37]

While male and female complementarity dictates female subordination socially, on the cosmic level Hildegard sees a complementarity of masculine and feminine that manifests God's design for cosmic harmony. This cosmic complementarity is represented for Hildegard on many levels. Maleness represents God and God's word, while femaleness represents earth and flesh, the matter through which God shapes all things. Here flesh, matter or earth *(terra)* is not evil, but rather, in its "virginal" form, is the bodily substance that God's Spirit fills with life, moisture, and "greenness." The beauty and delight of God's creation lie in the harmonious union of these two principles, God's life-giving power and matter or *terra*.[38]

Wisdom *(Sapientia)* or Love *(Caritas)* is the feminine expression both of God and of creation, mediating the union between the two. Hildegard's final great work in her seventies, *The Book of Divine Works*, is a reworking of the whole drama of creation, incarnation, and redemption to focus on the role of Wisdom/Love, who mediates between God and creation. It is through Wisdom/Love that God created the cosmos in the beginning, and it is in Wisdom/Love that God will bring it to completion in the end.[39] The axis of this union of God and flesh mediated by Wisdom is the incarnation of the Word through the Virgin Mary, who gives the divine Word his humanness through her virginal flesh as one who is totally an instrument of the divine Spirit.[40]

Finally Ecclesia, bride of Christ and mother of Christians, who receives the vivifying power of Christ's redemptive sacrifice on the cross as her bridal "dowry," manifests this reunion of divine Spirit and virginal matter.[41] Ecclesia is pictured in many of Hildegard's visions as a towering woman, holding reborn Christians in her arms and womb, while her head is assailed by corrupt and unfaithful church leaders.[42] In one vivid picture of the final conflict between God and the Antichrist, Ecclesia is even imaged as having the lower part of her body taken over by an ass's head protruding from her vagina.[43] But Christ will intervene to throw this final eruption of Satan into hell, while rescuing for paradise the faithful children reborn in the womb of mother church.

For Hildegard, Christian virgins are particular expressions of the true children of mother church. They are the reborn virgin Eve manifest in the Virgin Mary. In their holy life in community, Eden is partly restored. Hildegard even dressed her nuns in solemn liturgy in long white veils and golden crowns to symbolize their way of life as the restoration of Eden. She heard in the sweet music of liturgical chant an echo of the music of paradise.[44] In her letter to the prelates of Mainz imploring them to lift the interdict that had silenced liturgical music in her community, she suggests that these prelates imitate the devil, who ever seeks to silence music that reminds humans of paradise.[45]

Hildegard describes the music of paradise, lost in the fall but partly restored with the aid of musical instruments:

> God, however, restores the souls of the elect to that pristine blessedness by infusing them with the light of truth. And in accordance with His eternal Plan, He so devised it that whenever He renews the hearts of many with the outpouring of the prophetic spirit, they might, by means of interior illumination, regain some of the knowledge which Adam had before he was punished for his sin. And so the holy prophets, inspired by the Spirit which they had received, were called . . . not only to compose psalms and canticles (by which the hearts of listeners were inflamed), but also to construct musical instruments to enhance these songs of praise with melodic strains. . . . In such a way these holy prophets get beyond the music of this exile and recall to mind that divine melody of praise which Adam, in company with the angels, enjoyed in God before the fall.[46]

Hildegard has no doubt that virginity or chastity is an essential expression of redeemed nature, the restored paradise and anticipated life in heaven when all death and suffering will be overcome. She strongly supports the Gregorian reforms that imposed celibacy on the priesthood. For her the various celibate ecclesiastical orders—priests, monks, and nuns—stand on a higher level of holiness than married laypeople, although ecclesiastics can also become instruments of the devil.[47]

Although she includes married laypeople in the redeemed, she sees them as a lower order who produce children for the church; she visualizes them as lying in the clouds in the lower part of Ecclesia's body, rather than in her bosom.[48] In her description of the final defeat of the devil and the gathering of the redeemed into the heavenly paradise, she speaks of prophets, apostles and martyrs, virgins and widows, anchorites and monks, and princes being gathered into heaven. Married lay commoners are too unimportant to mention.[49]

For Hildegard, gender difference is not annulled by Christ, but rather virginity annuls the fallen nature and restores the paradisial union of body and spirit of both men and women. Virginal women not only are included in equal honor in this procession of the redeemed, but they have a special mysterious meaning as representatives of virginal Eve restored in Mary, the church as Virgin Mother of Christians, and finally that divine Wisdom and Love that ever unites God and matter in symphonic harmony in its once and future form, anticipated here and now in the virginal flesh and sweet song of vowed women religious.

## Thomas Aquinas

When we turn from the visionary cosmology of Hildegard of Bingen to the scholastic theology of the great Dominican master, Thomas Aquinas, writing a hundred years later (1225–74), we find ourselves in a significantly different world, intellectually and socially. Intellectually, Aquinas represents the great medieval synthesis of the Augustinian tradition of theology and the philosophical method of Aristotle. Where Hildegard reports visions, Aquinas reasons as a logician, weighing the arguments of authorities pro and contra to disputed questions. Hildegard belongs to the earlier medieval world of rural monastic estates ruled by men and women of noble families; Aquinas to the university, mendicant orders, and emerging cities of the thirteenth century.

In the 1230s the major collection of canon law was promulgated, closing loopholes by which abbesses had exercised elements of pastoral office in the early Middle Ages. Women were strictly forbidden from public teaching or preaching, touching sacred vessels, incensing the altar, or taking communion to the sick. Spiritual guidance of nuns, including confession, and external control of finances of nunneries were more firmly put in the hands of supervising priests.[50]

While such matters were disputed in Hildegard's day, she was able to employ the combination of her prophetic office and her extensive connections with prelates and princes of noble families to wrest control of her own community from the monks of Saint Disibod, moving her monastery to another site, where she both governed its external affairs and controlled its pastoral and liturgical life. Although she still received a provost from Saint Disibod's, she prevailed in claiming that the nuns had the right to appoint this provost.[51]

Between 1158 and 1170 when she was in her sixties and seventies, she conducted four preaching tours throughout Germany, speaking to both clergy and laity in chapter houses and in public, mainly denouncing clerical corruption and calling for reform. We have the texts of several of such sermons, such as one she preached at Cologne in 1163. Hildegard sent a copy of this sermon to Dean Philip and the cathedral chapter of Cologne, who humbly asked for it so they could reform their lives by careful study of her inspired words.[52]

By one hundred years later it was hard to imagine such acceptance of public preaching by a woman, even a well-connected abbess and acknowledged prophet. In the mid-fourteenth century Catherine of Siena would intervene with popes, prelates, and princes to end the Avignon captivity of the papacy and Great Schism, but she did so in a more private manner, by audiences and letters.[53] Women's religious writing would increase after the twelfth century, but the genre would be primarily personal spiritual experiences, not the sketching of a vast cosmology. The shift of scholarship from monasteries to universities (where women were barred from study) would also bring a decline in the educational level of nuns. Although the nuns of Helfta in the thirteenth century maintained university level education for their women,[54] the Beguine mystic Mechthild of Magdeburg, who ended her days at Helfta, dictated her revelations in her Low German dialect, not Latin.

This more exclusively male world of canon law and university life is evident in Aquinas' treatment of gender in his theological anthropology. Indeed, so removed was he from contact with women or sexuality, first as a young monk and then as a Dominican in the university of Paris, we have a sense that such issues are for him a theoretical abstraction, in contrast to Augustine, behind whose views one always senses the existential anxiety of his own experience. Further, Aquinas' incorporation of Aristotle's sociobiology worsened the definition of women's "natural" inferiority. His use of Aristotle's definition of the soul as the "form" of the body suggests a more integral body-soul union than that of Augustinian Platonism, but this also implies a more negative view of women's capacities of soul, as affected by the definition of her bodily inferiority.[55]

For Aquinas the soul is naturally immortal and can exist apart from the body. Its essential quality is intellect, through which it also exercises sovereignty over bodily things. But the soul is also the "form" of the body and can only use the senses and exercise sovereignty through being united with the body, and so is incomplete by itself.[56] This definition of the soul allows Aquinas to maintain the Augustinian distinction between woman as *homo* and woman as *mulier*. As asexual soul in relation to God, woman possesses the image of God and is made to enjoy eternal life in communion with God in heaven.

Considered as female, however, woman was created not as an end in herself, but as helpmeet to the male in the work of procreation (not as a friend or companion to the male for which Aquinas follows Augustine in opining that another male would have been more appropriate).[57] Aquinas combines this Augustinian view with Aristotle's definition of the female as defective in her bodily, volitional, and intellectual capacities. The male seed provides the form and active power in procreation, while the female only provides the "matter" that is formed. Normatively every male seed would produce another male. So the very procreation of the female comes about through a defect in this process of formation of the female matter by the male seed, resulting in an incomplete or defective being, a female.

The female by nature is inferior or defective in physical strength, volitional self-control, and intellect and cannot exercise sovereignty over herself or others. Therefore, the social hierarchy in which the male rules and the female obeys is biologically necessary, parallel to the relation of active mind and passive matter. This definition makes woman's inferiority inner and not just a matter of her procreational role. Aquinas accepts the view that women have inferior capacities for intellect and self-control and cannot image and represent human nature normatively.[58] Contra Hildegard, Aquinas views women as more swayed by passions and prone to lust than men.[59]

This view affects Aquinas' Christology and view of priesthood. Christ had to be male to represent the headship of the New Adam over regenerated humanity, because only the male possesses "perfect" (complete) humanness of soul and body. So also only males can be priests. Women are not only barred from priestly ordination juridicially, but by nature they cannot validly receive this sacrament because their intrinsic defectiveness means they cannot exemplify excellence or exercise sovereignty.[60] This inferiority and subjugation of woman would have existed in paradise because it reflects biological nature, which for Aquinas has not changed with the fall. In paradise the body would have been mortal, although undying because of its perfect submission to God. Procreation would have taken place as today, including defloration of the woman. The chief difference in paradise was that there would have been a perfect submission of the body to the intellect, and of humans to God. This perfect ordering of higher over lower Aquinas calls "original justice."[61] It would have meant a complete state of virtue, although not a spiritual body or face-to-face communion with God, which comes about only through grace that transcends nature.

The fall destroyed this original justice, and thus weakened but did not destroy the inclination of the soul to virtue. The body, no longer submissive to the intellect and to God, asserted its natural mortality. Eve is more guilty than Adam for the fall because she sinned not only against God in disobedience, but also against her neighbor, Adam, in seducing him—although the fall could have happened only through Adam's consent, since he, not she, possessed the higher reason that can exercise headship over humanity as a whole.[62] Woman not only shares in the general human loss of original justice, and falls into mortality and lust, but is punished for her additional guilt by the pains of childbirth and male domination over her (worsening her original subordination that would have been by mutual assent).[63]

Aquinas' follows Augustine in teaching that original sin is passed down in the sexual act, but he changes the focus. The male seed itself cannot transmit original justice, since it no longer possesses it, so the male procreative act generates a fallen human without this original virtue. Sexuality, which would have been pleasurable in paradise, has been worsened into disordered lust, but lust per se does not transmit sin, it simply gives evidence of the disordered, sinful state.[64]

Since the male seed alone transmits original sin as an expression of its generative power, Christ born without the male seed takes mortal flesh, but not original sin, from his mother, Mary.[65] (Why women, who do not transmit original sin since they are only the passive and not the active power in generation, are more prone to lust than men is not explained. Here as elsewhere we see the fissures between Aquinas' Augustinian and Aristotelian legacies.)

Although women by nature are barred from priesthood, God can bestow prophetic gifts on them, according to Aquinas. This is possible because the prophetic gift pertains to reality, while women's lack of eminence that bars them from priesthood is a matter of symbolism; that is, they cannot *represent* excellence. But this does not mean that some women might not possess it; indeed Aquinas opines that some women are better in soul than many men.[66] Here we sense a bit of historical experience that counters Aquinas' Aristotelian anthropology, which, if strictly followed, would suggest that all women by nature would be inferior to all males, not just in body and social role, but in soul (intellect, moral self-control).

Yet, since women are barred from public teaching, women with prophetic gifts cannot impart them in public. They can only communicate them to men in authority, not only to authorize their validity, but to disclose their contents publicly.[67] Aquinas also bars women from the exercise of any temporal jurisdiction since they lack the capacity for sovereignty, although he does allow that an abbess can exercise limited spiritual authority over her community as *delegated* to her by male authorities. This view puts Aquinas at variance with other theories in his time (and later) where women are barred from spiritual authority but, as ruling queens, exercised temporal authority.[68] So woman would have been in a state of subjugation in the original creation, which expressed her inferior biological nature and procreative role, worsened into domination and painful childbearing in the fall. But when Aquinas treats salvation and its ultimate expression in heaven, gender hierarchy seems to vanish. Here woman exists simply as *homo*, made in the image of God, as end in herself, rather than procreative aid to the male.

Although for Aquinas the soul is naturally immortal and cannot die, the future state of its immortal life, whether in bliss or perdition, is a matter of supernatural grace dispensed by God to the elect, not a possession of the soul by nature.

As elect, gifted by and cooperating with grace, to be taken into finally eternal communion with God (the beatific vision), women stand on an equal footing with men. For Aquinas, there is no gender discrimination in election. In heaven, therefore, women are as likely to be in the highest ranks of the blessed as the most eminent male, since the hierarchy of the blessed is a matter of the fulfilled image of God (which woman possesses equally) and cooperation with God's gifts of grace (merit), not human hierarchies, including that of gender.[69]

Here again we find in Aquinas a teaching of spiritual equality that contradicts his Aristotelian anthropology, which would suggest that women's defects, which are not only of body but include inferior capacities for intellect and virtue, should confine her to the lower ranks of the blessed, much as (as Aquinas suggests elsewhere) there is a hierarchy of rank among angels. Thus we find in Aquinas' theological anthropology a maintenance of Augustine's distinction between women's equality as image of God in her inner nature as *homo* and her subjugated status as woman in her procreative role. But this distinction has become more contradictory, due to the incorporation of an Aristotelian anthropology in which women's inferiority is a defect, not only of body but of soul, mind, and will.

## Mechthild of Magdeburg

With Mechthild of Magdeburg (1210–83), we enter a world of female visionary imagination and religious life different from Hildegard's, but also far removed from the intellectual world and university life of her contemporary Thomas Aquinas. Born in Saxony to a family of knightly class, Mechthild was well acquainted with the culture of princely courts, but also with the growing urban life and the new urban preaching and mendicant orders, the Dominicans and Franciscans, whom she saw as God's gift to reform a sinful age.[70]

Mechthild recounts her first "greeting" by the Holy Spirit when she was twelve; it was such an overwhelming experience that she could never thereafter tolerate giving in to any sin. These experiences continued daily.[71] When she was in her early twenties she joined a Beguine community in Magdeburg, where she lived for forty years. The Beguines represented a new form of female urban religious life in the thirteenth century in which groups of women took simple vows of chastity but were free to marry. They lived together in houses in the midst of urban life, supporting themselves through handwork and also serving their neighbors through charity, nursing the sick and teaching. They fell under suspicion of heresy, mostly unfounded, through their uncloistered way of life, but were valued by city fathers for their services; these officials often furnished some of the Beguines' support.[72]

Mechthild reflects this new context of women's religious life both in her compassion for the weak and suffering (in this life and in purgatory)[73] and in her sense of personal vulnerability to clerical foes who were offended by her claims of visionary authority.[74] Like Hildegard, Mechthild is certain of the truth of her visionary gifts and struggles against those who challenge it, but she lacks both the aristocratic hauteur and the access to the highest levels of power of church and state that protected the abbess.

When she was forty Mechthild received a command from God to write down her visions under the title of *The Flowing Light of the Godhead*.[75] Like Hildegard, Mechthild protests her unworthiness and lack of learning but affirms that God's demands take precedence over her weakness. She too consulted with her confessor, a Dominican, Heinrich of Halle, who both affirmed the divine origin of the command to write and copied down what she told him. Over the next twenty years Mechthild dictated a succession of revelations, which Heinrich organized into six books. The seventh book was dictated in her old age after she entered the convent of Helfta. Mechthild recorded her visions in her own Low German dialect. Heinrich of Halle, who organized the complete German version, also translated the whole into Latin about the time of her death.[76]

Although Mechthild was supported by her Dominican confessor and later by the aristocratic nuns of Helfta, she speaks often and bitterly of foes who challenged the veracity of her visions and her right to make them public through writing. When some men told her that her book should be burned, she took her complaint to God, who assured her that "the truth cannot be burned by anyone" and that her book was protected by God's own hand, which is stronger than any man's. In the vision God even identified her book with

God's trinitarian nature: the parchment on which it was written as God's humanity, the words that flew into her soul as God's divinity, and the voice of these words as the Holy Spirit.[77]

God's choice of such a lowly vessel to communicate God's revelations duplicates the kenosis of God in the incarnation, just as God chose to build "a golden house in this filthy slough, to live here with your mother and all creatures." Echoing Paul's principle that God chooses the lowly to confound the wise, Mechthild is told that many a wise master is a fool in God's eyes. Rather God typically imparts special graces to "the lowest, the least, the best concealed place," just as a mighty flood "flows by nature into the valley."[78]

Mechthild not only resists those who challenge her visions, but develops a general view of the state of Christianity of her day as corrupted by sinful clerics and religious. She perceives behind the facade of many "spiritual people" a hypocrisy and self-centeredness that not only fails to understand the true message of spiritual life, but corrupts others. Mechthild compares herself to Christ, who must drink the cup of gall created by these false Christians: "The Devil has many a cupbearer among spiritual people, cups so full of poison that they cannot drink it all alone but must pour out the bitterness for the children of God."[79] Such criticisms undoubtedly fueled some of the persecution that Mechthild experienced.

Mechthild shares with Hildegard and the orthodox Christianity of her day general assumptions about salvation history. Her theological world moves between the drama of God's creation of humanity and Adam and Eve's fall, through the faithful witnesses from Abel and the prophets to the central mystery of redemption through Mary and Christ, to the apostles and saints of mother church, to the present time when many church leaders "stain" the church through their corruption. For her too the coming drama of the Antichrist, the sufferings of the saints in that time, the final judgment and eternal transformation of the world loom just ahead.[80]

But where Hildegard's visions survey this historical and cosmic sweep, in Mechthild the focus is on the intense, intimate drama of the soul, Mechthild's own soul, in its ecstatic flight to and union with God as its beloved, and in its suffering alienation, which imitates the kenosis of Christ in tormented flesh, as the paradigmatic center of the salvation drama. In her description of this love drama between the soul and God, Mechthild draws on the heritage of

Christian interpretation of the Song of Songs blended with elements drawn from the German *minnesinger* poetry of the love relation between a lady and her noble lord. The blending of these two traditions, the mystical reading of the Song of Songs and the poetry of courtly love, in Mechthild as well as other Beguine mystics, created a new genre of religious language, which Barbara Newman has called *mystique courtoise*.[81]

For Mechthild God's decision to create humanity is driven by desire to be fruitful and to love. In one vision Mechthild envisions the Trinity in conversation, deciding to create humanity as a Bride for God to love and be loved in return:

> Then the Eternal Son said with great politeness: "Dear Father, my nature, too, should bear fruit. . . . Let Us pattern mankind after Me, although I foresee great sorrow since I must love man eternally." The Father replied: "Son, I, too, am moved by a powerful desire in my breast, and I hear the sound of love. We shall become fruitful in order to be loved in return. . . . I will create a Bride for Myself who shall greet Me with her mouth and wound Me with her look; only then will love begin." And the Holy Spirit said to the Father: "Yes, dear Father, I will bring the Bride to Your bed." . . . Then the Holy Trinity leaned over the creation of all things and created us, body and soul, with untold love.[82]

Adam and Eve together were given the noble nature of the Son. To Adam was given a share in the Son's wisdom and earthly power over all earthly creatures. To Eve was given the Son's "loving honorable modesty which He Himself bore in honor of his Father." "Their bodies were created pure, for God did not create anything to make them suffer shame, and they were dressed in angel's garments." Mechthild seems to share the Origenist view of the early Augustine that originally Adam and Eve would have conceived children in some ethereal and sinless manner that would not have changed the virginal nature of their bodies: "They were to conceive their children in holy love, as the sparkling sun shines on the water without troubling it."[83]

With sin, however, Adam and Eve lost this original sinless and incorruptible body. Their bodies became corruptible and sin-prone. In a dramatic image Mechthild speaks of the fallen body as having "sinful sap," "which Adam extracted from the apple, which flows naturally through all our limbs." Eve received in addition an accursed (menstrual) blood, "which began with Eve and all other women from the apple."[84]

Mechthild attributes to the fallen body both the tendency to sin—to turn from God and to indulge bodily desires—as well as finitude, pain, and illness. The soul in herself retains her natural likeness to God and thus her desire to ascend and reunite with God as her beloved. But her ties to the fallen body drag her down to the earthly realm and tempt her with desires for false loves of bodily indulgence. Yet in ecstatic experience the soul temporarily frees itself from its ties to the body and tastes its original and renewed love relation with God, which has been lost with the fall but restored through the incarnation of Christ in Mary's sinless flesh.

Mary, whose body was uncorrupted, preserved this original love relation of the soul with God during the period between the fall of Adam and the incarnation. Mary as God's bride exemplifies what God intended and continues to intend the soul to be. Thus Mary speaks:

> So the almighty Father chose me for a Bride, in order to have something to love, for His beloved Bride, the noble soul, was dead. . . . Then I alone became Bride of the Holy Trinity and the Mother of orphans, and brought them before the eyes of God, so they might not sink.

Mary is a mediatrix who mothers and suckles all the faithful with the "pure, unspoiled milk of true, tender mercy," not only Christ and Christians, but also the prophets and sages before Christ was born, and Mary continues to do so until the Day of Judgment. [85]

The soul can taste, at least in momentary glimpses, its true noble nature, and dance and play in heaven with its beloved. Again and again Mechthild describes this love play with its beloved in language drawn from courtly love as well as the Song of Songs. In one vision, the soul complains to *Minne*, or Lady Love, imagined as the go-between that captures and wounds her with desire. The dialogue ends with the soul acknowledging her defeat by Love, telling her to take a letter to her beloved: "Please tell my love that His bed is ready and I lovingly long for him."[86]

In another vision, the soul appears in court as a timid servant girl looking longingly at a prince. In imagery drawn from Sacred Heart and eucharistic devotions, God eagerly bares his red-hot heart to her and takes her into it. The two embrace and mingle together "like water and wine."[87] Although God is infinitely greater than the "poor soul," in the love relation they become equal. God even subjects himself to the soul and does her will, as the lord kneels to the lady in courtly love.[88] God's great love for the soul is a continual kenosis in which God pours himself out for the soul, so much so that God is as "lovesick" for her as she is for God: "She is consumed by Him and takes leave of herself; when she has had enough, He is more lovesick for her than He ever was before when He desired more."[89]

Although this love quest and play, culminating in mutual dissolution into one another, is the heart of Mechthild's visions, nevertheless, it can only be momentary as long as the soul is tied to the body. The soul must not only fall back into its distance from God, but it must even embrace alienation from God as its highest self-abnegation of its own desires for the sake of love for God.[90] In this paradoxical move, Mechthild also sees the soul embracing innocent bodily suffering (although not sin) as the way to purify its attachment to the body and to participate in the crucifixion of Christ, who not only entered the flesh but suffered all the torments of the flesh to express his loving quest to redeem humanity's soul and body.[91]

Thus Mechthild describes her early ascetic efforts to subdue the body through fasting, flagellation, and vigils,[92] as well as sufferings that came to her through illness and, most of all, through betrayal and persecution by her foes, as imitation of Christ's redemptive suffering. Thus Christ speaks to Mechthild not only as bride, but as one who must share in his sufferings and so become his female counterpart as dying and rising Christ:

> You shall be martyred with Me, betrayed by envy, sought out by falsehood, captured by hatred, bound by slander, blindfolded so the truth may be withheld from you, slapped by the wrath of the world, brought before the court in confession, boxed on the ears with punishment, sent before Herod in court, undressed in wretchedness, flogged with poverty, crowned by temptation, looked down upon in degradation; you shall bear your cross despising sin, shall be crucified renouncing all your desire, be nailed to the cross with holy virtues; wounded by love, you shall die

> on the cross with holy constancy, be pierced in your heart by constant union, removed from the cross in true victory over all your foes, buried in obscurity, and, finally, in a holy conclusion, you shall rise from the death and ascend into heaven, drawn by God's breath.[93]

In the salvation drama of humanity's creation, fall, and redemption, Mechthild does not believe that women are in any way inferior to men in their spiritual nature. She suggests in her account of the creation of Adam and Eve that the Son apportions his gifts to the couple with wisdom and power for Adam and love for Eve. Eve receives a double punishment in the fall of cursed sap and cursed blood. Mechthild accepts women's marginalized and powerless place in society as a given but relates it, not to divine punishment, but rather to divine favor, giving women greater likelihood of sharing Christ's sufferings and receiving God's grace, which flows down to rest not on the "mountain," the powerful and learned, but in the "valley," the unlearned and powerless woman, herself.

Humanity's nature and destiny as bridal soul of God is both symbolically feminine and also more accessible to women, both in their modesty and humility in society and also because it was to Eve that Christ gave the gifts of his capacity to love and honor God. Thus the gifts to Adam of power and wisdom are, in some way, more of a temptation to pride than a means of reuniting with God, than the gifts given to women. But Mechthild can also speak of the soul as God's image as masculine as well as feminine: as virile man in battle, as comely maiden at court before her lord, and as pleasing bride in the nuptial bed with God.[94] When Mechthild speaks of Adam or "man" collectively, it is with the male pronoun but with the assumption that women share equally in this human nature, in its nobility and its fall.

In speaking of her writing, Mechthild mentions the surprise of her scribe, Heinrich, at the "masculine style" of her book.[95] Despite her protests that she, "a sinful woman," is only following the commands of God in writing her revelations, this passage suggests that, to her foes and friends alike, Mechthild was not their notion of gentle, humble womanhood, but appeared unnaturally masculine as she battled for her right to record her visions and to follow her own course of life, responding to her critics with fierce denunciations of their faults.

Masculinity and femininity are, thus, fluid categories for Mechthild. Women possess God's image equally with men. They have in no way a lesser nobility or capacity for spiritual interchange with God. Indeed, in some way, they are in a superior position, because they are less tempted by worldly power and have a natural affinity for the love relation with God for which the soul was created and in which it finds its consummation. This consummation, although tasted fleetingly while the soul remains tied to the fallen body, will be completed after death, when the body no longer ties down the soul.

After the Day of Judgment, the soul will receive back its original unfallen body. Following the "noble youth, Jesus Christ, the pure maiden's child," as comely and full of love as he was at eighteen, God's bridal souls, adorned with the wreaths of their virtues, will be carried to the eternal wedding with the Trinity. Then "the highest dance of praise begins . . . from bliss to love, from love to joy, from joy to clarity, from clarity to power, from power to the highest heights." There they are greeted by the Father: "Rejoice dear Brides, My Son will embrace you. My divinity infuse you. My Holy Spirit will lead you always further in blissful vision, according to your will. What more could you wish for?"[96]

## Julian of Norwich

With Julian of Norwich we move to the fourteenth century into the thriving city of Norwich, England. We also encounter a third form of religious life for women, the anchoress. Julian (her religious name, taken from the church of Saint Julian to which her anchorhold was attached)[97] was born about December of 1342, probably to a prosperous family of Norwich.[98] She must have adopted a serious devotional life as a young person, for she tells us that she had prayed for three gifts from God: to see Christ's passion as if she were actually present; a sickness to the point of death; and three wounds, contrition, compassion, and a full-hearted longing for God.[99] Such prayers express the desire to be totally focused on the relation to God in Christ, in the presence of Christ's passion and as if at the point of the consummation of her own life.[100]

Beginning on May 8, 1373, when Julian tells us she was "thirty and a half years old," she experienced the answer to these prayers. For seven days she lay ill to death.[101] Beginning on the seventh day (May 13) she experienced sixteen "shewings" of Christ's dying on the cross, as well as of God's relation to and love for us.[102] Having seen Christ's suffering in vivid detail to the final point of expiration, suddenly he was transformed into risen life; so she too was suddenly restored to health.[103] Perhaps shortly after this experience, Julian wrote down these visions, the interpretations given to her of them, and her first reflections on them, in a text of twenty-five chapters. She spent the next twenty years pondering the meaning of these visions and writing a much expanded version of her *Shewings of God's Love*.[104] The former is known as the "short text"; the latter is known as the "long text."

It is not known when she actually entered into the life of an anchoress, but it is likely that she did so shortly after these visions, the solitude of the anchorhold giving her the space for a dedicated life of prayer, study, and reflection on them.[105] The life Julian chose as an anchoress attached to the Church of Saint Julian at Norwich meant that she was enclosed in a room for the rest of her life, never to emerge until her death. But it was not an isolated or miserable life. A window into the church allowed her to participate in the liturgy, and another window into an attached parlor allowed her to counsel many who came seeking her advice and prayers, such as Margery of Kempe, who records her visit to Julian about 1412–13.[106]

Donations and local religious authorities provided for her physical needs, looked after by a servant and her assistant. It was expected that she would dress and be fed simply but adequately. So Julian's main task was to construct her own self-disciplined life of prayer and meditation.[107] Norwich was well-supplied with good religious libraries, including that of the Augustinian friars across from her church, and so it is likely that Julian's daily routine included the extended study of theological classics.[108] The church sat at a busy crossroads linking Conisford with the center of Norwich. Julian was there perhaps for more than forty years during a tumultuous time of war and plague.[109] Although set apart in her cell, Julian would receive the outpourings of daily troubles from those who came seeking her counsel. Such a holy woman was highly regarded by her contemporaries as one whose presence benefited the whole community.

Like Hildegard and Mechthild, Julian also felt the need to justify her extraordinary visions and her writing as a woman normally excluded from higher theological education and public teaching authority. She does so by describing herself as a "woman, ignorant, feeble and frail," yet nevertheless commanded to write what she has experienced because God has chosen her to be a conduit of God's teachings for the benefit of the whole Christian people, and in no way simply to exalt herself. As she puts it: "Because I am a woman should I therefore believe that I ought not to tell you about the goodness of God since I saw at the same time that it is His will that it be known?"[110] It is not she who teaches, but Jesus who teaches through her.

Her description of herself as "leued" (ignorant) and "vnlettyrde" have puzzled commentators,[111] since Julian's writing shows a woman of high literary skill in her Middle English dialect and considerable theological sophistication. It probably should be read to mean that she was self-taught beyond the elementary school level, thus not schooled in the Latin scholasticism of universities (not available to her).[112] It also expresses a typical self-disparagement by which medieval woman claimed their authority by claiming it not in their own names but in the name of God, who had chosen to make them God's instrument.

Yet Julian does not simply supersede her own voice with the divine voice, but distinguishes between what has been revealed to her in visions and in words by formed divine inspiration in her understanding and her own pondering on questions for which she has an as yet incomplete understanding. Thus she often qualifies her reflections by phrases such as "as I see it" or "as I understand it."[113] Julian draws her theological reflection from three sources: natural reason, the common teaching of holy church (Scripture and tradition), and the inward workings of the Holy Spirit, which she sees as parts of one whole, "for these three are all from one God."[114] There is no indication that she felt incapable in any of these three areas as a woman. Indeed, aside from the brief justifications of her authority just cited, she does not discuss herself as a woman, but operates simply as a human person fully engaged in living the redemptive life, seeking to understand it and to share the benefits of her insights with the Christian people.

The central message that Julian understands to have been revealed by Christ's revelations to her is that of absolute assurance that God's persisting love for humans will triumph over all evil; that "all shall be well."[115] Julian's own central question to Christ is, "How can this be?" in the light of so much sin and suffering in the world and the church's teachings that many sinners will fail to repent and will be ultimately damned. The questions of theodicy—how an all-loving and all-powerful God could have allowed humans to fall in the first place, why evil continues and whether it will be fully overcome—fuel a lifetime of theological ponderings from which Julian emerges with a profound theological understanding of the basic categories of Christian faith, at once traditional and original.[116]

Not only is the trinitarian God all-good in every way; the God whom Julian comes to name as Father, Mother, and Lord, has created a world and formed human persons as the apex of creation in a way that fully manifests this divine goodness. For Julian all that is, is God; God is the true substance and being of all that is created. Nothing has being except through participation in the being of God. Because all that is manifests the being of God, all that is is good in its true nature. Evil has no substantial reality.[117]

Yet evil surely exists; and indeed, for Julian, it is the central theological problem. How can it be reconciled with this revelation of unmixed divine goodness in which all creation participates as its true "ground of being"? Here Julian differentiates the human being as *substance* and as *sensuality*, terms we might translate as essence and existence, rather than as soul and body.[118] As substance the human being is the image of God, the created manifestation of divine being and so is completely good, by nature united to God's being. But, as sensuality, human existence has a certain autonomy that can be grasped in its created state as an end in itself, apart from God. When humans do this they fall into alienation from God and from themselves; human psychosomatic existence becomes split from its substance or true nature united to God. Although Julian does not dwell on the story of Adam's fall,[119] and never mentions Eve, one can infer that she assumes that this split of substance from sensuality results in a loss of an original immortality and perfection that humans would have enjoyed when their physical existence was united to their spiritual substance in union with God's uncreated being.[120]

This fall into sin (alienation) is manifest in woundedness. Humans experience every distress of mind and body. For Julian, sin, while "nothing" in itself, is felt in human life as *pain*[121]—the pains of mental anguish, self-blame, shame, and of physical suffering of the mortal body. Significantly, Julian never describes sin in terms of either pride or pleasure. For her there seems to be neither self-esteem nor delight in the sinful state. Rather, the primary way in which humans are caught in bondage to sin is in their self-absorption in their own distress, physical and mental. This distress leads them to forget their true nobility as God's image, and God's continuing love for them, and to slide into a despairing sense of hopelessness and worthlessness.

Julian insists that God is not angry with us and does not blame us for our fall into sin. These negative emotions are our own projections onto God from the context of our encapsulation in the fallen state where we see only our own dilemmas and fail to recognize that God continues to love us and to wish us only good. The supreme expression of God's "courteous" love is that God, the Son, from whom we have our substance, together with the whole trinitarian God, also chooses to take on our sensuality, our bodily existence. Descending not only into the body, but taking on all the woundedness to death of the fallen human condition, Christ provides the conditions for our restoration to union with God and with our own true selves, indeed in a higher form than if we had remained in our original innocence.

God permitted and continues to permit humans to fall into sin because God allows humans freedom; moreover, in order for humans to attain their full spiritual maturity in union with God, they also have to experience what it means to fall out of that union into the distressful condition of separation from God.[122] But God has never ceased to love us and to sustain us in being, even as we became blind to this sustaining love. God, from the beginning, intended to provide the remedy. Divine Wisdom, from whom we have our spiritual substance, took on our bodily existence and bore all its woes in the crucifixion. Thereby God provides the means by which we can heal our division, "oning" our souls to God and drawing our sensuality back into union with our souls, anticipating the day when this union will be complete and every form of mortality and distress will cease.

Julian develops this theology of human fall and redemption through a parable of the fallen servant.[123] The servant, who is Adam and all humans, stands before his loving Lord eager to do God's will. This eagerness to obey is his true nature and impulse. But, in his alacrity to please God, he rushes off at top speed and falls into a ditch, where he becomes wounded, torn, and muddied. He then becomes so absorbed in his shame and distress that he fails to look up and see that his Lord has in no way stopped loving him. He moans in fear, imagining that God is angry with him, and so the servant is unable to recognize God's continuing love and gracious goodwill for him.

How does the servant break out of this dilemma and recognize both God's continuing love and his own continuing worth as God's true child and created image? This is possible only through God's greatest work of mercy. God as second person of the Trinity becomes the servant, "falling" into the "womb of the virgin," taking on the torn and muddied body of the fallen servant and bearing all its distresses. Christ now stands beside the loving Lord, carrying all rescued servants as his crown of glory. Through Christ's supreme act of love, the servant is restored to his position of honor before his Lord.

Christ, as creator of our soul and body, takes on the distresses of our fallen bodily condition—but without sin (separation from God). This, then, is Julian's answer to the problem of evil. But it is not simply that Christ has remedied our fall through entering our fallen bodily condition, but also that the sinful condition itself continually points us to the means of our healing. Because sin is experienced as pain, we cannot rest in sin but are continually impelled by our distress to seek to overcome it. The pains of sin purge and purify us and stir up repentance, compassion for others in pain, and a desire to find our true rest, which we can find only by resting in God.

Thus, for Julian, the wounds of sin are at the same time the medicines of sin, for our true nature remains that of God's created image.[124] We are never really separated from God, nor do we ever lose our true nature as God's created image. We have become blind and have forgotten who we are, but we have not ceased to be, in our true essence, the noble manifestation of God's loving goodness. Thus our quest to overcome the distresses caused by sin can only find its true solution as we awaken to a recognition of God's continuing love and are led back to God as the true ground of our nature and only real happiness.

The pains caused by sin, rightly understood in the light of God's continuing love, not only become means of purgation and healing, but also a means of participating with Christ in the healing of the sins of humanity. By bearing our pains in union with Christ, we become partners with Christ in redemption.[125] Thus Julian's vision of redemption is never of the isolated self seeking its own flight to God, but of a human being whose healing union with God is at the same time expressed in outpouring compassion for others, becoming a servant for others as Christ has become for us.[126]

Yet the dilemma of the ultimate resolution of evil remains for Julian. How can be it that *all* will be well, when evil and suffering continue to abound—as she herself could plainly see even from her anchorhold—in a society torn by plague, famine, war and division, even in the church? Julian does not contest the church's teaching that damnation awaits the unrepentant sinner, yet she holds out a belief that the mystery of God's love is still incomplete.[127] At the end, when our healed union with God and ourselves is completed and all sin and suffering are overcome, there will be a transformation that we do not yet fully know. We can be assured that God's love indeed means that *all* will be well, but here and now this truth must be held in faith rather than in full understanding.[128]

Julian's exploration of the trinitarian nature of God as both mother and father has aroused renewed interest in modern times, especially among feminist theologians. Although both patristic and medieval theologians occasionally speak of God as mother, particularly in connection with Christ, through whom we are both reborn and fed through the Eucharist, Julian develops this maternal aspect of God the Son far more fully than any previous theologians.[129] In eleven chapters in the long text she elaborates on this union of fatherhood, motherhood, and lordship in God:[130]

> Thus in our making God almighty is our kindly Father and God all-wisdom is our kindly Mother, with the love and goodness of the Holy Spirit, which is all one God, one Lord.... Furthermore I saw that the second Person who is our Mother substantially, the same dear person is now become our Mother sensually. For of God's making we are double; that is to say, substantial and sensual. Our substance is that higher part which we have of our Father, God almighty. And the second Person of the Trinity is our Mother in kind, in our substantial making—in whom we are grounded and rooted; and he is our Mother of mercy in taking our sensuality. And thus our Mother means for us different manners of his working, in whom our parts are kept unseparated. For in our Mother Christ we have profit and increase; and in mercy he reforms and restores us; and by the power of our passion, his death and his uprising, oned us to our substance. Thus our Mother in mercy works to all his beloved children who are docile and obedient to him.... Thus Jesus Christ who does good against evil is our very Mother. We have our being of him, where every ground of

> Motherhood begins, with all the sweet keeping of love that endlessly follows. As truly as God is our Father, so truly is God our Mother.[131]

Julian's exploration of God's motherhood is rooted in key aspects of her theology. The persons of the Trinity are for her a dynamic relationship not just with each other, but with us. We are created, restored, and brought to fulfillment in interrelationship with God as Father, Mother, and Lord. Her identification of the Second Person with Wisdom reclaims the feminine aspect of this biblical symbol.[132] She also uses the traditional christological symbols of baptism and Eucharist to see Christ as the one in whom we are reborn and fed, as a mother brings a child forth from her womb and feeds it from her own body.[133] But central to her view of God as Mother as well as Father is her understanding of divine love as incapable of real anger or rejection of God's children, no more than a mother could reject her child, even though she might need to appear stern at times to discipline it. But behind even this discipline is a love that can never cease. Julian sees this kind of divine love as motherlike, or rather divine Motherhood as its fullest reality, which we see palely revealed in human mothers.[134]

While this sense of God's motherhood reflects something of Julian's experience of women as mothers (or at least her view of what a mother's love should be), her understanding of sin also reflects a significant shift in perspective that perhaps also reflects her experience as a woman. In sharp contrast to the Augustinian view of sin as overweening pride and concupiscence, Julian views our bondage to sin primarily as our entrapment in an overwhelming sense of fear and worthlessness and as manifest in pain, not pleasure. But once we glimpse God's continuing love and our own worth in God's eyes, we can become secure in our trust in God. Our wounds can become our medicines for growth in contrition, compassion for our fellow Christians, and reunion with God and with our own true selves. Or as she puts it at the end of the short text: "For God wants us always to be strong in our love and peaceful and restful as he is towards us, and he wants us to be, for ourselves and for our fellow Christians, what he is for us."[135]

4. Quaker Woman Preacher, from print after painting by Egbert van Heemskerk. University of California Press.

## Chapter Four

# Male Reformers, Feminist Humanists, and Quakers in the Reformation

IT IS NOTORIOUSLY DIFFICULT TO GENERALIZE ABOUT THE changing status of women in any era, but particularly in that complex shifting of religious, economic, and political patterns that took place from 1500–1700 in Western Europe. Generalizations about women's status in this era need to be contextualized by geographical region, social class, and marital status. Particular changes, such as the abolition of celibacy in Protestant areas, not only affected men differently from women, but also affected different groups of women differently.

An educated abbess, such as Caritas Pirckheimer in Nuremberg, experienced the abolition of celibacy as an assault on her women's monastic community and on a way of life in which she had religious status and educational and leadership opportunities as a woman.[1] Catherine Zell, wife of the Reformer Matthew Zell in Strasbourg, saw the abolition of celibacy quite differently in her tract in defense of their marriage. For her it united ordained ministry (for men) and married life, acknowledging the true dignity of marriage against a celibate tradition that had disparaged it as a second-class status in the church. Clerical marriage also ended the scandalous hypocrisy in which bishops officially condemned but tacitly allowed clerical concubinage, while collecting fees on the illegitimate children of these unions.[2]

It is generally agreed by social historians studying various regions of Western Europe that single women were losing economic opportunities and women in general were suffering a narrowing legal status in this period, compared to the eleventh to fourteenth centuries. Guardianship for adult unmarried women had died out in the later Middle Ages. In that period, in many regions, single women or widows could hold land in their own names, make contracts, and represent themselves in court. This changed with the Renaissance revival of Roman law, which defined women as incapable of legal responsibility due to their "imbecility." Early modern European law codes strengthened the subjugation of all women to a male guardian, whether father, husband, or other.[3]

This increasing legal subordination paralleled declining opportunities for women to exercise political roles on the basis of inheritance of land. As self-governing fiefs were superseded by more centralized kingdoms and trained bureaucrats took over the running of states, political leadership and economic management roles that noblewomen had played as heirs or wives of heirs disappeared. In France in 1316 an interpretation of Salic law precluded a woman from inheriting the kingdom, thereby trying to exclude not only women but also various male heirs whose claims came from their mothers.

The sixteenth century still saw a number of significant queens as heirs in their own right, most notably Isabella of Castile; Mary, Queen of Scots; and Mary and Elizabeth Tudor. The Hapsburgs used female relatives to govern parts of their vast territories, deputizing as governors Margaret of Austria, Mary of Hungary, Margaret of Parma, and the Infanta Isabella Clara Eugenia. Several powerful queen mothers ruled as regents during the absence or minority of their sons, such as Catherine de Medici for her son Charles IX. These visible women rulers deeply challenged a European world that generally was narrowing women's political status in the family and political life.[4]

As citizenship was being defined, either in city-states or kingdoms, women were excluded from voting or holding political office, even though they paid taxes as workers and property-holders. Political theorists paralleled the sovereign power of rulers with that of male heads of households over their wives and children, enforcing the idea that women were subordinate in household and kingdom and excluded from exercising political power. Protestant Reformers generally saw female rule as inherently unnatural, unlawful, and contrary to Scripture, although they had to come to terms with female rulers who favored the Reformation in their territories. The most notable of such tracts was that by John Knox, *First Blast of the Trumphet against the Monstrous Regiment of Women*

(1558) against Mary, Queen of Scots, and Mary Tudor. He would subsequently have to live down this attack during the reign of Mary Tudor's half-sister Elizabeth.[5]

The opportunities for women to support themselves independently were also narrowing in this era. The lack of differentiation of economic activity and the household in the Middle Ages meant that women did all kinds of work, according to class context and the particular skills by which a household supported itself. Women and men in families worked together in skilled artisan work. Women belonged to some guilds in their own right, particularly in textiles, and could inherit the guild status of a husband as a widow. Many female household skills, such as pharmacy and brewing, were also marketed by women in the community.

The early modern period saw an accelerating process by which paid work was increasingly separated from domestic work and women were forbidden to engage in work in the paid economy. Baking, brewing, pharmacy, printing, even many areas of textile work, were separated into male-only workshops differentiated from the domestic roles of women, children, and servants in the household. Licenses and educational requirements, forbidden to women, heightened the exclusion of women from many kinds of work in which they had been previously engaged beyond the family on the basis of family-taught skills.

Women who baked, brewed, or spun might still depend on selling their wares, but their work was demoted to an informal economy outside of the licensed shops or they were allowed only to contribute low-paid piecework, such as spinning thread that was then sold to shops were men did the weaving. Women's healers became unlicensed "quacks." As paid work for men was separated more and more from domestic work, an unpaid sphere of "women's work" was defined as women's proper sphere as "housewife."

This differentiation of female housework and male paid work was sharpest in the emerging middle class. It meant that the widow of a middle-class artisan or businessman no longer shared in the skills by which he had made a living and had little possibility of continuing such work in his absence. Low paid drudge work was always available for the woman without male support, but it became increasingly impossible for a woman to support herself by skilled work.

The Protestant rejection of monastic life and the expansion of the definition of vocation to work roles in society had a very different effect on women than on men. Women lost the option of a religious vocation distinct from marriage, but they did not gain an affirmation of their work roles in society as vocations. Rather, for Protestants, woman's only calling was to be wife and mother. Women working outside the home were viewed with suspicion as rebelliously rejecting their proper sphere. Protestantism also removed the cults of Mary and women saints that gave women the comfort of female advocates in heaven, and its simplification of liturgy removed many avenues of female employment.[6]

Women's educational opportunities did not greatly improve in this era. The closing of convents in Protestant territories ended one institution that had provided education for some women—not only for vowed nuns but for boarders who went on to marry. Luther and other Reformers argued that civil authorities should open schools for girls as well as boys, so all could read the Bible. But those few schools opened for girls offered only an hour or two a day for one or two years, were limited to catechism and basic literacy, and stressed female subordination and household duties. The university remained firmly closed to women in Northern Europe, although a few women seem to have attended and even lectured in Italian universities.[7]

Some humanists, such as Erasmus, argued for women's equal capacity for education, and some literary fathers, such as Thomas More, raised educated daughters. The main educational opportunity for noble or upper-middle-class women was the availability of a good library in the home, made possible by the advent of printing, and a father who encouraged their study, even hiring a tutor to teach his daughters along with his sons. But publishing by women was seen as highly improper, and women were excluded from the new scientific and literary academies.

A woman's opportunities to communicate her learning and to discuss ideas in an educated circle that included males were very limited. The royal court, where learning was valued, and the seventeenth-century institution of the literary salon provided opportunities for a few noble or upper-class women to read and discuss, but women were primarily defined as patronesses rather than as producers of learning in these circles. The woman who got too serious about her own ideas, rather than being a graceful encourager of those of males, was likely to be ridiculed.[8]

## Gender in the Theological Anthropology of Luther and Calvin

The Protestant Reformers reflect this reaffirmed "headship" of men over women in their theological anthropology and their application of this to family, church, and society. Their emphasis on marriage as the normal state of life for all men and women, rejecting the classical and medieval Christian understanding of celibacy as a superior state of life that anticipated eschatological perfection, disposed them to denounce those elements of medieval celibate misogyny aimed at the disparagement of marriage. But this was combined with a firmly patriarchal view of the family. That the man should rule and woman be submissive to his divinely ordained headship in the family was axiomatic for them, even if at times the Reformers modified the hierarchical demand with appeals to the husband's cooperation with the wife in family responsibilities and greater emphasis on companionship rather than procreation as the central purpose of marriage.

Martin Luther pioneered the Reformation attack on celibacy and the restitution of marriage as the normal vocation for all, including the ordained, in his sermons and treatises on marriage as well as in other writings. Luther based his argument against celibacy on his theology of creation and the fall. God created humanity male and female because marriage is God's intended state of life for humans, for both procreation and companionship. In Luther's view, Adam and Eve would not only have had normal sex in the garden, but Eve would have borne many children. This is woman's primary purposes in God's creation. As Luther puts it in his 1519 sermon on marriage, "A woman is created to be a companionable helpmeet to the man in everything, particularly to bear children."[9]

The difference between the original paradise and the fallen state of sin was that, as originally created, Adam and Eve would have been physically, mentally, morally, and spiritually perfect. They would not only have had perfect knowledge of God, but also knowledge of nature that would have given them wise use rather than abuse of its resources. They also would have embraced one another lovingly and had sex without shame or lust. Thus Luther maintains the Augustinian view that sex in paradise would have been chaste and lust-free. Normal genital sex would have taken place pleasurably as the "loveliest thing," not deformed into lust—that is, rampant and selfish orgasmic appetite, which Luther compares to an epileptic or apoplectic fit.[10]

Woman, Luther insists, was created equally in God's image and was equally perfect in paradise. She too would have had spiritual knowledge and been co-administrator of the land and the animals with Adam.[11] But Luther modifies this emphasis on Eve's original equality with Adam in the image of God, in two ways. First, from the beginning, the male was ontologically different from the female in a way that clearly established male preeminence. Thus Luther says, in commenting on the text of Genesis, "male and female He created them":

> . . . for the woman appears to be somewhat different from the man, having different members and a much weaker nature. Although Eve was a most extraordinary creature—similar to Adam so far as the image of God is concerned; that is, in justice, wisdom and happiness—she was nevertheless a woman. For as the sun is more excellent than the moon (although the moon, too, is a very excellent body), so the woman, although she was a most beautiful work of God, nevertheless was not the equal of the male in glory and prestige.[12]

Second, Luther stresses Eve's difference from Adam in paradise in her roles as mother and homemaker. Her unfallen physical perfection would have been expressed not only in lust-free sex, but in greater fertility and the ability to bear children without pain or difficulty. She would have had many children with ease.[13] Adam and Eve would have lived a bucolic life raising their many children and tending the garden. Work would have been like play. There would have been no diseases, noxious insects, or savage animals. The pair would have lived all their (long) lives in perfect health as in the prime of youth.[14] Their children would have stood on their feet immediately after birth (like chicks do today). They would have acquired instant wisdom. Pairing off, they would have soon established their own families in their own gardens.

Worship would have taken place on the Sabbath, for the church was established already in paradise before the creation of Eve. With the creation of Eve, household government was established, but there would have been no need for civil government, for there would have been no crime. Civil government, for Luther, became necessary only after the fall to restrain sin.[15] In a short time Adam and Eve and their descendants would have filled up the number of the predestined humans, and then been taken into immortal life without ever experiencing death. Adam would have simply fallen asleep painlessly on a bed of roses and been translated into immortal life—where, as Luther assumes, along with the classical Christian tradition, sex and procreation would no longer be necessary.[16]

This happy married and fruitful life in paradise, however, was not to be. On the very first Sabbath (which Luther takes literally as a historical day), after God instructed Adam about the fruit of the tree of the knowledge of good and evil and Adam then instructed Eve in God's command, Satan approached Eve, bent on destroying this original perfection. Luther concurs with the view that Satan approached Eve because as a woman she was weaker and so more easily deluded than Adam, who would have stomped on the serpent and told him to "be silent." Eve's light-mindedness led her first to doubt and then to embrace the serpent's lies, "offering herself to Satan as his pupil"[17] (a language that echoes that of the witch hunters).

Luther concurs with the traditional interpretation from First Timothy that Adam himself was not deceived by the serpent. He was deceived by his wife, and was self-deceived by his desire to please her.[18] This fall from faith to disbelief worked an instant change in Adam and Eve's nature. They lost their earlier wisdom and courage and became stupid and fearful, as evidenced by their craven replies to God's inquiries. Adam tries to blame Eve and to blame God for having given him Eve, and Eve blames the serpent. Neither forthrightly acknowledges his or her sin and asks for forgiveness.

In the fallen world into which Adam and Eve were expelled, they and the whole creation have lost their former perfection. Every power given by God is now hideously deformed. Adam is punished by hard labor in a thorny earth, while Eve experiences great suffering in what was her primary expression of blessing, childbearing. She now falls under the domination of her husband. Since Luther assumed that Eve was always to be led by her husband as a lesser being, even in paradise, the punishment of domination means that what was formerly an acceptable companionship of greater and lesser now becomes a burdensome servitude.

> This punishment too springs from original sin, and the woman bears it just as unwillingly as she bears those pains and inconveniences that have been placed on her flesh. The rule remains with the husband, and the wife is compelled to obey him by God's command. He rules the home, and the state, wages war, defends his possessions, tills the soil, plants, etc. The wife, on the other hand, is like a nail driven into the wall. She sits at home. . . . If Eve had persisted in the truth, she would not have been subjected to the rule of her husband, but she herself would have been a partner in the rule which is now entirely the concern of men. . . . In this way Eve is punished.[19]

For Luther, women grumble and resist these punishments. This resistance reflects both their memory of their former glory and their sinful impatience with accepting God's punishment, but these trials are not to be changed. Women must accept their present subjugated, painful, and limited lot as their just punishment for having been the instigator of the fall. But they should also be comforted that their main glory of childbearing continues, and in this some remnant of the original blessings of paradise shines forth, in however a painful and deformed context. Even if a woman dies in childbirth, it is no matter, for it was for this that she was created.[20]

For Luther, as in the Augustinian tradition, a key aspect of the deformation of original nature wrought by sin is the corruption of sexuality into lustful appetite. Luther speaks of sex in its present state, deformed by lust, as like a disease, like leprosy or a fit, so shameful that people seek dark, hidden places in which to do it. Yet, for Luther, this is no reason to avoid marriage, but rather to insist that marriage is necessary for almost all. [21]

Driven by the mad raging of lust, all (men) would sin, with the exception of a few individuals who have been given the special grace to live chastely without sex. But Luther regards these as rare and no basis for building an institution of celibacy. Marriage is the antidote to succumbing to lust outside of marriage and hence to sin. Thus the woman is God's gift to man, not only as the means of companionship and offspring, but now, in sin, as the antidote to sin. To avoid sin, all men, with some rare exceptions, must marry.[22]

Luther's anthropology of gender in creation and fall sees male preeminence, and female auxiliary status to the male as companion and childbearer, to have been God's original order. This has been corrupted by sin into domination. The fact that Luther insists that both male and female share equally in the image of God does not alter this basic ordering of greater and lesser perfections and patriarchal family roles.

Luther also suggests a greater partnership of Eve and Adam originally in the governance of creation, which has been lost in sin, confining women to the home and giving all power outside the home to the male. But these corruptions of the original relation of the genders in creation are construed by Luther as divine punishments, not as male injustice. Thus they are not to be remedied but rather to be endured by women:

> Thus that ordinance of God continues to stand as a memorial of that transgression which by her fault entered into the world. That subjection of women and domination of men have not passed away, have they? No. The penalty remains. The blame is passed over. The pain and tribulation of child-bearing continue. Those penalties will continue until judgment. So also the dominion of men and the subjection of women continue. You must endure them.[23]

For Luther, redemption offers no real alleviation for women of male domination in the family and in society, although the Christian male will seek to be kind rather than cruel to his wife and share in domestic work, including the humble task of diapering babies.[24] But the firm exclusion of women from political life that characterizes God's decree during the fallen era is not to be changed in the church. Here too women are not to be heard as preachers or leaders. Luther admits that God did raise up some women prophets in the Old and New Testaments, but these reflected emergency situations.[25] They were unmarried women, so their speaking did not violate the rule of subjugation to the husband. The prophet daughters of Philip in the New Testament spoke only in private.[26]

Thus, for Luther, women are defined as sharing equally in the image of God and as having had a more equal (although still lesser) status in original creation. When the present historical era of sin and fall is overcome, women will be translated into heaven, where they will share equally in immortal life. But here and now, redemption does not change their lesser status and the basic purpose for being that they were given in creation, nor does it change their more severe disabilities and exclusion from public life that are God's punishment of them in the fall.

Calvin's theological anthropology of gender in creation, fall, and redemption comes out in practice in much the same place as Luther's. Calvin, however, thinks of women's secondary status in creation and subjugation in the fall in more juridical terms, while Luther inclines to an ontological view of women as innately different and lesser as women. Also Calvin was more aware of challenges to biblical justifications of women's subordination from Renaissance feminists, such as Aprippa von Nettesheim, and of claims to speak to the church from influential Protestant women. Calvin thus sought to define more precisely his views that women were both "equal" and "second" in creation and have been subjected to a worsened servitude due to sin.

Calvin hardly mentions women in the *Institutes*. He assumes that the male generic covers the female and so whatever is said about "man" includes woman. At one point he declares testily: "Why, even children know that women are included under the term men!"[27] In his commentary on Genesis 1–3, Calvin insists that Eve shared equally in the image of God with Adam, understanding the term "image" as the "perfection of the whole," but particularly in terms of moral and spiritual perfection related to the inner self, the mind and heart.[28]

Calvin rejects Chrysostom's view that the divine image has primarily to do with dominion "given to man that he might, in a certain sense, act as God's viceregent in the government of the world," but concedes that "this truly is some portion, though very small, of the image of God."[29] Yet it becomes apparent that, for Calvin, it is exactly in this small portion of the image, having to do with government, that the dominion of the male over the female resides.

Refuting what he sees as a misinterpretation of 1 Cor. 11:7, where Paul denied women the image of God, Calvin insists that Paul was not speaking here of the inner soul where woman shares the image equally with man, but "alludes only to the domestic relation. He therefore restricts the image of God to *government*, in which the man has superiority over the wife, and certainly he means nothing more than that man is superior in the degree of honor." This distinction between equality in the image and yet superiority in honor related to government seems to be Calvin's intention when he speaks of woman also having been created in the image of God "though in the second degree."[30]

Calvin rejects the misogynist view of woman as a "necessary evil," insisting that "woman is given as a companion and an associate to the man, to assist him to live well." For Calvin, this helping relation is decidedly one of dominant and subordinate "partners," even though each has obligations to the other: "On this condition is the woman assigned as a help to the man, that he may fill the place of her head and leader." As intended by God, this marital relation of unequal partners would have been completely harmonious since each would have accepted his or her place in the "divinely appointed order": "The man would look up with reverence to God; the woman in this would be a faithful assistant to him; both with one consent would cultivate a holy, as well as friendly and peaceful, intercourse."[31]

With the fall, marriage has become filled with "strifes, sorrows and dissensions," which Calvin seems to attribute primarily to women's insubordination: "Hence it follows that men are often disturbed by their wives and suffer through them many discouragements." Good Christian wives, "being instructed in their duty of helping their husbands," are exhorted to "study this divinely appointed order."[32] For Calvin, too, the fall corrupted what originally would have been a chaste sexuality into lust; thus marriage is doubly necessary, both for its original purpose of companionship and procreation and as antidote to sin, although he admits that a few men have been given the gift of celibacy. As Calvin puts it in the *Institutes*, "Now, through the condition of our nature, and by the lust aroused after the Fall, we, except for those whom God has released through special grace, are doubly subject to women's society."[33] This phrase reveals how much Calvin actually thinks only of males when he speaks generically.

In Calvin's description of the fall, he plays down notions that Eve was approached by the serpent because she was morally or intellectually weaker or that Adam was less guilty. He makes Eve's primacy in sin an example of how humans generally are approached by Satan "at that point where he sees us to be the least fortified."[34] Adam too, "being drawn by her into fatal ambition . . . became partaker of the same defection as her."[35] The basic sin of both was unbelief, apostasy from God's command and authority, from which flow all other sins and evils.

Although both Adam and Eve sinned equally, their punishments are different, for each is punished in the context of his or her different responsibilities; Adam as tiller of the soil and Eve as wife and childbearer. These punishments are transmitted to all their posterity. Yet in describing Eve's punishment of subjection to her husband, Calvin suggests that her sin was insubordination not only to God but to her husband: "Thus the woman, who had perversely exceeded her proper bounds, is forced back to her own position. She had, indeed, previously been subject to her husband, but that was a liberal and gentle subjection; now, however, she is cast into servitude."[36] Thus Calvin seems to see the forcible subjugation of women as necessary to make women obey their husbands when they, through fallen faithlessness, fail to do so voluntarily.

Unlike Luther, who sees the fall as depriving women of a role in the government of public affairs in which she would originally have shared, Calvin attributes women's exclusion from government to the original divine ordinance in which sovereignty in domestic and state affairs was given exclusively to the male. This same order of creation means that women are not to preach or teach in church.

Calvin's view is evident in his commentaries on key passages on women in 1 Corinthians and 1 Timothy. In commenting on Paul's denial that women have the image of God (1 Cor. 11:7), Calvin reiterates his belief that women share equally in the image of God in those matters that have to do "solely with the mind," with "Christ's spiritual kingdom in which external distinctions are not regarded." This is what Paul was referring to in Gal. 3:28 when he said that "there is no difference between the man and the woman." Women lack the image of God only in those "external arrangements and political decorum—which is a part of ecclesiastical polity." Here "the man follows Christ and the woman the man, so they are not upon the same footing, but on the contrary this inequality exists."[37]

The exclusions of women from teaching and prophesying in 1 Cor. 14:34 and 1 Timothy 2, for Calvin, reiterate this basic rule that women, both in society and in the church, are excluded from public leadership by the order of creation set up by God from the beginning. Rejecting Luther's view that Adam was superior by right of primogeniture, Calvin insists that women are excluded because the woman is under subjection in the original order of creation, and this has been redoubled as punishment for her sin: "He (Paul) assigned two reasons why women should be subject to men: because not only did God enact this law at the beginning, but he also inflicted it as a punishment on the woman."[38]

Calvin, however, also has to explain those instances where women have been allowed to teach and prophesy in Hebrew Scripture and in the New Testament, as well as the examples of reigning queens who exercise powers of government. He explains this in three ways. First, he suggests that there might be occasions when a woman may speak in church and when the law against women speaking, like that of covering her head, might be regarded as a matter of public decorum that can be set aside. But he thinks of such a case as both an emergency situation and also as an occasional laywoman's testimony, not a formally appointed role of teaching.[39]

This argument is inadequate for the Hebrew prophetesses and the women prophets in the New Testament who exercised ongoing roles. Here Calvin distinguishes between God's appointed order of creation, set up from the beginning and due to last until the end of history, in which women are excluded from public authority, and the absolute power of God which transcends God's established order and by which God can choose to suspend it. The divine sending of prophetesses to teach the people of Israel or the church is an example of this exercise of God's absolute power, by which God, in emergency situations, can suspend the ordinary law of nature by which women are excluded from teaching.[40]

Finally, there is the troubling case of female rulers. Calvin believes that when women are legal heirs according to the customs of the people, they are to be obeyed. But the very existence of such female rulers testifies to a crisis situation in which the sinfulness of men is so rampant that God sees fit to humiliate them by having them obey a woman. Yet the law remains that female rule itself, in society and especially in the church, is a sign of a violation of the ordinary laws of nature by which women are commanded to "be silent."

> Woman, by nature (that is, by the ordinary law of God) is formed to obey; for *gynaikokratia* (the government of women) has always been regarded by all wise persons as a monstrous thing; and therefore, so to speak, it will be a mingling of heaven and earth, if women usurp the right to teach.[41]

Thus Calvin's anthropology of gender defines women according to three statuses: (1) an inner equality of soul as image of God; (2) an external subjugation in matters of government, both being established in God's original order of creation; and (3) a worsening of women's subjugation into servitude in the Fall in which women are forced to accede to a submission that would originally have been voluntary. Women's exclusion from public leadership in society and in the church is not changed by salvation. Rather the redeemed Christian woman once more learns to obey voluntarily, internalizing her duty and so no longer having to have it forced upon her.

Woman will be saved equally with man and share equally in eternal life, according to God's grace renewing her inner equality in the image of God, but this in no way suspends those laws of creation by which woman is subject to the man as long as the temporal order of creation continues. The occasional suspensions of this rule of exclusion, for prophetesses and for queens, are exceptions allowed by God, because God is sovereign over his own laws and can occasionally choose to suspend them in crisis situations, to instruct the people by sending a prophetess or to punish them by sending a queen to rule them.

Calvin also allows an occasional situation where a laywoman might say something in public. Here the rule against women speaking can be seen as a matter of decorum, normally to be observed but sometimes to be set aside. Thus in the *Institutes* he compares the laws of women covering their head and of keeping silence, saying:

> Is that decree of Paul concerning silence so holy that it cannot be broken without great offense? Not at all. For if a woman needs such haste to help a neighbor that she cannot stop to cover her head, she does not offend if she runs to her with head uncovered. And there is a place where it is no less proper for her to speak.[42]

But these cases are of an emergency nature and fall short of a woman occupying an office. None of these exceptions for Calvin in any way suspend the ordinary laws of God by which the woman is "formed to obey."

## Renaissance Feminism and the Debate about Women

From the fifteenth through the seventeenth centuries a literary debate argued the respective virtues or vices of women. A misogynist tradition long rooted in late medieval sermons and popular stories and songs denouncing women's slippery and manipulative natures was translated into a satire on courtly love in Jean de Meung's continuation of the *Romance of the Rose* (1275–80).[43] Christine de Pizan was the first female author to answer these attacks. In her *City of Ladies* (1405) she lifts up a catalog of wise female rulers and learned and virtuous women and argues that women's defects come, not from their natures, but from their subordinate status and lack of education.[44]

Misogyny played a major role in the depiction of women as prone to witchcraft in the literature and artistic imagery of witch persecution.[45] The handbook of witch-hunting, the *Malleus Maleficarum* (1486) written by two Dominicans, Heinrich Kraemer and Jacob Sprenger, authorized to carry the witch-hunts into Germany, elaborate the Thomistic view of women as intrinsically defective into a picture of the female by nature as prone to demonic influence:

> When a woman thinks alone, she thinks evil . . . They are feebler both in mind and body. It is not surprising that they should come more under the spell of witchcraft. . . . And it should be noted that there was a defect in the formation of the first woman, since she was formed from the rib of the breast which is bent in the contrary direction to a man . . . And since through the first defect in their intelligence, they are always more prone to abjure the faith, so through their second defect of inordinate passions, they search for, brood over and inflict various vengeances, either by witchcraft or by other means. Wherefore it is no wonder that so great a number of witches exist in this sex.[46]

This picture of woman as prone to witchcraft was continued in Protestant thinkers, although both Lutherans and Calvinists juxtapose the witch, not with the virginal woman, but with the good wife. Luther himself inaugurates this view by depicting women as naturally weak and fearful and therefore turning to witchcraft for aid. But this is a false protection. Only when women accept their God-given subordination to their husbands and become obedient wives will they be safe from these temptations to use magic to assuage their fears.[47]

Calvinist authors wrote an extensive literature on marriage in which they defined the roles of male and female partnership, male headship, and female obedience. The rebellious wife who rejects her proper role is linked both with Eve's sin and with female proclivity to witchcraft. The English Puritan divine, William Perkins addressed these parallel views of women in his treatises on marriage, *Christian Oeconomie* (1590), and in his *Discourse of the Damned Art of Witchcraft* (1596). For Perkins the rule of the husband over the wife was ordained in paradise and is the basis of all other government in church and state. The duty of the wife in this relationship is to "submit herself to her husband and to acknowledge and reverence him as her head in all things . . . (and) to be obedient unto her husband in all things; that is, wholly depend upon him, both in judgment and will."[48]

The contrary of these duties of the good wife are the sins of bad wives: "to be proud, to be unwilling to bear the authority of their husbands; to chide and brawl with bitterness, to forsake their houses."[49] In this rebelliousness lie the seeds of proneness to witchcraft. Perkins believes that most witches are female because they are weaker and so "sooner entangled by the Devil's illusions with the damnable art than the man." The devil prevailed first with Eve and continues to find easy marks in women. But the fact of weakness is no reason for mercy, for Perkins. Women who enter a covenant with the devil should receive the full sentence of judgment: "Though it be a woman and the weaker vessel, she shall not escape, she shall not be suffered to live, but must die the death."[50]

Replies to this construction of the bad wife as witch seldom questioned its misogynist assumptions. Thus Reginald Scot, in his 1584 treatise *The Discoverie of Witchcraft*, also believes that women are weak and prone to delusions, but he argues that witchcraft itself is such a delusion and not an actual pact with the devil. Scot, in contrast to Perkins, argues for mercy and forbearance toward these women whose imaginary trafficking with the devil is a sign of mental instability.[51]

There also arose a literary tradition of defense of women, mostly written by men, but increasingly women took up the pen in their own defense. One of the most daring of these treatises was written by Cornelius Agrippa, a polymath scholar of the early sixteenth century. In 1509 he gave a lecture on the "Nobility and Superiority of the Female Sex," which he published in 1529 in a more elaborated form. In this treatise Agrippa turned the traditional biblical arguments about Eve's creation and fall upside down.[52] Agrippa begins by accepting the traditional view that, in their inner spiritual nature or soul, women and men were created equally in the image of God and destined for equal glory in heaven. In those things that pertain to specific femaleness, however, Eve was not inferior but superior to Adam.

Agrippa argues this superiority of Eve by pointing out that her name means "life" while Adam's means "dirt," showing that she is closer to living spirit, while he is closer to inert matter. He even hints that Eve's name echoes the name of God and represents the female aspect of God as Wisdom.[53] Her superiority is indicated by the fact that she was created in paradise, while Adam was created outside it. Also, she was created from better material, living flesh rather than clay. Her creation after Adam indicates her perfection, as the crown of creation, the culminating work of God. Moreover, it was Adam who received the order not to eat of the fruit of the tree of knowledge of good and evil, while Eve was innocent of this command. Thus it is he who was truly guilty in the fall. The devil approached Eve first, not because of her weakness but because he was envious of her greater beauty and perfection.

Agrippa goes on to argue that Christ came as a male, not because the male is the normative and "perfect" sex, but because the male was more guilty for sin and so more in need of redemption. Mary signifies the higher perfection of the female sex. Christ's perfection springs from having been the son of the Virgin without aid from the male. Moreover, it is women, not men, who were faithful to Christ to the end and to whom he appeared first at the resurrection. The gospel message was given first to women, and women have carried it forward through the ages.

The right to preach was given to women by the Holy Spirit at Pentecost, and women in the apostolic age, such as Anna and the daughters of Philip and Priscilla, taught in public. It is male tyranny against the explicit word of Scripture that has denied women the right to preach and has kept women from the education by which their superior gifts might be evident.

> Yet there are some who use religion to usurp authority for themselves against women, and they justify their tyranny by means of sacred Scripture. The curse of Eve is constantly in their mouths: "You shall be under your husband and he shall rule over you." If one answers them that Christ took away the curse, they will object again from the sayings of Peter, with whom Paul also agrees, "Let women be subject to their husbands."[54]

Agrippa argues that male monopoly of ministry belonged to the old order in which Jew was set above Greek, but in the new age of redemption brought by Christ "there is neither male nor female but a new creation." A male-only priesthood was allowed under the old covenant because of man's hardness of heart, but this was superseded in Christ. And yet male tyranny continues to deny women their rightful place in both political leadership and culture.

> Thanks to the excessive tyranny of men, prevailing against divine right and the laws of nature, the freedom given to women is now banned by unjust laws, abolished by custom and usage and extinguished by upbringing. For as soon as a woman is born, she is kept home in idleness from her earliest years, and as if incapable of higher employment, she is allowed to conceive nothing beyond her needle and thread. . . . Public offices too are denied her by law. No matter how intelligent, she is not allowed to plead in court. . . . So great is the wickedness of recent legislators that they have made void the command of God for the sake of their traditions, as they pronounce women, who in other eras were most noble by virtue of their natural excellence and dignity, to be of baser condition than all men. By these laws, therefore, women are forced to yield to men like a conquered people to their conquerors in war, not compelled by any natural or divine necessity or reason, but rather by custom, education, fortune and tyrannical device.[55]

Agrippa here suggests that this male domination is recent, imposed on women in his own times, while women in earlier pagan and even medieval times had greater dignity and power. He pleads that such unjust laws should be dissolved so that women can take their rightful place in both political and cultural affairs, to "allow them their privilege with which God and nature had invested them."[56]

Agrippa's treatise was translated into Italian, French, German, and English in the sixteenth century and often reprinted in the next two centuries. Many of his arguments appear in later pro-women writers, although few dared to emulate fully his reversal of the anti-female tradition. In the early seventeenth century a renewed debate about women's good or evil natures broke out in England with the publication of a tract by Joseph Swetnam arguing for women's inferiority and evilness, *The arraignment of lewd, froward and unconstant women . . . profitable to young men and hurtful to none* (1615).[57]

This tract drew three responses from women writers, all published in 1617: Ester Sowernam's *Ester hath Hang'd Haman*, which included a long poem entitled "A Defense of Women, against the Author of the Arraignment of Women," signed by a Joane Sharpe; and Constantia Munda's, *The Worming of a Mad Dogge or a Soppe for Cerberus*.[58] The identity of these authors is unknown and they are probably pseudonyms. A fourth tract, by Rachel Speght, *A Mouzell for Melastomus, the synical Bayter of Evah's Sex*, was written by the teenage daughter of an evangelical minister, who refutes Swetnam's arguments with counterarguments from the Bible.[59]

Speght argues for the complete parity of women and men in creation, fall, and redemption. Both were created equally in the image of God, and both were made for the same redemptive end, to glorify God. In paradise they would have held joint authority over creation. Both sinned equally, although Adam as the stronger was more responsible for sin. Eve was compensated by God with the promise that the Savior would come from woman's seed, and both are represented by Christ, for although Christ came as a male, he was born from woman. Moreover Christ loved women equally and appeared first to women in the resurrection. Speght mingles arguments for parity with suggestions of women's superior moral virtue, repeating the arguments that Eve was created from a more refined material. But her basic view is that the marriage relation is to be one of mutual companionship as the closest model of the restoration of paradise. Man's role as head in marriage is to be one of love and protection, while women are to submit only in those matters that are good, but not in anything that goes against virtue. No obedience is owed in wrongdoing.

The other authors of these replies to Swetnam also emphasize biblical and theological arguments. They take their stand on the biblical doctrine of woman's equal creation with man as the image of God. Since it is God's creation of woman that established woman's essential goodness, for Swetnam to claim that woman is essentially evil is an insult to God as Creator. In her treatise, Sowernam repeats many arguments found in Agrippa, claiming that women's superiority is shown by the fact that Eve was created in paradise, while Adam was created prior to being placed in Eden. This creation in paradise is reflected in woman's continuing tendency toward the ideal.

Eve was also created of better material, from flesh rather than mere mud. Moreover, she was created last, after Adam, as the crown of creation. God created in ascending order of importance, first the planets, then plants and animals, then man, and finally woman. It was God who brought the woman to the man and founded marriage. As God intended it, marriage was to be a model of love and mutuality. Men who rail against women thus rail against God's gift to them. The serpent wished their downfall because he envied the happiness of the primal pair. But it is Adam who is more at fault. Eve responded to the serpent innocently, believing his lies. It is Adam who caused the fall, not so much because he ate the apple but because, having done so, he tried to excuse his fault by blaming Eve. Thus Adam is the type of all men who rail against women and seek to exculpate themselves, thereby causing the destruction of paradise.

God, however, had mercy on woman. God not only blessed her with the promise of children, but also assured her that it would be through the seed of woman that the Savior would be born. God announced the eternal enmity between the woman and the serpent, showing that women are inherently averse to evil and malicious ways and inclined to good. Sowernam goes on to cite a long list of biblical heroines of the Old and New Testaments, showing how women have ever been a blessing to men and bringers of salvation. This list culminates in the faithfulness of the women at the cross and the tomb, when all the male disciples had deserted their Lord. Sowernam sums up the biblical part of her argument against Swetnam:

> Thus out of the second and third chapters of Genesis and out of the Old and New Testaments, I have observed in proofe of the worthinesse of our Sexe: First, that woman was the last worke of Creation, I dare not say the best; She was created out of the chosen and best refined substance; She was created in a more worthy

> country; She was married by a most holy Priest; She was given by a most gracious Father; Her husband was enjoyned to a most inseparable and affectionate care over her; The first promise of salvation was made to a woman; There is inseparable hatred and enmitie put betwixt the woman and the Serpent; Her first name, Eva, doth presage the nature and disposition of all women, not only in respect of their bearing, but further, for the life and delight of heart and soule to all mankinde. I have further shewed the most gratious, blessed and rarest Benefits in all respects bestowed upon women: all plainly out of Scriptures. All of which doth demonstrate the blesphemous impudencie of the author of the *Arraignment,* who would or durst write so basely and shamefully, in so general a manner, against our so worthy and honored a sexe.[60]

Unlike Agrippa, neither Sowernam nor other pro-women writers dare carry the argument into a denunciation of women's legal subordination and exclusion from public cultural and political life as unjust male tyranny. They accept the basic pattern of women's subordination in the family, arguing merely for respect and affection. Although the debate over women has sometimes been seen as primarily a literary clash of wits, the underlying import was quite serious. The misogynist diatribes against women as inherently vicious gave husbands the right to beat their wives and, at its most extreme, led to torture and death of "witches." The women defenders of women hold up instead a more idealized view of the companionate marriage in which the husband treats his wife as a cherished good to be loved and respected, while the wife can submit to a husband who is her friend and protector.

The Renaissance tradition of feminist humanism diminished under the Stuarts but did not die out. It was carried on by women of the upper middle class and gentry who focused mainly on expanded education for women. Margaret Cavendish, the duchess of Newcastle, was a leading feminist humanist in the mid-seventeenth century. She belonged to the type of gentlewoman who cultivated a self-taught scholarship in the retirement of her country estates. The duchess longed to be recognized as an equal by the male scholars of Oxford and Cambridge universities and often addressed her writings to them, but mostly she was seen by them as a silly eccentric.[61]

At the end of the seventeenth century a more sustained theological argument for women's education was developed by Mary Astell, who came from a leading Newcastle merchant family. Astell had been tutored as a child by a curate uncle who taught her poetry and classics and introduced her to the writings of the Cambridge Platonists. Astell remained all her life a faithful High Church Anglican, a Jacobite in politics, and a Christian Platonist in her theological anthropology. At the age of twenty-one Astell set out for London, where she found help from William Sancroft, the archbishop of Canterbury. Support for her writing came from the High Church publisher Rich Wilkins, who would handle all her work for the rest of her life. She also entered into a philosophical dialogue with John Norris, the last of the Cambridge Platonists who was so astonished by her insights that he published their correspondence under the title *Letters Concerning the Love of God* (1695).[62]

Astell found a lifelong circle of patrons among London noblewomen interested in education. She became a mentor for young aspiring women scholars. Astell's career is notable because she remained single and lived alone all her life, supporting herself through her writings and as a teacher and principal of a charity school for girls. She sought to be accepted by the male thinkers of her day as a philosopher and commentator on social and political issues, but was recognized mainly for her writings on marriage and women's education.[63]

Astell's first book, for which she would remain best known, was *A Serious Proposal to the Ladies* (1694),[64] in which she appealed to leisure class women to abandon frivolity and to cultivate education to develop their immortal souls in this life and for the life to come. She proposed a new educational institution for women that would combine the features of a convent and a women's college with the buildings and grounds of an aristocratic estate. Astell sought to convert such upper-class women both to a love of learning and to the dedication of their means to found such an institution.

Astell never argued for political rights of women and regarded the hierarchies of class and gender as the unchangeable basis of social order, culminating in the hopefully enlightened rule of the legitimate monarch. But she deeply resented the domination of ignorant and morally inferior men over women of quality such as herself, especially when such men were presumed to have power over women simply because they were males, while women were denied the possibility of self-improvement because they were women.[65] Her solution was female celibacy. The only way women can free themselves from constricting male domination is to reject marriage and create in its place a female-centered world of intellectual and spiritual cultivation.

For Astell, the theological foundation of women's equality and autonomy is their souls. The soul, for Astell, is a created intellectual spirit, essentially genderless, given by God to men and women alike. Both women and men are called to develop their intellectual and moral properties to the highest level through study, prayer, and good works in this life, and thereby to fit themselves to enjoy the highest communion with God for all eternity. Following the Cambridge Platonists, Astell saw no split between nature and grace, rationality and spirituality.[66] Human reason is a spark of the divine Reason. Through moral self-discipline and rational contemplation, the soul can ascend to an ever more perfect communion with God. To deny women education, therefore, is ultimately to deny women the opportunity to cultivate their souls for that fullness of eternal life to which they are called by God.[67]

Astell does not envision that all those in her school will remain celibate. Most young women will come as students and leave for marriage, being thereby fitted to be better wives and mothers and doers of charity in their communities. A celibate elite of women teachers will live permanently in the community, which will have a regular life of prayer, as well as study. An unabashed "lover of her sex," Astell speaks of this community of women as knit together by bonds of loving friendship. It is a redemptive community, paradise regained and a holy mountain of redeemed life. Thus education is for Astell ultimately a means of salvation and a foretaste of the heavenly community.[68]

## Women in Radical Protestantism: Civil War Prophets and Quakers

A very different genre of writings comes from seventeenth-century English popular female prophets. Many of the women who spoke and wrote as prophets were from the "middling classes" and had some independent means,[69] although some were former servants and a few, such as Lady Eleanor Davies, were from the gentry. Prophetic preaching and writing by men and women flourished particularly during the period of the English Civil War and early Protectorate (1645–53), when public censorship disappeared.

In her study on women and ecstatic prophecy in seventeenth-century

England, Phyllis Mack lists thirty-eight well-known women visionaries who were active in the 1640s and early 1650s, most of them associated with the Baptists, some with movements such as Ranters, Levelers, and Fifth Monarchists.[70] Modeling their language after the books of Daniel and Revelation, these women (and men) writers see themselves as living in a time of apocalyptic crisis and crying out to the nation to repent before the time of judgment comes.

One such prophet and popular pamphleteer was Mary Cary (later Mrs. Rande), who published a series of visionary writings that applied the language of biblical apocalyptic to English politics. In her *A Word in Season to the Kingdom of England* (1647), Cary declared that God had delivered England from the grip of Satan through the defeat of the Royalists and the execution of King Charles, and God now expected England's new leaders to bear good fruit. If they would avoid divine displeasure, Parliament and magistrates should stop oppressing the poor and mistreating the saints (like herself) who were preaching the gospel. All should submit to the yoke of Christ as their King.[71]

Cary and other female prophets do not make a special case for women's right to preach and prophesy. Rather, they declare that the Holy Spirit is no respecter of persons. God gives the power of prophecy to women equally with men, in order to rebuke erring kings and prelates. Cary and other female prophets place particular emphasis on Acts 2:17-18. God does not tie up the Spirit in law nor confine it to priests, Levites, and the learned. As promised in Scripture, in these last days God is pouring out God's Spirit on all flesh, and God's sons and daughters are prophesying. Divine judgment is about to be unleashed against the servants of Satan, and the saints, while presently suffering, will soon be delivered to reign over a redeemed earth.

For Cary, the Holy Spirit annuls all social hierarchies of class, education, and gender. She spends no time seeking to persuade men of women's right to an education or authority to speak. Prophecy transcends all human offices or credentials. Its power gives women of the meanest class supreme confidence to speak out against the highest leaders in the land. "I am but a weak instrument," Cary declares, "but I am all by the power of the Lord."[72]

The heirs of this spirit of millenarian prophecy during the English Civil War were the Society of Friends, or Quakers, begun by George Fox in 1647. The Quakers spread rapidly in the 1660s, uniting radical witness in society with disciplined familial community. Rooted in the English northwest, they soon had strong groups in the south, including London, and carried their message abroad to Holland, North America, and the Caribbean and eastern Mediterranean.[73] Most Quakers came from the yeoman and small-business classes, but some were former servants and others were drawn from the landed gentry. Margaret Fell, converted by George Fox when he visited her home in 1652, together with her seven daughters, was herself was an Askew, an ancient landholding family. She married Thomas Fell, a barrister member of Parliament and a judge. Inheriting the Fell estate at the death of her husband in 1658, she made her home, Swarthmore Hall, the organizational and communications base for the Quaker movement worldwide.[74]

Quaker life and discipline encouraged literacy among members, women as well as men. Women's Meetings kept books recording their decisions and disbursements and circulated their decisions to other women's Meetings, with exhortations to persevere in the faith. Quakers networked with each other through letters, journals, and travel diaries intended for community reading and wrote tracts defending their theology and vision. Women from the first were a significant part of these "publishers of the Truth," both in public witness and print. Of the 650 Quaker authors during the first fifty years of its history whose works are preserved, eighty-two are women, some of whom authored numerous tracts.[75] For example, Margaret Fell wrote twenty-four tracts, while Dorothy White (1630–85) wrote twenty known tracts. Her topics range from confrontation with the evils of English society, in *An alarum sounded to Englands inhabitants* (1661), to advice and comfort to suffering friends in *Universal Love to the Lost* (1684).[76]

Quaker women, like Rebecca Travers, did detailed work to refute attacks on Quaker theology and to defend its understanding of scriptural authority, revelation, and Christology. Elizabeth Bathhurst wrote a systematic theological presentation of Quaker beliefs in 1679, *Truth's Vindication*. In 1683 she authored a collection of biblical passages, *Sayings of Women*, showing that God, in both Testaments, spoke through women as well as men.[77]

Underlying this active ministry of Quaker women as preachers, missionaries, writers, and leaders of women's meetings was a Quaker theology of spiritual equality of women and men in creation, an equality that was restored through redemption in Christ. As one Quaker theological document put it, Adam and Eve were originally created:

> of one mind and soul and spirit, as well as one flesh, not usurping authority over each other . . . and the woman was not commanded to be in subjection to her husband till she was gone from the power . . . the power and image and spirit of God is of the same authority in the female as in the male.[78]

Quakers accepted the traditional Christian view that women were created equally in the image of God, but rejected its qualifying claim that subjugation of woman to man was also established by God in relation to her sexual, reproductive, and domestic roles as wife and mother. For the Quakers all such "usurping of authority over each other," whether man over woman or master over servant, is the expression of a sinful power "under the law" and "under the curse" that began with the fall. But in Jesus Christ the law has come to an end, the curse has been overcome, and the original spiritual equality of all persons, male and female, is restored.

Margaret Fell, in her tract *Womens speaking justified, proved and allowed of by the Scriptures* (1666), echoes arguments found in earlier pro-women tracts, such as those by Speght and Sowernam. Not only did God originally "put no such difference between male and female as men would make," but God showed a special mercy on Eve as the more innocent of the pair and the more truthful in confessing her fault to God at the fall, while Adam tried to blame both God and Eve for his disobedience.[79] Fell, and Quakers generally, put great stress on God's curse on the serpent (Gen. 3:15): "I will put enmity between thee and the woman and between thy seed and her seed." Following the tradition that the "seed of the woman" is a prophecy of Christ, born of woman, Quakers divided humanity between "two seeds," the redeemed who are in the "light," who belong to the "seed of the woman" and those who are "Satan's seed."

This passage for Fell is the foundational mandate from God for women's preaching, for if the woman who belongs to Christ does not speak, then the seed of Satan will prevail. Moreover, those who oppose women's speaking thereby manifest that they belong to Satan and not to Christ:

> Let this word of the Lord which was from the beginning stop the mouths of all that oppose women's speaking in the power of the Lord. For he hath put enmity between the woman and the serpent; and if the seed of the woman speak not, the seed of the serpent

> speaks; for God hath put enmity between the two seeds. And it is manifest that those that speak against the woman and her seed speaking speak out of the enmity of the old serpent's seed.[80]

Not only in the time of Christ, but even "in the Age of the Law," God empowered female prophets who testified to God's truth, Fell argues, citing the standard examples of Hulda, Miriam and Hannah, Ruth, Esther, and Judith. With the coming of Christ the power of the serpent has been dealt the decisive blow, God's Spirit has been poured out on all flesh, raising both sons and daughters into the restored humanity of the resurrection. Not only did Jesus himself manifest his love to many women, such as the woman of Samaria, Mary and Martha, but he appeared first to Mary Magdalene, Joanna, and others, making them the apostles of the resurrection to the male apostles who lacked their same steadfast faith.[81]

Thus for Fell the good news of redemption itself hinges on acceptance of "the message of the Lord God that he sends by women," and hence on acceptance of women's preaching. "What had become of the redemption of the whole body of mankind if they had not believed the message that the Lord Jesus sent by these women, of and concerning his resurrection?" Fell concludes: "And thus the Lord Jesus hath manifested himself and his power, without respect of persons, and so let all mouths be stopt that would limit him, whose power and Spirit is infinite, that is pouring it upon *all* flesh."[82]

Fell deals with the familiar Pauline passages in 1 Cor. 14:34 and 1 Tim. 2:12 by claiming that the women referred to in these passages had not yet been converted and hence did not have the spiritual authorization to speak. These are women still "under the law," who manifest their unregenerate nature by their "broidered hair or gold or pearl and costly array" (1 Tim. 2:9) and by being "idle, gadding about from house to house . . . gossips and busybodies" (5:13). But the restrictions rightly imposed on these women (and on men!) do not apply to righteous regenerate women, who not only may but must speak in the power of the Spirit:

> But what is all this to such as have the power and Spirit of the Lord Jesus poured upon them and have the message of the Lord Jesus given unto them? Must not *they* speak the word of the Lord because of these undecent and unreverent women that the Apostle speaks of, and to, in these two Scriptures?[83]

Fell's interpretation of Paul reflects standard Quaker exegesis of these texts. Mary Cole and Priscilla Cotton in 1656 wrote a tract from prison, *To the people and priests of England we discharge our conscience,* defending their public preaching, in which they likewise argue that the women whom Paul enjoined to keep silent are those not yet converted. But those who are in the Spirit, whose head is Christ, to which Paul referred in 1 Cor. 11:5, are mandated to pray and prophesy in public—albeit with covered heads—to cry down the false church and state of Babylon. Cole and Cotton add that men also, particularly priests and bishops of the established church, are enjoined by Paul to keep silent and listen quietly to the women and men who have received the Spirit. The same argument is found in the Quaker catechism of 1671, *Some Principles concerning the Elect People of God in Scorn called Quakers,* in the section "concerning women speaking in church."[84]

Fell and other Quakers argue that gender subordination did not exist in God's original design of creation, but appeared only as an expression of sin, annulled in Christ. But they also spoke in a deeply gendered world both in domestic and public life and in religious and cultural symbolism.[85] They argue their spiritual egalitarianism by transforming the traditional Christian gender imagery that made the female both the symbol of evil as "Whore of Babylon" and symbol of the church as "bride of Christ." Quakers dealt with these female symbols of evil and good by insisting that both are female generics that include men and women equally. The "Church of Christ," Fell declares, "is a woman"; she goes on to argue that "those that speak against the womans speaking speak against the church of Christ and the seed of the woman, which seed is Christ."

It is the church that is spoken of when Jeremiah declares, "For the Lord has created a new thing on the earth, a woman encompasses a man" (Jer. 31:22).[86] For Fell, all Quakers are symbolically female as bride in relation to their bridegroom Christ, but the femaleness of the church also proves that women are included in representing and speaking for Christ as his bridegroom.[87] Quaker men and women are symbolically female also because redemption dissolves all arrogance, mightiness, and usurping of power of one over another, and the adoption of traits of meekness and gentleness traditionally associated with women. The Christian paradox that God chooses the lowly of the world to confound the mighty is here used to include women, but also Quaker men who have engaged in a kenosis of dominating power and so have become "womanlike"; one Quaker man even signed his letters "Your sister in our Spouse."[88]

For Fell, unregenerate men and women equally are referred to by the negative female images, such as "Whore of Babylon," although men more than women have the opportunity to behave in those modes of "whorishness" expressed in "usurping power" over others:

> In this great city of Babylon, which is the woman that hath sitten so long upon the scarlet-coloured beast, full of names of blasphemy . . . and this woman hath been drunk with the blood of the saints and with the martyrs of Jesus; and this hath been the woman that hath been speaking and usurping authority for many hundreds of years together.[89]

This double female symbolism of the true church as Bride of Christ and the unregenerate as Whore of Babylon, both understood generically as men and women, shapes early Quaker religious rhetoric. Speaking of religious nurture to one another, Quakers typically use the mother-child language of babes being suckled, or the marital imagery of brides embraced by their beloved, for both men and women. But when denouncing powerful and unjust men in church and state, Quaker women as much as men employ an apocalyptic language where such men are called Jezebels and idolatrous whores. Although Quakers cite female biblical prophets to justify women's right to speak, when they actually speak as prophetic denouncers they do not do so in the persona of these female prophets, but as male biblical figures such as Moses, as mouthpieces of an angry and judging God.[90]

Quaker religious language dissolves the connection between female and male gender symbolism and biological sex, but, as Phyllis Mack points out, it does so on a different basis than modern feminist gender deconstruction.[91] For Quaker spirituality, the deep inner person, the soul or conscience, lies below not only bodily difference or formal social roles, but also below the experiences of the self in thoughts or feelings. The soul transcends all surface constructions of the self, not only socially, but as one's own ideas and emotions.

The soul is the image of God, rooted in God's being. As Sarah Jones, a poor widow of Bristol, puts it in her 1650 exhortation to other Quakers, *This is lights appearance in Truth to all the precious lambs of Life, Dark vanished, Light shines forth,* redemption means "that ye sink down into that eternal word and rest there, and not in any manifestations."[92] Social class, gender difference, all the external babble of social gestures and the inner babble of thoughts and feelings, are for Quakers those "manifestations" that are not the "eternal word that was before manifestations were." Redemption dissolves the outer differences of roles and reroots the person in the divine power of God, which is both the true source of its creation and its destiny in immortal life.

When the soul "sinks down and rests" in the eternal by a spiritual emptying of the self of all vain surface appearances, this divine word lays hold of the self and impels it to speak, despite the "weakness" of the person who in society may be a mere woman, servant, or child. So the Quaker prophet who thunders at the powerful of church and state also negates the ego as the source of this presumption. Thus Margaret Killam, haranguing at a "steeplehouse" declares: "I was made in much meekness to declare the truth."[93]

Sarah Chevers, in her epistle to Friends, describes this process of self-emptying as both the filling of the emptied self with divine power, and also as a streaming forth of the reborn self to others in the "light." For Quakers, self-dissolution into God creates a power that is directed back into social relations, both in denunciations of false and oppressive society and in the building of community between those "tuned into" this Spirit of God:

> The much more are we broken down into self denial, sealed down forever into the true poverty, and upright integrity of heart and soul, mind and conscience, wholly ransomed by the living word of life, to serve the living God . . . we cannot hold our peace: The God . . . of glory doth open our mouth and we speak to his praise, and utter his voice and sound forth his word of life, and causeth the earth to tremble . . . my heart, soul and spirit that is wholly joined to the Lord, stream forth to you.[94]

Quaker spirituality in which the gendered self is dissolved into a pregendered soul rooted in God, as its original and true "ground of being," has affinities with some medieval women mystics. But Quaker women were not celibates who rejected social and sexual roles of family life;[95] they lived ordinary lives, marrying, producing and raising children, tilling fields, selling goods, and keeping books on their business as well as religious transactions.

This combination of self-dissolution into the transcendent "light" that impelled a person into a career of preaching, missionary travels, confrontations with authorities, and imprisonments, and living ordinary lives as spouses, parents, and workers created tensions for both men and women, but particularly for women. The two roles were in more dramatic tension for women than for their male colleagues. The same woman who sunk herself into God and barred her back to the whip, after having cried down the minister at a "steeplehouse" as a "painted beast,"[96] was expected not only to maintain the sentiments of a fond wife and nurturing mother, but to be available to provide the services thereof for her husband, children, and itinerant Friends who might arrive at her house.

From 1662 until 1688 the Quakers experienced severe persecution. Thousands of them were imprisoned, suffering beatings and abominable jail conditions, and hundreds died. Quaker women suffered alongside men, and often bore the brunt of sadistic savagery from authorities who found their combination of calm faith and unbending determination particularly aggravating. Quaker women accused of being witches were stripped and pricked for "witch's teats."[97] During the years of persecution, Quakers shaped a distinctive form of institutional life that enabled them not only to survive but to express enlarged roles for women in ministry. The system of men's and women's Meetings developed in the 1660s gave Quaker women a recognized sphere of ministerial work, but one that built on traditional complementary gender roles of men and women in the family.

The Quaker combination of transcendent gender equality and conventional gender complementarity is illustrated in a document sent between 1675 and 1680 from the Lancaster County women's Meeting (probably headed by Margaret Fell's daughter, Sarah) to be read at "women's Meetings everywhere."[98] The document defends the institution of women's Meetings—which was being challenged by some men and even women Friends as defying the apostolic injunctions against women's speaking in church[99]—with the same theology found in Margaret Fell's 1666 treatise. Here too it is argued that the original image of God, restored in Christ, includes male and female equally; in redemption women have been freed from all sinful domination.

The document goes on to describe the ministerial roles of women in the women's Meetings in terms that institutionalize the collective power of matriarchs in the family. These roles consist in disciplining those who are disorderly (particularly other women and girls): the supervision of marriage, both to prevent Friends from marrying outside the fold and to assure suitable partners, and the administration of funds to care for the poor, poor widows with children, the sick, infirm, and aged.

These roles hardly seem to warrant either resistance to women's Meetings or the radical egalitarian theology used to defend them. Yet the women's Meetings aroused more fear among Friends that traditional gender differences were being transgressed than all the women of the earlier period who had cried out against authorities in the voice of an angry prophet and who left husband and children to travel long distances as missionaries, risking stripes, prison, and death. The difference was that those roles were understood as charismatic "gifts" allowed women occasionally, but the women's Meetings gave women a public office in the church. This was seen as a dangerous challenge to the Christian tradition that women are not to hold official church offices.

Quaker women at the end of the seventeenth century present us with a paradox. Retired to a more inward life in her community, the Quaker woman resembled the Puritan Goodwife playing her helpmeet role in both family and church. Yet under the plain dress and speech lurked a crucial shift in theological anthropology. Quakers believed that God created humans, male and female, equally in the image of God and redeemed them into a spiritual equality for a future immortal life. But, unlike other Christians, they did not believe God had established a mandate for social subordination "in the beginning." They saw subordination of class and gender as sinful usurpation, the wrongful fruit of the fall, already overcome for those who are "in Christ."

As apocalypticists, Quakers did not at first translate this theology into social reform, but expected injustice to fall under the rod of divine judgment. At the end of the seventeenth century they withdrew from "the world" to cultivate their own sanctified community, allowing an enlarged space for women in church leadership, but tacitly accepting class and gender hierarchy as the present shape of things "under the law." It would be another century, as Quaker theology was joined to political liberalism, before a new generation of Quaker women leaders would arise to apply this theological shift to political reform to overcome slavery and female subjugation in society.

5. Statue of Lucretia Mott, Susan B. Anthony, and Elizabeth Cady Stanton by Adelaide Johnson, donated to the U.S. Congress by the Women's Party in 1921 to celebrate the victory of women's suffrage. The inscription hails the victory as "one of the great bloodless revolutions of all time that liberated more people than any other without killing a single person." Copyright © *Chicago Tribune*.

## Chapter Five

# Shakers and Feminist Abolitionists in Nineteenth-Century North America

EIGHTEENTH-CENTURY WESTERN EUROPE presented a face of deceptive stability. In politics absolute monarchs reigned; in the established churches tied to these rulers, Reformation or Counter-Reformation orthodoxies prevailed. But volatile forces that presaged the disintegration of this European ancien régime boiled under the surface. Left-wing mystical and millennialist forms of Christianity were by no means subdued, but they experienced many pockets of renewal, their persecuted leaders fleeing from country to country, bringing their subversive message with them. At the same time new empirical sciences and rational philosophies questioned the authority of revealed religion and social classes.

In this chapter I trace these two lines of religious and social thought as they flowed to the new revolutionary nation of the United States in the late eighteenth and early nineteenth centuries. In America they found a wider audience and a larger field for experimentation than was allowable in the "old countries" of England and Western Europe. For most male leaders of mystical-millennialist and rationalist movements, changed gender relations and new opportunities for women were not on the agenda. Yet these questions often intruded themselves from the margins, especially from female adherents of these movements. I will focus on a representative movement in those lines of thought in which gender questions became central: the English-American millennialist sect of the Shakers and the women's rights movement that arose from the abolitionist struggle of the 1840s, led to a large extent by women of Quaker background.

## The Shaker Tradition: From England to North America

The Shakers (United Society of Believers in Christ's Second Appearing) arose from a small millennialist sect of "shaking Quakers" that began to gather in 1747 near Manchester, England, led by James and Jane Wardley. In 1758 they were joined by Ann Lee, a twenty-two-year-old illiterate mill worker, who would become the leader of the group and lead it to the United States. Various revival movements of the day impinged on this group. Although most Quakers no longer welcomed the volatile forms of spirit possession and social confrontation of the previous century, some Quakers revived these patterns. The Wardleys may have originated from such a Quaker gathering.[1]

The Wardleys were also influenced by the Camisards. These were radical French Calvinists who fled to England in the early 1700s from persecution in their homeland, bringing with them a tradition of spirit possession and millennialist expectation and gathering English followers eager to experience such outpourings of the Spirit.[2] There were also mystical groups, such as the Philadelphians, influenced by the German mystical theosophist Jacob Boehme, who taught that God was both masculine and feminine. For them, the English mystic Jane Lead was the female vehicle of this androgynous God.[3]

Women played important roles in all these movements, as Camisard prophets, as Philadelphian mystical teachers, as a founding leader and inspired prophets among the Shaking Quakers. The Methodist revival movement also awakened spirit possession and millennialist hope, and Ann Lee attended George Whitefield's revivals in her spiritual search. Methodists were conventionally patriarchal in their views of ordained ministry and society, but women often functioned as local preachers and class leaders.[4] Thus "in the air" in all these movements was the idea that women might be both leaders and inspired vehicles of the Spirit at the time when the millennial completion of Christ's work of salvation was imminent.

Ann Lee did not at first assume a leading role in the Wardley Society. She had not yet broken with the Anglican church at the time of her marriage in

1762 to a blacksmith, Abraham Stanley.[5] In the next years Lee experienced a series of four difficult pregnancies and the deaths of all four infants. These experiences induced extreme feelings of sinfulness and horror of sexuality. Becoming more zealously involved in the Wardley Society, Lee engaged in confrontations with the mobs who objected to the loud worship of the sect, resulting in several imprisonments. It was during one of these imprisonments that Lee experienced a divine vision that showed her that the original sin by which Adam and Eve fell from grace into depravity was the sexual act.[6] She also became convinced that she was the chosen instrument of Christ to announce this saving truth to a world damned by lust.

Lee's role as inspired vehicle of Christ's redeeming grace, available only to those who adopted complete abstinence from sexual expression, was accepted by the Wardley Society. After several additional attacks on her and her community by church and civil authorities, Ann decided to emigrate to America when a vision told her that the true church of Christ was to be established there.[7] In May 1774 she sailed to America with a band of seven followers, including her brother, William Lee, and her husband (who later deserted the sect to remarry). After living in poverty in New York for two years, the group was able to secure land and move to the area of Niskeyuna, eight miles northwest of Albany.

From this settlement Lee and her followers conducted preaching tours to nearby towns in New York and New England. They were often met with hostility and outright violence from mobs and local authorities who saw the Shakers as strange and dangerous, suspecting them of witchcraft and religious and political subversion due to their millennialist claims, female leadership, celibacy, and pacifism. This region, however, was also swept by religious revivals, led by Methodists and New Light Baptists. Shakers began to draw converts from these revivals, from those who were disappointed in the inability of established churches to maintain the enthusiasm of spiritual outpouring. Both William Lee and Ann Lee received violent beatings from angry mobs, causing his death in 1784, followed by Ann's a few months later.

The Shaker movement survived the crisis of the death of its spiritual mother through the work of a series of leaders who created the organizational pattern and the theological self-understanding for its future development into the nineteenth century. Lee was succeeded by one of her original

English band, James Whittaker, who continued the process of preaching tours and founding local societies, but he died two years after Ann Lee.[8] The mantle of leadership then fell on one of Lee's American converts, Joseph Meacham, a former New Light Baptist, who chose Lucy Wright to be co-leader with him.[9]

It was Meacham who shaped the Shaker communal organizational structure to reflect what he saw as the Gospel Order of the Millennial Church of Christ's Kingdom. Patterned after a vision of a restored Jerusalem temple, Shaker societies were given a three-court structure of different kinds of celibate families. The inner court was composed of mature believers who had consecrated themselves and all they owned to the community. The second court was composed of young people in formation or those who still had worldly obligations, and the outer court carried on the worldly business of the society.[10]

Each local society was divided into families with a collegiate leadership of two elders and two eldresses who acted as spiritual leaders, while two deacons and two deaconesses managed the temporal needs of the family. Several families were grouped into a Society led by a collegiate episcopate also comprised of two elders and two eldresses. The mother Society of New Lebanon, in turn, had an oversight role over all the other Societies. This was led by Meacham and Lucy Wright (Wright headed the whole movement alone for twenty-four years after Meacham's death in 1797).[11] Integral to Meacham's organizational plan was the idea that the millennial Church must be led by parallel male and female leadership, representing the dual spiritual parentage of Christ as Father and Mother.

Meacham also set patterns of religious life, worship, and doctrine for the new society. His millennial laws put into practice the key Shaker ideals of confession of sins, celibacy, community of goods, and sexual equality. Meacham also reformed Shaker worship from spontaneous expressions of Spirit possession to ordered sacred dance carried out in parallel lines of men and women.[12] In his major written work, Meacham interpreted the place of the Shaker church in Christian history as the fourth and final stage of a series of redemptive dispensations following the original fall of Adam and Eve from paradise.[13]

Meacham's work as theological interpreter of the Shaker gospel would be followed by three other important writers in the nineteenth century, John

Dunlavy,[14] Calvin Green,[15] and Benjamin Seth Youngs. Youngs played the major role in writing what is called the Shaker Bible, *The Testimony of Christ's Second Appearing*, first published in 1808, a monumental work that places the Shaker church and its beliefs in biblical and Christian history and theology.[16] Youngs was born in 1774 in Schenectady, New York, and joined the Shakers with his family in 1794. Youngs belonged to a new generation of Shakers who never knew Ann Lee personally, but he was an active participant in revival preaching in the early nineteenth century that brought thousands of new converts into the Society.

Before outlining the theological interpretation of the Shaker gospel found in the *Testimony*, it is useful to discuss how this mature theological system evolved from the self-understanding of Ann Lee herself. Since her memoirs were written by her successors (mostly male) in the generation after her death, we are dependent on them for any reconstruction of what she taught about herself and her work. The "quest for the historical Ann" is almost as problematic as the quest for the historical Jesus, since most of what we know of her has been refracted through memories shaped by the believers who constructed this later theological and organizational work.[17]

Ann Lee probably did not envision such a highly organized communitarian system, with its parallel male and female leadership, nor place the Shakers in a dispensational redemptive history, with its systematized theory of a dual-gendered God and parallel male and female Christs.[18] But she did provide the core inspiration for this later theological and organizational superstructure in several ways. First, the central Shaker belief that sexual lust was the root of all evil, and celibacy its cure, was rooted in her personal experience and transformative prison vision. Second, she linked this revelation with the advent of the millennium. Thus a new era of redemption that is the "beginning of the end" starts with her revelation and its reception by believers.

Finally, and most importantly, it is she who is the chosen instrument of this revelation through which the final era of redemption begins. Thus Ann Lee understood herself as having a unique relation to Christ and a unique role in both embodying and conveying it to others. This was not simply a message, but the power of spiritual transformation through which the final era of redemption is to happen and its church gathered. Lee seems to have conveyed her special relation to Christ and role in redemption in feminine metaphors traditionally used in the Christian tradition for the church. She was the "bride of the lamb" and, through this bridal relation to Christ, the mother of the reborn who gathered through her maternal ministry.[19]

Although bridal language was common for female (and even male) mystics, and women (and even men) who saw themselves as nurturing the spiritual life of others might speak of themselves as spiritual mothers, Ann's use of this language conveyed a new and decisive role. For earlier Christians, being bride of Christ and mother of Christians were derivative of a relationship to the church established by Jesus, while for Lee, this language signifies a unique role that she plays in relation to Jesus Christ—a role that founds a new community of the reborn on the basis of a new outpouring of the Spirit not previously available.

Shaker "mothers and fathers" in ministry represent a spiritual parentage derivative of Ann Lee's bridal relation to Christ by which she is mother of Christ's renewed children. A story told in Shaker tradition of the conversion of James Meacham conveys what is likely to have been Lee's own self-understanding of this special bridal-maternal role. Meacham challenged Lee's leadership with the Pauline Scriptures that forbid women to teach or have authority over men, saying: "for it is a shame to a woman to speak in the church. But you not only speak, but seem to be an Elder in your church. How do you reconcile this with the Apostle's doctrine?"

Mother Ann answered:

> The order of man in the natural creation is a figure of the order of God, for man in the spiritual creation. As the order of nature requires a man and a woman to produce offspring, so, where they both stand in their proper order, the man is first and the woman is second, in the government of the family. He is the father, and she the mother, and all the children, both male and female, must be subject to their parents; and the woman, being second, must be subject to her husband, who is the first; but when the man is gone, the right of government belongs to the woman; so it is in the family of Christ.[20]

Meacham is described by the Shaker documents as stunned by this reply, immediately perceiving a whole new worldview:

> This answer opened a vast field of contemplation to Joseph, and filled his mind with great light and understanding concerning the spiritual work of God. He clearly saw that the New Creation could not be perfect in its order, without a father and a mother. That, as the natural creation was the offspring of a natural father and mother, so the spiritual creation must be the offspring of a spiritual father and mother. He saw Jesus Christ to be the Father of the Spiritual Creation, who is now absent; and he saw Ann Lee to be the Mother of all who were now begotten in the regeneration; and she, being present in the body, the power and authority of Christ on earth was committed to her; and to her appertained the right of leading and governing all her spiritual children.

Although one can doubt whether Meacham saw all this at once, if Lee's analogy of herself as the spousal representative of her absent husband Christ is historical, it provided the kernel of the Christology that would be elaborated in the *Testimony*, with its androcentric patriarchal assumptions given a twist that provides a unique female role in redemption for Lee and her daughters. Lee draws here on the conventional marriage law of her time. The married woman was assumed to be subject to her husband and united to him as "one," but through this subjection to and union with her husband, English law created the legal fiction that the wife represented the husband when he was gone, either through death or distant travel.[21] Lee, in effect, claims this relation to Christ for herself.

Traditional Christology paralleled the New Adam with the New Eve,[22] the "begetting" role of Christ on the cross with the bearing role of the Church,[23] Christ as bridegroom with the church as bride,[24] but there was no particular woman in the New Testament story who represented this bridal and maternal relation to Christ (although much of this bridal and maternal imagery would be transferred to Mary).[25] Church leaders might claim to represent the apostles, especially Peter, the "Prince of the Apostles," but did not personally embody the Bride of Christ. By claiming this role, Ann Lee created a special role for herself as representative of Christ in the stage of redemptive history after his departure and positioned this marital relation as the font of a new spiritual family that she headed uniquely as their mother in Christ.

The theology of the *Testimony* has struck feminist readers as disappointingly rooted in patriarchal assumptions.[26] But the combination of androcentric dominance and secondary female parity was reflected in Ann Lee's self-understanding (if she was the source of this analogy), with the important difference that she spoke of herself from the perspective of the wife of an absent husband whom she represents, while her male interpreters define her from the perspective of the husband whose dominant rule governs her subordinate one.

The *Testimony* is organized by a scheme of four successive dispensations of revelation and salvation: the patriarchal, the Mosaic, the First Appearing of Christ in Jesus, and the Second Appearing of Christ in Ann Lee. The story is also structured by a theory of correspondences between the natural and the spiritual levels of existence and a scheme of material figures and spiritual fulfillments. The nature of God and the way of salvation are prefigured in earlier dispensations in outer material forms, then made present partially in the beginning of the New Creation in Jesus, but in full spiritual power only in the Second Appearing.

This means that the first creation of the world and its primal couple, Adam and Eve, were not created in their final spiritually transformed and immortal form, but in a way that tested their ability to grow into a higher promise to be realized only at the end. Adam was created dual, a living soul in the image of God and an animal body that he must rule over, even as he must rule over the beasts of the material creation. He was also created dual in the sense of being both male and female, but was not complete until the woman was taken out of him and stood as his companion. Only as male and female is Adam fully "man."[27]

Eve is seen as a subordinate image of Adam. She too is both animal body and living soul, and is taken from Adam to share in dominion over the animal world. But she is also in some way closer to the animal world over which they are to rule jointly, and she exercises this rule only under her husband's direction. Only if this right order had been maintained—male over female, soul over body, human over beasts—would the original creation have been kept in its intended harmony.

But this was not to be. Eve, being closer to the bestial nature, succumbed to the temptation of the serpent, and Adam in turn to her temptation. The essence of the fall is the upsetting of right order; human submits to beast, male to female, soul to body. The lower rules over the higher. Lust expressed in the sex act is the basic expression of sinful corruption of right order and is the root of all sin. Wars, oppression, slavery, pride, and gluttony—all forms of human disorder and violence—are rooted ultimately in lust, the succumbing of the rational soul to the animal instincts.[28]

Since the sex act was the fundamental expression of the fall, Youngs struggles with the question of whether there could have been sinless sex and procreation. He finally acknowledges that, in the creation of male and female, God intended reproductive sex to exist. But this was supposed to happen only at God's order, when Adam and Eve were mature and could carry out this act without lust, solely for the purpose of offspring.[29] By leaping for the "fruit" prematurely, they lost for themselves and their offspring the possibility of mature, lust-free, reproductive sex.

Youngs's view of both the fallen and the redeemed condition wavers between exemplarism and collectivism. Sin is passed on because corrupted parents can only produce corrupt offspring, but each human also sins for himself or herself by acting in the same way as Adam and Eve. The capacity for sinless sex was not lost, but in practice became rare or nonexistent without new dispensations of spiritual power.[30] Moreover, reproduction itself is not the highest end of humanity. It was necessary to create the mortal bodily nature of humans, but as living souls humans were pointed toward spiritual regeneration leading to immortal life, in which there will be no marrying or giving in marriage. Sex and reproduction belong to a lower natural order that is to be surpassed by the higher spiritual order truly fitting to humanity as living soul rather than mortal animal body.[31]

In the first two dispensations of salvation, the patriarchal and the Mosaic, humanity learns the ethical disciplines to control and limit the animal body with its lusts. Periodic outbreaks of rampant depravity are disciplined by God, and a series of virtuous figures—Abel, Noah, Abraham, and Moses—receive God's promise of salvation and prefigure the redemptive order whose spiritual power still lies in the future. In Jesus, however, there is the beginning of the new spiritual creation that transcends the natural, material creation and points to the final end of humanity in immortal life.

Jesus was the first exemplar of the new creation that has overcome both the animal nature and its fall, being himself produced without sex. With no father but God, Jesus stands on a new plane of spiritual life, although partaking of the human body through his mother.[32] He also took up and bore the cross of this physical body. For Shakers, Jesus' cross meant his crucifying the flesh to live a celibate, lust-free life, culminating in full spiritual rebirth or resurrection.[33] The true disciples among his followers likewise were celibate, but the full power of spiritual life was not yet available.[34]

Jesus, the first Christ, exemplified the fullness of redemptive life, but power of the Spirit to live this life for the whole church was not yet available. Consequently, the early church soon compromised and accepted marriage as preferable to the greater evil of fornication.[35] This compromise gradually led to a full capitulation of the church to sin. The first age of the fall before Christ is paralleled by a second more blasphemous age of the fall of the church, the reign of the Antichrist, when those claiming to represent Christ actually represent the devil. The reign of the Antichrist begins with the fifth-century popes and continues through the Reformation to the eighteenth century.[36]

For the Shakers, the Magisterial Reformers represent no real improvement but are simply the multiplication of the horns of the ecclesial Antichrist.[37] Even worse, the Reformers reject the gospel order of celibacy, exemplified by Jesus, in a wrongheaded reaction against the abuse of celibacy as a cover for fornication by the church of Rome.[38] A few true followers of Christ continue from the time of the early church to the present time, but they are marginal figures persecuted by the dominant church, such as Marcion and Priscillian, the Albigensians, the Waldensians, and the Anabaptists.[39] In the seventeenth and eighteenth centuries the imminent advent of the second coming of Christ in spiritual power was anticipated by an increase in prophetic movements: the Quakers, the French Prophets, and the Wesleyan revival.[40]

With the coming of Ann Lee and her foundation of the Shakers, the fullness of salvation begins. But, for Shakers, this second coming itself is only the seed of a millennial process in which all people must be gathered into the regenerated humanity.[41] The *Testimony* presents several key arguments why this second coming must take place through a woman. First, there is the order of creation of male and female. Thus the new humanity also must be exemplified in a male and a female. Just as the original Adam was incomplete until the woman was taken from his side and stood beside him as his companion, so the New Adam is incomplete without the New Eve, the regenerated woman.[42]

Youngs evokes Paul's anthropology (1 Cor. 11:7), where man is said to be the head of the woman while the woman is the *glory* of the man, as a proof text for the claim that Christ's second coming in *glory* can only refer to Christ's coming in the woman.[43] Youngs ransacks the Old and New Testaments for all references to twoness and female counterparts to messianic figures to prove that this dual coming of Christ was already predicted in the Scriptures.[44] The sequence of the fall is also used in a theory of spiritual reversal. Just as woman sinned first and, through her, the man, so in the order of redemption the male must come first and then the woman. Only then does redemption come down to that lower part of man where sin originated and, by reversing it, restore original right order.[45]

Finally Youngs elaborates a view of God's androgyny as the ultimate foundation for why both the natural and the regenerated humanity must be both male and female.[46] This, he believes, was unknown in previous revelation but has been disclosed through the second coming of Christ in the woman. Only with Ann Lee is the Mother or Wisdom side of God revealed. He argues that the androgyny of God was implicitly revealed in Genesis, where God's making of humanity in God's image, male and female, implies that God is both male and female. But only with Ann Lee is God's feminine nature disclosed, not simply as a theory, but as a vibrant religious experience.

Youngs and other Shaker writers ridicule the traditional Christian view of the Trinity as three male persons. This they regard as absurd and unnatural. Throughout all nature every species exists as male and female, so God who is the author of nature must be male and female, for the natural world mirrors on a material level the spiritual world.[47] This does not mean, however, that God is two separate persons, male and female. This notion of separate persons in God is an error. Rather God is one in substance but in a dynamic relation of two dimensions, power and wisdom. These two dimensions in union are reflected in humanity as male and female, but here too the two must become united in community.

Also Shakers insist this coming of Christ in the woman and the revelation of the feminine aspect of God is necessary for justice to women. Women are denied their rightful place both in human society and in the church when only males represent humanity, Christ, and God. This emphasis on the male is the source of all distortions, wars, and violence. Justice and harmony in human relations are possible only when the woman is restored to her rightful place as partner to the man, sharing dominion both in the natural world and in its transformation in the higher order of regeneration.[48]

Only when there is acknowledged to be both a father and a mother in Christ can the children of regeneration be born and grow into a community through which the mass of fallen humanity will eventually be transformed. Although Jesus and Ann Lee together represent this completed manifestation of the new creation, there is no substitutionary atonement for sin in Shaker theology. Every man and woman must take up their cross, crucify the flesh, and be transformed into the new humanity of celibacy, community of goods, gender equality, and peace, before there can be a fully redeemed humanity.[49]

Although this new creation has started with the Shakers, and they are the foundational examples of it, redemption remains incomplete until all are transformed in a like manner. Only when this millennial process of transformation is complete will the whole world be transformed into an eternal new creation freed from mortality. At the beginning Shakers imagined this would happen by a process of evangelism in which everyone would eventually become Shakers. But toward the end of the nineteenth century, as the numbers of Shakers dwindled, some Shakers revised this view of themselves. They began to see themselves as only a seed planted that must take root in many other movements throughout the world. Perhaps, like the seed, they must even die so that many plants might arise and flourish in a great harvest of world transformation.[50]

Although the millennial order developed by Meacham provided for gender parity in ministry and administration, this was also organized by the traditional gendered division of labor in which men did the outside work and women the inside work. This put cooking and cleaning in the hands of women, as well as many other kinds of skilled housework in what was a subsistence communal economy, but it meant that men did the overall administration of the Society in its financial dealings with the world. But, as the numbers of Shakers dwindled and the Society became mostly female at the end of the century, this pattern changed. Women took equal roles of administration.[51]

It was in this later period of the Society that Shaker women came into their own as writers and interpreters of Shakerism in publications intended both for internal reading and for the "world." A group of progressive Shakers, who styled themselves Alethians (from the Greek word for truth), adopted an ecumenical stance toward the "world" and looked to the various progressive movements in society, such as feminism, vegetarianism, the peace movement, antiracism, and socialism, as exemplifying the redemptive progress by which the world was to be gradually transformed.[52]

Anna White, eldress of the Society of New Lebanon, was one such Shaker woman who sought to interpret Shakerism in relation to the progressive movements of her day. Prominent in the peace movement, White led delegations of Shakers to meetings of the Universal Peace Union and associated herself internationally with the Alliance of Women for Peace. Having obtained hundreds of signatures for the Petition for International Disarmament, White was appointed New York vice president of the Alliance.[53]

In her history of Shakerism, White revises the androcentrism of classical Shaker theology to present the theory of a dual God and Christ in feminist terms. In her view Shakerism from its beginning manifested the full equality of women with men, an equality that the rest of the world is only recently beginning to recognize.

> Woman appears in her rightful place, at once the equal of man in creation and office at the hand of God. Ann Lee's followers, 1900 years after Jesus uttered the words, "Neither do I condemn thee, go and sin no more," and sent Mary to tell the Good News of a risen Lord and living Savior, alone of all humanity, have taught the doctrines that have placed woman side by side with man, his equal in power, in office, in influence and judgment. To Ann Lee may woman look for the first touch that struck off her chains and gave her absolute right to her own person. To Ann Lee may all reformers among women look as the one who taught and through her followers teaches still perfect freedom, equality and opportunity to woman. The daughters of Ann Lee, alone among women, rejoice in true freedom, not alone from the bondage of man's domination, but freedom also from the curse of that desire "for her husband," by which, through the ages, he has ruled over her.[54]

## Abolitionist Feminists

The women's rights movement that arose from women's involvement in the antislavery struggle in the two decades before the American Civil War drew on a combination of radical evangelical and Quaker theological and social principles and American political egalitarianism. The American Declaration of Independence assumed an Enlightenment secularization of the Christian doctrine that all humans are created in the image of God, declaring that all human beings possess a common original human nature. Despite differences of individual talents or social circumstances, all humans have a common "species nature" that endows them with "reason and moral conscience."[55]

This common human nature is the basis for the claim that all humans should possess the same "human rights." Feudal societies, divided between aristocrats and commoners, denied this common humanity and equality of rights, setting up a system of class-based privileges and disprivileges. For revolutionary liberalism these traditional differences of rights reflected not the "natural order" but an evil distortion of "nature." The overthrow of feudalism and the creation of new societies founded on constitutional governments would restore original equality, codifying it in a new society of equal rights of citizens before the law. This secular, political equivalent of fall and redemption was enshrined in the American tradition in the ringing statement: "We hold these truths to be self-evident, that all men are created equal."

But the framers of the American Declaration of Independence and Constitution did not seriously consider including "all humans" in this definition. They were alarmed when some observers, such as Abigail Adams, the wife of John Adams, suggested it might include women, raising the further specter of other excluded groups: propertyless white men, Negro slaves, and Indians.[56] What the delegates to the Constitutional Convention meant by "all men" was white propertied males, not their slaves and dependents. It would take another 140 years, a civil war, and a series of reform movements for these excluded groups to be incorporated into the American legal definition of self-representing citizens. Although Angelina and Sarah Grimké were not the first feminist lecturers in the United States (they had been preceded by others, such as the controversial British feminist Frances Wright in the 1820s[57]), it was they who put the issue on the agenda for a sector of the abolitionist movement at the end of the

1830s. The Grimké sisters were remarkable figures in the abolitionist movement of this period because they were white Southerners raised in a prominent and prosperous slaveholding family of Charleston, South Carolina.[58]

Increasingly repelled by her personal experiences of the household treatment of slaves, Sarah Grimké was drawn to the Quakers by her reading of the memoirs of John Woolman, an eighteenth-century Quaker abolitionist. In 1821 Sarah decided her new convictions demanded that she leave Charleston and move to Philadelphia, where she joined the Fourth and Arch Street meeting of the Society of Friends. Sarah's sister Angelina, thirteen years her junior, followed a similar path of moral and religious disassociation from the dominant forms of Christianity and from Charleston slave society. She joined Sarah in Philadelphia in 1829 and applied for membership in the Arch Street Society of Friends.

Philadelphia Quakerism in this period was rent by a schism between the prosperous establishment Quakers, represented by the Arch Street Society, and the Hicksites, who sought to revive the earlier, more democratic patterns of Quakerism.[59] Establishment Quakers, although still allowing women the right to preach and attend women's Meetings, put the Society's effective administrative power in the hands of the dominant males. While admitting blacks to membership, they followed the common practice of other churches in forcing them to sit on special "colored benches" in the back of the meeting. They frowned on social activism, including abolitionism, among their members, particularly when it involved participating in non-Quaker gatherings. These patterns of sexism, racism, and sectarianism would eventually drive the Grimké sisters out of the Quaker fold, despite its importance to them in midwifing their escape from slave society and more conservative forms of Christianity.[60]

Early in 1832, Angelina pioneered the sisters' involvement in the abolitionist movement by following its literature and news. In 1835, despite misgivings from Sarah, Angelina broke with the strictures of the Arch Street Friends to attend meetings of the Female Anti-Slavery Society, led by Hicksite Quaker Lucretia Mott, and a speech given by British abolitionist George Thompson. A letter from Angelina to radical antislavery leader William Lloyd Garrison urging him to stand firm against mob violence was published by Garrison and launched Angelina in abolitionist circles. In the summer of 1836 Angelina wrote her first major antislavery tract, *Appeal to the Christian Women of the South*.[61]

Overcoming her misgivings, Sarah joined her sister in the fall of 1836 to be trained as field agents for the American Anti-Slavery Society. This training, under the guidance of Theodore Weld, longtime abolitionist organizer, launched the sisters as antislavery speakers. For the next eighteen months the sisters would speak extensively in New York, New Jersey, and Massachusetts, often confronting mobs and hostility from local clergy. New writings poured from their pens: letters to clergy of the Southern states, writings addressed to free colored people and to Northern whites.[62]

The sisters adopted the radical Garrisonian demand for "immediate emancipation" rather than the gradualism exemplified in the Colonization Society, which planned to send freed Negroes back to Africa on the assumption that whites and blacks could not live together as free and equal citizens in the United States. The Grimké sisters were remarkable not only in drawing on their Southern experience of oppression of slaves, but in their direct solidarity with this experience of black suffering. They insisted that not only slavery but race prejudice should be overcome. They acted out these principles with personal friendships with blacks and an insistence that black men and women be leaders in the antislavery movement, not just objects of concern.[63]

These principles drew further retaliatory fire, now directed both at the sisters' abolitionist principles and also at their defiance of the traditional role of women by public promotion of these principles as women. Early in 1837, Catherine Beecher, conservative educational reformer, attacked the sisters' immediatism and their failure to play the traditional feminine role in her *Essay on Slavery and Abolitionism, with Reference to the Duty of American Females*.[64] That same summer, the Congregational clergy of Massachusetts, who had already closed their churches to abolitionist speakers, attacked the sisters for violating the New Testament teachings that women must be subordinate to males and silent in public.

Angelina undertook a series of letters to answer Catherine Beecher, including three concluding letters refuting her views on women's role.[65] Sarah also wrote a series of letters in response to both Beecher and the Massachusetts clergy, "On the Equality of the Sexes and the Condition of Women," from July to November of 1837. These letters laid out a biblical exegesis and theology for women's equality and analyzed the oppressive status of women in society.[66] In the 1830s abolitionist preachers like Weld drew on the patterns of revivalist meetings, defining slavery as a national sin and calling for personal and systemic conversion from this sin in light of an impending divine judgment and millennial transformation of society.[67] The Grimké sisters applied this denunciation and call to conversion from personal and social sin, framed in the context of divine judgment and millennial hope, to women's oppression in patriarchal society.

The core of the sisters' argument against slavery and for equal rights for blacks and for women in society rested on their reading of the Genesis teaching on creation of all humans, male and female, in the image of God. Reclaiming the biblical roots of the liberal doctrine of egalitarian "original nature," the Grimké sisters would insist in writing after writing that God's creation of all humans in the image of God meant God created all humans with the same moral nature, equal in rights and responsibilities. While creation in the image of God made humans collectively the agents of divine dominion over the nonhuman world, no dominion was placed by God of one human over another, neither master over slave nor male over female.[68]

When a relation of dominion of one group of humans over another is created, the humanity of the subjugated group is denied, reducing them from the status of persons to that of property. This is a grievous sin against God's intention for humanity, and the source of all evil between humans. In Sarah Grimké's words:

> We must first view woman at the period of her creation. "And God said, let us make man in our own image, after our likeness; and let them have dominion over the fish of the sea, and over the fowl of the air and over the cattle and over all the earth and over every creeping thing that creepeth upon the earth." . . . In this sublime description of the creation of man (which is a generic term including man and woman) there is not one particle of difference intimated as existing between them. They were both made in the image of God; dominion was given to both over every other creature, but not over each other. Created in perfect equality, they were expected to exercise viceregency intrusted to them by their Maker, in harmony and love.[69]

Moving then to the story of the fall, Sarah Grimké reads Genesis 3 as showing that the primal pair played different roles, the woman initiating, but more naively; the male accepting, but more culpably, since he was more aware than she of the divine command. For Grimké this means that woman is in no way more guilty for the fall than man. The pair lost their original innocence, but not their original equality due to any divine chastisement. It is human sin that has brought to the surface the evil impulse to domination of human over human that the male has unjustly exercised over the female:

> The lust of domination was probably the first effect of the fall, and as there was no other intelligent being over whom to exercise it, woman was the first victim of this unhallowed passion.[70]

Sarah sums up her case in these pithy words:

> But I ask no favors for my sex. I surrender not our claim to equality. All I ask of our brethren is that they will take their feet from off our necks and permit us to stand upright on that ground which God has designed us to occupy.[71]

Sarah Grimké believed that it was Christ's mission to restore this original equality in the image of God between all humans, overcoming the evil systems of domination of male over female, master over slave. This is the meaning of the great text of Gal. 3:28. But Sarah Grimké also struggled with contrary texts in Paul, which deny women's equality in the image of God, demand that women cover their heads, and teach the subjugation of wives to their husbands. She was particularly affronted by the claim that the husband represents Christ in relation to the wife. These texts are totally contrary to what Grimké believed to be the essence of the biblical message that all humans are equal before God and no one can be God to another person. She vacillated between trying to find an alternative reading in which these texts refer only to local circumstances, not general principles, and a denunciation of them as wrong.[72]

Sarah Grimké began her letters with the claim that female equality can be read from the Bible against later church teachings that have contravened its true message. But in the process of studying the Bible as she wrote the letters, Sarah began to doubt whether the biblical writings are consistent. She asserts as normative the equality of all persons in creation and redemption to critique contrary teachings in Scripture itself. Paul is questioned as still harboring "Jewish" views of male domination and hence not able to understand the radical nature of the gospel fully.

The suggestion that the husband could represent Christ in dominion over the wife was for Grimké unthinkable, for it suggests that one human is usurping the relation of God toward another human. This is contrary to what she took to be the fundamental biblical teaching that all humans are equal before God and none can usurp the place of God for another. She concluded that these texts in the New Testament are either being misread or represent a sinful flaw within the pages of Scripture itself.[73]

Sarah and Angelina, in their writings on women, strongly reject the dominant view, evoked by both the Massachusetts clergy and Catherine Beecher, that women are not only subordinate, but have fundamentally different modes of virtue. Both sisters insist that whatever is right for a man to do (e.g., speak in public, exercise political power) is also right for a woman to do. The contrary principle also holds: Whatever is wrong for a woman to do should also be wrong for a man to do. If some kinds of power are oppressive, then it is equally wrong for men as for women to exercise such power.

By discarding the false notion of separate male and female spheres and duties, women need no longer ask themselves "how far they may go without overstepping the bounds of propriety":

> They will be enabled to see the simple truth, that God has made no distinction between men and women as moral beings; that the distinction now so much insisted upon between male and female virtues is as absurd as it is unscriptural, and has been the fruit of much mischief: granting to man a license for the exhibition of brute force and conflict on the battle field, for sternness, selfishness and the exercise of irresponsible power in the circle of the home; and to woman a permit to rest on an arm of flesh, and to regard modesty and delicacy and all the kindred virtues as peculiarly appropriate to her. Now to me it is perfectly clear, what WHATSOEVER IT IS MORALLY RIGHT FOR A MAN TO DO, IT IS MORALLY RIGHT FOR A WOMAN TO DO, and that confusion must exist in the moral world, until woman takes her stand on the same platform with man and feels herself clothed by her Maker with the *same rights* and of course that upon her devolve the *same duties*.[74]

This insistence that both men and women are moral agents called to the same standards of virtue in society led the sisters to challenge the binary theories of masculine and feminine natures and roles. It is not simply that the female nature has been deprived of its full rights and ought to be able to exercise the same public roles as males; the humanity of the male also has been distorted by the lust of domination and aggression. Both masculinity and femininity are false distortions of humanness. Women need to be converted from their timidity and deference to men, and men need to be converted from their prideful claim to superiority, in order to restore both men and women to their original and intended humanity of equal and shared moral rights and duties in all spheres of society, both domestic and public.

This surfacing of the "woman question" in abolitionism was highly unwelcome, even to many radical male abolitionists. Although they might agree that women had a right to speak in public, they saw discussion of women's rights as an issue to be diversionary from the all-important topic of abolishing slavery. The sisters pointed out that it was their opponents, not they, who dragged them into this issue by insisting that they must not speak in public as women. This made it necessary to deal with the women's issue explicitly in order to defend their public speaking on behalf of abolition.[75] But the conflict was not to be so easily settled. It would split the American antislavery movement in 1840 and create a lasting schism between women's rights and black enfranchisement after the Civil War.[76]

In the spring of 1838 Theodore Weld confessed his love for Angelina Grimké and the two were wed in May of that year in a ceremony that reflected all their egalitarian principles.[77] Although Weld intended to be an equal partner in marriage and in public life with his wife, the realities of women's role as housekeeper and child-raiser in a household struggling with limited financial resources soon caught up with them, together with sister Sarah, who lived with them. Neither sister would play the same role of public lecturer after Angelina's marriage.[78] Yet the Grimkés' three-year public career launched the "woman question" among abolitionists, a question that would be taken up by their successors, Quaker minister Lucretia Mott and women's rights leaders Elizabeth Cady Stanton and Susan B. Anthony.

Lucretia Mott, born on January 3, 1793, was only five weeks younger than Sarah Grimké. She married at eighteen, and when the Grimké sisters retired from public life in 1838, Mott was already a grandmother and was emerging into a public leadership role in American reformism that would continue until her death in 1880. Mott had been sensitive to issues of women's rights since her school days. She deepened these concerns in the 1820s by reading Mary Wollstonecraft's *Vindication of the Rights of Women*, a book that would remain foundational for her views of women's rights.[79]

In 1827 Lucretia Mott followed her husband, James Mott, into the Hicksite side of the Quaker schism. Lucretia regretted the schism in principle, but the Hicksite return to the foundations of Quakerism in the experience of the inner light against all dogmatism of Bible and creed suited her unfolding liberal views of religion.[80] Although she often risked disownment (even from the Hicksites) for her theological radicalism, activism, and antisectarianism, she was able to survive these criticisms and remain a lifelong Quaker minister in good standing.

The Motts espoused antislavery views from their earliest years of marriage, adopting in the mid-1820s the principles of "free produce" (boycotting products produced by slave labor).[81] In 1830 they were converted by William Garrison to the demand for immediate emancipation against the gradualist and implicitly racist views of the Colonization Society. In 1831 Lucretia Mott organized the first meeting of the Philadelphia Female Anti-Slavery Society as part of a drive of the Garrisonians to involve women in antislavery work. This society broke sectarian and racial boundaries from the first, including as members both black and white women from different Christian churches.[82]

Through the Female Anti-Slavery Society, Lucretia Mott laid a basis for many friendships across racial lines. She opened her home to interracial gatherings, preached at black churches, and mobilized white women to support black women's concerns, such as financial support for Sarah Douglass' school for black children. Interracial socializing was inflammatory in Philadelphia, and mob violence heightened against antislavery meetings, climaxed by the torching of the new Pennsylvanian Hall in May 1838. Mott arranged for pairs of white and black women to exit from the threatened hall arm in arm,[83] and she continued her practices undeterred by the violence. These experiences gave her increasing confidence in her own and other women's leadership abilities.

The Grimké sisters had already surfaced the "woman question" within the American Anti-Slavery Society, but the society split in 1840 when Lucretia

Mott was made an official committee member. For Mott the turning point on women's issues was the June 1840 meeting in London of the World Anti-Slavery Convention. Mott and several other women were among the American delegates to this convention, but the British organizers objected and refused to seat the women. This touched off a vehement debate. It also linked Lucretia Mott with Elizabeth Cady Stanton, who attended as the young wife of anti-slavery leader Henry Stanton. The two women spent hours talking about women's plight and resolved to form an organization to promote women's rights when they returned.[84]

Stanton's many pregnancies delayed these plans, but finally on July 19, 1848, Lucretia Mott and Elizabeth Cady Stanton opened the first Women's Rights Convention in Seneca Falls, New York. They presented to the convention a Declaration of Sentiments modeled after the Declaration of Independence:

> We hold these truths to be self-evident that all men and women are created equal. . . . The history of mankind is a history of repeated injuries and usurpations on the part of man toward woman, having in direct object the establishment of absolute tyranny over her.[85]

The Declaration went on to demonstrate this thesis by listing all the laws by which the female was defined as rightless, excluded from the vote, property holding, education, and from other ways of participating in public society.

The three hundred women who attended this convention adopted the Declaration enthusiastically, adding to it a series of resolutions that claimed women's equality both before God and before the law. Mott proposed the closing resolution that "the speedy success of our cause depends on the zealous and untiring efforts of both men and women for the overthrow of the monopoly of the pulpit and for the securing to women an equal participation with men in the various trades, professions and commerce." Stanton's resolution that "it is the duty of women in this country to secure to themselves their sacred right to the elective franchise" was the only one that passed with less than a unanimous vote. Mott's principles of resistance to participation in unjust government gave her pause in the face of this demand, but she soon endorsed it on the grounds that if voting is immoral, it is as much so for men as for women.

Three years later, Susan B. Anthony, a teacher of Hicksite Quaker background, met Stanton and the two formed a lifelong collaboration in the struggle for women's rights. Despite Mott's insistence that younger women take over the movement, Stanton and Anthony continued to regard her as their mentor and to invite her to speak and to chair their meetings. One of Mott's last public addresses was in July 1878 on the thirtieth anniversary of the Seneca Falls convention, when she was eighty-five years old.[86] The three women continued to be closely associated as the historical leaders of the women's suffrage movement.[87]

In Mott's speeches and sermons delivered over forty years, in settings ranging from her own Cherry Street Quaker meeting in Philadelphia, to Unitarian churches and the Free Religious Association (an organization of religious liberals from many traditions, including Jews), antislavery, temperance, women's rights and peace society meetings, Mott laid out a consistent religious basis for her involvement in these many reform issues. The foundation for all these calls for personal and social transformation was the Quaker principle of the inner light.

For Mott the inner light was simultaneously a revelation of the true inner spiritual nature of human beings and the presence of the divine in the depths of the self. Access to the inner light was not limited by gender, race, or creed. It was the true nature of all humans present across all religious and social divisions, manifesting a universal divine presence that taught the same principles of truth, justice, and love in all times and places.[88]

This divinity present in every human is not a spiritual power given only to baptized Christians through Christ after the fall that alienated humans from God. Rather, for Mott, it is natural; it is the true nature of humans as created by God in God's image. It has not been lost, but is still fully present in the depths of every person, although we need to get in touch with it through quiet listening and opening ourselves to its transformative power.

Mott vehemently rejected all Christian doctrines, such as total depravity, imputed sin inherited from Adam and Eve, imputed salvation through Christ's sacrifice on the cross, the divinity of Christ, the Trinity, and the inerrancy of Scripture, as well as ceremonial forms, such as baptism, Eucharist, Sabbath observance, and even Quaker plain dress and silence. In her view all these doctrines and forms externalized sin and salvation, God and revelation, as things outside the person that could be taken on as outward ideas or forms without inward transformation and committed action for redemptive change in society.

This does not mean that Mott repudiated any importance of Jesus, the biblical testimony, sin, salvation, and millennial hope. Rather, for her these truths only became meaningful when they were freed from their doctrinal or external forms and reintegrated into the reality of divine goodness as the true nature of every person. Ideas of the fall and the inheritance of sin from the primal parents fundamentally deny this innate goodness as our original and true nature, given to us by God in creation.

For Mott, the doctrine of total depravity fixed the human being as alienated from God and incapable of being or doing good and thus gave a powerful excuse for evil as the prevalent way of being human. Sin thus understood as an inheritance of a fallen nature from Adam and Eve was an abstraction that did not force anyone to examine the real sins of selfishness and violence to others in which one was actually involved in one's daily life, as a part of an unjust and violent society.[89]

For Mott, the doctrine of vicarious atonement through Christ's death and resurrection was the other side of this same "gloomy doctrine" that justified a formalized "do nothing" Christianity. The individual, defined as incapable of turning to God and doing good through his or her own God-given nature, was assured of and outwardly imputed a salvation done by an external agent, Christ. They need not be transformed inwardly or commit their lives to be and act rightly in their own lives to create a society of justice for all, overcoming real sins, like slavery, that deny a group of humans their humanity.

For Mott, Jesus was not divine in a way that set him apart from the rest of us as an incarnate god, but rather he was divine in the same way all of us are: that is, the divine was present in his soul as it is in all of our souls.[90] Jesus differs only in that he opened himself very fully to this inner divine presence and thus manifested a transformed self committed to truth, justice, and love, but the same transformation is equally available to all of us. Jesus is an exemplar of what we are all called to be in his goodness, truthfulness, and demand for justice for the most despised, not in his dying on the cross and being resurrected.

Like all true prophets who are in touch with the inner light, Jesus was a nonconformist or "heretic" toward the clerical systems of his day. It is this nonconformity to injustice and clericalism that caused him to be attacked and killed by the religious and political powers of his day. We too, when we are in touch with the inner divine self and act rightly, can expect to suffer and be condemned as heretics by the defenders of clerical "priestcraft."

The Bible is authoritative insofar as it shows us the common truths to which we are all called, but it also contains erroneous views that glorify war and justify slavery. Its truths must be evaluated in the same way as any other book, in the light of the primary testimony to God's truth in the depths of the self in touch with the divine presence.[91] In addition, the clergy distort the actual teaching of Scripture in order to use it to justify slavery, the subjugation of women, war, and intemperance. Their claim that the Bible is inerrant prevents people from realizing they can read it and evaluate its good and bad points for themselves.

All of these doctrines of inherited sin, vicarious atonement, an exclusive divinity of Christ, and biblical inerrancy, as well as various ceremonial forms, are tools of clerical domination by which a priestly caste set themselves up to lord over others, preventing ordinary people from thinking for themselves; blocking the real message of the gospel, which is the call to a real transformation of the self and society into living ways of love, justice, and peace. This creates a system of religious hierarchy that justifies other forms of domination, denying the truth that we are all equal in this process of experiencing God's revelation in ourselves and doing our own work of redemptive change to overcome the real and concrete evils in and around us. For Mott, at the top of the list of such evils were slavery, oppression of blacks and Indians, subjugation of women, intemperance, and war.

Women's oppression is one case (among others) of wrongdoing in which unjust treatment of some people in society was defended by distorted religious teaching. These evils must be repudiated by an understanding of true religion. God created women and men equally in the image of God and gave women exactly the same inner divine nature and capacity to experience inwardly the reign of God as the male. Mott repeats the Grimkés' themes that men and women together were assigned to govern nonhuman nature, but no domination was given to one group of humans over another. The lust for domination over others arose with the fall. Male domination over women is a prime example of this sinful usurpation of power over others.[92]

The sinful domination of men over women has been acted out over the centuries by laws that reduce women to a rightless dependency, denying them education, the vote, and jobs. It has also been expressed by distorted cultural ideas that declare that women are by nature incapable of such public political, educational, and economic participation. The Christian clergy has reinforced these ideas of female inferiority and weakness with false readings of the Bible that prevent people from realizing that women played leadership roles in biblical times. Women were prophets in Old and New Testament times and were affirmed by Jesus as equally called to preach.

Mott explains away contrary texts in the New Testament, such as 1 Cor. 14:34–36 and 1 Timothy, by opining that these were local situations, not general principles for all times.[93] Although she is prepared to claim that the Bible in both Testaments is egalitarian to women, she is also quick to deny that this argument establishes scriptural inerrancy. It is simply a proof of relative enlightenment of the people who wrote the Bible. Christians can claim this fact to refute clerical misuse of the Bible to justify women's subjugation. But the Bible must be read like any other book to discern its good and bad ideas. As Mott likes to put it, we must take "truth for authority, not authority for truth."[94]

Mott also insists that the New Testament view of marriage is that of equality in relationship, not male headship over the wife as his property. The basic principle of marriage in the Bible, one renewed in the Quaker tradition and being discovered by all enlightened people today, is one of "equality in independence, mutuality in dependence and reciprocity in duties."[95] Marriage so redefined will cease to be oppressive to women and be a real and full partnership of equals, a relationship she sees as exemplified in her own marriage.

In order for women to recover their true spiritual powers given to them by God, all the oppressive laws against women must be rescinded. Women, like men, must be able to vote, run for elective office, pursue all areas of education, and be employed in all skilled jobs. Mott also sees the emancipation of women as an internal process within women, not just a cancellation of unjust laws that limit them. Women, like blacks, have been inwardly retarded and damaged by oppression. It will require a process of education and spiritual development to really open them to their full inner powers. Oppression has not changed women's essential nature, but it has meant that women have been socialized to operate in a partial and distorted way. So they need a developmental process to reclaim their full selves.[96]

Like the Grimké sisters, Mott rejects notions of female superiority as well as inferiority. Once women gain power, they too, like men, can abuse it. Thus both men and women must be spiritually developed to gain their truer selves. Since women have been distorted to dependency and men to domination, this process of spiritual development of both men and women will blend the qualities assigned to each into a larger whole in a way that will make all humans and society better.[97]

Mott sees this redemptive process as this-worldly. She is agnostic toward life after death, placing biblical millennialism in a framework of a doctrine of progress in society toward an ever better and more just way of life.[98] Once slavery was overcome, women's rights would soon follow (although she was aware that the abolition of slavery had not overcome the oppression of blacks, and argued that the antislavery societies should continue in order to work against de facto continued enslavement).[99] Mott's reform commitments after the Civil War focused particularly on peace, in the hope that arbitration could replace war as a means of relationship between nations. "War no more" was for Mott the final horizon of hope for human social progress.[100]

The half century from 1870 to the winning of suffrage in the United States in 1921 saw some shifting in the ground for the struggle for women's rights. The focus of the women's movement became increasingly a strategic campaign to win the vote, rather than a broad utopian agenda of social transformation embedded in millennial hope. The belief that civil rights for all are founded on the "natural" or essential equality of all humans was surrendered by many of the new women's leaders. Instead they argued that woman's moral superiority calls for her enfranchisement in order to uplift society. This argument was racist and classist, acquiescing in disenfranchisement of blacks and hostility to immigrants, while arguing for a doubled vote for the "better" class of Americans by including females of this group.[101]

The religious basis for the struggle for women's rights also changed. Some, like Elizabeth Cady Stanton and Matilda Joslyn Gage, shifted from apologia to attack on the Bible and Christianity as the primary tools of female subjugation, while a new generation of evangelical feminists, such as Frances Willard and Anna Howard Shaw, repudiated such critique of the Bible and took Christianity to be the primary basis both for women's equality and their moral superiority.[102] Susan B. Anthony sought to prevent conflicts over religion from splitting the newly united front of radical and evangelical feminists, by bracketing religious questions altogether. For Anthony women's suffrage was a matter of political and social rights, while religious views are private matters that can only be divisive when they intrude into public affairs.[103]

Elizabeth Cady Stanton grew up in a Scotch Presbyterian family. Her teenage conversion experience during a revival led by Charles Grandison Finney led to a period of depression and physical sickness. She was rescued by her brother-in-law who demythologized the revival experience as based on emotion-fed delusions.[104] As she adopted the feminist cause, she experienced the Christian clergy as chief opponents who constantly used the Bible to argue for women's subjugation. Unlike Anthony, who grew up in a liberal Hicksite Quaker household, Stanton's experiences convinced her that Christianity was a major force for women's degradation and so could not be ignored.

This conviction led to her decision in the 1890s to assemble women biblical scholars to answer the question: "Have the teachings of the Bible advanced or retarded the emancipation of women?" The result was *The Women's Bible*, a comprehensive commentary on all the biblical texts in both testaments relevant to women.[105] This publication was greeted by a storm of criticism, and was officially repudiated by the newly amalgamated National-American Women's Suffrage Association in January 1896, despite Anthony's plea for tolerance of religious differences.[106] For the majority of women members of the NAWSA, the linking of women's suffrage with an attack on the Bible was personally offensive and threatened to retard their efforts to win middle-ground American opinion.

The biblical commentaries assembled by Stanton, the majority written by herself, actually follow a well-trodden path of nineteenth-century feminist critique. Genesis 1:26-28 is seen as establishing an essential equality in the image of God of women and men, with dominion given both jointly, but no dominion of one over the other.[107] Stanton adds to this her belief that the text also proves the androgyny of God. Divine androgyny is reflected in the natural laws of the universe that strive for a dynamic harmony of male and female elements.[108]

By contrast to Genesis 1, Genesis 2 is denounced as an effort by "some wily writer" to obscure this original androgynous equality by adding a different creation story in which the female is secondary and auxiliary to the male.[109] Genesis 3 does not prove female sinfulness but rather woman's superior dignity as one impelled by a thirst for knowledge, in contrast to a passive and cowardly Adam. Women's subjugation in society does not reflect a punishment by God, but wrongful domination by men, who have sought to justify this injustice by the doctrine of the fall.[110]

In the Genesis 3 commentary, Stanton inserts her view that for most of the 85,000 years of human development women reigned supreme in a matriarchal form of society. Only with the barbarian era did the male "seize the reins of government," imposing a patriarchal system of society. Human society is now progressing to a higher state as women are being emancipated to enter into shared rule with men, the Amphiarchate.[111]

For Stanton the New Testament is also questionable in its testimony about women. Jesus was completely egalitarian and a radical of his time whose views are reflected in the Galatian text that in Christ "there is no male or female." But Paul was ambivalent toward women. He accepted a situation in the early church where women held equal ministry with men, but he also expressed his own views of women's inferiority by arguing that women lacked the image of God. Paul's views were worsened by interpolations by later priestly hands that obscure this early shared ministry and impose teaching of women's silence and subjugation.[112]

*The Women's Bible* presents the scriptural record as mixed in a way not very different from views of the Grimkés or Mott, but it was more explosive because, unlike the works of these earlier writers, it came down clearly on the side of a condemnation of the Bible as a purely "man-made" book whose primary effect has been to justify women's subjugation. Stanton believed the Christian clergy were so wedded to these texts that the church could not be reformed to support women's emancipation. Christianity, and the Bible as its basis, must be transcended by a new rational religion more in tune with the laws of nature and the progress of society.[113]

Stanton sided with a view of God as androgynous and believed that progress would bring about increasing harmony of the male and female principles in nature and partnership of men and women in society. But she fiercely denounced the prevailing view of male-female complementarity that saw feminine superiority in a special talent for altruism and self-sacrifice. For her the greatest evil effect of Christianity has been in convincing women that self-sacrifice is their particular duty and calling. Against this view, she asserts that the first duty of women (as of men) is to self-development, not self-sacrifice.[114]

Stanton developed this theme of women's duty of self-development in a famous speech delivered to Congress in 1892, "The Solitude of the Self."[115] In this speech she laid out a view of the self rooted in heroic individualism. All persons must face life's vicissitudes alone, with no one to take responsibility for their fate except themselves. This is as true for women as for men, but false teachings on female weakness and dependency hold out the illusionary promise that woman can count on man to take care of her. This means that women are cheated out of the self-development that will enable them to be responsible for themselves. Women have the right to political, economic, and cultural equality, because women as much as men finally stand alone in the face of misfortune and must be able to take charge of their own lives.

While Stanton's post-Christian radicalism, with its call for a rational religion to birth a more just society, struck responsive chords in a few other suffrage leaders, such as Matilda Gage,[116] her heroic individualism departed radically from the reigning views about "women's nature" in American society of the period, including those of many in the suffrage movement. Most of these women not only wished to argue that the Bible was the great charter of female emancipation; but they were also deeply wedded to a view of women as superior to men, innately altruistic and loving.

Churchman Horace Bushnell, in his treatise *Women's Suffrage: the Reform against Nature*, had used this view of women's innate altruism and moral superiority to argue that women were unfitted for the rough-and-tumble of political life.[117] But evangelical feminists, like Willard and Shaw, drew on this view of women's loving maternal nature to insist that women must enter public life in order to uplift it and cleanse it of its evils, such as intemperance, prostitution, corruption and insanitation, degradation of immigrant working people, and war.

Thus, late nineteenth-century American feminism presented a contradictory melange of arguments about gender and religion. For some, Christianity is the basis of women's emancipation, while for others it is irreformably patriarchal and must be discarded by those who hope for real equality for women. Some feminists clung to a belief in an essential likeness of men and women as the basis for women's equality, while others combined claims to equality with a belief in female superiority.

Some feminists linked women's emancipation with a millennial vision in which all forms of evil would be overcome, culminating in an end to war, while others sought a more strategic view to gain for middle-class white women entry into the same political, economic, and educational rights as the men of their families, accepting the disenfranchisement of blacks and hostility to immigrants. All these ambiguities and conflicts about the goals and foundations of women's rights would return in new forms in the rebirth of feminism in the 1960s.

6. *Christa,* Edwina Sandys. Copyright © Edwina Sandys, 1974; Bronze (54" x 40" x 8").

Chapter Six

# Feminist Theologies in Twentieth-Century Western Europe

THEOLOGY IN WESTERN EUROPE IS OFTEN SEEN TODAY as a latecomer to feminist questions and largely derivative from models imported from North America. It is true that there has been an important influence of North American feminist theology on that developing in Western Europe in the 1980s. Also feminist theology in Europe seems "behind" because it finds much less ready access to positions in theological faculties than is the case in North America. Yet important women founders of European feminist theologies, such as Elisabeth Gossman, began their work in the 1960s in a European context.[1]

## Feminist Theology and German Protestantism

American women who studied theology in the 1950s or '60s in a Protestant or ecumenical setting also read German theologians and biblical scholars as the normative theology on which Americans at that time felt themselves dependent. Karl Barth, Rudolf Bultmann, and Paul Tillich were the "great names" for their American theological teachers. Thus one needs to situate the rise of feminist theology in Europe and America in the 1960s in this context. Only later did American women begin to rediscover their own nineteenth-century women forebears.

German Protestant theology was shaped by a distinctive history that has marked its meaning for the post–Second World War period. The German

Reformation begun by Luther laid down significant challenges to Roman Catholic theology and church power, but it was soon recast in a scholastic form and united to new national state churches, becoming as dogmatic and sacralizing of the established social order as the older Catholic Christendom.[2] Liberal Christianity arose in the late eighteenth and early nineteenth centuries to challenge this fossilized Protestant orthodoxy and to open Christian thought to modern science and historical criticism. The great liberal biblical critics, such as Herman Reimarus, broke the hold of biblical literalism.[3] Liberal theologians, such as Friedrich Schleiermacher, sought to demonstrate to the "cultured despisers" of religion that Christianity could be open to personal religious experience.[4]

With the devastating violence unleashed in the First World War, followed all too soon by the shock of the rise of Nazism and the vast military destruction and genocidal death camps of the Second World War, the old liberalism was seen as having failed. In his 1919 commentary on Romans, Karl Barth enunciated his great "No" to liberalism's union of Christian faith and human religious experience.[5] Dialectical theology under Barth called for a return to an understanding of God as "wholly other" than our religious aspirations, a God who comes down from above in judgment and grace, breaking apart our human efforts to reach up to God.

During the Nazi era Barthian theology was seen as forming the great bulwark against German Christianity, the co-optation of the German Protestant church as a civil religion of the Nazi state. Young theologians and pastors, such as Dietrich Bonhoeffer, led the Confessing church to reject the German Christians and to risk imprisonment and death for a Christianity true to the gospel.[6] Barthian theology emerged from the Second World War with heroic credentials.

As dialectical theology hardened into neoorthodoxy in the 1950s and '60s, some began to question its adequacy to address the modern questions of historical relativism and social justice. The neoorthodox "No" to all human social projects as equally sinful before God seemed to level all differences between the competing systems of capitalism and socialism and to render meaningless all efforts to create more just societies. Yet neoliberal forms of theology, such as that of Tillich and Bultmann, also were detached from these social struggles, despite Tillich's early socialism.

Both liberal and neoorthodox theologies were closed to feminism such as had existed in Germany in the late nineteenth century and first third of the twentieth. Schleiermacher appeared pro-woman, but his model of gender was based on the reigning anthropology of masculine-feminine complementarity. Schleiermacher saw the core religious sentiment in humanity as the "feeling of absolute dependence"; in that context, he saw women as more naturally religious than men, having from their very nature those submissive traits that made them open to recognizing their helplessness and absolute dependence on God. Men, in order to be religious, had, in this sense, to become "feminine."[7]

But Schleiermacher could only imagine this male-female complementarity in the context of the bourgeois marriage of his day. Any ideological or social critique of this system of gender relations was unimaginable. A feminist movement that wanted to free women from their enclosure in the family and to give them political rights, higher education, and professional employment could only be seen as an "unnatural masculinization" that undermined woman's true nature and role as the feminine "angel in the house."

Barth, in his volumes on creation in the massive *Church Dogmatics* that he was writing in the 1950s, enunciated a renewed Calvinist theology of the "orders of creation" that was even more explicitly hostile to feminism. Barth drew on the Martin Buber tradition that saw the male-female pair in Genesis as the primal I-Thou relation that parallels the human I-Thou encounter with God. He insisted that only together is this primal pair the image of God. Neither male nor female can stand alone as an autonomous human. They are "Adam" only together, in their relation to God, and they are male and female only in relation to each other.[8]

This notion of the male-female pair in I-Thou relation as the primal meaning of humanity sounds egalitarian and mutual. Barth would declare that neither gender is in any way inferior to the other. But he also insists on a social ordering of the male-female pair that demands fixed traditional social roles. In his words, "Man is A, he is first. Woman is B, she is second. This means preceding and following, super and subordination." This relation is in no way exchangeable. Man must stay in his place and woman must stay in hers.[9]

These social roles of male headship and female subordination are construed as a divinely created order. So for a woman to wish to step out of her place to do "masculine" things, such as becoming a minister or a political leader, is for

Barth a violation of the will of God, who has laid down this fixed and unchangeable order of creation. It is in these terms that Barth denounces feminism in his *Church Dogmatics*.[10] This Protestant construction of the primal male-female pair as only together constituting the "whole" human also excluded homosexual relations as lacking the possibility of "wholeness" in relationship and violating the primal creational order.

The most distinctive feminist theologian to emerge from this German context is Dorothee Soelle. Soelle, despite years of teaching at Union Theological Seminary in New York City, always thinks theologically in her context as a German of the Left. It would, however, be more than a decade of Soelle's writing before Soelle would explicitly own feminism as one of her social contexts for theological reflection. Both German male theology and also the German Left were unreceptive to feminism, socialism decrying any feminism apart from the "worker's struggle" as bourgeois and reactionary.[11] Soelle's late embrace of feminism, however, reflected primarily her preoccupation with the meaning of the Nazi experience for Christians.

These preoccupations biased Soelle against American feminist theology in the 1970s. But, through her dialogue with women at Union Seminary, she recognized that her theology had always been implicitly feminist. The questions she had been asking as a political theologian were along the same lines as the critique and reconstruction of theology being formulated by feminists.[12] But Soelle had to develop her journey to liberation theology before she would add "feminist" to her self-understanding as a liberation theologian of the German Left.

In her developed theology in the 1980s Soelle would speak of herself as working out of three interconnected social contexts: as a German, as a Protestant Christian, and as a woman.[13] As a German born in 1929 Soelle takes the Holocaust as the primary question for any German theology after this event. No German can do theology authentically if he or she does not take this radical challenge to German national culture seriously.[14]

The Holocaust also raised for Soelle issues of the ongoing threats to life on earth from the postwar capitalist economic order. An economic system that provides an affluent life for a First-World elite, while condemning the majority of people in the Third World to desperate poverty, is the new system of global oppression. Also the rivalry between East and West for global resources has created a system of militarism capable of exterminating all life on earth. This threatened future holocaust of the entire planet must be the context for theology in the late twentieth century, a theology that is not an end in itself but is done in and through political praxis.[15]

In Cologne in the late 1960s Soelle was part of a group of engaged Christians who conducted monthly "political night prayer." These services consisted of reading important recent news and analyzing it, followed by a Scripture reading, a brief sermon bringing the Scripture and events together, prayer, and then a discussion of "what can we do?" Out of this practice of political prayer, Soelle shaped her political theology.[16]

Soelle began her political theology in the context of a critique of Bultmann. Bultmann's existentialist hermeneutic had been very important for Soelle's theological development, allowing her to situate Christian theological categories in the context of real human experiences in a new way, beyond Barth's rebuke to the old liberal correlation of theology and experience. But Bultmann's view of sin and grace remained resolutely individualistic, as he refused to see social systems as places of sin or grace.[17] His project of demythologizing remained limited, overcoming a past mythic worldview but refusing to own problems of social ideology that might be stated in nonmythic form, whether in Scripture or in contemporary culture. Soelle took the insights of existentialist hermeneutic of the gospel in a different direction, adding ideology critique of ancient and modern cultures to demythologizing, situating the existentialist "call to decision" in response to the gospel in the context of political resistance to oppression.

Sin, politically interpreted, means a critique of the real contradictions of society, a critique of the ideologies that blind us to these contradictions and make us "swallow the lies" of the dominant society. Forgiveness, politically interpreted, means real concrete acts of repentance as social struggle to overcome oppression and make a more human world.[18] This political understanding of sin and grace led Soelle to a critique of both orthodox and liberal theologies (including Barthian neoorthodoxy and Bultmannian existentialism) in terms of the ideological elements of their theologies that refused real engagement in questions of justice.

Soelle's theological method thus came to be characterized by a systematic ideology critique of both orthodox and liberal theology and the enunciation of a feminist liberationist alternative. This method is found scattered through her writings of the last two decades, but is most systematically laid out in her introduction to theology, *Thinking about God*, developed from lectures in the late 1980s.[19]

Ideology critique, for Soelle, means a deconstruction of the orthodox idea of God and human nature, or the human "predicament," showing that the view of both God and "man" in Protestant orthodoxy and neoorthodoxy sustained a violent, unjust world and allowed the Christian to ignore and tacitly support systematized evil without ever naming it as "sin." Because of its privatization of the religious questions in terms of the individual self—its splitting of church from state, individual from society—liberal theology, from Schleiermacher to Bultmann, failed to challenge these orthodox patterns despite its apparent greater openness to the modern world, its acceptance of the autonomous authority of modern science and historical criticism of the Bible.

Reflection on this critique of Protestant orthodoxy from a feminist perspective has illuminated for Soelle the particular ways that this concept of God was part of a gendered system of male power over female. Soelle has denounced what she calls the "phallocratic" Christian imagery for God as Lord, Sovereign Power, and patriarchal Father. This God, imaged primarily in terms of power (all-powerful) rather than justice or love, is the theological identity myth of powerful males, supported by a church of ruling-class males.[20] This idea of God not only supports the patriarchal family and church, but undergirds economic and political systems of empire, from the Pax Romana to the Pax Americana.

Such a God directed Germans to exterminate the Jews in the name of obedience to authority and continued to justify the Holocaust after the war by claiming that God's all-governing providence would not allow any such things to happen unless they were the "will of God." For Soelle this "God Almighty" is an idol, and worship of this God must be rejected in order to discover the "powerless God of Love" that speaks through Jesus Christ.[21]

To reject the God of the rulers is to deconstruct the classical dualism of transcendence and immanence. Barth's "No" to liberalism renewed a concept of God as "wholly other," far removed in a transcendent realm inaccessible to human experience. Mystical traditions of communion with God were rejected as false human efforts to possess God.[22] God's saving word is seen as always coming to humans from "above." We (women particularly) are called to submit to a divine will that we can never fully understand. This split virtually denies divine immanence. The result is an orthodox Protestant spirituality fixated on the themes of human sin, powerlessness, and the call to submission, in which the created world is left devoid of the presence of God.

Nineteen-sixties theologians celebrated the connection between a biblical view of divine transcendence and the secularization of the "world."[23] But the impact of this driving out of any sense of the sacredness of creation by a "wholly other" God is to hand over all created things to the market forces of a technocratic economic and military order. The ideology of secularity disconnects human society and the earth from God. Humans need no longer be restrained in their rapacious use of all "things," including human beings reduced to commodifiable objects, by any sense of a Creator God to whom we are accountable for our use of the earth.[24]

The underside of this view of God as disconnected and all-powerful male ego, ruling from outside, is a belittled human being who is called to become "acceptable" to this God by acknowledging his or her worthlessness and impotence. The human stands before God always as convicted sinner, whose sins have been paid for by the blood of the cross and who thereby is atoned for and accepted by a God who nevertheless endlessly reinforces human unacceptability.[25]

For this theology of "forensic justification" the greatest sins are "works" of spirituality and political hope. Humans can never feel joy in the living presence of a God who wells up in our well-being. Nor should we hope that by alleviating poverty, lessening racism or sexism, and preventing the threat of nuclear holocaust, we are in any way bringing the world closer to being the reign of God.

For Soelle, this theology of divine transcendence and human impotent sinfulness nicely supports a "do-nothing" practice of "redemption" that rules out both action and contemplation. Christians gather endlessly in their churches to reiterate the rhetoric of sin and salvation without changing anything either within themselves or in the world around them. The same theology carries over in secular cultural form in technocratic society, supporting an awestruck submission to a rapacious market system, defined as "natural law," and a belief that we are helpless to change anything.[26]

In the 1990s the old Christian orthodoxy and secular military and market orthodoxies are merging in right-wing Christian movements, such as those in the United States, that believe simultaneously that America is God's elect nation to rule the world, and that "religion has nothing to do with politics"; that is, salvation has only to do with the individual soul after death and nothing to do with making a more just society. Soelle calls these kinds of New Right Christianity "Christofascism."[27]

Far from not taking sin seriously, as orthodox Christians often claim, feminist liberation theologians take sin far more seriously than does the established church. For Soelle, the alienated human reality that is enclosed in its egoism and passivity and out of touch with God has three dimensions: an inward personal dimension, a structural systemic dimension, and an ideological dimension. Soelle thinks of the alienated individual as more victim than aggressor, although there are individuals who hold great power and engage in real decisions and actions that erect and erect again the world of militarism and exploitation.

But most individuals are more collaborators with evil than active decision-makers. Some belong to the *kaputter typ* (broken-down type)[28] that have died inside and lost any sense of how to relate. Others are the self-satisfied bourgeois who simply go along as cogs in a machine of rapacious exploitation, gaining their little bits of profit from it without questioning the evil purposes of the larger reality,[29] much as so many "good Germans" went along with Nazism and later justified themselves as "just doing what they were told" and "not knowing what was happening."

Soelle faults the Christian church as playing a major part in shaping this ethic of collaboration, confusing obedience to authorities with obedience to God. Unquestioning compliance with orders itself became a virtue, without asking about the meaning and purpose of what was ordered. Questioning, dissent, rebellion against authority—these are seen as the essence of sin. The primal sin of Adam (more specifically, of Eve) was disobedience to authority, to be atoned for by redoubled submission. Christians are taught not to question authority to discern whether it is of God.[30]

Both inward deadness and unrelatedness, and the religious and secular ideologies that sacralize submission to dominating power, have their source in this system of power. Systems of oppression spring from and collectivize human arrogance, greed, fear, and hate. These negative tendencies have their roots in human persons but go far beyond the bad side of individuals to become a collective system of death that holds humans themselves in bondage. Soelle sees sin in its collective form as a demonic counterworld to God's creation, the world of the "man-eating ogre" that masquerades as God's creation and claims God as its Lord but is actually counter to all that is truly of God. Like the death camps, it masks its evil reality with false slogans, such as "Work makes one free," over its gates.[31]

Authentic theology begins, for Soelle, in pain, in recognition of the hurt to oneself and others caused by this violent "world."[32] Theology stirs up dissent from the official ideologies of the dominant world that try to sacralize it as God's will or the natural order, calling all good Christians and citizens to bow before it. Sin can never be known in the abstract, but only as one dissents from this system and begins to recognize its effects on oneself and others. Breaking loose from obedience to "this world" and disbelieving in its "God" are the first gifts of grace; naming it as evil is the first act of conversion. In this sense Eve is the first liberator. Dissent from the orders of a patriarchal "God" not to ask questions is the first act of conversion, appropriately led by women to whom these orders have been especially directed.[33]

When the patriarchal Cosmocrator has been unmasked as an idol, the dissenter may become permanently estranged from Christianity, if these ideological notions of God and "man" are assumed to be the real Christian message. Many Marxists, feminists, and other dissenters from sacralized injustice have entered this first stage of critique. They have rejected the patriarchal God and been ejected from the patriarchal church as unbelievers, but they have known no prophetic community to welcome them as daughters and sons of God on a journey of authentic faith and life.

For Soelle this dissent against the idols of "this world" is not apostasy, but the first step to knowing who Jesus Christ and God really are. But the church has done such a good job of confusing Christ with Caesar and God with Satan that most people find it difficult to go on to the next step of liberated and liberating faith. Without Christian communities where kerygma, diakonia, and koinonia (word, service, and community) are constituted on the ground of prophetic faith, feminists and other skeptics fall into alienated skepticism toward the gospel or catch glimpses of a liberating view, but without a sustaining community.[34]

Soelle's "theology for skeptics" declares that it is by passing through a rejection of the patriarchal God of the rulers that we are able for the first time to glimpse the real Jesus Christ,[35] the powerless Jewish prophet who announced good news to the poor, the setting at liberty of those who are oppressed to the marginalized of his day. Jesus also called the mighty of religion and state to repent and enter the reign of God behind these lowly victims of their power. This Jesus did not come to suffer and die, to masochistically offer his blood to a sadistic God to pay for our sins,[36] but to liberate us into a new community of joyful life.

Jesus died on the cross because the mighty of religion and state did not accept his call to repentance and solidarity with the poor, but sought to shore up their system of power and its ideological justifications by silencing the voice of the prophet. His resurrection means that they did not succeed in silencing him. He rose and continues to rise wherever prophets arise,[37] breaking through the system of lies and offering a glimpse of the true God of life who stands against the systems of worldly power. The cross is not a payment for sin or a required sacrifice of our well-being, but the risk Jesus and all people take when they unmask the idols and announce the good news that God is with those who struggle for justice and communicate loving life.[38]

Human beings are not powerless, worthless wretches, but free beings made in God's image and called to be co-creators with God in redeeming creation from sin. Jesus is our representative, not as an otherworldly divine figure who has nothing in common with us, but as one who expresses what we are called to be as humans: courageous strugglers against evil, tellers of truth to power, healers and joyful livers of life to the full who infectiously communicate well-being to one another. This is who Jesus was, and this is what Jesus calls us to be, as healed women and men.

Soelle reinterprets ideas of God in relation to humans and creation, and ideas of who we are called to be in relation to God and our fellow earth creatures. Her rejection of an ideological definition of divine transcendence as detached otherness and sovereign power "from beyond" clears the way for an alternative understanding of God's relation to us as transcendent immanence. God is totally immanent, not in the sense of sacralizing "what is" as systems of unjust power, but rather as the life-giving presence that sustains us, "in whom we live and move and have our being." God's immanence is radically transcendent, not as far away, detached, and unavailable, but in the sense of being radically free from our ideologies of domination, the grace that continually frees us from our blindedness by lies.[39] For Soelle God is the power of life as loving interrelationship who is present in and through those times and places where such life is happening.

Soelle deconstructs and reconstructs our calling as Christians (humans). We are not called to masochistic self-negation, but to fulfillment and well-being.[40] But we have to discover what true well-being is. We have been offered a false well-being as prosperity purchased by the exploitation of others. Making profit at the expense of others means living with a suppressed guilt that makes us hostile to others, continually seeking to dominate and repress them lest they unmask our thievery and take away our stolen goods. The world economic system, defended by global militarism, has been constructed upon this wrongful profit. This system threatens to undo creation and turn the whole earth back to nothingness.

True well-being is found when this false "success ethic" is renounced and we learn to live more and more freed from it. Then we can begin to taste the joys of true well-being lived in mutual service and shared life. When life is lived in solidarity with others in shared well-being, every act of sustaining life becomes a sacrament of God's presence, whether that be bread broken and shared, sexual pleasure given and received between lovers,[41] tilling the ground, making useful product, or giving birth to a baby. God does not call us into a reign beyond this world in heaven, but to the fulfilling of the promise of life on earth, when "God's will is done on earth as it is in heaven"; that is, justice is done in love among all earth creatures.[42]

For Soelle, then, the essential dualism that divides the world is that of death-dealing dominance against life-giving love. The God revealed in Christ is life-giving love. This is also the authentic nature of humans and the creation that humans are called to liberate and heal as co-creators with God. There is no essential difference between men and women in this task, for Soelle, but there are differences in social location. And women too can be deluded by and become collaborators with dominating power.

But because women as a gender group have been marginalized by this power, and have been socialized to identify more with love and relationality, Soelle hopes that women will be readier to break with lies and power systems and align themselves with the struggle for justice and love. The struggle is finally one of women and men for life on earth, not a struggle of women against men. The good news of the gospel, rescued from patriarchal distortion, is that God in Christ is with us and in us in this struggle.

## Feminist Theology and Catholicism

In this section I turn to three leading Catholic feminist theologians in Europe: Kari Elisabeth Børresen from Norway, Catharina Halkes from the Netherlands, and Mary Grey from England. All three come from historically Protestant European countries, and this has given them a wider base for teaching and research than would have been the case in Catholic countries. In the historically Catholic areas of Western Europe (France, Italy, and Spain), there is still in the late 1990s no real conversation between feminism and theology. The Vatican has made contraception and abortion and women's ordination indiscussible topics and has required new bishops to take oaths not to be open to change on these issues.[43]

Although a feminist theologian might not focus on these topics as her primary issues, this means that hierarchical Catholicism views feminist theology with deepest suspicion. This has made it very difficult for Catholic women to teach it in Catholic theological faculties. In France, where there has long been a lively feminist philosophy, which is influencing feminist theory and theology elsewhere, there is virtually no dialogue between feminism and Catholic theology. Even Catholic women's circles who want to expand women's roles in ministry and theological teaching in the church fear to use the term "feminist."[44] In Italy feminist scholars work on religion through other fields, such as anthropology, history, and ancient and medieval studies.[45]

### Kari Elisabeth Børresen

Kari Elisabeth Børresen, born in Norway in 1932, was raised in an intellectual Catholicism brought by French Dominicans schooled in the reform theology of Marie-Dominique Chenu and Yves Congar. When she went to study in France in 1950 she experienced a culture shock at the androcentrism of "normative" Catholicism there, so different from her own experience of Catholicism, family, and society in Oslo. This experience impelled her into a lifetime of research on the theological roots of this androcentrism.

Børresen has done her feminist theological work under the rubric of history of ideas, receiving her Ph.D. in that field from the University of Oslo in 1960 and her *Habilitation* in 1968. Her doctoral thesis on gender in the anthropology of Augustine and Thomas Aquinas, *Subordination and Equivalence*, has been recognized as a classic of feminist theological history.[46] Børresen's work in patristic and medieval studies has continued to focus on the history of theological anthropology in terms of the inclusion of women in creational and redemptive Godlikeness.

Børresen's work has been widely recognized in Scandinavia and internationally. Since 1982 she has been research professor of the Royal Norwegian Ministry of Culture and professor of medieval studies at the University of Oslo. She was a visiting professor of the faculty of theology of the Gregorian University in Rome (1977–79) and the University of Geneva (1981). She has participated in the Women and Religion Program of Harvard Divinity School and for several years was a member of the Center for Theological Inquiry in Princeton, New Jersey. She has coordinated international research on women in Christianity as convener of the first and second European Research Conferences on Women in the Christian Tradition for the European Science Foundation (1992, 1995).

Børresen emphasizes that the New Testament legacy of Paul's theology excluded women from creational Godlikeness as image of God, but included women in redemption in Christ through an androcentric neutralization of femaleness. This idea was continued in patristic asceticism whereby redeemed virginal woman overcame her weak femaleness and became "virile and manly." The Antiochene church fathers, such as John Chrysostom, continued Paul's denial that women were created in God's image. This tradition was passed on to some medieval theologians and influenced canon law through the writings of Ambrosiaster, which were incorrectly transmitted under the authority of Augustine.

Børresen has shown that, for Christianity, the breakthrough to inclusion of women in the image of God was initiated by Clement of Alexandria, who defined the image as the asexual intellectual soul's capacity for virtue. This view was continued in the Cappadocian church fathers, Basil and Gregory Nazianzus, and found its fullest expression in Augustine. In these church fathers the neutralization of femaleness in Christ was backdated to creation, distinguishing a spiritual or intellectual equivalence of the human soul as image of God, contrasted with woman's specific femaleness in creation, in which she was created subordinate.

This subordination pertains only to woman's biosocial roles in the created order and will disappear in heaven when these are no longer relevant. The church fathers grounded redemptive equivalence in the original creation of the asexual soul as the image of God. But they did so by a view of both creation and redemption that was androcentrically sex-neutralizing and so continued to justify the subordination of woman as female.[47] Thus creational equivalence restored in Christ was prevented from having social consequences for church or society.

The next major shift in Christian anthropology came with medieval church mothers, such as Hildegard of Bingen, culminating in Julian of Norwich. These women mystics evoked the Wisdom tradition of female-identified divine immanence. They identified Christ's incarnation with female vulnerability and so feminized Christ's body. Through these ways of including the female, they inserted female metaphors into the description of Christ and God. This "Matristic achievement," as Børresen calls it, potentially overcomes concepts of a male God and the androcentric concept of the human in which Godlikeness and femaleness are incompatible. Women's inclusion in the image of God is fully overcome only when God can be imagined as female.[48]

This development has yet to be accepted by the Christian churches, even those that now ordain women. Moreover, the Roman Catholic Church has shifted from emphasizing women's subordination in creation to denying that women are christomorphic and can represent Christ. Women's equivalence in the creational image of God is accepted in a form that tacitly consents to the modern social developments of women's equality in society. But creational equivalence is split from redemption in Christ. The masculinity of Christ is used to deny women's ability to image "Christ" and to confine women to imaging the subordinate female-identified church, thereby continuing to deny women's ability to be ordained; that is, to represent Christ and God in the cultic acts of the priesthood. The papal emphasis on Mariology perpetuates an anthropology split between "masculine" and "feminine" natures, an anthropology that exalts women's "difference" while denying her capacity to represent Christ.[49]

Børresen sees the breakdown and transformation of theological androcentrism as an "epistemological revolution," comparable to the breakdown of geocentrism with Copernicus and anthropocentrism with Charles Darwin, of immense significance for contemporary Christianity and society. Full recognition of female Godlikeness entails a further development of Julian of Norwich's incorporation of female symbolism into the picture of God.[50] Only when God is understood metaphorically as both male and female, fully and equally, can women be fully integrated into the image of God as female. Only then will their redemption in Christ affirm their humanity as female, rather than symbolically negating it. Dichotomies between Godlikeness and humanity, male and female, Christology and sacramental ministry, must be healed for theological talk to become fully human.

Børresen speaks of this process of integrating women into the divine image, culminating in an incorporation of the female image into God, as both a human process of inculturation and a divine pedagogy. The denial by patriarchal culture and theology of female godlikeness falsifies humanity, male and female, and God. God is engaging in an ongoing paedagogy, leading church fathers and mothers to a fuller understanding of both God and their own natures as made in God's image. This divine pedagogy takes place in and through our own development of consciousness by which we recognize and incorporate into our theology this fuller sense of ourselves and God in interrelation. Our cultural development and divine pedagogy are two sides of one dialogical process of humans, men and women, with God our Teacher.[51]

## Catharina Halkes

Catharina Halkes, born in 1920, grew up in the village of Vlaardingen near Rotterdam, where Catholics were an embattled minority vis-à-vis their Calvinist neighbors. War and family problems delayed her higher education until 1945, when she entered the University of Leiden to study linguistics and literature. Halkes's study of theology was through active pastoral involvement in Dutch Catholic women's groups, such as Young Women for Catholic Action and the Catholic Women's Guild. Through these movements Halkes began to focus on lay empowerment and cooperation of men and women in pastoral work. This led to her return to university in 1964 to study pastoral theology. She joined the faculty of the Catholic University of Nijmegen in

1967, where she was appointed pastoral supervisor in the Department of Practical Theology in 1970.[52]

The Second Vatican Council (1962–65) found Dutch Catholics eager for church renewal. Actively involved in the renewal movement, Halkes became part of a working group advising the Dutch bishops that sought to incorporate women and married men into ordained ministry in a declericalized model of church. Halkes's 1964 book, *Storm after the Silence,* called for an inclusive model of ministry. The Dutch Pastoral Council (1969–71), which brought together bishops, priests, nuns, laymen and laywomen in a national synod, seemed to be on the verge of church reform that would incorporate these changes.[53]

But from the mid-1970s Dutch Catholicism suffered increasing intervention from the Vatican to stifle these progressive trends. Dioceses were split and conservative bishops appointed. Progressive Dutch Catholics found themselves shut out of official circles. Yet this period also saw the burgeoning of both feminist theology in theological faculties and the spread of Women and Faith groups on the diocesan level. The pope's 1985 visit to Holland, when Halkes was forbidden to give an address, impelled the formation of the Eighth of May movement, where progressive Dutch Catholic feminist, peace, and justice groups network independently of the bishops.[54]

Reading American feminist theology, Halkes sought to introduce it to Western Europe with an address at an international congress on women's studies at Nijmegen in 1975. In 1977 she became lecturer in "Feminism and Christianity" at the University of Nijmegen, publishing her first major book of feminist theology, *Met Miriam is het Begonnen* (*It All Began with Miriam*) in 1980.[55] In 1983 the first European chair in feminist theology was established at that university and she was appointed to it. The years from 1978 to 1986 saw a remarkable spread of feminist theological studies in Holland, with virtually every theological faculty, Catholic and Protestant, making this a mandatory part of the curriculum. Pastoral courses in feminist theology for women engaged in parish work also became common.[56]

Thus Holland became a major success story in Europe for incorporating feminist theology into the theological curriculum. Yet the hardening of the hierarchical church against democratic feminist trends was alienating the younger generation of Dutch Catholic women (and men). Older Dutch Catholics, such as Halkes, who had weathered fifty years of struggle to shape an ecumenical, progressive, feminist Dutch Catholic church, feared they were losing the next generation. Younger feminist theologians were losing interest in the church and no longer felt that the Christian themes could guide an inspiring vision for social transformation. Halkes's recent writings reflect her concerns to restate what she sees as the full vision of the Christian message in its positive potential for human emancipation and transformation. In her 1989 *En alles Zal Worden Herschapen*, Halkes put this transformative vision in its fullest context as an ecological feminist theology.[57]

Halkes' view of redemption reflects a developmentalist perspective from her work in pastoral theology. Humans, created in the image of God, are by nature *capax Dei*, capable of knowing and manifesting God, and are called into a process of transformative development to become fully mature and responsible caregivers in their relations with one another and the earth. No dominion is given by God of one gender or social group over another. The call to growth into maturity and responsibility is given equally to all human persons.[58]

To be called to responsibility means that God creates humans free and capable of making choices. The story of the expulsion from paradise reflects both the gift and the risk of freedom. For Halkes it symbolizes, not a loss of freedom, but a necessary step toward actualizing that freedom without which there cannot be freely chosen responsibility. Yet the risk of freedom also means the possibility of wrong choices. The terrible history of patriarchy, of racism and colonialism, of unjust economic relations between social groups, of ecological disaster, which are worsening in the late twentieth century, are expressions of these wrong choices.

Christian theology reflects the ideological distortion that has sought to justify these wrong choices. Yet Halkes is confident that these distortions can be stripped off to reveal a gospel message that is fundamentally emancipatory for women and men in their relations with one another, personally, socially, and ecologically. The basic Christian theological symbols of creation-incarnation-resurrection-eschaton are, for Halkes, one continuous trajectory, calling us into a process of renewal and transformation whose goal is the reign of God on earth where all creatures live in just relations in community.[59] The heart of the Christian message is this call into the redeemed future, which is never fully realizable on earth, but which pulls us ever to continue to stretch forward, which "keeps us upright and gives us direction."[60]

For Halkes, the incarnation of Christ is the center point in this trajectory from creation to Kingdom. In Christ, God became human to make the human divine. This means both renewal of the human potential for manifesting God, given to humans from the beginning, and direction toward its full realization in God's reign. Christ is the representative of God united to humanity, not as something other than what we are, but as the fulfillment of what we are all called to be as humans. As Halkes puts it:

> In its historical context this incarnation of God is a unique event which can repeat itself every day, however, if people live and act receptively to the divine secret, thus revealing God. But how? By growing in authenticity toward the adult humanity of Jesus, by acting justly, with charity and responsibility toward people, relations and the entire creation, in order that everything and everyone may achieve her/his potential.[61]

If Jesus represents realized humanness as God's image, the outpouring of the Holy Spirit at Pentecost empowers the renewed struggle to make christic humanhood our own. The Holy Spirit founds the church as a community of persons in solidarity with each other, reaching out to all other humans and to all God's creation in an ongoing process of redemptive transformation. This ongoing process entails both growth into our full and equivalent humanity as persons, and also the overthrow of all hierarchies that have been unjustly erected by sin: sexist, racist, and classist hierarchies. Sons and daughters prophesy; the divisions of male and female, slave and free, Jew and Greek are overcome. The Christian community is called to journey to ever fuller equality and mutuality of all persons.

For Halkes the emancipation of women from patriarchy is intrinsic to the good news in Christ, but it is equally a call to men to be transformed. Since women and men have been socialized differently in patriarchal societies, each must embark on different journeys out of their respective histories. Women must enlarge and politicize those qualities of relationality and care that they have been directed to develop as women while men must renounce dominance and embrace the work of everyday care for others from which they have distanced themselves through male privilege.[62]

Redemptive transformation occurs not only on the interpersonal level—it also involves transformed social structures. As unjust privilege and disprivilege have been organized into systems of power, these must be changed to make possible a just sharing of power. This cannot be done without changing the model of power itself, from domination of some over others to mutual empowerment. The self we are called to be cannot be determined by these past ideologies, but directs us toward an ever-expanding future. This means being open to the criticism of those of other races and cultures. Whites and middle-class people are called to hear perspectives coming from other experiences and cultural identities and to overcome the social structures that incarnate injust relations between whites and Third World people.

For Halkes the Christian vision of redeemed humanhood in community is not fixed on an idea of "equality" based on partial male or Western identities. Because it is both utopian and transformative of all unjust relations, it is ever open to differences of both gender and cultural experiences. This perspective, however, does not fix differences as static separations, but encompasses plurality in a process of inclusive transformation toward a fullness of humanity in community that is open-ended, rooted in a capacity for divinity that goes ever before us in expanding realization of our potential.[63]

Just as the transformative journey must go beyond the interpersonal to transformation of social structures, so it must also go beyond human society to ecological relations. The fullness into which humans are called through Christ and empowered by the Spirit makes all humans partners and also puts humans in the midst of the whole created world as caretakers of creation. Unjust relations distort persons, society, and the relations of humanity to the rest of nature. So the process of metanoia, of conversion, must also mean a conversion from distorted relations to the rest of creation into a sustaining and caretaking relation that allows all other creatures to flourish equally with us.

All of these transformations are interlinked. Male domination over women has distorted not only personal relations and social structures, but also relations with nature. Nature has been imaged as like the female in patriarchal ideology.[64] The transformation of power relations from male domination to man-woman mutuality thus must govern transformation on all three levels: personal, social, and ecological. To be engaged in this transformative conversion is the human calling, growing ever more fully into our potential as image of God, becoming the "likeness of God," a redeemed humanity with creation that is God's reign realized, the face of the earth renewed and God's glory manifest.[65]

This is the vision that has guided Catharina Halkes's lifework and thought. But it is one that she fears falls on deaf ears at the end of the twentieth century at a time when it is most needed. These Christian symbols seem to have lost their power among the younger feminist theologians who now fill university theological faculties of Holland, although a Christian feminist vision and hopes for church reform remain more vibrant among women working on the grassroots pastoral level.

## Mary Grey

Mary Grey (born in 1941) can be seen as a member of a bridge generation between the founding "mothers" of European feminist theology and a younger generation skeptical of their efforts to reclaim Christian symbols for feminism. Standing in continuity with the Christian feminism of Catharina Halkes, she began to construct her thought in the mid-1980s in dialogue with a twenty-year legacy of feminist theology in Europe and North America, including new questions coming from French feminism and postmodernism. Grey received her doctorate in theology at Louvain in 1987 and was Halkes's successor in the chair of Feminism and Christianity at Nijmegen in Holland from 1988 to 1993. She lectures often on the Continent and was president of the European Society for Women in Theological Research, 1989–91.[66]

Grey is also engaged with First World–Third World issues. She and her husband have been founders of the Wells for India project, which works with local groups, particularly women, in the Dudu area of Rajasthan, India, to provide water for drought-striken villages. This work has opened up a series of other projects: tree planting, provision of spinning and sewing machines, schooling, and health care. The Wells project also became involved in providing a home for children of prostitutes, when a group of prostitutes brought their children to the directors of the project and asked for a place where they could be cared for and saved from the fate of their mothers. Thus Grey does her theological reflection in the context of both a wide network of feminist theology across Europe and also with vivid awareness of the plight of women in Third World poverty.[67]

Grey's theology of redemption works out of a creation-based model of "right relation." For Grey evil or sin is all the "manmade" systems of "unmaking the world," exemplified by war, poverty, and pollution of the earth. These social patterns of violence or "wrong relation" that create oppression, injury, and untimely death have penetrated all levels of the human-constructed world, from personal psychology of men and women to global exploitation that threatens planetary life. They have distorted culture, including theology, making God in the image of Logos, or the logic of domination, and silencing the real face and voice of God as Sophia, the creating and redeeming energy of right relation.[68]

For Grey the Sophia nature of God as right relation is also our authentic human nature, but we have lost touch with it from being immersed in and indoctrinated into the culture of violence. Men and women have been socialized into this culture in different ways: men to identify with the logic of its dominating power, and women to acquiesce and sacrifice themselves to it. Thus the journey of redemptive healing is different for women and for men because of this different socialization.

Men have to let the voice of dominating power, and their own identification with it, be shattered in order to hear the voice of Sophia, which is also their deeply buried authentic being. Women must journey out of self-abnegation and cooperation with male domination. Women are not only victims of this system of violence—as affluent women they benefit from it, collaborate with it, support it, and act as secondary oppressors to those under them.[69]

Grey concentrates primarily on the female redemptive journey, although she makes it clear that both men and women must be redeemed, but in different ways. The goal of redemption is a new right relation of men and women that can found partnership in building a different society, a different relation to creation. Grey parallels the stages of women's redemptive journey with the classical categories of the religious journey in the mystical tradition.[70]

In the first stage of awakening, women catch a vision of a larger self. They then must pass through a *via purgativa* in which they burst the bonds that have held them to narrow and oppressive roles. They begin to strip off layers of a false self, by which they identified themselves as auxiliary and self-negating beings, and to protest against violence to themselves and others. In the *via illuminativa,* they begin to gain a fuller sense of the vision of life into which they wish to journey. But this is followed by a dark night of the soul in which they face abandonment and rejection by those who want them to remain as they were before. They struggle with loneliness and anxiety about the truth of their vision in the face of rejection. They wonder if God, imaged as male power, is angry or is dead.

Gradually they emerge from the dark night of the soul, as from many death experiences, into a recognition that this despair and doubt are the birth pangs of the fuller self. It is a suffering and death that issues into resurrection, into birth into a fuller self that is unified with the relational energy of God. Grey believes that women's socialization into relationality puts them closer to the true relational nature of God than men socialized into dominance. But women have to break with the distortion of relationality into self-sacrifice and develop a self-affirming sense of their identity into order to integrate their female virtues into a fuller self in which autonomy and connectedness with others are merged. They can then move into larger areas of creativity and service in society as an active agent of change.[71]

God is the relational power of the universe that is in and through all things, ever empowering renewed life. Creation and redemption are not split into two opposing times or actions of God, but form one ever-insurgent process that creates and re-creates, overcoming the forces of disconnection and violence.[72] Grey does not see this relational energy of the universe as reduced to natural evolution, but redemption as healing interconnects with the evolutionary thrust toward more qualitative ways of relating. There is no dualism here. In redeeming one encounters creation; in liberation one discovers original grace.[73]

The true God of relational energy unites creation and redemption but is "wholly other" from the logic of domination. The systems of domination created by "men," and the god made in their image, are alien to God. Sophia, God as relational energy, is marginal in this world and is silent in its circles, including its religious systems. Sophia is powerless in the context of dominating power and silent in the discourses of such power. Yet She speaks and acts insistently in the depths of our being, seeking to disrupt this dominant logic, to undermine its power, and to open us to an alternative logic and power of relationality.[74] The voices of Sophia often come from the margins, speaking in the persons of children and fools and talking in riddles and stories, rather than syllogisms and mathematical formulas.

Jesus is our Christian paradigm (although, Grey hints, he is not the only one) for a humanity totally unified with divine Wisdom and manifesting the authentic self in relation.[75] Jesus is redemptive as exemplar of the true person united with Sophia-God. His death on the cross has been distorted into a model of victimization that has been preached to women and oppressed people especially to encourage their acquiescence in victimization, while dominant men accept Christ's sacrifice as redeeming them from their sins by paying for these sins to a God made in the image of male domination.

This is not the true meaning of the cross, of Christ's suffering and death. Rather Christ's suffering and death is the risk taken by all people who protest injustice and call the powerful to conversion. We too risk crucifixion when we enter the path of authentic living, for those who identify with dominating power wish to silence the voice of prophets, to drive them from their midst and finally rid the world of them by killing them. The cross signifies, not God's will, but the refusal of repentance by the powers of domination.[76] Yet Christ survives crucifixion. He passes through and beyond it to resurrection and insurgent new life that mediate the power of risen life to us. He is our hope that we too can pass through the death throes of the old systems of violence into newness of life.

The church was born in Pentecost to be the continuation of Christ's resurrected presence. It is to be the redemptive community of loving and life-giving relationality that carries on through the Spirit, calling the powers of dominance to repentance and living the resurrected life of loving and caring relationships. This means the true church is at the margins of the dominant society and often gathers those who are marginalized by it.

This also implies that the church, which has made itself in the image of empire and patriarchy, is contrary to the true message of Christ. The true church is often found on its margins. Today it is expressed in new feminist gatherings, such as Womenchurch. Yet the church is called, not simply to be countercultural and on the margins, but also to be leaven, calling the church of patriarchy to repentance and to discovery of its authentic calling.[77]

This struggle for newness of life is, for Grey, both personal and political, both local and global. It underlies our personal journeys into authentic life as persons in relation. It sustains local struggles for water, health care, decent work, care for the earth, and saving of children from prostitution. It is the underlying impetus for struggles for changes of political and economic systems in order to make relations between men and women, between races and social groups, and between nations, more equitable. It is calling to us today to come down from our imagined dominance over the earth and to join with our fellow creatures of the earth in one interconnected community of life.[78]

The sustaining energy of this struggle to make and remake the world is God. This God is not a God of dominance that is separated out of and ruling over the universe in a projected image of the distorted male ego.[79] God is Sophia, the Wisdom of right relation, the God of insurgent life and renewal of life that is the life-giving and loving relationality in whom we live and move and have our being, even as we seek to smother Sophia's voice within us. It is She who is our true source of life, of revelation, redemption, and future hope, in whom we are called to remake ourselves and our world.

## European Feminist Theology in the 1990s

In the 1990s European feminist theology presents a very diverse face. In some theological faculties, such as those in Holland, feminists are well established in the completion of doctoral degrees and introductory teaching, although professorial chairs for women at universities are rare. Some of this new wave of women scholars are disinterested in the concerns of pioneer foremothers, such as Catharina Halkes, which brought together pastoral work in the church with social justice. They have given up on the church, and some are tired of "guilt" over European affluence in relation to Third World poverty. They wish to pursue more purely theoretical issues in feminist theology, in dialogue with postmodernism or French feminist philosophers such as Luce Irigaray.[80]

Yet in other areas of Europe, such as France, Italy, and Spain, the word "feminism" itself is virtually banned in theological faculties. The discussion of women's ordination is "off the map" for church women accepted by the hierarchy. Church women's groups continue to speak only of the "cooperation of men and women in the church" on the level of local churches where laywomen and nuns often do the major pastoral work.

Then there is the newly opened world of Eastern Europe, where women have scarcely begun to be able to poise the question of feminism at all. Here women have lost ground in jobs and education in an economy that converted rapidly from communist systems, where certain principles of affirmative action for women held sway, to a brutal form of competitive capitalism. Questions of feminist theology are barely discussible in societies where the churches have survived underground for half a century and are often picking up old sectarian rivalries where they were left off a generation ago.[81]

The specter of mass rape of women in Bosnia has become the major area of angst for Western European women in the churches, women who watched this horror with feelings of helplessness and guilt, wondering why there was so little word from the churches on this question. While the Third World constitutes the areas of outreach to poor and oppressed women for progressive North Americans, many Western European women feel that their primary area of solidarity should be with their sisters in Eastern Europe.[82] When European feminists gather with feminists from North American and Latin American countries, even with some representation of women from the former East Germany, Poland, Hungary, and the former Yugoslavia, these women are at very different places.

There is also a significant divide between feminists in academic studies and those whose work lies primarily on the pastoral level. Unlike the situation in Roman Catholic churches, the ordination of women in Protestant churches in Scandinavia, Germany, and Holland was settled in the late 1950s and early '60s. Women are present as pastors in growing numbers in these churches and are moving into the positions of provost and superintendent. The episcopacy is also opening to women. Moreover the continuing reality of state churches in these countries, which Americans are apt to regard as a cause of their decline, has a paradoxically positive effect for women, including lesbians.

Some state churches are compelled to follow state guidelines of nondiscrimination toward women and homosexuals. So, unlike the United States, where the issue of ordained gay men and lesbians seems to be an intractable source of conflict, in Sweden and Germany lesbian women serve in the ministry with little fanfare. In Frankfurt in late April 1996 I attended a party held in the pastoral residence of a city church where two lesbian pastors lived together; they had just been accepted to serve in a co-ministry in the parish church. While this was regarded as a first by the young crowd of men and women, most of whom were in ministry or in theological studies preparatory to ordination, it was not in danger of being reversed by church authorities.[83]

For these young women and men with interests in feminism and theology, the foundation for creative work lies not in university-based theological faculties but in grassroots feminist pastoral theology centers. A leading example of such a grassroots center for feminist pastoral theology in Germany is the Frauenstudien und Bildungszentrum of the EKD (German Protestant Church), located in Gelnhausen. Here German Christian women pursue work in feminist liturgy and "Bible drama" in a free-flowing version of Womenchurch. Feminist spirituality and social transformation can be explored in creative symbolic expression through dramatic play with biblical stories and worship. But this center is not outside the institutional church; it is partly funded by the World Council of Churches and is affiliated with the state Protestant church. Its work is to provide feminist religious resources for women working in pastoral ministry in parishes, as well as for women who come together in autonomous gatherings.[84]

In Western Europe the question of Christian feminism versus a post-Christian "Goddess" or "pagan" feminist thealogy and spirituality plays out differently than in the United States (and still differently in Latin America, Asia, and Africa, as we will see in the eighth chapter). In the United States pagan feminists of European background cannot go back to an indigenous landscape of pre-Christian spirituality, for this world is not their own. The small cadre of Amerindian women exploring their traditions from women's perspective do not welcome Euroamericans seeking to encroach on traditions that are not their own and that have been historically devastated by European colonialism in the Americas.[85]

Consequently American pagan feminists look to the Mediterranean or Celtic worlds to discover a pre-Christian spirituality of their ancestors, but often in a way that is unrooted in their own experience. For Europeans, especially in the Germanic world, this question of return to pre-Christian spirituality is complicated by the negative example of Nazism. It is hard to celebrate pre-Christian Germanic myth as a positive resource for the good, with the recent example of the appropriation of this myth by Nazism in the near background. Some German women are exploring Goddess feminism, but in a way that avoids the Germanic question by looking to Mediterranean Old Europe.[86]

In the Celtic world, especially in Ireland, one finds the most positive union of pre-Christian spirituality, feminism, and ethnic identity. Untainted by the Nazi bad example, Celtic spirituality offers a realm where the imagination of post-Christian feminists can flow freely, yet in a context where many remains of mysterious barrows and standing stones dot their own landscape and history. Celtic identity can stand as an alternative to many layers of oppression of Irish and Welsh peoples: pre-Christian vis-à-vis Christianization, Celtic Christianity vis-à-vis Romanized Christianity, and Irish national independence against British colonial occupation.

In Ireland a post-Christian feminist like Mary Daly can find a very different welcome from that which often greets her in the United States. Irish feminists have not experienced the divide between Christian and post-Christian Goddess feminists in the same way as have feminists in the United States. In Ireland feminist theologians can move across the landscape from later forms of Christianity to Celtic Christianity and back to pre-Christian Celtic spirituality as shared ground. Those whose emphasis is more on one than the other are united in their common marginalization by established clerical Catholicism.[87]

A figure like Mary Daly can be welcomed by this feminist community as one of their own. They can all thoroughly enjoy her insightful digs at Catholic clerical "snooldom," while her exploration of a magic Background of "fairyland" that breaks through the Foreground of imposed Roman Catholic and British forms of patriarchy is familiar territory in Ireland (see chapter seven). Second-sight experiences are somewhat expected in places like Newgrange in Ireland, and no one confuses such encounters with a mental breakdown, as they are wont to do in Boston. It is not surprising, then, that Mary Daly, fleeing the fragmentation of feminism in the United States, has found welcome relief and reaffirmation of her vision with frequent trips to Ireland in the late 1980s and '90s.[88]

Although feminists in the church present a very diverse face in Europe, England, and Ireland, some are nevertheless able to present a common front at key moments. One such key moment was the European Women's Synod held in Gmunden, Austria, July 21–28, 1996. Here Catholic and Protestant women from across Europe, north and south, east and west—drawn particularly from pastoral work rather than academic research—gathered to express common concerns as women toward developments in Europe and in the world. The idea of a women's synod reflects a protest against the marginalization of women's concerns both in official ecumenical church gatherings, and also in the development of the bodies of the European Economic Union. Thus the synod united religious and ethical with political and economic concerns.

The concluding statement of the European Women's Synod reaffirmed the principle established at recent United Nations meetings that "women's rights are fundamental human rights," and demanded that this principle be implemented in Europe as well as on a global level. All forms of violence against women were repudiated. These include the violence of poverty, violence against blacks, migrants, and Gypsy women and men, against sexual violence in armed conflict and in everyday life, and against lesbian and bisexual women. The neoliberal model of the economy, promoted by the policies of the World Bank, the International Monetary Fund, and the European Economic Union, with its effects of growing polarization of wealth and poverty in the world, including between Eastern and Western Europeans, was strongly protested.

The European Women's Synod declared that its struggle for justice and well-being was rooted in a

> creation spirituality that draws on traditions of the past as well as contemporary liturgical work done by women. We affirm the spirituality of women's experience as a new mysticism and prophecy born in the solidarity and struggle for justice, peace and the integrity of creation.[89]

The synod statement aimed to integrate spiritual and psychological development of the person with political and economic justice. The group sought to envision just social relations and ecological harmony against all systems of violence at the personal, social, and ecological levels. Militarism and the continued development and trafficking of advanced weaponry were condemned. The women called for women to work together in networks of solidarity across east and west, north and south, to create "an economic order for Europe which respects the integrity of creation, all human communities and the survival of future generations. We commit ourselves to the development of sustainable lifestyles and societies."[90]

Thus, despite differences of economic conditions, religious pluralism, and sexual lifestyles, many European women in 1996 could forge a common voice on what a redeemed humanity on a redeemed earth should look like, at least to the extent of being clear about what social patterns stand as unacceptable countersigns to such hopes. They were beginning to imagine how they might mobilize their power as women across Europe to be a counterweight to the systems being put in place by the European Economic Union.

7. *Creation,* Sergio Velasquez. Nicaraguan Cultural Center.

Chapter Seven

# Feminist, Womanist, and Mujerista Theologies in Twentieth-Century North America

WHEN THE LONG AMERICAN STRUGGLE FOR women's suffrage was finally won, the United States Congress accepted from the National Women's Party a sculpture by Adelaide Johnson, paid for by the Women's Party, honoring Lucretia Mott, Susan B. Anthony, and Elizabeth Cady Stanton. It was dedicated and installed in the Capitol rotunda in 1921, but the next day the all-male leaders of Congress had it removed to a broom closet, where it remained until 1963. It was then moved to a gloomy corner of a lower chamber in the Capitol called the "crypt." The inscription on the statue that celebrates women's fight for equality as "one of the great bloodless revolutions of all time which liberated more people than any other without killing a single person," was whited over by the congressmen. The statue is positioned so that the names of the three women cannot be read. The saga of this statue is symbolic of the ongoing erasure of the memory of women's history in American society.[1]

In the mid-1960s when the "second wave" of the American women's movement began, few Christian women who took up the task of feminist theology knew the work of their foremothers of the nineteenth century, much less of the seventeenth century or before. They were reinventing the questions and experimenting with answers without benefit of knowing the thought already forged over several centuries by their foremothers. The new wave of feminism has given birth to major new scholarship on women's history that has gradually recovered the writings of these women.

Yet the nineteenth-century women's movement left an ongoing legacy for women in the church, not only with the vote, but also with the beginnings of ordination and theological education. Some women in the Congregational, Unitarian, Universalist, and other churches were ordained in the nineteenth century; many more became home or foreign missionaries. Some women began to gain theological education in time to participate in Elizabeth Cady Stanton's feminist revision of the Bible. This inclusion in ministry and theological education slowly built up pressure for the widening of women's participation in church leadership, pressure that bore fruit in 1956 when women were accepted for ordination in the Methodist Episcopal Church and the Presbyterian Church, USA.[2]

In 1954 Harvard Divinity School admitted the first women to its M.Div. program, but school officials were reluctant to give the only two women in the graduating class the top honors that they had earned, on the grounds that this would put the men in a bad light.[3] From the 1960s the number of women students in theological education has expanded to fifty percent or more in many American seminaries, more and more women have been ordained, and the number of women teaching in theological faculties has grown steadily.[4]

Feminist theology has become a normal part of the offerings of the curriculum of most theological schools, although usually still as an elective rather than a way of rethinking the whole curriculum. Every field of theological studies, from Bible and church history to theology, ethics, pastoral psychology, and worship, now has an extensive literature to draw on for its courses. Yet most male students and faculty still do not read this literature as a necessary part of their education and scholarship. Women in the Christian churches have come a long way since 1960, but the danger of erasure of the memory of this achievement, like that of their foremothers of the nineteenth century, remains.

In this chapter on Christian feminist theology in the United States from 1968 to 1996, I start with three women theologians who began writing in the 1960s and who continue today (1998) to develop their thought: Letty Russell, Mary Daly, and this author. I will then discuss three younger theologians whose work revisions feminist theology in various contexts: Carter Heyward, Delores Williams, and Ada María Isasi-Díaz.

This is by no means a comprehensive coverage. Many other feminist theologians could have been chosen as equally important, such as Sallie McFague or the Asian American feminist theology represented by Rita Nakashima Brock.[5] There is also an expanding literature of feminism in specific fields, such as biblical studies, and feminist theology built on the stellar work done by feminist biblical scholars such as Phyllis Trible and Elisabeth Schüssler Fiorenza. I have chosen these six as representatives of two closely connected generations of feminist theologians from the 1960s to the 1990s.

I realize that Mary Daly since 1973 would object to being called either a Christian or a theologian. I include her here, not to co-opt her into a company that she has rejected, but as a "sign of contradiction" to the whole enterprise of Christian feminist theology who is too important to be overlooked.

## Letty Russell

Letty Russell would describe herself as having spent her whole adult life "trying to figure out how to subvert the church into being the church."[6] In 1954 she was one of the two women admitted to Harvard Divinity School and in 1958 one of the first women to be ordained by the Presbyterian church. She spent her formative years in ministry from 1952 to 1955 and 1958 to 1968 in the East Harlem Protestant Parish in a poor black ghetto of New York City as an integral part of a creative experiment in inclusive ministry across racial and class lines. Her first book, *Christian Education in Mission* (1967), reflected this experience in designing an alternative way of being church in East Harlem.[7]

In the early 1970s Russell began to reflect theologically on her many experiences of marginalization as a woman in theological education and ministry. This led her to integrate the feminist perspective into the paradigms of black and liberation theologies that she had absorbed from the black civil rights movement and from Latin America. Her first explicitly feminist book was *Human Liberation in a Feminist Perspective: A Theology* (1974).[8] Over the next twenty years Russell moved from East Harlem to become a professor of theology at Yale Divinity School. She continues to expand her connections with Third World liberation movements, particularly with Third World feminists in the church.

Russell's books on partnership, on feminist interpretation of the Bible, authority in feminist theology (*The Household of Freedom*, 1987), and on feminist ecclesiology (*The Church in the Round*, 1993) represent the ongoing growth of her theology.[9] Russell is notable not only as a theologian of continuing practical/prophetic insight, but as an enabler of other women, particularly Third World women, to do theology. She has helped sponsor many projects, programs, and initiatives that have given women theologians forums to dialogue together and to develop their theology in their own contexts. This many-sided work of enablement is the basis of praxis and reflection for Russell's feminist liberation theology.[10]

Russell's theological methodology can be summed up by her phrase "thinking from the other end." By "other end" she means thinking from the perspective of redemption or New Creation.[11] For Russell, much influenced by Jürgen Moltmann's *Theology of Hope*, the norm of Christian theology does not lie in the past, either in some ideal moment in the Bible or the early church or in the beginnings of creation, but in the future.[12] This does not mean that there are no reference points for Christian theology in paradigmatic memories of the past, in the Exodus community of Israel, in Jesus Christ, and in the "original" creation. But rather all these past moments are to be understood as "memories of the future."

The normative future is the norm of total liberation, the "revolution in which everyone wins."[13] This does not mean that the liberation of everyone into just relations of well-being in communion with God and creation does not involve overcoming vast evils of racism, sexism, classism, war, poverty, and violence on many fronts; it means rather that one does not confuse the overcoming of these evils with the demonization, defeat, and destruction of particular groups of people; for example, white men, capitalists, Christian clergy. One overcomes systems of evil while reclaiming the persons captive in those systems, the oppressed and the oppressors, for a new liberated humanity on a redeemed earth.

Russell's vision of redemption insists on being all-inclusive, without in any way being Pollyannaish about the many-sided insidious nature of the evils in which all humans are caught in one way or another. This does not mean conflating white men, white women, black and Third World men and black and Third World women, the rich and the poor across all these divisions, into a leveling universalism in which "we are all equally oppressed." We are emphatically not all equally oppressed, in Russell's view. Sexist, racist, and classist oppression means there are real differences between men and women across these many divides of race, gender, and class. But there is also no simple division of some normative group of the oppressed who therefore are "without sin" and all the other "bad guys."

Even those most oppressed by the many dimensions of violence can nevertheless be caught up in emulation of the dominant class and lateral violence against their neighbors.[14] And affluent white men can sometimes be converted from their privileges of race, class, and gender and enter into real solidarity with the poor. White, middle-class, educated, professional American women—Russell's own context, of which she is always clearly aware—stand in a position of status ambiguity, sharing some experiences of oppression with other less privileged women, but also sharing privileges of class, race, education, and professional status that put them on the side of the oppressors.[15]

White middle-class women can become enablers of other women and oppressed men, but only by being critically aware of the myopias induced by their context of privilege. Thus, for Russell, thinking theologically from the "other end" is always complemented by thinking socially from the "bottom," from concrete listening and being taught by women and men of oppressed classes and races.

The vision of total liberation or the New Creation is something none of us has experienced. It has never existed in history, either in the early church or in some ideal time at the beginning of creation. Nor have any modern revolutions produced it, although many have worked out of its hopes and some have made advances for human well-being. Thus the norm of the New Creation by which we must judge the Bible, Christian theology, and social struggles is one that is constantly rising out of an unquenchable hope for a better world, a refusal of humans to settle for oppression as the last word of human life and history.

This means that hope takes many different forms in the context of different oppressions. Even among women, what a white middle-class American woman may imagine as liberation—i.e., equality with men in a high-status profession—may be very different from the hopes of a poor Indian woman—i.e., enough food for her family.[16] We also work out of the many "memories of the future" of our particular histories: the winning of suffrage or ordination for women, a successful organizing of a strike led by union women at a factory, the liberation of a colonized country from colonialism.

For Christians the paradigmatic memory of the future is Jesus Christ, the one who stood on the side of the oppressed, was crucified for this by the powers-that-be of religion and state and yet continues to be alive in our midst, beckoning us into a still unrealized future. Although Russell continues to see Jesus Christ as the normative memory of the future for her (for all Christians, including Christian feminists), she becomes clearer in her later books that this is a contextual norm. Jesus Christ is the normative memory "for me/us," but this does not exclude others going forward on the basis of other religious memories.[17]

Ultimately our liberating memories of the future are rooted in God working in history, seeking to make us God's partners in redeeming creation. It is we—all humans, all creation—who are "God's utopia," God's future.[18] Our memories of the many ways we have experienced redemption are finally memories of our response to and partnership with God when we acted for transformation and justice, when we celebrated its signs of presence in our midst.

A feminist liberation theology, then, is about reflection on the praxis of acting to overcome injustice across class and race lines in the particular context of how women are oppressed and are struggling for liberation across these divisions. It is about questioning and rereading the Bible from the perspective of the liberation of all women and men from this whole nexus of oppression. It is about questioning and rereading theology from this perspective. It is about reshaping the church, its ministry and mission, to become *a* (not *the* or *the only*) genuine sign and means of this praxis of liberation, and a place where it is continually remembered and celebrated, equipping the community for continued praxis.

This concern for a theology that enables the praxis of liberation means that Russell has spent a lot of her work on the issue of partnership. By partnership she does not just mean equality between a man and a woman in marriage, although this too is included.[19] Rather, she means a multiplicity of relationships by which we as white women with black women, with black men, with white men, with women and men across many divisions, learn to grow and to be converted out of relations of privilege and unprivilege, power and powerlessness, domination and subjugation, into genuine mutuality.

Conversion, for Russell, from domination/subordination to mutuality is always a two-sided process.[20] The subjugated must be empowered into their full potential to be and act; the privileged must learn to listen to the other and give up privilege. The goal is not an exchange of places but a new relation of mutuality. This involves both inner transformation of mind, spirit, and worldviews and a transformation of social structures and systems of power. Russell does not just talk about this process in general; she has spent much time trying to do it and then to reflect on the processes of this journeying into mutuality in the context of a variety of particular relations: a woman and a man in marriage, two women in a bonded relationship, clergywomen with clergymen, clergy with laity,[21] a woman theologian with her students, a white Christian woman leader in the church in dialogue with Third World women, Christian women developing their own theologies and leadership in their contexts.

Conversion into partnership, for Russell, is a process that takes place in specific ways in concrete contexts. Conversion from domination/subordination into partnership is what becoming a sign of the New Creation really means in various particular contexts. Her theology is rooted in continual engagement in the praxis circle: seeking to live out this process of conversion, reflecting on her learning from this process in order to return to praxis again better equipped to do it, and to help others to do it.

In her forty-five years of thinking out of this engagement in the praxis of liberation, Letty Russell would claim no dramatic victories, many setbacks, but many moment-memories of grace. She (we) cannot give up, not because we know "we can do it if we try," but because we know we are part of God's struggle on our behalf. The assurance for our hope, the ground of our undefeated persistence, lies in our faith that we are joining God in a struggle for the redemption of creation, and God will never give up on us.

## Mary Daly

Mary Daly's life and "faith journey" are in marked contrast to those of Letty Russell, who despite severe criticism of the evils of society and the church, including patriarchalism in the Bible, continues to see her struggle securely grounded in Jesus Christ, a grounding that continues to enable her to fight to "subvert the church into being the church." Daly grew up in an Irish Catholic family in Schenectady, New York, and all her education—from grammar school through three doctoral degrees—came from Catholic faculties. Already as an undergraduate at the College of Saint Rose in Albany, New York, she was attracted to the study of Catholic philosophy. But as a woman she was regarded in the Catholic world as unfit for this highest study.

After earning a B.A. and an M.A. in English, all the while being rebuffed in her search to study philosophy, in 1952 she entered a new doctoral degree program for women in sacred theology at Saint Mary's College, Notre Dame, Indiana. She completed this program in Thomistic theology, only to discover that her degree was regarded as a second-class "women's degree" by Catholic universities. After several years of teaching at a Catholic junior college, rebuffed by Notre Dame and by Catholic University in her efforts to enter their doctoral programs in philosophy, she went to the University of Fribourg, Switzerland, in 1959. There she obtained a doctorate in theology and then a second one in philosophy from the Catholic faculty.[22]

In 1966 Daly returned to the United States to take up a teaching position in the faculty of theology of Jesuit-run Boston College, where she has continued to teach for the rest of her academic career. Even though her three doctoral theses reflected her mastery of impeccable Catholic scholastic theology as taught in the pre–Vatican II era, Daly began to ask feminist questions when she read Simone de Beauvoir in 1954. She returned from Europe with a contract to write her first book, on women in the church. In *The Church and the Second Sex* (1968) she documented the long history of women's marginalization in the Catholic church and its theological teaching, from the perspective of one who sought to reform Catholicism to include women in teaching and ministry.[23]

Although it was a tame, reformist work by her later standards, the Boston University leaders responded to the publication of this book by giving her a terminal one-year teaching contract. The students erupted in protest. After considerable struggle the Jesuits reversed this decision and granted Daly a promotion with tenure. From this experience in 1968 until 1972, Daly grew into an increasing conviction that Catholicism in particular and Christianity in general were irreformable for women. It was not simply that the Bible and Christianity had been deformed by patriarchy, but they simply *were* the theological ideology of patriarchal domination of women. In order to be liberated, women must reject Christianity, root and branch.

She expressed this conviction on November 14, 1971, when she was invited to be the first woman to preach at Harvard Memorial Chapel. She used the opportunity to denounce Christianity as irredeemable for women and to call for women (and men) to make an exodus from the church. Almost all the women who attended this service walked out with her, as well as a few men. Although many who participated in this act did not take it literally, for Daly this was a definitive repudiation of the Christian church as an institution.[24] As she wrote her next book, *Beyond God the Father* (1973), Daly clarified in her own mind that this also meant repudiating any possibility of redeeming Christian symbols for feminism. She changed her language in this book from characterizing the women's movement as the true church and the true expression of Christ, to calling the women's movement "anti-church" and "anti-Christ."[25]

By 1975 Daly became convinced that not only Christianity, but all patriarchal cultures, as these had ruled the world from the time of an archaic overthrow of woman-centered cultures, must be rejected. Feminists and feminist philosophers must position themselves as radical outsiders to the whole patriarchal enterprise of culture and social systems of recorded history. Feminist philosophers must document the evils of this vast system of the "Most Unholy Trinity: rape, genocide and war," repudiating all expressions of its culture and institutions, disenchanting its hold over women's minds, bodies, and spirits, leaping into an alternative consciousness and creating a feminist community of women outside of it.

Her next two books, *Gyn/ecology: The Metaethics of Radical Feminism* (1978) and *Pure Lust: Elemental Feminist Philosophy* (1984), undertake this documentation and shape the symbolic language for this process of "exorcism and ecstasy," the disenchantment of patriarchal evil and the leap beyond it into an alternative community of radical feminists in communion with the natural "elemental" world.[26] This elemental world is one of animal familiars—cats, cows, and spiders; of trees, mountains, stars, and galaxies that give us intimations of true life, a world of mysterious happenings where one can touch remnants of archaic times before patriarchy conquered.[27]

Daly has shaped a provocative alternative language for this process of exorcism and ecstasy. Her 1987 book, *Webster's First Intergalactic Wickedary of the English Language*, sought to provide not only the definitions of this new vocabulary, but a code language of chants and incantations by which radical feminists could free themselves from patriarchal evil and move into communion with elementary "be-ing." Her most recent book, *Outercourse: The Be-Dazzling Voyage* (1992), is an intellectual autobiography in which Daly recapitulates this journey into radical feminism and charts the interconnections between its various stages or "galaxies."[28]

Although there appear to be great discontinuities between Daly's three doctoral dissertations (which faithfully probed Catholic scholastic theology and philosophy), her first Catholic "reformist" book, and then her subsequent books repudiating Christianity and all historical patriarchal cultures, a basic line of continuity connects these different stages of her thought, as Daly makes clear in her autobiography. This line of continuity is Greek ontological philosophy hidden in the depths of Catholic philosophical theology of the Middle Ages.[29] The dualism between illusionary images and true being that underlies this Greek philosophy, a dualism that is at once ontological, ethical, and epistemological, remains the infrastructure for Daly's development of an increasingly radicalized thought-praxis that divides the world of false and demonic images, manifesting oppressive nonlife, from the world of communion in true be-ing, or what she would call the "Foreground" and the "Background."[30]

For Daly the Foreground is a realm of false imitations and distortions of true be-ing. It rests on no real energy or life of its own, but its energy is drawn vampirelike from sucking the life-energy of women while attempting to reduce women themselves to nothing, to robotlike instruments of male sadistic power.[31] It builds up a false and destructive world of toxins that pollute the channels of natural life of women, plants, animals, and planets. It is necrophilic, hating all living beings and seeking to replace them with machinelike imitations, which it celebrates as superior to anything living.

The Foreground demonizes thought, constructing elaborate mazes of misleading ideology that reverse the real thought that is rooted in life. It silences and paralyzes women, erasing the memory of archaic time when women, in harmony with elemental be-ing, ruled.[32] Daly sums up this demonic counterworld with the word "sadosociety." It is both lecherously violent and boring, expressed in "boro-cracy" and "stag-nation." Its sadistic leaders are aided by a vast army of collaborators or "snools," who both cringe in submission to their dictates and enjoy being secondary torturers of others. Female collaborators or "hench-women" gain secondary power through faithful service to snools and sadists.[33]

The task of elementary feminist philosophy is to disenchant or "a-maze" this maze of reversed delusionary thinking, enabling women to catch a glimpse of the true reality of be-ing hidden behind it. The "craft" of the feminist philosopher is like piracy and alchemy, stealing back the wealth stolen by the "phallocrats" and turning the dross back to gold.[34] This craft is also a vehicle of escape, a ship on which to sail out of the "cocko-cratic" system and its "academentia." Women gather on the other side in biophilic sisterhood with each other and with the elemental world.

The demonic powers of cocko-cracy pursue them with a million strategies to recapture the escaping slaves. They label them as the "lunatic fringe," as "bitches" and "witches," seeking to scare off other women from hearing their prophetic truth. The snools deny jobs to feminists and try to commit them to mental institutions and prisons. Part of the craft of these escaping women is to unmask these labels and reveal their truthful depth. Radical feminists embrace the labels of "Hag" and "Nag," "Witch," "Bitch," and "Lunatic," discovering their liberatory meaning as wise, wild, and strong women, female wolves who bay at the moon and female horses who romp into freedom. They glory in being "Positively Revolting Hags";[35] that is, wise women who are in total revolt against sadosociety and reject all its "works and pomps."

The promise on the other side of cocko-cracy is to live fully in communion with the Background, with the realm of true be-ing, communing with the auras of animals, plants, and planets, sailing on the subliminal sea of buried knowledge, and finally "jumping over the moon" to take up permanent residency in the free space of elemental life beyond the poisoned touch of snools. Here "gynergy," the creative energy of women in communion with be-ing, is fully realized and can ply its craft unimpeded.[36]

Yet the atrocities of sadocracy continue and have grown worse in the 1980s and '90s. The fragmentation of the women's movement turns into its dismemberment. The pollution of the earth worsens with oil spills, acid rain, and contamination from nuclear plant breakdowns, such as Chernobyl. The rape, torture, and massacre of women escalate,[37] while the prophetic naysayers are marginalized and turned into Cassandras whom no "good woman" can believe. Discouragement sets in, but ultimately Daly is hopeful that the bold exorcizers of patriarchy will win.

Daly takes heart as she experiences radical feminists continuing to gather on the fringes of sadocracy, conducting trials and judgments of its criminals.[38] They bond together in joyous assemblies in Ireland, Germany, Italy, and

Boston. They keep on keeping on, growing from strength to strength, even as snooldom redoubles its efforts to muzzle them. Nothing less than the true life of the planet is at stake. In the prophetic words of Susan B. Anthony, "Failure is impossible."[39]

In my view Daly's radical judgment on the threat to human and planetary life from the present system of political, economic, and military rule is by no means exaggerated. Daly also pinpoints, with brilliant accuracy, the many strategies of reversal, diversion, and deflation of critical thought and vision that have gone on in the cultures of domination, and which continue to rule the airwaves of media, government, and academia. Anyone concerned for the liberation of humans and life on the planet can learn something from Daly about how to keep the tools of our outrage and critical awareness well sharpened.

Daly's insightful analyses unfortunately repel, not only the many men and women who are deeply invested in exploitative society, but even the many women and men across classes, races, and religions who share much of her critique of this society. This is, in my view, because she and her movement have fallen into the trap of "sectarian closure";[40] that is, mistaking a particular group of women (American, Western European, mostly lesbian, professionals), and their anger and alienation, as the "elect," the critical minority who are in a privileged touch with the "pure land" of life against death.

Other women who are not attracted into this community by virtue of being committed to primary bonds with men as husbands and sons and as colleagues in struggle; any men who want to support women but without denying that they too have positive life and spirit; anyone who wishes to plumb the depths of historical religions, such as Christianity (or Buddhism, Judaism, or Islam) to find their liberating insight rather than rejecting them as totally demonic—these are all written off as deluded collaborators with evil, if not worse, as "snools" and "henchwomen." Thus a critique of systems and ideologies of evil becomes turned into a weapon of contempt toward persons, or, as Letty Russell would put it, the critique *ad rem* becomes an attack *ad personam*.[41]

This does not mean that real persons do not construct evil systems, collaborate with them, and need to take responsibility for their acts or failure to act. Rather it means one cannot liberate a person without addressing him or her as a "thou" rooted in Being (or what Jews and Christians call the *imago Dei*). When persons are demonized as incapable of anything but evil, they do not respond well. Daly's thought virtually denies that males have any potential for true life, labeling their power as derivative blood-sucking from the energy of women who alone have life rooted in true being.

This view of males does not seem to be Daly's practice at all times. In her autobiography she expresses deep appreciation for her father and a few male teachers and friends, and she protests that she has never excluded a male student who really wanted to study with her. By holding separate sessions for men and women, she has given the few men in her classes special attention.[42] Yet her system of thought, as it culminates in *Pure Lust* and the *Wickedary*, seems to offer no basis for commonality between women and men rooted in a shared humanity. Nor does she have patience with women who continue to maintain primary relations with men, including their own sons.[43]

This means that all men (with rare exceptions) and most women are cut off from Daly's in-group, if they take this rhetoric literally. The solution, I believe, is not to take it literally. Rather, one must take it as one symbolic, prophetic language that points out the systems of lies and violence with ruthless accuracy, calls us to divest ourselves of them and shape a new community in communion with the real sources of life. But this means translating Daly's prophetic call into language that affirms the grounding of all persons in life, which encourages life-giving connections with many partners across many cultural traditions, breaking out of present encapsulations in lies and violence. By reconnecting Daly's call for exorcism and ecstasy with an all-embracing love and concern for women and men across many races, classes, and cultures, Cassandra's speech might be deciphered and heard as good news for a growing majority.

## Rosemary Ruether

I also grew up a Roman Catholic but in a less ghettoized form than Mary Daly. This has contributed to a different approach to relating my developing feminist theology to Christianity and to the Catholic and other churches. My family was religiously ecumenical and included a Catholic mother, an Episcopalian father, and a Jewish favorite uncle. My mother was serious and free-thinking in her spiritual life, in a way that suggested that there were both valuable and questionable aspects of Catholicism. I did not attend Catholic schools after my sophomore year in high school.

At Scripps College in Claremont, California (1954–58) I became a classics major and moved easily into a history-of-religions approach to all religions. I learned a positive appreciation of the pagan traditions of antiquity and became interested in studying the Hebrew and early Christian traditions because of their socially critical, prophetic traditions. But this did not mean that I rejected as wrong the pagan traditions with their visions of sacred nature. Rather, I continue to believe that we need both spiritualities; both prophetic social transformations and encounters with the sacred depths in nature.[44]

My academic training fostered a methodology of historical-critical sociology of knowledge very different from the abstract scholastic theology in which Daly was trained. These experiences have disposed me to see both positive and negative aspects of the Jewish and Christian traditions and the ancient pagan traditions, and to be skeptical of exclusivistic views on either side; that is, either Christians who see the biblical tradition as totally superior to inferior paganism, or feminist neo-pagans who regard the biblical traditions as totally evil, in contrast to a paganism imagined to be totally pro-woman in harmony with nature.

Like Letty Russell I became deeply involved in the civil rights movement in the early 1960s. I worked for the Delta Ministry in Mississippi in the summer of 1965, and then taught at Howard University School of Religion from 1966 to 1976, thus shaping my praxis/thought in its formative stage in the context of the African American struggle. Since the early 1970s I have had an expanding connection with the struggles of Third World peoples for justice, increasingly in the context of Latin American, African, Asian, and Arab feminists.[45]

From these experiences I, like Letty Russell, see the perspective from the "bottom" as key to my feminist liberation methodology. From my summer in Mississippi until today I find that the crucial way to see the dominant system of patriarchy, including its racism, classism, and colonialism, in critical perspective is to put myself constantly in those places where, in solidarity with its victims, I can see it from the underside. This does not mean victims are infallible or without their own delusions and potential to misuse power. Poor people can trash each other for limited resources. When some from the underside begin to reach the upperside, a few can become manipulative as they grasp the ways liberal tokenism presents to them of using their status as "representatives of the oppressed" to make their way into unjust power and affluence.

Nevertheless, those from oppressed groups committed to the struggle for justice for their community continue to be for me a "cognitive minority" whose insights are crucially revelatory for those like myself, from the white middle class of the United States, who seek to see global social reality truthfully and to act and think out of that perspective. Also, like Russell's, my theology combines the view from the "bottom" with the view from the "other end," from the side of the vision of redemptive transformation of creation. But, unlike Russell (and closer to Daly in this), my understanding of the New Creation as the norm for theology is rooted in an ontology of primal "origins."

This does not mean I believe there was some perfect time when all was well with humans on earth in an archaic paradise before the rise of patriarchy. I agree that many of the most egregious evils that have led to the present crisis of the planet were planted with the rise of patriarchal societies of the early urban era. Many indigenous peoples rooted in earlier cultures, such as the Andean Indians, have precious traditions of ecological spirituality to share with us. But archaeological studies that have uncovered pre-Incan Andean tombs, where slaves and concubines were buried with their lord, show that all was not well in these earlier cultures.[46] Again, for me, this is a matter of relative differences rather than absolutes on either side.

When I think of ontological origins that underlie future hope, I am thinking of deep ontological structures that underlie human and all living beings and that dispose us to biophilic mutuality as our authentic mode of being. The ultimate "ground of being" of these deep ontological structures, and the future promise that they hold, are what I call God. But God is not a "being" removed from creation, ruling it from outside in the manner of a patriarchal ruler; God is the source of being that underlies creation and grounds its nature and future potential for continual transformative renewal in biophilic mutuality.

Our ontological grounding in God/creation has ethical consequences. Only when we act in this manner of biophilic mutuality with one another (across not only gender, class, and race, but also species lines) is there well-being, while the exploitative domination of some by others violates this ontological ground and leads to violence, hate, escalating oppression, misuse of the earth, and eventually a social system that will destroy itself. Even though such systems may be able to survive by force for some time, the longer they survive in this way the more destructive they become.

If biophilic mutuality is our "nature" rooted in God, from whence come these tendencies to oppressive and destructive violence? I see this as a perversion of the life instinct of self-preservation that tends to limitless self-aggrandizement. This tendency is found even in the plant and animal world, but it was kept in check in the animal world, including among humans, until about eight millennia ago by cooperative interdependence that incorporated competitive limits of each by the others, at a time when the human species did not hold commanding power. But with new human developments of control over food supply (hunting, domestication of plants and animals), humans were able to break free of some of these limits by exploiting other animals, the earth, and each other. Slavery, hierarchy, sexism, the treatment of land and animals as property, all developed as aspects of a system of society called patriarchy.[47]

I, like Daly, believe we are at a terminal stage of these patterns of patriarchal exploitation, a stage at which we either choose to learn new ways of relating that recapture biophilic mutuality on a new, consciously chosen, level, or else we will destroy ourselves and much of the life forms of the earth with us. I see God, the divine ground of being, as the ground of our hope in this struggle for transformation, but this is not a God who is "in charge" and will intervene to save us despite ourselves and bring in a reign of God from the sky. Rather the deep ontological structures that dictate biophilic mutuality as the only way to generate well-being give us the potential for making a new future, but one we could miss through our greed, hatred, and delusions.[48]

If we do the latter, the same ontological structures will bring judgment and nemesis upon our evil ways and systems, for these finally cannot survive. But unfortunately, when the powerful destroy themselves, they destroy the innocent as well. It is not certain that God can rectify this, for God can only call us to our better selves and give us the ongoing basis for it; God cannot force this conversion upon us (I agree with process theology here).[49] Unlike Daly, I believe failure is possible, although not fated. It is this understanding of reality that underlies my feminist ecological liberation theology.[50]

## Carter Heyward

Carter Heyward was catapulted into the American religious scene in 1974 when she and ten other Episcopalian women were ordained as priests by three retired bishops. This "irregular" ordination was a dramatic moment in the struggle for women's ordination in the Christian churches. The Episcopal church came to the brink of voting for women's ordination at their General Conventions in 1970 and 1973, but, by a voting technicality, the majority vote in favor was counted as a victory for the "no" vote. A group of Episcopal women who had completed their preparations for ordination, together with several bishops, decided that the time had come to protest this injustice by going ahead with their ordination. Heyward told the story of her own growth toward claiming her priesthood, and the events surrounding the 1974 ordination, in her autobiographical book, *A Priest Forever*.[51]

In the 1976 national convention of the Episcopal church, women's ordination was finally accepted. The American Episcopal Church now has several thousand women priests and a growing number of women bishops. The irregular ordinations of Heyward and the others were regularized. The esteem in which she was held by the progressive wing of the church was signaled by the invitation to join the faculty of Episcopal Divinity School, where she has continued to teach to the present. Yet pioneers who led the fight, such as Heyward, remain marked by their decision to defy church law. This entails not only a reputation as rebels, but a searing experience of the way abusive power can lurk under paternalistic "kindliness."[52]

Heyward's theology is an ongoing in-depth exploration of the many aspects of abusive power as sin and its redemptive counterpart as mutual relation. In her doctoral dissertation, completed at Union Theological Seminary in May of 1980, *The Redemption of God: A Theology of Mutual Relation*,[53] Heyward lays down the major lines of her theological view that continues to inspire her thought and practice to the present. Heyward's theology, founded in a feminist liberation perspective, entails a denunciation and an annunciation. The sin denounced can be defined as "wrong relation."

Such wrong relation consists both in the exercise of power over others, denying mutuality and reciprocity, and also in the disconnection of people from each other, ignoring our actual connections. Patriarchy, as the primary systemic and ideological expression of sin, typically brings together both aspects of wrong relation; it both uses power abusively, violating the well-being of the other physically, psychologically, and spiritually, and it assumes a series of disconnecting splits—mind versus body, self versus other, individualism versus community—that create barriers to recognizing connection.

A false individualism and disconnection, together with dominating power over others, is reflected in patriarchal Christian theology, in its view of God and God's relation to humankind as one separated from us, ruling over us, exercising punishing or saving power over us without mutuality or reciprocity. Heyward's theology analyzes and critiques this theology of separation and domination as it justifies and sacralizes these same kinds of relations in society, including in the church, and in other "helping professions" such as psychotherapy.

Redemption, for Heyward, includes all expressions of human creativity that break through disconnecting and dominating relations and spark experiences of mutual relation, even if partially or momentarily. Mutual relation reintegrates in dynamic mutuality all the false splits set up by patriarchal culture, ideology, and society. The split between body and spirit is overcome. Mutual relation is holistic. One is and becomes whole in mutual relation that is at once intensely physical and intensely spiritual. Sexuality and spirituality are no longer opposed but are experienced as one erotic energy connecting us with one another. Sexual and spiritual ecstasy are one.

The self-other split of Western psychology is likewise overcome. The male-female dualism that directs men toward separation and autonomy, while directing women to lose their selves in altruism, is transcended. Mutual relation is simultaneously other-related and self-related. The more we enhance and empower others, the more we enhance and empower ourselves, and vice versa. Competitive relations based on power over others are changed for an empowerment that grows ever greater for each in relation to the other. This does not mean a fusion or loss of individuality. We each become distinct and recognize our distinctiveness as we learn to commune in mutuality.

Mutual relation also transcends and integrates the love-justice dichotomy of Western ethics. To make love is to make justice, for Heyward. There can be no just relation that is not loving, and no loving relation that is not just. To develop toward an increasingly just society is at the same time to create societies based on love. This entails breaking down the private-public, individual-social splits of Western society. We are individuals and at the same time in community. The critique of unjust relations is both personal and systemic. Sexism, racism, classism—all forms of advantage and disadvantage over others—must be overcome.

As a white, Southern, middle-strata Christian professional, Heyward recognizes her own social ambiguity and conditioning in wrong relation, how she has learned both to accept abuse as a woman and to exercise it, unknowingly, toward others who are black, poor, Jewish, or of other racial, class, and religious groups disadvantaged by the dominant social system. Growing out of wrong relation is a long process of conscientization and transformation. It also means overcoming the economic, political, and military systems of wrong relation to create social systems that can incarnate justice for all.

Heyward has sought to explore the justice-making aspects of her theology of mutual relation by in-depth work on racism, with black women colleagues especially.[54] She has also connected herself with struggles for international justice against American military neocolonial interventions in poor countries. The book *Revolutionary Forgiveness* reflects her élan toward justice for small, poor countries seeking to define their own development freed from American dominating power. Heyward and a group of students at the Episcopal Divinity School lived in Nicaragua for two months in 1984 and then reflected on their experience in a class. Writing the book together as the "Amanecida (daybreak) Collective," the group sought to reflect their understanding of feminist liberation theology as both a theology rooted in practice and a theology done in community.[55]

Such a theology of mutual relation must finally reshape the model of God and God's relation to us. God is not a separate power or being over against us, situated in some space outside of "the world," disconnected from reciprocity with us. Rather, God is the ground or matrix of mutual relation. There can be no split between loving God and loving ourselves or between loving God and loving our neighbor. Rather, God is incarnate in that process of mutual relation in which we love our neighbors as ourselves. As we learn to love one another we are at the same time empowered by God, who grounds our power of mutual relation, and God is born and grows in our mutual relation.[56] God births us and we birth God in mutual relation. Heyward names this reciprocal relation between us and God as "godding," becoming godlike and creating God in our loving and justice-making relations with one another.

As Heyward was completing her doctoral dissertation, she also "came out" as a lesbian.[57] "Coming out" itself becomes for Heyward a metaphor for redemption against sinful relations manifest in heterosexism. Unlike many gay and lesbian understandings of identity, Heyward rejects sexual essentialism. We are not born either homosexual or heterosexual; we are simply born to be sexual as an expression of our loving relationality. Compulsory heterosexuality is a false distortion of the self and society that privileges the white heterosexual male as the dominant and normative person, but this is a social construction of wrong relation in unjust power, one that is foundational for the other patterns of abusive power.

Redemption is coming out to our full-bodied sexuality by which we can ecstatically open ourselves to the other, whether that other is defined as male or female, same gender or other gender. Gender identities are themselves social constructions, rather than our "natures." If Heyward chooses to define herself as a lesbian, it is not because she feels she is biologically confined to respond sexually to women and not to men. She has also experienced loving relationships with men and at one point contemplated marriage with a man.

Rather, in heterosexist society, she chooses love relations with women as a preference that can be less oppressive and more liberating because it breaks with the dominant heterosexual social conditioning and power relations. But lesbians also must know themselves as capable of wrong relation with each other. They may be less conditioned to such abuse, but women too must grow into increasing reciprocity and mutuality with each other, overcoming the deep patterns that dispose them to abuse or accept abuse, even with other women.[58]

Heyward's theology of mutual relation follows themes common to contemporary feminist theology. She differs primarily in the radicality of her willingness to explore the full implications of this view, both in dissolving the idea of deity as a separate "person" from our mutual relation and also in the explicitness of naming sexuality as spirituality. This second aspect of her thought is further developed in her 1989 book *Touching Our Strength: The Erotic as Power and the Love of God.*[59] But it was with the publication of her 1993 autobiographical account of her relationship with a woman therapist, *When Boundaries Betray Us: Beyond Illusions of What Is Ethical in Therapy and Life,*[60] that feminists committed to her general position began to wonder about danger zones in her thought.

In this book Heyward tells of her love for a woman therapist and the refusal of this therapist to reciprocate on the grounds of professional ethics, and at the same time her reluctance to break off the relationship. Heyward uses this experience to denounce patterns of professionalism that are controlling and that deny real mutuality in such relations. This denial of intimacy and mutuality on the ground of professional ethics is for her inherently abusive and makes such a relation "untrustworthy." Heyward recognizes that vulnerable people, such as children and women, need boundaries to be protected from abuse by powerful "helpers," but she believes that in relationships where both have strongly developed selves, such boundaries can be discarded.

This book brought a storm of criticism from reviewers, especially from those defending the necessity of professional boundaries to create "safe space" for therapy. Feminist reviewers also were troubled by Heyward's seeming rejection of the decision of another woman that more personal intimacy between them would be inappropriate, both professionally and for the personal well-being of each.[61] What does this say about Heyward's understanding of "mutual relation"? Others have agreed with Heyward that such professional ethics can be overdone to the point of denying that therapy needs to be a reciprocal process of mutual change.[62]

The radicality of Heyward's understanding of doing theology as an expression of her own ongoing experimental praxis, in which she exposes her personal struggles, means her thought can become vulnerable to the personal question.[63] But it would be doing a profound disservice to Heyward's theology, as well as her person, to forget that her understanding of God as mutual relation is experienced in but never reducible to individualized relationships of the moment. God as "surprise" is the power for ever-new breakthroughs in lived experience and self-critical reflection in the quest to incarnate "right relation." Thus Heyward's God keeps her horizon ever open to learning new things from moments of failure as well as joy.

## Delores Williams

Delores Williams is an African American woman who grew up in Louisville, Kentucky, and was active in the civil rights movement. She married and had two of her four children before completing her college education. She then went on to do seminary and doctoral studies at Union Theological Seminary and presently teaches there as a professor of theology and culture. Her frequent lectures and publications put her at the forefront of the development of womanist theology.[64]

The term "womanism" has developed among African American women, particularly in religious studies, to indicate the reflection on Scripture, theology, and ethics from the context of African American women's experience.[65] Delores Williams defines womanism as rooted in the recovery of the survival and resistance history of black women in the United States, in the context of the black family and community. Womanists love and affirm themselves, not in isolation, but as those who have often been the primary defenders of the well-being of the black family and who are fiercely identified with the struggle of the whole black community against oppression.[66]

Womanism, for Williams, is nonseparatist and multidialogical. It does not separate the well-being of the self from that of the family, family from community, or black women from black men. Womanists engage in a plurality of dialogues, with black male liberation theologians and with feminists who work in Asian, Hispanic, and Euroamerican contexts, without diminishing the primacy of their own concerns as black women. Womanism can be critical of the myopias of black males and also of feminists, not simply in order to confront others, but for the sake of a greater solidarity in struggle for justice.

Womanists enlarge the definition of the systems and ideologies of oppression to include expressions of racism that white women are guilty of within the systems of white classism and racism, and expressions of sexism that white men and black men have been guilty of toward black women. For black women these expressions of racism, sexism, and classism are not separable but exist as a multidimensional oppression that black women have experienced in concrete particularity.[67] Williams also includes ecological destruction in her account of the systems of evil, and sees particular analogies between violence to and the defilement of the earth and the treatment of black women's bodies.[68]

Black women remember all aspects of this oppression in telling their story of resistance and survival. They recall their experiences of rape, sexual abuse, beating, exploited labor in house and field under slavery at the hands of white men, and the roles played by white women in this exploitation. They are also clear about the way in which the image of the white woman has been set up as the model of acceptable "feminine" femaleness to stereotype black femaleness as debased and incapable of respectability and beauty.[69]

They are also aware of how sexism has existed within the black community. They remember domestic violence, sexual abuse, and exploitation of their labor by black men, including black ministers, even while being blamed for the strength by which they have fought for the survival of their families, as if this very strength had somehow debilitated black men.[70] They are also aware of the way in which black women and men have sought to assimilate themselves into models of white bourgeois respectability in ways that marginalized the poor black woman. The American system of evil, what Williams calls "demonarchy," encompasses all these aspects of violence, debasement, and denial of dignity that have converged in the personal lives and historical experience of black women.[71]

This multilayered experience of oppression is the hermeneutical norm for black women in judging the appropriateness of biblical interpretation, theology, and ethics. Whatever ignores or reinforces aspects of this experience of oppression is by definition part of the system of evil and is not salvific. Womanists, therefore, while affirming the liberation intent of black theology, also question its ignoring of the experience of black women and its disregard for the sexism of the Bible and the Christian tradition. Through the womanist hermeneutical lens, much that black theology has affirmed in the Bible and theology as liberatory is seen as ambivalent, even conducive to oppression of women generally and of men and women of disadvantaged groups, such as slaves and those of other races.

Williams questions the uncritical way in which the African American community has accepted the Hebrew Bible as analogous to their own story, rather than writing their own story as canon or at least making their own story a more explicit norm for judging the adequacy of biblical models. Thus, for example, black male liberation theology has claimed that God in the Bible is unequivocally on the side of the oppressed, while overlooking the sexism of the Bible that oppresses black women.

Black theology has also ignored the justifications of slavery in both Hebrew Scripture and the New Testament. A people whose history in the United States is rooted in being brought here in chains as slaves, whose masters used these very passages in Scripture to justify slavery as acceptable to God, cannot overlook this problem in the Bible.[72]

Black theology has also been insensitive to racism against non-Jews in the Bible, in its uncritical identification of blacks with ancient Hebrews. The negative stereotyping of Egyptians in the Hebrew symbolism cannot be overlooked by an Afrocentric quest for roots that include African Egypt. Black theology cannot ignore the injustice of the biblical Hebrews to the Canaanites who were conquered, deprived of their land, expelled, and massacred by Hebrew settlers. The Exodus story cannot be looked at only from the isolated point of identification between African Americans who were enslaved and the Hebrews liberated from slavery. It must look at the whole story of Exodus, including a story of settlement in a "promised land" that was oppressive toward the people living in the land at the time of the Hebrew invasion. Williams is sensitive toward the oppression of Palestinian people by a Zionist "promised land" ideology in the twentieth century and draws from writings of Palestinian theologians in these remarks.[73]

Williams takes the story of Hagar in the book of Genesis as paradigmatic for the interpretation of the womanist perspective. Hagar, like the female ancestors of African American women, is a slave of African (Egyptian) background. As a slave she is the property of her mistress, Sarai, who can use her any way she wants. As a foreigner she is not the beneficiary of laws limiting the use of Hebrew slaves by other Hebrews. Her oppression at the hands of Sarai includes sexual abuse and forced surrogacy, to bear the child for Abraham that Sarai is not able to bear.[74]

Hagar is also exposed to domestic violence at the hands of her mistress when she, through her son, is seen as a rival to the position of Sarai as wife. She is twice thrown into the wilderness at Sarai's demands because of this perceived threat. There she is abandoned without resources and has to find her way in a situation where she and her son were expected to die. In the wilderness she has direct encounters with God, who assures her that through her son she will be the mother of a powerful nation, a promise parallel to that of Abraham. But she is also, at the first expulsion, ordered by God to return and subjugate herself to Sarai. Then she is definitively expelled and left to make her way alone with her son after Sarai bears her own child.

Thus, for Williams, the God that Hagar encounters in the wilderness is not entirely on the side of Hagar as one of the oppressed, but mostly sides with the interests of Sarai. Moreover Hagar's interpretation of her experience of God as a "God of seeing" may draw on her Egyptian experience of the divine, and so the more positive aspects of this experience come from non-Hebrew traditions. Williams understands this to mean that the Hebrew God is an ambivalent figure for black women, who need to turn to their own experience and to African traditions for additional theological resources.[75]

African American women have shared the experiences of Hagar in all these aspects of sexual and physical abuse, forced surrogacy, and abandonment to make their way in the wilderness, without social resources other than their own initiative and creativity. Like Hagar their creativity has enabled them to encounter a divine power in this wilderness, one that has empowered them to "make a way out of no way." Williams particularly resonates with Hagar's experience of forced surrogacy, which she sees as a specific experience of African American women who in slavery times were made the surrogate sex objects, childbearers, and child-raisers replacing white women, as well as having to do the hard field labor of black men.[76] Although the white patriarchal slave system may have been the defining context for this, white women often have been the immediate oppressors, just as Sarai was the primary oppressor of Hagar.

Redemption, for Williams, must be judged in terms of the experiences of black women's oppression and their struggle for survival and quality of life for themselves and their children. Black women encounter a redeeming God, not through Christ's sufferings on the cross, but in wilderness experiences in which they find a God and a relationship with Jesus that has empowered them to embrace their own power and integrity. In the wilderness their experiences of God have enabled them to resist such oppression and to struggle to "make a way out of no way."

Williams names redemption for black women, not in terms of the sweeping idea of "liberation" of black theology, which is so far-reaching that it hardly touches the day-to-day struggles relevant to black women. Rather, empowerment to struggle on a daily basis for "survival and quality of life" is her symbol for the concrete redemption black women and their families need here and now,[77] although they continue to hope for a larger liberation from all the structures of racist, classist, sexist, and heterosexist oppression.

Williams is critical of the traditional theology of atonement centered on Jesus' suffering sacrifice on the cross as a surrogate for sinful humanity. Such a model of atonement reinforces unjust suffering, including the surrogate suffering that has been black women's particular oppression. The cross needs to be recognized as a symbol of evil. It is the expression of the rejection of Jesus' ministry of life as good news to the poor by the powerful who sought to silence him, and the hope aroused through his life, by subjecting him to a horrible death by public torture.

The cross needs to be recognized soberly as the risk that anyone struggling against oppression may experience at the hands of those who want to keep the system of domination intact, but it is not itself redeeming.[78] What is redeeming is not Jesus' death, but Jesus' life, his vision and ministry of justice and right relation restored in communities of life. Jesus is a model and helper for black women as one who resisted the temptations toward unjust power in the wilderness and chose to speak the word of life against the systems of death. It is as one who ministers on behalf of life that Jesus can be claimed as "mother, father, sister, and brother" for black women seeking to find "a way out of no way" for survival and quality of life, and not because he was subjected to a horrible death on the cross.

Williams is also deeply critical of what she calls the "African American denominational churches" as institutions that have all too often reinforced the oppression of black women by their sexist denial of their ministry, their exploitation of their work for the church, their otherworldly theology and failure to be prophetic voices against social oppression. She contrasts this record of the African American denominational church with the true black church. This is not an institution, but it is what happens wherever black people are rising and claiming their positive powers against the "demonarchy."[79]

Yet black women cannot give up on the African American denominational churches, for they have also been a vital resource for black women's empowerment, despite their failings. Black women must continue to call these churches to renewal to become the "black church," which they have claimed to be but have often not been.

## Ada María Isasi-Díaz

Ada María Isasi-Díaz was born in Cuba in 1943 and came to the United States with her family at the age of eighteen fleeing the Castro regime. She joined a religious order and spent three formative years as a missionary in Lima, Peru. This experience was key for her commitment to a liberation perspective on behalf of the poor. With the rise of the Catholic women's ordination movement in 1975, Isasi-Díaz became deeply aware of sexism in the church.[80] After working as a national coordinator for the Women's Ordination Conference, she did master's and doctoral studies in theology at Union Theological Seminary in New York.

Isasi-Díaz had also become increasingly aware of anti-Hispanic ethnic prejudice in North America. She began to formulate a *mujerista* perspective on theology together with other Hispanic women across the United States, particularly with Chicana grassroots activist Yolanda Tarango, with whom she wrote *Hispanic Women: Prophetic Voice in the Church.*[81] Isasi-Díaz presently teaches theology and ethics from a Hispanic woman's perspective at Drew Theological and Graduate Schools in Madison, New Jersey.

For Isasi-Díaz *mujerista* theology is first of all the liberatory praxis of Hispanic women oppressed by ethnic prejudice, sexism, and poverty in the United States. Its dimension of theoretical reflection is never separated from praxis but is an integral part of praxis. *Mujerista* theology is communal by nature. Theologically educated professionals like herself may serve as enablers of *mujerista* theology, but it is done by the community of Hispanic women engaged in liberatory praxis.

This methodology of doing theology in community is expressed by gathering retreats of Hispanic women who reflect together on questions of daily life, survival, and faith. Isasi-Díaz and Tarango drew the data for their first book together (written bilingually in English and Spanish) from this work in group reflection. Isasi-Díaz carried this same methodology into her second book, *En la Lucha: Elaborating a Mujerista Theology.*[82] She is presently working with Hispanic women across the United States to study the experience of the body as a primary site of both oppression and liberation for Hispanic women.[83]

In *Hispanic Women,* Tarango and Isasi-Díaz presented a methodology of conducting these retreats that interconnect storytelling, analysis, liturgizing, and strategy.[84] Storytelling enables Hispanic women to gain their own voice, to articulate their life experience in a way that is often denied them both in the larger Anglo society and in their own communities. Analysis is a way of reflecting on these stories that locates the issues of oppression and resources for resistance and liberatory praxis.

Liturgizing puts this resistance and hope in a context of celebratory self-expression in a way that allows Hispanic women to claim their experience in worship. This is particularly important since Hispanic women often experience the official liturgies of the Roman Catholic Church as alienating and disempowering, defining them as unworthy before God for not being able to "live up" to its rules, particularly on issues of sexuality, marriage, birth control, and abortion.[85]

The fourth step of strategy brings reflection back to concrete praxis, to actions that women can take to better their lives. These four steps are not a linear process but a continual spiral of interconnected elements. The enablers facilitate this process, record developments, and extract from the process the "generative themes" that emerge as the basis for *mujerista* theology, but they are committed to doing this in dialogue. They need to check back with the participants to see if the way they have interpreted their views accords with the women's own self-understanding.

In her book *En la Lucha*, Isasi-Díaz focused particularly on the issues of ethnic identity, moral agency, and praxis in *mujerista* theology. Ethnic identity is a complex issue for Hispanic women in the United States. Hispanic people in the United States come from a variety of countries: Caribbean islands such as Puerto Rico and Cuba, Mexico, Central and Latin America, as well as Spain and Portugal. For the purposes of her work, Isasi-Díaz has concentrated on the three major U.S. Hispanic communities of Chicanas-Mexicans, Puerto Ricans, and Cubans.[86]

These three have quite different relations to the United States. Some, like Chicanas of the U.S. Southwest, live in what was once the Mexican northwest, taken over by the United States in the mid-nineteenth century. They are not "immigrants" but people conquered in their own historic lands. This Chicana population from Texas to California is fed by continual emigration from Mexico. Puerto Ricans come from an island taken over by the United States in 1898 and have U.S. citizenship status and the right to live anywhere in the United States, while the Cubans came and continue to come as refugees from the Castro regime. While the first waves of Cubans were welcomed in the context of U.S. anti-Castro policies, more recent waves, often poorer and blacker, have been less welcomed.

In addition to these different relations to the United States, Hispanics are diverse among themselves, drawing on different historic experiences and representing different mixtures of indigenous, African, and European racial-cultural backgrounds. In Mexico and the Caribbean islands, people from Europe (Spain) were the ruling class and set themselves above those of mixed race (mestizo or white/Indian) and mulattos (white/African), with Indians and Africans at the bottom of society. These divisions remain among Hispanics in the United States, often defining class as well as race differences, but Hispanics have sought to overcome these divisions but celebrating a shared *mestizaje/mulatez*, a common peoplehood rooted in the amalgamation of the three races.[87]

In the United States most Hispanics are drawn together by a common language, Spanish (although for many indigenous peoples Spanish is a second language, and Brazilians speak Portuguese). They also find themselves treated as "people of color" regardless of whether they are actually solely of European ancestry. Thus Spanish "accent" becomes "color" in the United States, although the more African- and Indian-looking Hispanics experience racial and ethnic prejudice especially. Hispanics also experience pressure to assimilate culturally and linguistically. Becoming "American" means speaking English without a "foreign accent" and living like one's Anglo neighbors.

This means that Hispanic identity is both a given and a choice in the United States. The Hispanic community has to choose to retain its own language and culture against pressure to assimilate and prejudice against those who do not; they also seek a new identity that affirms its *mestizaje/mulatez* across white, Indian, and African mixtures and across the diverse communities of Puerto Ricans, Cubans, and Mexican-Americans/Chicanas. For Isasi-Díaz *mujerista* theology is rooted in this praxis of both claiming one's particular Hispanic identity against pressure to assimilate and creating a new intercommunal solidarity across Hispanic groups, embracing their *mestizaje/mulatez*.[88]

For Isasi-Díaz, theory and theology are not separate "second steps" from lived liberative praxis. One cannot abstract a *mujerista* theology apart from praxis. Praxis has always to be seen on the level of daily life in continually changing strategies by which Hispanic women, in the context of their families and communities, seek survival and well-being in the midst of a society that assaults them through structures and ideologies of ethnic prejudice, economic exploitation, and sexism.[89]

Evil or sin in *mujerista* theology can be defined as all of those structures and attitudes that assault Hispanic women physically, culturally, psychically, and spiritually, as poverty and violence and as diminishment of their sense of dignity and self-worth. Sin assaults Hispanic women from many sources. It comes from the Anglo community that exploits their labor and disregards their culture. It also comes from men in their own families and communities who exploit their labor, abuse them sexually, and reduce them to sex objects, baby-machines, and maternal nurturers, often with little economic means to carry out these many demands on their bodies and spirits.

Sin also comes from the institutional churches, particularly Catholicism, which have traditionally enforced rules of marriage and sexuality that sacralize demands for women to be passive and maternal servants of men. These churches judge Hispanic women as sinful because their struggles to survive may mean that they turn to prostitution, marriage without benefit of clergy, divorce, or separation, birth control, and abortion. About 20 percent of U.S. Hispanics are Protestants, many joining more fundamentalist or Pentecostal churches, but these churches also have authoritarian patterns of clerical power, enforced by a biblical literalism in the hands of the pastors, which can deprive Hispanic women of their culture and sense of autonomy and self-determination.[90]

Redemption for Hispanic women rests on an unshakable belief in their self-worth despite these many-sided assaults; a sense of self-worth that Isasi-Díaz identified as "being created in the image of God." Through this sense of self-worth Hispanic women conduct a struggle for survival and well-being for themselves and their families in spite of all odds. Redemption is the renewal, energizing, and affirmation of deeply rooted faith in their own worth that drives their praxis of survival and quest for well-being. *Mujerista* theology is itself about supporting this praxis and affirming Hispanic women's moral agency; that is, their sense of their right and capacity to be self-determining agents of their own lives on behalf of their own and their families' well-being.

The churches, Catholic and Protestant, are, for Isasi-Díaz, more adversaries than aids in this liberatory praxis. For religious support *mujerista* theology turns more to Hispanic women's traditions of popular religion, itself a mix of popular Spanish Catholicism, Amerindian, and Afro-Caribbean practices.[91] Integral with the affirmation *mestizaje/mulatez* is the embrace of this mixed heritage of popular religion that the official missionary work of Catholicism and Protestantism has aimed at eradicating in order to bring Hispanics into the "correct" Christianity.

Isasi-Díaz acknowledges that popular religion needs to be criticized for those elements that enforce superstition, fatalism, and acceptance of suffering.

But it is a valuable resource for Hispanic women's moral agency and liberative praxis precisely because it puts faith and practice in their own hands, where they relate to the divine directly without church structures that enforce control over them. *Mujerista* theology creates new communities of faith that promote Hispanic women's reflection on their stories, analysis and strategy for liberative praxis that celebrates this faith in liturgy and fiesta, drawing on the most creative aspects of popular religion.[92]

Liberation or redemption, for Isasi-Díaz, does not end simply with carving out a small sphere of enhanced well-being for Hispanic women in their local contexts, although it remains rooted in this concrete reality. But she also envisions a challenge to the macro systems of racism, sexism, and exploitation that govern the entire U.S. American social, political, and economic system. It is this macro system that holds in place exploitation of Hispanic women in their local contexts. Liberation thus demands justice for all in the United States as its agenda. Its praxis of liberation remains rooted in and reaches out from the local context to build coalitions to promote justice in the whole society. Defining this praxis of justice is difficult from the context of a marginalized Hispanic community in the United States, but it is a demand that *mujerista* theology cannot surrender as its larger horizon.[93]

The diversifying of American women's theologies of liberation in many communities—Euroamerican Protestant and Catholic, lesbian, African American, and Hispanic, as well as others we have not covered due to the limits of this chapter (such as Asians), is sometimes deplored as divisive fragmentation qua "identity politics." But this divisiveness has come, I believe, not from those claiming nonwhite or non-heterosexual identities, but from the myopias of white middle-class heterosexual feminists who want a unitary "feminism" based on their own identities as the hegemonic culture and group.

Lesbians, womanists, and Hispanics like Heyward, Williams, and Isasi-Díaz have made clear that they are not separatists in terms of gender, sexual identity, or ethnicity. They are open to coalitions for joint struggle, but based on an egalitarian mutual acceptance of difference. Although more work on this needs to be done, a sense of a community of struggle enriched precisely because of its "many-splendored wonder" of contextualization in many differences is developing and is experienced in women's communities of theological dialogue and teaching. This is the power and hope of women's liberative theologies in North America.

8. *Kwan In.* Painting used by Chung Hyun Kyung in her multimedia presentation for the WCC assembly in Canberra to illustrate her image of the Holy Spirit.

Chapter Eight

# Feminist Theologies in Latin America, Africa, and Asia

FEMINIST THEOLOGIES ARISING IN LATIN AMERICA, Africa, and Asia have generally developed in relation to the liberation theologies of their regions. Latin American liberation theology was pioneered by priest-theologians, such as Peruvian Gustavo Gutiérrez[1] in the mid-1960s. It developed in response to the crisis of poverty and revolutionary violence in their regions and the failure of the capitalist developmental model promulgated by North American and Western European corporations and governments to promote social justice.

In 1976, in the wake of the rise and destruction of the socialist reform government of Salvador Allende in Chile, Latin Americans such as Sergio Torres,reached out to Asian and African theologians to found the Ecumenical Association of Third World Theologians (EATWOT). Latin American liberation theology focused on questions of poverty and economic oppression within their countries and particularly between Latin America and the "First World." They were challenged by Asian and African theologians to be more sensitive to questions of race and culture as well.

Questions of sexism and gender, however, were virtually ignored by these male theologians from all three regions. By the late 1970s a growing cadre of women theologians were attending the international meetings of EATWOT: Mercy Amba Oduyoye from Ghana, Virginia Fabella and Mary John Mananzan from the Philippines, Marianne Katoppo from Indonesia, Sun Ai Park from Korea, Ivone Gebara and Elsa Tamez from Latin America. They began to challenge the lack of attention to gender in Third World theologies. The issue surfaced at the 1978 Assembly in New Delhi when the plea of Marianne Katoppo for inclusive language brought jokes and trivializing comments from the men.[2]

In 1983 an international dialogue between Third World and First World theologians was convened in Geneva, with a mandate to make the delegations from Asia, Africa, Latin America, North America, and Western Europe gender-inclusive. The result was a considerable number of women theologians from the five regions, who gravitated toward each other to discuss feminist issues in theology and social analysis. This brought further resistance from some of the male Third World theologians who wanted "their women" to stay "in their place;" i.e., behind the agenda of the men.

This resistance took the form of claims of the priority of race, class and cultural issues. It was said that white women were beneficiaries of white racism along with white men, and so there was no reason for Third World women to trust them. Further, feminism was a First World movement, and its intrusion in the Third World was an expression of cultural imperialism. From a more Marxist orientation, class or economic hierarchy was said to be the major contradiction that needed to be dealt with, and gender was of secondary importance.[3]

At the end of the conference the women theologians from the Asia, Africa, and Latin America rose together and demanded a Women's Commission within EATWOT that would meet separately in order to allow Third World women to dialogue and develop their own feminist theology in their own contexts. "We have to decide for ourselves what feminist theology means for us," they said. "It is not for First World women to tell us how to do it, nor is it for Third World men to tell us it is not our issue."[4]

This proposal was accepted by the EATWOT leaders, and a four-stage process was planned: national, regional, and intercontinental meetings of Third World feminists. These took place in 1985 and 1986. The papers from these conferences made their way into major publications.[5] These were to be followed by a world consultation that would bring the Third World women theologians into a new stage of dialogue with First World feminist theologians. This was delayed as women in each region began to intensify their own regional organizing for meetings and publications. The world consultation finally took place in December 1994 in Costa Rica, bringing together forty-five women theologians from fourteen countries.[6]

By 1994 some of the definitions of First and Third World were themselves in question. The paradigm of the dialogue expanded somewhat to add Eastern European women, an Arab woman and a delegation of women theologians of both European and indigenous ancestry from the Pacific. The boundaries of the two "worlds" were further complicated by the presence of a white South African and a Japanese feminist theologian, both seen as "First World" within the "Third World." (The term "Third World" for the three regions has been retained in this chapter because the theologians from these areas have not, so far, seen it as necessary to rename themselves[7]).

This process of developing Third World feminist theology led by the Women's Commission of EATWOT is of great importance. Without it, it would have been much more difficult for women theologians of these regions to develop and publish their thought. Thanks to this support, Asian, African, and Latin American women were able to gather regionally and internationally, to organize regional networks of communications, develop a sense of their own identities as women theologians from Asia, Africa, and Latin America, and to receive the stimulation of South-South dialogue.

It should not be supposed that the EATWOT process was the only impetus for the development of Third World feminist theologies. There were already secular feminist movements in many of the countries of these regions by the 1970s. In some countries in Latin America and Asia there had been women's movements at the turn of the century working for women's legal and property rights and access to higher education. In the 1970s a new wave of feminist movements began in Third World countries. As in North America and Western Europe, this "second wave" of feminism has often focused on questions of rape, domestic violence, and reproductive rights. The issues have taken distinct forms in different countries. For example, in India the feminist movement has played the major role in exposing the practices of female feticide (the killing of fetuses), and dowry murders.[8]

The interconnection of the secular feminist movements and the rise of feminist theology among women in the churches has varied regionally. In Asia there was a positive relationship. Aruna Gnanadason, leading India

Christian feminist, emerged from the Indian women's movement, while Filipina Mary John Mananzan, a Benedictine nun, was both the chair of the major secular feminist movement, Gabriela, and founder of the Women's Institute at Saint Scholastica's College, of which she was the president.[9] In Korea the student movement, feminism, and Minjung theology grew up together. Already in 1980 Sun Ai Park founded the all-Asia Christian feminist journal *In God's Image*.

Latin American feminism's militant anticlericalism and focus on sexual and reproductive issues taboo for Catholics kept Catholic feminist theologians leery of ties to these movements in their countries.[10] The secular feminist movement was perceived as middle class, even though feminists often were engaged in services to poor women on issues of violence and reproductive rights. In Latin America in the wake of increasing unemployment and cutbacks in basic food, health, and educational services from the state, popular women's movements arose to create neighborhood kitchens and to serve other survival needs. Women in religious orders were involved in supporting these popular women's projects. Feminists working in the churches in liberation theology often felt more comfortable supporting these popular women's movements than in the circles of secular feminists.

The ecclesial base for doing feminist theology has also varied in the three regions. Protestant women whose churches began to ordain them had a claim to education in their denominational seminaries, but only a few of these seminaries, such as the Seminario Bíblico in Costa Rica and the Lutheran Seminary in São Leopoldo, Brazil, have made themselves centers for feminist theology. Catholic women had less access to seminary theological education. Some Catholic universities, as well as Protestant colleges, however, have developed women's studies or religious studies departments open to feminist theology.[11] Catholic women have also founded their own feminist organizations for grassroots ministry, publications, and conferences, such as Talitha Cumi in Lima, Peru, and the Con-spirando Collective in Santiago, Chile.[12] Women in Catholic religious orders play a role in supporting both these initiatives.[13]

## Feminist Theology in Latin America

In an interview in 1993, Brazilian theologian Ivone Gebara traced the development of feminist theology in Latin America over the previous twenty years.[14] In the 1970s Latin American women, stimulated by the new secular women's movement and the translation of feminist theology from Germany and the United States, began to recognize that "we are oppressed as historical subjects. We discovered our oppression in the Bible, in theology, in our churches." The first phase of response to this discovery was the search for positive female role models in the Bible: prophetesses and matriarchs; Mary, Magdalene, and other women disciples.

The second phase of feminist theology began a "feminization of theological concepts. We began to discover the submerged feminine expressions for God in the Bible. We discovered God's maternal face in texts such as Isaiah 49."[15] There was also an expansion of women's teaching and ministering roles in the churches, as academics, catechists, and leaders of base communities on the grassroots level. Male liberation theologians began to include a few women in their conferences and publications to give the "woman's perspective" (typically confined to topics such as family, anthropology, and Mary, not the "big" topics like the Trinity and Christology).[16]

For Gebara, both of these stages of feminist theology were still "patriarchal feminism," which did not challenge the hierarchical paradigm of humanity, God, and the cosmos, but simply added women to it. Women were thought of as having distinct (even morally superior) moral insights and ways of being compared to men. One needed to add the "feminine dimension" to theology and pastoral life. Gebara sees herself and others engaged in a third and more radical step in feminist theology: not simply adding the women's perspective, but dismantling the basic patriarchal paradigm that has shaped all relations—of humans to each other, to nature, and to God.

These first stages of Latin American feminist theology also were much dominated by the patronage (and limits) of male liberation theologians. More radical gender critiques of society, the church, and theology were muted to stay within the limits of the "woman's voice" that male liberation theologians were willing to hear. But, by 1990, there was a sense that the older liberation theology paradigm was in crisis. The Sandinista defeat in Nicaragua and the fall of

Eastern European communist states gave the sense that all the struggles and sacrifices that had been made by Latin American people for revolutionary change over the past thirty years were for naught. Poverty was worse than ever, while the ability to even imagine an economic order alternative to triumphal global capitalism was being declared impossible.[17]

This sense of crisis of the old hope of socialist revolution and its theological reflection led to a recognition of a need for a new, more inclusive paradigm of liberation that would recognize multiple aspects of oppression and sites of struggle. Critiques from feminists and theologians from other regions of lack of sufficient attention to gender, race, and culture theology were given more attention by male liberation theologians, such as Leonardo Boff and Pablo Richard.[18]

The 1992 observance of the "Five Hundred Years of Resistance," as an alternative to the celebration of "Columbus' discovery of America," gave a forum to the indigenous peoples to voice their experiences of genocidal oppression and cultural suppression during the years since the Spanish "invasion." Afro-Caribbean and Afro-Brazilian peoples also began to gain a voice to tell their story and to denounce the racism of Latin American white and mestizo culture and society. A Latin American black feminist theology has begun to emerge, especially from Afro-Brazilians, such as Silvia Regina Silva.[19] The ecological movement began to be taken more seriously as a Latin American problem, rather than a pseudo-problem imposed by the wealthy nations. In fact, impoverishment of the people and of the land had gone hand in hand in Latin America since the Spanish and Portuguese invasion, although this crisis was now more aggravated by modern industrialism.[20]

Elsa Tamez, a Mexican Protestant biblical scholar and president of the Seminario Bíblico (recently renamed Universidad Bíblica Latinoamericana) in San José, Costa Rica, has taken the question of cultural oppression in relation to the indigenous peoples of the Americas as a central preoccupation. Her quest to vindicate the indigenous voice, not just as victims of social oppression but as a people with a legitimate religious tradition that needs to be heard and integrated into Christian theology, breached the walls between Christian exclusivism and other religions, particularly toward indigenous "pagan" peoples. This exclusivism had been foundational to Christian evangelization of the Americas, as much for Protestants as for Catholics.

Tamez' pamphlet, "Quetzalcóatl y el Dios Cristiano"[21] was based on the theme of "conflict between the gods" that had been explored by theologians such as Pablo Richard.[22] Richard had argued that the "God problem" of contemporary Christianity was not between atheism and belief in God (as liberal Christianity assumed) but between the true God and the idols. The true God is the God of Life, the God of the prophets and of Jesus, who calls us to preferential option for the poor. Idolatry is not primarily a question of "false gods" of other religions, but rather the corruption of biblical faith so that the biblical God is converted into a tool of the rich and powerful to sacralize their wealth and power, to call for submission to this unjust regime of military, economic, and political dominance in the name of submission to "the will of God." Liberation theology must denounce this false God of death and announce the true God of life.

Tamez used this theme to analyze the relationship between the Christianity of the Spanish conquerors and the defeated Aztec and Náhuatl peoples of Mexico. Eschewing any simple dualism between Christianity and the indigenous religion in which one is good and the other bad, even in reversed form, Tamez seeks to show that the God of Life was already known in pre-Aztec Náhuatl religion in the form of Quetzalcóatl, but this figure had been corrupted in later militarized Náhuatl society, culminating with the Aztecs, who imposed their war God, Huitzilopochtli, upon the traditions from the earlier god. Traditions of self-sacrifice in the interests of the well-being of the people were perverted into a violent practice of human sacrifice of war captives.

When the Spanish arrived, justifying their conquest in the name of bringing salvation from the "true God" to the "Indians," they were repelled by these practices of human sacrifice. They used them to reinforce their view of indigenous religion as totally demonic, but they failed to recognize that their own version of Christianity was just as much a perversion of Christianity into a religion of war, violence, and human sacrifice. Tamez draws on sixteenth-century documents to show that the Indians submitted to Christianity out of powerlessness, with full recognition that it spelled "bad news" for themselves. Yet they also were able to glimpse positive elements of the biblical God of life and justice behind the swords of the Spanish, similar to their own faith.[23]

It is time, Tamez believes, for Christians, in turn, to recognize the true religious principles in indigenous religions. A liberating theology must be based on a mutual respect for the liberating elements in both traditions and a struggle against the death-dealing aspects of both traditions, rather than an assumption of essential superiority of Christianity to indigenous religions. In her talk for the 1994 global dialogue of feminist theology in Costa Rica, "Cultural Violence against Women in Latin America,"[24] Tamez lays out a complex analysis of Latin American culture. She says that Latin Americans need to claim all the layers of their traditions as mestizo people of both indigenous and European ancestry. This does not mean romanticizing indigenous cultures as totally egalitarian toward women against Spanish patriarchy, or seeing Latin Americans as innocent victims vis-à-vis northern aggression. Rather there must be a frank appraisal of the themes that mandated violence against women in the indigenous cultures. These were overlaid by Spanish patterns that were violent toward their own women, and doubly so toward indigenous women victims of triple oppression of impoverishment and racial and sexual contempt.

Tamez wants to develop a Latin American feminist hermeneutic of culture that can differentiate what is oppressive and what is liberating in both indigenous and Christian cultures. She also calls for a relation to feminists of the north that must be based on mutual respect for each other's differences of culture. Only on this basis can there be alliances between feminists internationally to fight against the violence of oppressive foreign cultures coming from the powerful nations. Latin American Christians need to develop a nondiscriminatory discourse that honors true elements in other religions, and to work toward egalitarian relations between men and women in their own churches and societies.

While Elsa Tamez has focused on cultural critique, Mexican theologian María Pilar Aquino has sought a more expanded analysis of economic injustice. She analyzes gender oppression in the context of the multidimensional aspects of racial, class, cultural, and ecological violence wrought by neoliberal global economy, as the framework for her feminist liberation theology. In her 1992 book, *Nuestro Clamor por la Vida (Our Cry for Life)*,[25] Aquino sought to sketch the foundations for a Latin American feminist theology. In this book she uses liberation theology methodology as foundational, deepening it by situating Latin American women's oppression and praxis of liberation as its central optic.

For Aquino, an adequate shaping of a Latin American praxis of liberation must be situated in a comprehensive analysis of the historical, ideological, and socioeconomic forces that have determined woman's oppression. This means reclaiming the many layers of Latin American women's history: indigenous women's spirituality, their subjugation, but also resistance to Spanish colonialism; the shaping of divisions between women, indigenous, black, mestizo, and white, but also breaking across these divisions in praxes of solidarity. It also means overcoming the split of public and private of modern ideology that falsely naturalizes women's oppression in the household and informal economies and fails to recognize these patterns of women's work as an integral part of the total system of socioeconomic exploitation.

Oppression is cultural as well as social. Feminist liberation theologians must analyze the logocentric modes of discourse that silence women's voice and experience. They should shape a new mode of "sentient intelligence" to allow women to articulate their resistance to oppression and their hope for well-being. Ideological critique includes critique of the androcentrism of the Bible and theology. Women must uncover the oppressive content of biblical stories and theological symbols and shape alternative readings of Scripture.

For Aquino the possibility for this lies in Jesus' liberating praxis for all, women equally with men. Jesus' announcement of "good news to the poor" points to God's re-creative "liberating purpose for creation, history, the world and humanity."[26] Redemption is an ongoing praxis to realize this fullness of life, overcoming all oppressive hierarchies. Latin American feminism is about reading this critique and hope from the optic of the multiple dimensions of oppression of Latin American women. At the end of her book, Aquino sketches unfinished tasks to deepen this work of reflection on liberating praxis for Latin American women: less dependency on male liberation theologians, more critical feminist theory and social analysis, deepening critique of the patriarchal elements of the Bible, closer collaboration with the Latin American feminist movements, more interclass and race collaboration, more reclaiming of indigenous spirituality and Latin American women's history.[27]

In her most recent writings Aquino has done more work "across the border" in the circles developing a North American Hispanic theology.[28] She has also been concerned to develop a fuller critique of the neoliberal global market economy, with its privileging of an economic elite, mostly white and male, and its deepening poverty for all others, female, black or brown, Third World, and the earth itself. In her 1996 essay "Economic Violence in Latin

American Perspective" she shows that this neoliberal market economy that claims to have triumphed as the only possible economy and way of life, in the wake of the fall of socialist alternatives, is not only creating poverty and violence for most humans outside this elite, but also rests on an idolatrous claim to universal truth and normative ethics for human fulfillment.[29]

For neoliberal ideology the competitive individual seeking to maximize "his" profits and consumer reach is the only model of human activity and fulfillment. The market is good, just, and "democratic" because it automatically rewards all who adopt this way of life, but it also punishes all those who stand outside it. The false claim of neoliberalism is that *all* can win in this system, concealing the obvious reality that the system works by only a small minority winning at the expense of all others. By refusing to admit this, it conceals its true elitist (racist, sexist, classist) face, and makes poverty the individual failings of the poor for which they alone are responsible.

Aquino calls for a feminist liberation theology in which women (and men) from Latin America would join hands with those from other areas of South and North to critique this system and expose its true face of violence for most humans and to the earth. This critique must also entail creating an alternative universalism, not based on the false universalizing of the power claims of one elite group, but on the aspirations of all humans within Planet Earth to shared life and well-being.

This means dismantling the claims of neoliberalism to be the only possible economy, showing that it is in fact ultimately impossible and destructive for all, for the system that presently impoverishes almost all must itself end in general destruction. Revolt against its false claims to promote prosperous democratic societies must re-create a new imagination about what could be a livable future that would be inclusive of all living beings on earth. A feminist liberation theology speaks on behalf of this alternative livable future, against the false system that points to general death.

While Elsa Tamez breaks across the Christian-indigenous cultural division to shape a new liberating theology of life, and Aquino seeks a broader and deeper analysis of the multilayered system of oppression as the context for inclusive liberating praxis, Brazilian theologian Ivone Gebara has focused in her recent writings on dismantling the patriarchal cosmovision of dualistic hierarchy that sustains ideologies and social systems of domination of some

(Christian white male ruling-class humans) over others (non-Christians, non-whites, women, the poor, and the earth).

Gebara too sees all theology, including feminist theologies, as arising in distinct contexts and needing to own those contexts, speaking both within and outside of their particularity, and yet also seeking to point from that context to what interconnects us all—as humans, as earth creatures, as parts of the cosmos. She speaks as a privileged Brazilian woman (white, middle class, educated) but one who has chosen to identify with the poorest black and indigenous Brazilians of the northeast of her country both as an option for the poor and as the context from which the oppressive system can be more truthfully discerned from its underside.[30]

The northeast of Brazil where Gebara has chosen to live and work is a region of violent contrasts of wealth and poverty that have been shaped by colonialism and capitalism; a few with great power, the majority powerless; a few with vast landholding and most landless. As a context for doing theology it does not afford monastic or ivory-tower solitude and quiet that has been the traditional Christian place for cultivating spirituality and theological reflection. Rather, it is a place of noise and garbage. The noise is both the noise pollution of a dysfunctional modern industrialism and the noisy responses of the poor who live in this world. Garbage is the waste discarded disproportionately by the wealthy; they scarcely let it touch their own pristine precincts, but this is the garbage in which the poor must live. To live one's spirituality, to do one's theology, in the midst of such noise and garbage is to do them in the midst of oppression, but also with consciousness of the vitality of the poor who somehow manage to survive and even celebrate in it and despite of it.[31]

For Gebara women are coming to theological voice at a unique time, when history is irrupting in their lives and they are becoming aware of becoming historical agents. It is also a time when the historical systems of domination built by humans over millennia, and their religious ratifications, are coming apart and revealing themselves as unviable. Women theologians must dare to see through the successive layers of distortion that justify this dominant system in our theology and to reflect on our inherited symbols from the context of our real questions, the questions of defense of life in the midst of violence. They must overcome their timidity in approaching these monumental theological constructs that claim such authority and respect and to ask the questions of daily life, shaping new ways of speaking, even if they are halting and less than systematic.

For Gebara this daring to ask questions in the face of great systems of authority begins with a deconstruction of theology, revealing its reality as anthropology. We must constantly reclaim our own theological projections and recognize that all theology, including the Bible, is a human cultural construct. Christian theology, the Christian Scriptures, are one such construct[32] among others. There is no God "out there" revealing "His Nature" and "His Plan" to us. It is we ourselves, the thinking part of the cosmos, who are thinking, imagining, and constructing systems of interpretation. Christian theology must be done ecumenically in relation to the many other human religions, recognizing ours as one human construct among others. We must deconstruct our traditions to see how our ways of structuring our stories validate violent power of some over others, and we must find ways to retell them that can be mutually life-giving.

Gebara has particularly focused on the symbol of God as Trinity in her work of deconstruction and reconstruction.[33] For Gebara, the Trinity is not a distant separate God living someplace else, controlling creation from outside. Rather, the Trinity is a symbolic expression of the basic dynamic of life itself as a process of vital interrelational creativity. Life as interrelational creativity exists on every level of reality. As cosmos it reveals the whole process of cosmic unfolding and interrelation of planets and galaxies. As earth it shows us the dynamic interrelational process of life unfolding in the biosphere.

Each species ramifies into many differences, including human beings with their many races and cultures. We must celebrate this diversity of human plurality of races and cultures, and affirm their interrelation with one another in one human community on earth. Likewise, interpersonal society and finally the person herself exists as a dynamic of plurality, interdependency, and creativity, of unity and diversity in interaction. While she sees this dynamic of life in vital interrelationality as the real meaning of the Trinity, for Gebara this also raises the question of the origin and reproduction of evil.

For Gebara, the reality of the life process is by its very nature fragile, limited, and threatened, reproducing itself in a dynamic of pain and joy, birth and death and birth again.[34] In this sense evil (tragedy) is a natural part of life and inseparable from it. But humans are threatened by this fragility, this relation of life and death, diversity and connection. There is a constant urge to secure life permanently against death, to secure power as control to ward off vulnerability, to ward off difference by subjugating the "other" to our uniformity. Women, other races, other cultures, and the earth itself have all been victims of this urge to control and secure life, to assert power and uniformity against death, vulnerability, and difference. Women have been victimized especially because they represent the vulnerability of the life process, its threatening power and otherness to men.

Out of this urge to control and secure life and power, powerful groups of people, particularly males of those groups, have arisen to shape systems of domination attempting to secure a monopoly of power over life for themselves and they have reduced women, other races, and the earth to subjugation, thereby distorting the dynamic of interrelation into extreme imbalances of power and powerlessness, dominance and violation, wealth and poverty.[35] We live at a time when this system of distortion has reached its nadir, threatening to destroy the whole planetary life system. These systems of unbalanced power are what evil means in the second sense of sin—of unnatural evil, unnecessary and finally destructive evil, the evil that humans have constructed but which humans cannot and should not accept. Humans can and must seek to overcome this evil, both for justice and for the defense of life itself.

For Gebara, religion plays an ambivalent role in this construction of a system of sin, or unnatural evil. Most religions have been a projection of this urge for control and domination by the powerful. We create a powerful, patriarchal, invulnerable God who reflects the desire of men for control of life without death. The powerless, in turn, imagine countermyths of great Messiahs who will defeat the evildoers by violence and bring in a permanent state of bliss without death. Messianic countermyths, including much of the hopes of liberation generated by liberation theology, tend simply to reproduce the system of violence.

The Jews produced Messianic hopes to counteract the oppression they suffered at the hands of great empires, but they did so in a way that assumed counterviolence. For Gebara, however, Jesus was a very different prophetic figure. Far from reproducing the cycle of violence, he sought to break through it. Taking the side of the victims of oppression, he also called us to a new community of mutual service. The dominant system could not tolerate his message and killed him to silence it. But his followers also betrayed him by turning his new vision of shared love into a new warrior, imperial Savior who would secure the new Christian system of dominating power.[36]

For Gebara, a feminist theology must not project either a paradise of the beginning or a paradise of the future that reproduces the flight from finitude and difference. Rather, we need to withdraw all these projections and seek to dismantle the systems of violence and domination—not to create a future paradise secured from pain, limits, vulnerability, and death, but to learn to share with one another our fragile goods, our vulnerable joys and sorrows in a way that is truly mutual. We need to overcome domination and exploitation of each other in order to learn to embrace each other and celebrate our joys in the midst of sorrows, birth in the midst of pain, and the resurgence of life in the midst of death.

We must, as Gebara puts it, "take the side of the serpent" (of the Genesis story), refusing the orders of the patriarchal God that keep us in a state of childish dependency.[37] We can then recognize that the fragile fruit of the tree of life is indeed lovely and good for discernment, and eat the fruit with relish, making it a part of our bodies. This is the possible redemption of life on earth. But it is possible only when we put aside the impossible redemptions of final conquest of limits in a realm of immortal life untouched by sorrow, vulnerability, and finitude.

## African Feminist Theology

The Circle of Concerned African Women Theologians, which emerged in the late 1980s has become the major vehicle for the exchange and development of African Christian women's theological work.[38] The context in which these African women do their work is that of postcolonial (now post-apartheid) Africa, yet an Africa still very much shaped by the colonial experience and ongoing neo-colonial relations with the Western world.

Like Latin America, sub-Saharan Africa was Christianized as an integral part of European colonialism, but this took place in the mid- to late nineteenth century rather than five hundred years ago. The African populations still retain their historical indigenous languages and cultures, even if their relation to these cultures is disoriented through Western Christianizing. Thus the question of the relation between Christianity and indigenous culture is a central one for

African Christian theology, while this issue emerged late and is still marginal for Latin Americans.

Although North Africa shaped the earliest Christian theology of the first centuries, Islam superseded Christianity in North Africa in the seventh century, and only pockets of ancient African Christianity continue in the Coptic tradition from Egypt to Ethiopia and the southern Sudan.[39] Catholic missionaries arrived in the sixteenth century, but they had little impact on the interior of Africa until the mid-nineteenth century. At that time Catholic and Protestant missionaries flooded Africa, closely connected with the colonizing nations.

In 1880 the European nations partitioned Africa among themselves, the British taking much of East Africa from Egypt to the Cape, as well as Ghana and Nigeria in West Africa, while the French carved out most of West Africa. The Belgians took the huge center of the Congo, and the Portuguese and Germans occupied large areas in the east and west of southern Africa. The Italians, who held Libya, made a short-lived grab for Ethiopia in 1936. The European partitioning of Africa drew the borders of modern African states, and Europeans brought the languages and cultures that shaped the colonial institutions of church, education, and government.

Although some European missionaries belatedly began to appreciate African culture, the primary impact of missionary education was to treat Africans as people with a totally worthless and evil culture that had to be expunged in order for the people to be Christianized and incorporated into the culture of the colonizers. This negative view of African culture was mingled with racism toward the African person. European cultural colonialism of Africans moved ambiguously between "uplift" to become like Europeans and proletarianization to be made into workers in mines and plantations, with the assumption that higher professions were beyond the Africans' capabilities.

African women received a double version of these negative views, shaped by a combined European racism and sexism. The African woman was seen as highly sexed and needing to be "tamed," while at the same time she was viewed as oppressed by working in the fields or by practices such as polygamy and clitoridectomy, and needing to be protected. For European missionaries this double view meant that the African woman needed to be domesticated: washed, clothed in garments that concealed her body, trained to work in the kitchen and become a housemaid in the European manner.[40] But the higher education extended to an African male elite was usually assumed to be beyond African woman's reach.

Europeans not only divided Africa, politically and culturally, but also reshaped its internal society and economy by taking the best land for themselves for export agribusiness, either marginalizing African farmers on poor land or incorporating them into these farms as low-paid labor. African families were often broken up as women became maids in white households, while men became workers in fields and mines. The old, the young, and the sick often were sent to marginal zones reserved for Africans.[41] This distortion of the African socioeconomic structure remains to a large extent today, creating extremes of wealth and poverty and skewing development in the neocolonial era.

Missionary churches were slow to hand over control of their structures to Africans and even slower to make higher theological education and ordination available to African women, even when this was happening in their home churches in Europe or America. At the end of the nineteenth century, breakaway movements occurred in which African men shaped independent churches under their own leadership, drawing on the polity and liturgical tradition of the denominations from which they had come. There was no change in the patriarchal leadership patterns in these churches. These churches often took the name "Ethiopian" in order to claim a relation to the ancient African or Coptic Christianity that remains today in Ethiopia.[42]

In the 1920s and continuing until today a more radical movement of African independent churches has grown, often referred to as Spirit, Prophet, or Aladura (praying) churches. These churches draw on the religious patterns of healing, spirit-possession, and prophecy of the African traditional religions, as well as its cultural styles of music, dress, and organization, although often understanding themselves as transcending the power of the "evil" spirits of African religions by being filled with the "Holy Spirit" that comes from the "true God" of Christianity.[43]

Women generally have larger roles in these Spirit or Prophet churches than in either mission or Ethiopian churches, and some of these churches have been founded and led by women. These churches, however, are far from egalitarian in gender roles. Women, while playing roles in ministry, are usually not in the top leadership and administration, but are located on the lower levels of the church hierarchy in those roles having to do with charismatic gifts to discern the causes and heal the spiritual and physical maladies that afflict those who come to them for help, a role similar to the traditional shaman/healers in African culture.[44]

These Spirit churches, which arise mostly from poorer and urbanized sectors of society, primarily provide spiritual and physical means of survival, rebuilding community and identity for those uprooted and disoriented in the new Africa. They have generally not been leaders in movements of liberation, in the sense of transforming social structures.[45] Since some of these churches also carry on African customs, such as polygamy and pollution taboos, their usefulness for African feminist theology is ambivalent, although they are highly significant as examples of a new "folk" amalgamation of Christianity and African tradition.[46]

From 1958 to 1965 the French, British and Belgians departed from their colonies in Africa, while seeking to put in power African male elites who would be amenable to European neo-colonial control over the resources of the area. Some Europeans, particularly where there was a significant settler population, hung on to power, forcing prolonged wars of liberation in countries such as Zimbabwe, followed by destructive civil wars in the cases of the former Portuguese territories of Mozambique and Angola.[47]

South Africa, with the largest and most entrenched white settler population, is a special case. There the whites attempted the rigid system of separate development for whites and blacks known as apartheid. Only a prolonged struggle, led by the African National Congress for over eighty years, succeeded finally in dismantling the legal and political expressions of apartheid in the 1990s. But the legacy of this racist system lives on in screwed land tenure and the gap between a wealthy white elite, who own most of the resources, and the impoverished African majority (despite an emerging African middle class).

In the postcolonial period in Africa since the 1960s two major expressions of African Christian theology have emerged: African theology and black theology. African theology was founded by religious anthropologists, such as John Mbiti[48] and E. Bojaji Idowu,[49] under the rubrics of "indigenization" or "inculturation" of Christian theology into African culture. These scholars did careful research to reclaim distinctive African religious-cultural worldviews exemplified in distinct cultural groups. They sought to rescue these cultures from the heritage of vilification by Western missionaries and show that they contained coherent and positive spiritual values, in many cases strikingly similar to those found in the Bible (the Hebrew Scriptures particularly). Once these cultures were accorded their due respect, it would be possible for Africans to shape an integral inculturation of Christian theological themes into the African cultural worldview and traditional ritual practices.[50]

Black theology was developed in South Africa during the heat of the anti-apartheid struggle, sparked by the Black Consciousness movement of the 1970s, as well as the influence of black theology in the United States. This theological movement understood itself as calling for liberation, not inculturation. Liberation meant throwing off the racist system of apartheid and creating a nonracial, just democratic society in South Africa. Black Christian leaders, such as Allan Boesak, Desmond Tutu, and Itumeleng Mosala, were leaders of the black theology movement.[51]

As leaders of these two movements met in international gatherings, each criticized what they saw as the limitations of the other. Black theologians attacked African theology for viewing African culture as a static heritage of the past into which Christianity was to be incorporated, without recognition of the ongoing changes of this culture and the need for liberating transformation of injust cultural and social patterns, both from African society and from Western colonialism.[52] Some African theologians, particularly John Mbiti, attacked black theology as an American import inappropriate in Africa.[53] Neither group paid much attention to women or gender injustice.[54]

Among a new generation of African theologians, including women theologians, this dispute is being resolved by a recognition that both inculturation and liberation are necessary.[55] There is a need to incarnate Christian theology into African culture, and to transform that culture to overcome oppressive aspects, while moving to a new cultural and sociopolitical liberative future freed from the heritage of racism, poverty, and gender inequity inherited by African societies across their history. Africans cannot afford to split this agenda into segregated and warring pieces, but need to create an African liberation theology that can embrace all of its aspects, even if some thinkers may choose to concentrate on cultural and others on socioeconomic issues.

African feminist theologians are very much at the heart of this new union of theologies of inculturation and liberation, seeking to look at both aspects through the focus on African women's oppression and liberation. A significant and growing community of African women theologians is emerging, led by Ghanaian theologian and church leader Mercy Amba Oduyoye, together with many sisters, such as Rosemary Edet, Daisy Nwachuku, Teresa Okure, R. Modupe Owanikin, and Bette Ekeya (Nigeria); Anne Nasimuyu-Waskike, Musimbi Kanyoro, Judith Mbula Bahemuka, and Teresia Hinga (Kenya), Isabel Phiri and Anne Nachisale Musopole (Malawi); Elizabeth Amoah (Ghana); Bernadette Mbuy Beya (Zaire); among others.[56]

These African women theologians and sociologists cross denominational lines. They are Catholics and mainline Protestants for the most part, and belong to a new educated professional class. Most have gotten their doctoral degrees in Europe or the United States, but find their major base for work in Africa in religious studies departments of universities, rather than as ministers in the churches or faculties of seminaries that train those going into ordained ministry. Secular modern Africa, represented by university departments, seems to be more open to what they are doing than the institutions of the churches in Africa, although the international church supports their work. Mercy Oduyoye has been Deputy General Secretary of the World Council of Churches, while Musimbi Kanyoro has been Executive Secretary for Women in Church and Society of the Lutheran World Federation, also based in Geneva.

In two major books, *The Will to Arise: Women, Tradition and the Church in Africa*, edited by Mercy Oduyoye and Musimbi Kanyoro, and Oduyoye's book, *Daughters of Anowa: African Women and Patriarchy*,[57] as well as numerous articles in journals and symposia, these women are shaping their critique of culture and Christianity and their vision of gender liberation and equity in an African context. This work of cultural critique has only begun. Much more investigation into the many cultures of Africa, from women's perspective, is needed. Women's reconstruction of theological symbols, as well as religio-cultural practices, is still largely in the future.

African feminist liberation theologians claim the sovereign right to evaluate all the cultural patterns they have received—from traditional African cultures, from Christianity, and from Western secularism—in terms of how they promote or impede women's development.[58] They further claim the right to be the primary arbiters of what promotes or impedes women's development. It is not for African men to tell them that all African culture is sacrosanct and to critique any of it is to be a traitor to African tradition, nor is it for Western men or women to judge these cultures from outside.

Only African women can determine what cultural patterns have debilitated them and which ones have been life-enhancing for them. If the goal is to be enhanced mutuality for African women and men together, African men must be willing to listen and learn from African women, rather than to dictate on these matters. This doesn't mean that all African women will agree on what is good or bad about practices such as polygamy, menstrual taboos, and the like. But the conversation must begin by granting primacy to African women's judgment, based on their experiences as African women in their distinct contexts.

African women theologians find much that is debilitating to them as women in traditional African cultural practices. Many of these practices are shaped by an underlying assumption that women are both powerful and dangerous, so their lives must be severely restricted and shaped to be servants of African men in all aspects of work, sexuality, reproduction, and family life, not independent persons in their own right. The impact of the pervasive African belief in evil spirits, acting through witches who cause all misfortunes, falls predominantly on women. African women often find themselves blamed and subjected to hostile mental and physical treatment based on the assumptions that misfortunes that affect others in the community, including their relatives, husbands and children, are due to their evil thoughts or practices.[59]

For example, when a woman is pregnant, there is general rejoicing and rituals of support, since it is in giving birth that the African woman is seen as fulfilling her primary function. But if the birth process goes badly, it may be assumed that she has done something wrong to cause this. She may be interrogated as to whether she has been unfaithful, on the assumption that this is causing her difficulties.[60]

Traditional widowhood rituals have been particularly negative for African women. The underlying assumption is that the widow is somehow responsible for her husband's death and must exculpate herself. In some Nigerian societies the widow is confined to her house for a long period, while being subjected to hostile treatment by her husband's relatives. She must loosen her hair, wear an old, dirty dress, refrain from washing, eat little, and cry out aloud three times a day. Her children may be taken from her but neglected, and she is not allowed to care for them. After this prolonged mourning that exacerbates the mental and physical pains of her widowhood, she often faces penury, since she is allowed no inheritance from her husband.[61]

African women theologians are not the only African women taking in hand these negative customs toward women. National Councils for Women's Development have been established by many African governments. In Ghana the International Federation of Women Lawyers have been active in promoting new legislation that curtails these widowhood rituals and provides for inheritance for the wife.[62] But it is the task of women theologians to investigate the underlying religious views that support negative customs and to ask how these might be transformed by a worldview that is more life-enhancing for women in partnership with men.

Women theologians are also reclaiming African traditions that are empowering for women. These include stories of female life-promoting and protecting deities and of powerful women ancestresses and leaders of the community. They include patterns of binary leadership of women and men, and traditions of women's prophetic and healing powers, often emphasized in Spirit Churches. They also include the positive roles of women as mothers, economic producers, farmers, creators of market associations and women's cooperatives by which African women have provided the means of life for their families, although these traditions need to be freed from exploitation that gives the African woman twice as much work as the man, but no decision-making power.[63]

Christianity, together with Western colonialism, has often claimed to have liberated African women oppressed by traditional African culture, but African women are rejecting this claim. For the most part colonial powers removed African women from political and economic roles they had earlier enjoyed, to shape more patriarchal as well as racist societies. The Christian churches mostly operated to sacralize this more patriarchal pattern brought by the West, claiming that this reflected biblical teaching and the will of God.[64]

The Bible thus became an additional authority to justify blood taboos and the removal of women from social and religious leadership. The churches also repressed sexual initiation practices that gave women some control over their sexuality and childbearing and made them more vulnerable in their sexual and reproductive functions.[65] Finally, it justified passive acceptance of suffering by reference to shouldering the cross of Christ.[66]

While African Christian women theologians are vehemently questioning these ways Christianity reinforced and worsened patriarchy, they nevertheless draw their primary mandate for social change from Christian theology. The beliefs that women as much as men are created in the image of God and therefore are of equal worth;[67] that Jesus came to liberate all, with particular concern for those most oppressed; these are continually cited as mandates for criticizing both African and Christian forms of patriarchy. Christ is set in tension with Christianity and aligned with the struggle and hope for African women's liberation.[68]

The God who speaks through Christ is one who calls Africans to create societies of justice and well-being for all, overcoming cultural and social patterns that mandate white or male domination at the expense of African women. The faith of African women that Christ is on their side against all forms of oppression that have come to them from African traditional culture, the church, and the West seems unshakable. But the Christ reference can be fluid, embracing the story of the historical Jesus and stories of African women's suffering and salvific risk on behalf of their communities.[69] Thus the relation of Christ to the redemption of African society from sexism and all injustice is open-ended, pointing forward to expanding future hopes, rather than confined to fixed African or Christian pasts.

## Asian Feminist Theologies

Summarizing feminist theologies from such large and complex regions as Latin America and Africa is challenging enough, but to attempt to do so for Asia borders on the absurd. The very concept of Asia as a region is a Western cultural construct that lumps together a vast area containing seven major linguistic zones and more than half of the world's population.[70] If the Middle East is included, all world religions originated in this region. The rich religious patrimony of Asia includes Hinduism, Buddhism, Taoism, Confucianism, Islam, Sikhism, Jainism, Judaism, Christianity, and many local forms of animism.

Yet despite extensive missionary efforts, Christianity remains a minority religion of 2.5 percent of Asians. Only in the Philippines is it the majority religion, followed by South Korea, where a substantial minority are Christians.[71]

Christian Asians are acutely aware that they are rooted in several religious identities. Thus the question of religious plurality necessarily plays a central role for Asian Christian theology.

Economic contrasts are startling in Asia, where 42 percent of the population remains under communist regimes, while Japan sets the pace for an aggressive Asian capitalism. Grinding urban and rural poverty in areas such as India and Bangladesh contrasts with glittering citadels of modern industrial wealth in cities such as Hong Kong. While large areas of Asia suffered under European colonialism, China and Japan fought off colonial inroads and recall their own histories of imperial hegemony.

Asian women have been organizing inter-Asian consultations on feminist theology since the early 1980s. In December 1990, Christian feminists came together from seven regions to discuss their hermeneutical principles for feminist theology in their distinct contexts. I will discuss key aspects of three of these papers from countries where major networks of feminist theology have emerged: the Philippines, India, and Korea.[72]

Feminist theologians from these three countries are acutely aware of developing their thought in the context of many interrelationships. One of these is their double relationship to the male liberation theologians of their nations and to Western feminist theologians. As feminist liberation theologians they bring the gender issues to the liberation theologies of their nations. The Filipino women developed their thought and practice in the context of the Filipino theology of struggle forged under the oppression of the Marcos regime.[73] The Korean women situate themselves within Minjung theology shaped through the struggle against Korean military dictatorships in the 1970s and 80s.[74] Indian women look to male theologians who have focused on the enculturation of Christianity in a Hindu or Buddhist worldview, together with questions of social justice.[75]

But these male theologians largely ignored the gender issue in doing theology and sociocultural analysis and tended to view it as unimportant when women brought it up. Asian feminist theologians thus must take up the question of gender against the resistance of their male colleagues. In so doing, they have profited from reading the feminist theologies emerging from the United States and Western Europe. But these women theologians speak from a Western middle-class context. However indebted to them, Asian feminists must do their own contextualizations of gender questions in very different social and cultural worlds.

Feminist theologians from Asia also bring into dialogue a Christian, mostly Western, heritage with their Asian religions and cultures. Here they, like Africans and Latin Americans, are deeply aware of contradictory messages from their traditions. For Indian women Hinduism with its caste system and purity taboos has been deeply oppressive. Patriarchal oppression of Indian women has often been accentuated by Christianity, despite its contributions to the protest against customs such as child-brides and widow-burning. Yet Indian women also want to claim a positive feminist tradition from their indigenous culture, often looking back to the pre-Aryan goddesses and to female symbols such as Shakti (female-identified cosmic life power) as resources.[76]

Korean women likewise recount a history of patriarchal oppression especially by the Confucian system, but they claim a feminist spiritual tradition from ancient pre-Confucian Shamanism.[77] Christianity also comes to them with a double face, reinforcing Korean male domination with biblical patriarchy, yet conveying to them ideas of democracy and a liberator Jesus who sides with the Minjung (oppressed masses). Filipino women speak of two stages of patriarchalization brought by Christian Western power: first by the Spanish, who ruled for four hundred years, and then by American colonialism and neocolonialism that shaped the twentieth-century Philippines. They claim women-centered or androgynous creation stories, goddesses, and priestesses from precolonial times, as positive cultural resources by which to critique an oppressive Christianity, but also to lift up its liberating potential.

These Asian women theologians are aware of the cultural and social plurality with which they work within their own countries. Indian women can only be ambivalent toward a male Christian theology that sought to enculturate itself in Hindu spirituality, ignoring its oppressive aspects for women. They see their feminist critique as standing in solidarity with the struggles of untouchable peoples (Dalits), who likewise have been oppressed by Hindu casteism.[78] Similarly Filipino feminists reach across cultural divisions in their lands to support the struggles of tribal groups to retain their own languages and cultures.

All three groups of Asian feminist theologians do their reflection in the context of similar patterns of violence and oppression of women in their own patriarchal cultures, reinforced by Christianity and Western colonialism. Rape, wife battering, incest, sex tourism, poverty, and exploitative conditions of low-paid labor are shared horrors suffered by women across these regions. But there are issues particular to the cultures and histories of each country.

Indian women have focused on forms of violence particular to their region: suttee or widow-burning, dowry deaths (the burning of wives in order to seek a new bride and dowry for the husband's family), and female feticide.[79] Korean feminists have made the struggle for reunification of North and South Korea a particular concern.[80] They have also made the rights of comfort women (Asian [mostly Korean] women enslaved by the Japanese as prostitutes for the military during the Second World War) to compensation from the Japanese government a focus of struggle. For Korean feminists the experience of the comfort women has become a "root story,"[81] representing their oppression through the centuries and today. For Filipinas a major issue has been the large number of women of their country forced by poverty into immigrant labor, often virtually enslaved as prostitutes or maids in wealthy Asian countries such as Japan and Hong Kong.[82]

Asian feminist theologies move from analysis of these similar or distinct cultural and social oppressions suffered by women to a vision of liberating hope. Here each group of Asian women seeks to find a dynamic synthesis between the woman-empowering traditions of their indigenous heritages and liberating themes in Christianity. When seeking biblical models, the midwives who begin the process of exodus from bondage in Egypt, Hebrew prophetesses, and a Jesus who sides with the poor—particularly poor and despised women—figure as touchstones.

The Filipina theologians see themselves as making a feminist contextualization of the principles already enunciated by their national theology of struggle. This consists of a three-stage process: critical analysis of social reality, faith-based reflection on this reality, and commitment to liberating praxis, all done from the perspective of the poor,[83] specifically women of the Filipino poor. They lift up seven tasks for the future development of their feminist theology.

These tasks are: (1) an Asian cosmology that is holistic, integrating spirit and body; (2) an anthropology of mutuality of men and women, overcoming splits of mind and body, individual and society; (3) a Christology that emphasizes Jesus' humanness, not his maleness, and puts the cross in the context of the cost of discipleship to bring in God's reign (not the exaltation of passive suffering); (4) a Mariology that lifts up Mary as disciple rather than emphasizing her virginal motherhood; (5) a moral theology that focuses on the struggle against social and environmental sin rather than a sex-obsessed individualism; (6) a spirituality that integrates historical liberation and ecological wholeness; and (7) a gender-inclusive renewal of liturgy and language that draws on life-giving symbols and stories from indigenous traditions, as well as from Christianity.[84]

I will discuss three key aspects of this emerging Asian feminist theology: Christology, ecofeminism, and Korean women's Minjung theology. Christology is a major problem for a theology related to Asian spirituality. The major Asian religions, such as Hinduism and Buddhism, do not have a substantial God outside of the cosmos, but see cosmology as a dynamic process of phenomenal co-arising from a nonsubstantial void. Thus the very notion of a absolute Being outside of the cosmos who sends his son to become incarnate in a substantial body is problematic.[85] The Jesus story is repugnant to many Asians. One who died horribly on the cross strikes many Asians as one suffering from bad karma,[86] while Confucians might regard a person who counsels denial of family and state as lacking in filial piety.[87]

But it is the Christian claim of universal, exclusive truth that is most unacceptable for Asians. Jesus might be incorporated into their traditions as a holy man—a bodhisattva who realizes inner calm by seeing through the phenomenology of suffering to its inner nothingness but as only one exemplar among others of this redemptive state.[88] This traditional Asian soteriology is based on withdrawal from, not struggle to change, oppressive conditions that cause suffering. It is a spirituality of monks that promotes passive acceptance for those who suffer most from bad social conditions: women, untouchables, the poor.

A different Christology is arising in Asia among these marginalized peoples: Dalits in India, the Minjung in Korea, and women, who question traditional Asian spiritualities. Many of these can identify with a Christ who suffered and was broken in the struggle against injustice.[89] Asian feminist Christology arises out of this identification with the oppressed of Asia, especially oppressed women. Jesus is for them the one who took their side, who reached out to heal them from their broken condition. This Jesus reveals a God who does not justify injustice but opposes it and points to a new society where unjust suffering is overcome.

Asian Christian feminists live this Christology, not by trying to make other Asian Christians, but by joining with the poor, especially women, in a common struggle for life. Jesus is for them not *the* savior, but *a* savior, one pointer among others to a new future beyond poverty and violence. Although they choose to maintain a relation to Christ as revelatory for them of this new humanity of justice and love, Asian Christian feminists do not universalize him as the only savior. Rather they contextualize his story as a particular model of struggle and hope for just and loving community embodied for them here and now in Asian women who struggle to defend life against unjust suffering.[90]

Ecofeminism is another important theme for Asian feminists. The need to interconnect impoverishment of women and destruction of the earth appeared already in the early 1980s in Asian feminist thought and has been closely connected with the reclaiming of an Asian cosmovision that does not split the individual from the community or the community from the cosmos but roots the human community in a holistic cosmology. Indian ecofeminist Vandana Shiva, with her now classic book, *Staying Alive: Women, Ecology and Development,* has taken the lead in developing an Asian social ecofeminism.[91]

Shiva, who is Hindu in background and trained as a scientist, has focused particularly on the critique of the worldview of Western science, based on fragmentation, dualism and hierarchy. This worldview continued in secular form the hierarchical dualisms of Western Christian cosmology that located matter, women, and nonwhite people at the bottom of its system of domination and control. She sees this same patriarchal mind-set translated into Western colonialism, including its modern projects of technological development. Western agribusiness projects, such as the Green Revolution, have created a sector of wealthy farms in India at the expense of polluted soil and depleted water resources, and have marginalized women's role in agriculture. Shiva calls for a renewal of traditional forms of agriculture where women were the recyclers in the relations of forest, animals, and soil.

Shiva claims the Hindu concept of Shakti as a female-identified principle of cosmic life that interconnects humans, male and female, with nature and the cosmos, as the basis for a cosmovision alternative to that brought by

Western patriarchy. This theme of Shakti has also been taken up as central to women's empowerment in Indian feminist theology, as we saw above. Indian Christian feminist church leader Aruna Gnanadason has taken over the critique of Western patriarchal science and neocolonial development projects. She too sees the Shakti principle as key for an Indian ecofeminism and has sought to connect it with biblical stories of women as defenders of life:

> Nature, both animate and inanimate, is thus an expression of Shakti, the feminine and creative principle of the cosmos; in conjunction with the masculine principle, *Purusha, Prakriti*, creates the world. *Prakriti* is worshipped as *Aditi*, the primordial vastness, the inexhaustible, the source of abundance. She is worshipped as Adi Shakti, the primordial power. All forms of nature and life in nature are the forms, the children of the Mother of Nature who is nature itself born of creative play of her thought.[92]

Indian scholar Rita Shema has criticized these appropriations of Shakti for ecofeminism by Vandana Shiva and her followers. Shema too seeks a cosmological basis for an Indian ecofeminism in a Hindu worldview, but she feels the need for a more careful, critical evaluation of the dominant patterns of Hinduism that are dualistic and world-negating, placing women in the degraded sphere of the material world, cut off from higher spiritual aspirations. The theory and practice of purity taboos also located women, along with untouchables, in the sphere of the polluted, to be segregated from and avoided by men seeking spiritual liberation.

Particularly intriguing in Shema's work is the suggestion that the worldview and practices of purity taboos actually promoted environmental degradation in practice by the way they discarded materials seen as polluted in rivers or in segregated regions of the land and streets, rather than recycling waste material as a positive part of the life cycle. Shema looks to the Tantric tradition in Hinduism as one that broke down these divisions of the pure and polluted, spiritual and material, male and female, in a dynamic union, deliberately reversing traditional hierarchies to value the female as sacred, as well as the material realm traditionally seen as polluted.[93]

Shema believes this tradition is more helpful for a Hindu ecofeminism, but she recognizes the need for the development of a social and ecological ethic that could translate Tantric insights into a practice of positive care for the earth as a community responsibility. Traditional Hindu forms of spirituality have focused on the escape of the individual from the cycle of reincarnation and thus have failed to develop such a social ethic that looks to the material, social, and historical world as a place of redemptive transformation.

The most developed expression of an Asian and specifically Korean feminist theology is emerging from the work of Chung Hyun Kyung, formerly of Ewa Women's University in Seoul and now professor of ecumenics at Union Theological Seminary in New York. Chung presents a feminist contextualization of Korean Minjung theology. Minjung theology emerged from the popular struggles of students, workers, and some church people against military dictatorship in the 1970s. It expressed the experience of struggle for a just, democratic society that brought many young people to prison and basement torture chambers and some to their death during this period.

Minjung is distinctively Korean, its terminology and references hardly understandable apart from the Korean language, history, and popular culture. Minjung, from the Korean words for people (*min*) and mass (*jung*), is broader than the Marxist concept of the proletariat. It means all those in Korean society who are oppressed politically, exploited economically, despised socially, and kept uneducated.[94] It includes Korean women, who, despite class differences, have experienced all these forms of oppression. Korean feminists would speak of Korean women as the "Minjung of the Minjung."

Minjung theologians see the Minjung as subjects of history, those who are to become the revolutionary force to challenge, discredit, and transform the multiple forms of oppression, both from outside colonial powers and from internal hierarchies, into a more just and egalitarian society. This includes overcoming the split of Korea into North and South, imposed by the big powers in 1945, and the mutual transformation of two oppressive societies, communist and capitalist, into some new form that would blend the best of the democratic and socialist ideals. This division has become so entrenched that it has become politically dangerous on both sides of the dividing line to discuss reunification and to envision a new synthesis beyond these antagonistic roads of development.

Central to Minjung theology is the concept of Han. Han is the frustrated sorrow and anger at unjust suffering accumulated in the Minjung due to repression of any outlet for this anger or resolution to these experiences of injustice. Han is not simply the experiences of individuals. It is collective and transmitted from generation to generation. It can find dangerous expression in explosions of mass anger. It can also be expressed creatively in the masked dances and other forms of Korean folk culture by which the people mock the authorities and demystify their claims to obedient respect. Han also expresses a tenacity for life that arises in the midst of continuous expressions of defeat. Minjung theologians seek to convert Han into a constructive power both to protest injustice and also to engage in struggle to transform it.[95]

For Korean feminist theologians, women's Han is the deepest form of Han, combining all the experiences of oppression from outside colonizers and national elites together with the physical, emotional, and cultural oppression of women in the Confucian family system.[96] Chung sees the transformative expression of women's Han particularly in Korean shamanism, historically led by women and patronized by women across classes, even by some Christians. While Confucianism is the official religion of the patriarchal family, shamanism is the protest and survival religion of the wives, mothers, and grandmothers of these families, who take their daughters with them to the shaman *kut* ceremonies.

Han is released in *kut* ceremonies. This release of Han is called *han-pu-ri*, in which the accumulated angry ghosts of unresolved Han are laid to rest. Chung lists three essential aspects of *han-pu-ri*: (1) speaking and hearing by which the han-ridden ghosts are given voice and enabled to tell their stories publicly; (2) naming, in which the ghosts and their communities identify the sources of their oppression; and (3) action by which the unjust situation is changed, allowing the han-ridden ghosts to have rest.[97]

Chung translates these three steps in *han-pu-ri* into the methodology of Korean feminist theology. This theology has followed the process of listening to women's stories of oppression, analyzing the social structures that promote this injustice, engaging in theological reflection on oppression, checking back with the storytellers to be sure that their analysis is in accord with their experiences, and finally devising various actions to change the situation.[98]

Chung sees Korean feminist theology as drawing on four key sources. The first is Korean women's experience of victimization but also of resistance. The second is critical consciousness that analyzes such oppression as evil. In seeking alternative liberative cultural symbols, Korean women must lay claim to the full range of their traditions: Shamanism, Buddhism, Confucianism, Christianity, and modern political thought. They must not be intimidated by the orthodoxies of these traditions that forbid mixing them.[99]

This means a conversion from being objects to being subjects of traditions. Women must understand that in liberation struggle it is they and their lives that are the text, and the various scriptures and traditions provide material by which women can interpret their lives. Since it is the popular religiosity, not the official male institutional forms of these religions, that have been most accessible for women's self-expression, feminist theology should turn to these resources of popular women's religion. Their stance toward religious plurality goes beyond dialogue to solidarity between women in different religious traditions and finally to creative syncretism of their best liberative insights.[100]

Chung demonstrated all these key themes of her Asian feminist liberation theology in a landmark multimedia speech before the 1991 Assembly of the World Council of Churches in Canberra, Australia. There Chung's speech interpreted the theme of the WCC Assembly, "Come Holy Spirit: Renew the Whole Creation," from this perspective.[101] She began by summoning the han-ridden spirits of world history to be present in the assembly. These included Hagar, Uriah, and Jephthah's daughter, male babies killed by King Herod's soldiers, Joan of Arc and other women burnt as witches, indigenous people made victim of genocide in Western colonization, the Jews who died in the German death camps, those killed by atom bombs in Hiroshima and Nagasaki and others, including the earth, air, and water "raped, tortured and exploited by the human greed for money." These many han-ridden spirits Chung gathered as the icons of the Holy Spirit made present, calling for a resolution of their han through a renewal of all creation. As their names were called, artistic images that represented their suffering were played on a great screen behind her. Chung then performed a *han-pu-ri* ceremony, burning the paper with the names of the summoned spirits and sending the sparks into the air. In her speech Chung defined the process of transformation to renew creation as repentance: a repentance that is not just individual but collective, that includes changing our relation to the earth as well as to each other across many divided communities of dominators and dominated.

In her call for metanoia or repentant transformation, Chung defined three major shifts in consciousness and social organization that are necessary: (1) a change from anthropocentrism to life-centrism; (2) a change from the habit of dualism to the habit of interconnection; and (3) a change from the culture of death to the culture of life. These three changes are three aspects of an all-encompassing transformation that would relocate humans in the life-matrix of earth, see us all as interconnected in one community of biophilic mutuality, and commit us in all these relations to defend life, rather than endlessly destroying to maintain the power of some over others.

Chung ended her presentation with the majestic image of Kwan In, the compassionate goddess of Asian women's popular religion, as her vision of the Holy Spirit. As Kwan In, the Holy Spirit appeared as a calm, beautiful, and powerful female gliding through the air on the back of a dragon. Chung's presentation at the Assembly brought denunciations of heresy and syncretism from Eastern Orthodox and Protestant conservative leaders, while the majority greeted it with thunderous applause. After her talk Chung became a world celebrity but also received death threats from conservative Christians in Korea.

Controversy over the talk obscures the profound seriousness of its message. Chung's holistic vision combined protest against oppressions of sex, race, class, religion, and the earth with a comprehensive vision of a transformed ecofeminist community of life. She wove together liberating symbols from Christianity, Shamanism, and Buddhism in a cohesive new fabric, not a patchwork of old patterns. She demonstrated a way of doing feminist theology that returned from objectified discourse to the language of primal religious experience: dance, artistic image, and story. The purpose of her presentation was not simply to talk *about* the Holy Spirit, but to make the Holy Spirit tangibly present as the felt power of the divine through whom we might hope indeed that the whole creation will be renewed.[102]

# Conclusions

In this book I have traced the paradigm shifts in the understanding of gender and redemption from the New Testament until twentieth-century feminist theologies. I see the key paradigm shift that lays the basis for a feminist reading in Christianity beginning in the sixteenth century with the humanist Agrippa von Nettesheim and the Quakers in the seventeenth-century. From defining woman as created subordinate in the original creation and subjected to servitude due to her priority in sin, Agrippa and the Quakers affirmed a complete original equality and condemned woman's subordination as sinful domination.

The classical Christian paradigm defines women as created to be dominated and blames women as deserving redoubled domination for resisting it, while feminism defines women and men as originally equal and denounces male domination of women as sin. Redemption then becomes transformed gender relations that overcome male domination, rather than a call to women to submit to it as their means of salvation. From this foundational paradigm shift, a series of additional developments unfolded in nineteenth- and twentieth-century Christian feminism.

A second key shift took place from the seventeenth to the nineteenth centuries with a turn from an otherworldly to a this-worldly view of redemption. For traditional Christianity redemption means the reconciliation of the fallen soul with God, won by Christ in the cross, applied to the soul in baptismal regeneration, and developed through the struggle to live virtuously sustained by grace. Salvation is completed after death in eternal contemplative union with God (joined by the spiritual body in the resurrection).

Although hope for life after death remains a residual idea in modern Christianity, the focus of redemptive hope shifted (or returned) to a Hebraic hope for a this-worldly transformation of unjust relationships that would bring about a time of justice and peace within history (the reign of God). Nineteenth- and twentieth-century social gospel and liberation theologies have focused on this-worldly redemptive hope through some combination of personal conversion and progressive or revolutionary reform of social structures that will overcome poverty, tyranny, and war. Ecological sustainability has recently been integrated into this vision of a just and livable future.

Feminist theology developed within this modern tradition of this-worldly progressive hope, redefining the analysis of injustice in the context of gender hierarchy. Gender hierarchy is seen as central to a total system and ideology of patriarchy. Feminism sees patriarchy as a multilayered system of domination, centered in male control of women but including class and race hierarchy, generational hierarchy, and clericalism, and expressed also in war and in domination of nature. Elisabeth Schüssler Fiorenza has coined the phrase "kyriarchy" (the rule of the lord)[1] for this multilayered system of top-down power, rooted in the religious hierarchy (which in Christianity sees itself as representing Christ as Lord). Redemption means overcoming all forms of patriarchy.

Feminist theologians such as Ivone Gebara stress that overcoming patriarchy means dismantling an entire cosmovision based on a split universe, in which God is located in a spiritual realm outside of creation and ruling over it. Redemption is seen as sending God down from this higher spiritual realm to a lower, material world lacking spiritual life. Spirit and matter, God and body need to be reintegrated, locating the divine power of renewal of life-giving and loving relations in mutual relationality between all beings, not dominating control from outside.

Gebara also begins to dismantle the intrahistorical dualism that feminists accepted from biblical thought; namely, an original paradise of the beginning when all was in perfect harmony, and/or a reign of God at the end of history when all will again be in perfect harmony, contrasted with present evil. Gebara questions the literalism of a utopianism of the future when all evil will be conquered. Rather, she wishes to distinguish between a finitude of life and death, of joy and tragedy, contrasted to the construction of a system of domination based on the false attempt to secure the powerful from vulnerability, which turns most humans and the earth into victims. Here redemptive hopes lies in dismantling this distorted social construction to reclaim fragile joys and life-giving relations shared equally between all beings in the midst of life's limits.

The shift from otherworldly to this-worldly redemptive hope also entails a revised anthropology and Christology. Feminists reject the classical notion that the human soul is radically fallen, alienated from God, and unable to make any move to reconcile itself with God, therefore needing an outside mediator who does the work of reconciliation for us. Instead the human self is defined through its primary identity as image of God. This original goodness and communion with its divine "ground of being" continue to be our "true nature."

Evil is serious, but it is defined in terms of external structures and cultures of domination to which human persons fall victim or identify with as victimizers. Although some powerful humans invented these systems and ideologies for their own advantage, and many people victimized by them have acceded to them through socialization, this does not change our potential for good.

We are alienated or out of touch with this potential, but experiences of consciousness-raising, starting with those who are disprivileged, begin a process of conversion, getting back in touch with a better self and reconstructing personal and social relations. An external redeemer is not necessary for this process of conversion, since we have not lost our true self rooted in God. But "grace events" of loving outreach from others and shocks of rampant evil can awaken our awareness of inauthentic distortions, put us in touch with our authentic self and set us on the path of struggle for just and loving relations.

The role of Jesus becomes quite different in feminist theology. His is a root story for the redemptive process in which we must all be engaged, but he does not and cannot do it for us. Redemption cannot be done by one person for everyone else. No one person can become the "collective human" whose actions accomplish a salvation that is then passively applied to everyone else. His story can model what we need to do, but it happens only when all of us do it for ourselves and with one another.

Yet there is a remarkable persistence in the attachment of Christian feminists to the Jesus story. Across many cultures—Western European and

Euroamerican, African and Hispanic American, Latin American, Asian, and African—feminists, womanists, *mujeristas* continue to affirm their relation to Jesus, even as they reject the christological superstructure that has been erected by classical Christianity in his name. Only one feminist discussed in this book, Mary Daly, has definitively rejected an appropriation of Jesus, saying, "Even if Jesus wasn't a feminist, I am."[2] By implication, if Jesus could be shown to be "pro-woman," for Daly it would be irrelevant. Is the decisive step to being post-Christian the repudiation of any relevance of the Jesus story?

The other feminist theologians discussed in this book across many cultures remain "Christian," however radical in their repudiation of doctrines about Christ as redeemer, in their continued affiliation with the Jesus story as foundationally paradigmatic for their feminist theology. Why is this? Does this indicate some residual need for male authority? Some fear of breaking the final tie with Christianity? There may be an element of these fears and dependencies, but not enough to explain the resiliency of the Jesus figure for feminist theology.

Modern Jesus scholarship has radically stripped the Jesus story of its dogmatic accretions, revealing a Jesus whose life continues to strike a responsive chord for feminist liberation theology; namely, a man (not lord, but brother) who dissented from the religious and social systems of domination that marginalized the poor and the despised, most notably women. He incurred the wrath of religious and political authorities for these subversive teachings and practices, and the authorities sought to silence him by publicly torturing him to death.

But, just as the cross failed to silence his story, for Jesus rose to live on in a religious movement that kept his memory alive, so all the appropriations of him into constructions of ecclesial domination through the centuries also have failed to silence the subversive power of his name. The Jesus story, continually reenvisioned, still rises, beyond the deaths of patriarchal Christianities, and still lives as a touchstone for feminists who continue to seek and celebrate their liberation in "memory of him."

The Jesus story continues to be paradigmatic for Christian feminists because it is understood as exemplifying the redemptive paradigm of feminist liberation: dissent against oppressive religious and political structures; taking the side of the oppressed, particularly women; living a praxis of egalitarian relations across gender, race, class, and other status differences imposed by the dominant society; pointing toward a new time when these hierarchies will be overcome and anticipating redeemed relations in a community of celebration here and now.

Skeptics might wonder whether Christians in search of a "Jesus" to ground our faith are not, once again, looking down a long well and seeing our own face reflected in the bottom. However one construes the complex relation between "objective history" and subjective constructions reflective of our own desires, the Jesus story, told even by the minimalists of the Jesus Seminar, reflects this paradigm. Christian feminists resonate with this reading of the Jesus story as reflecting and grounding their own story.

If the Jesus story is claimed because it echoes our own story, why not discard it and tell our own story? The resistance to doing this, I believe, is due to several reasons. Most basically it expresses a desire to continue to belong to the church, not as a hierarchical structure, but as a community of faith; to have historical roots, to lay claim to a people, while at the same time calling that people to repent of its patriarchy and to understand its calling to redemption as liberation from patriarchy. A Jesus whose life message and praxis were redemption from patriarchy pulls the rug out from under Christian patriarchy and grounds a feminist Christianity as the "true" gospel of Jesus.

This is a powerful claim, powerful in a different way from telling our own individual stories in small communities. However paradigmatic for us in those small communities our stories may be, they do not have the historical weight of being claimed as the root story for two thousand years and by two billion people around the world today. To ground our liberative stories in the Jesus story is to lay claim to that whole people in prophetic judgment and call to repentance.

Yet the fact that Jesus was a male, and his maleness has been used by the patriarchal church to insist that women are not christomorphic—that they cannot, as women, represent Christ—is a major problem for claiming the Jesus story as the root story for feminist theology. One answer is to deconstruct the assumption of patriarchal theology that maleness is normative for being fully human and the image of God. Jesus' maleness is declared to be one "accident" of his historical reality among others, such as being Jewish, and a first-century Galilean. What distinguishes Jesus as normative is not his maleness but the quality of his humanness as one who loves others and opts for those most vulnerable and oppressed, namely women. One imitates Christ by living in a like manner, not by possessing male genitalia.[3]

While this deconstruction goes a long way toward answering the problem, it does not overcome the basic social-symbolic structure in which Jesus, a male, opts for women as objects of concern. This makes women paradigmatic as recipients of Jesus' liberative praxis, but not as agents of liberative action for themselves and other women (and men). Thus Christian feminist theology is pushed to go beyond the telling of the Jesus story as that of a "good man who really cared about us," and to dare to parallel the Jesus story with the stories of women who acted as liberators. Women become fully christomorphic only when one can tell stories of women who acted redemptively as parallel with the Jesus story.

Appearances of female Christs are not lacking in the Christian tradition. Indeed the need for a female Christ was impelled by the very development of a Christology that denied that women are christomorphic. Already in the Montanists of the second century the doctrine of the coming of the Holy Spirit was appropriated to image the appearance of the Christ-Spirit in the form of a female. The most developed theology of the second appearing of Christ as female was developed by the Shakers in the early nineteenth century.

But contemporary Christian feminism should be wary of the anthropology of complementarity on which the Shakers built their claim for a need for a female Christ to complete the revelation of an androgynous God and fulfill the redemption of a humanity that is both male and female. Do we want a female Christ who represents the feminine "lower half" of God and the feminine "lower side" of humanity? Or do we want both men and women to be fully human, however distinct in some biological and social experiences, and to have a female Christ as a fully empowered and empowering human?

I think it is not enough to say that Jesus represents both men and women because he was fully human, the sort of human we all want to be, if we cannot also say that women can be fully human and can represent the sort of liberative human we all want to be. Also one wants to be able to experience that sort of liberating woman in our own culture and ethnicity. Thus some Christian feminists begin to lift up female Christ figures of their own cultures.

Mercy Amba Oduyoye and Elizabeth Amoah tell the story of Eku, a Fante woman of Ghana, who led her people to a new land where they could find a good life; she risked her own life by tasting water from a pool to see if it was poisonous before allowing her thirsty people to drink. For Oduyoye the story of Eku as liberator for Ghanaian people parallels the story of Jesus.[4]

Many Christian feminists also question the focus on suffering and the cross as central to redemption. Others parallel Jesus and women as sufferers, a way of making women christomorphic found already in the medieval women mystics. Women are like Jesus because they suffer, and Jesus opts for women as those who suffer. But some want to ask, "What kind of suffering is redemptive?" Is the passive suffering of victims redemptive, or does the mandate for women to suffer in this way in order to be Christlike simply a justification and prolongation of evil?

Some theologians, like Delores Williams, have answered this question by a decisive rejection of victimized suffering as redemptive. What is redemptive is action to extricate ourselves from unjust suffering and changing the conditions that cause it. It is not Jesus' suffering and death that are redemptive, but his life as a praxis of protest against injustice and solidarity in defense of life. The praxis of Jesus we need to imitate is this protest and defense of life, not acquiescence to being crucified, which represents the victory of oppressors who sought to silence him.

Suffering is a factor in the liberation process, not as a means of redemption, but as the risk that one takes when one struggles to overcome unjust systems whose beneficiaries resist change. The means of redemption is conversion, opening up to one another, changing systems of distorted relations, creating loving and life-giving communities of people here and now, not getting oneself tortured to death.

This dismantling of the patterns of patriarchal Christianity, reconstructing a radically different understanding of the key touchstones of Christian theology; God, humanity, male and female, sin and fall, Christ, redemption—raises the questions of how feminist theology relates to Scripture and tradition. I believe that many Christian feminists remain stuck in a radical Protestant paradigm in which tradition is dismantled or bypassed by returning to what is seen as an original dispensation of revelation in Jesus of normative perfection. One leaps from an appropriation of this original "truth" to a reconstruction of theology for one's own time and context, ignoring the intervening history.

This radical Protestant paradigm forces one to falsify the earliest Christian movement as much more like our own vision than it really was, ignoring our actual heritage in a Christian history of ongoing reinterpretation that we continue. Although I believe there were touchstones in the early Jesus movement that can ground our vision, it also could only express its insights into new gender relations in a cosmology radically different from our own. We would not want to "go back" to those earliest paradigms of gender equality, as the alternative to the patriarchal paradigms that arose to repress them.

We need to own as ongoing revelation the process of continuous reinterpretation that lies behind our restatements of redemptive gender equality in new, more socially embodied terms. This does not mean "development of doctrine" in a traditional Catholic sense, which allowed for only small explications of ideas already implicit,[5] not radical paradigm shifts in understanding these symbols. Rather, we need a dynamic dialectical synthesis of the Catholic understanding of ongoing inspired development and the Protestant model of return to origins that dismantles distorted developments, seeing this not as a literal "return" to some first-century worldview, but as an insightful encounter with root stories that releases space for radically new envisionings.

A key impetus for radically new envisionings of redemptive hope lies in the growing plurality of women's voices in many cultural contexts. As women from African American, Hispanic American, and Third World contexts find their voices as feminist theologians, many distinct contextualizations of hopes for redemption from gender injustice develop. European or Euroamerican feminists are asked to let go of their unconscious assumption that they can represent women as a whole.

"Let a thousand flowers bloom of every color and form in the garden of feminist theology;" this might be one way of characterizing these cries. The differences among women who articulate their feminist theology in many particular histories and cultures need to be fully acknowledged. This has surely been happening in the past two decades. It is being affirmed, however painfully at first, as the genuine globalization of women's theologies, in solidarity with each other, that can happen only when a false universalization of one group of women is dismantled.

The second challenge coming from new communities of feminist theology is multireligious contextualization. What happens to Christian feminist theology when Christian symbols are one resource among others, along with

Shamanism and Buddhism (with Chung Hyun Kyung) or along with indigenous African and Latin American religions (with Elsa Tamez and Mercy Amba Oduyoye)? This barrier is being crossed with creative élan, although its meaning is yet to be fully explored. The praxis of multireligious solidarity and syncretism is emerging, not only as allowable but as required, especially for women whose historic cultural identities are multireligious, who can hardly say who they are apart from embracing all these aspects of themselves as persons and communities.

This incorporation of many religious traditions in new syntheses calls for monocultural Christian feminists, not to co-opt religious symbols that are not their own, but to be in solidarity with the justice and creativity of sisters engaged in multireligious contextualizations of feminist theology. It also calls European and Euroamerican Christian feminists to discover more about our own repressed plurality of identities.

Feminist liberation theology opens up as a human project, not an exclusively Christian project. Revisioned Christian symbols can be one cultural resource among others in a struggle for liberation that can meet and converge around the world only by being authentically rooted in many local contexts. This is the promise of feminist liberation theology. We are only beginning to live it, to imagine its fuller implications.

# Notes

## Introduction

1. By "canonical envelope" I mean that second strata of the New Testament, such as the Pastoral and Catholic Epistles, which interpret the New Testament writings as a whole in a patriarchal framework. See Elisabeth Schüssler Fiorenza, *In Memory of Her: A Feminist Theological Reconstruction of Christian Origins* (New York: Crossroads, 1983), 243–314.

2. Wisdom of Solomon, *Jerusalem Bible* (New York: Doubleday, 1966), 6–8.

3. See Barbara Newman, "Renaissance Feminism and Esoteric Theology," in her *From Virile Woman to WomanChrist: Studies in Medieval Religion and Literature* (Philadelphia: University of Pennsylvania Press, 1995), 224–43.

4. Mary Wollstonecraft, *The Vindication of the Rights of Women*, ed. Carol H. Poston, 2d ed. (New York: Norton, 1988).

5. See Rosemary Ruether, *Sexism and God-talk: Toward a Feminist Theology* (Boston: Beacon, 1983), 237–44; also see Rosemary Ruether, "Eschatology and Feminism," in *Lift Every Voice: Constructing Christian Theologies from the Underside*, Susan Brooks Thistlethwaite and Mary Potter Engel, eds. (San Francisco: Harper and Row, 1990), 111–24.

6. Ruether, *Sexism and God-talk*, 102–15; also see Lynda M. Glennon, *Women and Dualism: A Sociology of Knowledge* (New York: Longman and Green, 1979), 97–115.

7. See Rosemary Ruether, *Contemporary Roman Catholicism: Crises and Challenges* (Kansas City, Mo.: Sheed and Ward, 1987), 36–37, and 79 n.22. For the papal anthropology of complementarity, see John Paul II, "On the Dignity and Vocation of Women: Apostolic Letter" (Washington, D.C.: USCC, 1988).

8. Linda J. Nicholson, ed., *Feminism/Post-Modernism* (New York: Routledge, 1990).

## Chapter One

1. One example of such work is the Jesus Seminar, with its primary focus on development of a consensus among New Testament scholars on the authentic sayings of Jesus. See Robert W. Funk, Roy W. Hoover, and the Jesus Seminar, *The Five Gospels: The Search for the Authentic Words of Jesus* (New York: Macmillan, 1993).

2. S. G. F. Brandon played a key role in raising the question of the link between the Jesus movement and "Zealots" of the Jewish war period. See his *Jesus and the Zealots: A Study of the Political Factor in Primitive Christianity* (New York: Scribners, 1967). More recent studies include David Rhoads, *Israel in Revolution* (Philadelphia: Fortress, 1976); Richard Horsley and John Hanson, *Bandits, Prophets and Messiahs: Popular Movements in the Time of Jesus* (Minneapolis: Winston, 1985); Richard Horsley, *Jesus and the Spiral of Violence: Popular Jewish Resistance in Roman Palestine* (San Francisco: Harper and Row, 1987); Dominic Crossan, *The Historical Jesus: The Life of a Mediterranean Jewish Peasant* (San Francisco: HarperSanFrancisco, 1991).

3. Official Jewish thought would claim that acts of repentance can only prepare the people of Israel for an intervention that God will carry out in God's good time, but, particularly in times of heightened messianic expectation, the psychology of preparatory practice suggests that God will be "disposed" to more readily intervene when God sees the people preparing themselves through acts of prayer and repentance.

4. See Josephus, *Jewish Antiquities* 14.22–24 and 20.97, 98. Also see Baruch M. Bokser, "Wonderworking and the Rabbinic Tradition: The Case of Hanina ben Dosa," *Journal for the Study of Judaism* 16 (June, 1985): 42–92. Also see Crossan, *Historical Jesus*, 137–67.

5. Josephus, *Jewish Antiquities* 18.6, 9, and *The Jewish Wars* 2.66, 124. Judas, son of Hezekiah, was the leader of a popular insurrection in Galilee following the death of Herod. He should be distinguished from the revolutionary teacher Judas the Galilean, whom Josephus sees as the founder of the "Fourth Philosophy." See Crossan, *Historical Jesus*, 230–38. Also see Rhoads, *Israel in Revolution*, 47–60; and Horsley, *Jesus and the Spiral of Violence*, 78–82 and 87–89.

6. Mark 6:3 says, "Is not this the carpenter, the son of Mary and brother of James and Joses and Jude and Simon, and are not his sisters here with us?" To refer to a man by his mother's name alone usually indicated illegitimacy. It was a common way of naming children of slave women, who could not legally marry. Matthew 13:55 emends his saying to read: "Is not this the carpenter's son? Is not his mother called Mary? And are not his brothers James and Joseph and Simon and Judas? And are not all his sisters with us?" But the Markan version is surely the older one. See Jane Schaberg, *The Illegitimacy of Jesus* (San Francisco: Harper and Row, 1987). Winsome Munro took Schaberg's study a step further and suggested that Jesus was the son of a slave woman. This book-length manuscript was left unpublished when Munro died.

7. See Elisabeth Schüssler Fiorenza, *In Memory of Her: A Feminist Theological Reconstruction of Christian Origins* (New York: Crossroads, 1983), 118–19; also see Crossan, *Historical Jesus*, 259–60.

8. The temple structure was organized in concentric circles of holiness: from the inner Holy of Holies, accessible only to the High Priest in a state of purity, and on the Day of Atonement, Yom Kippur; to the outer courts for women and gentiles. See Josephus, *Jewish Wars* 5.198ff. Much of Rabbinic Judaism focused legal midrashim on structuring place, time, the body, and relationships in terms of separations of holy and unholy. This structuring tends to be obscured by Christian accounts that discuss Judaism in terms of doctrinal views parallel to Christian theological topics.

9. Rabbinic sources on women focus on careful observance of taboos, such as those involving menstruation, but these patterns of separation are not mentioned in the wealth of inscriptional evidence of Jewish women in the first centuries C.E., this raises questions about how much the taboos were actually observed by ordinary Jews. See Ross S. Kraemer, *Her Share of the Blessings: Women's Religions among Pagans, Jews and Christians in the Greco-Roman World* (New York: Oxford University Press, 1992), 93–127.

10. Ibid.; also see Judith R. Wegner, *Chattel or Person? The Status of Women in the Mishnah* (New York: Oxford University Press, 1988).

11. Schüssler Fiorenza, *In Memory of Her*, 127–28.

12. For an analysis of the Jewish woman as the "gentile within" in rabbinic law, see Judith Plaskow, *Standing Again at Sinai: Judaism from a Feminist Perspective* (San Francisco: Harper and Row, 1990), 171–90.

13. For an account of the temple of Jesus' time, rebuilt and greatly enlarged by Herod, see Michael Grant, *Herod the Great* (New York: American Heritage, 1971), 150–64.

14. For an understanding of the meaning of the "poor" in the Jesus movement, see Luise Schottroff and W. Stegemann, *Jesus and the Hope of the Poor* (Maryknoll, N.Y.: Orbis, 1986), 6–16.

15. For a critical evaluation of the "Abba" language in the Gospels, see Mary Rose D'Angelo, "*Abba* and Father: Imperial Theology and the Jesus Tradition," *Journal of Biblical Literature III, no. 4 (Winter 1992).*

16. Dominic Crossan characterizes the difference between John the Baptist and Jesus as an ascetic, apocalyptic stance versus a sapiental, immanentist communing with God present now. I suggest more of a future-present mingling of the two, in which apocalyptic expectation was also present, but the future was beginning now in "signs." See Crossan, *Historical Jesus*, 227–64.

17. Crossan sees the precipitating act that led to Jesus' arrest as the cleansing of the temple: ibid., 355–60. He eliminates the historicity of the triumphal entry into Jerusalem as a later addition from an apocalyptic Christianity. I see the triumphal entry as having a historical basis and being one signal to the authorities of Jesus' "subversive" nature, leading to Jesus' arrest: See Brandon, *Jesus and the Zealots*, 349–50.

18. See Martin Hengel, Crucifixion (London: SCM, 1977).

19. It is common in scholarly commentary to take Paul's account of the resurrection witnesses (1 Cor. 15:3–8), which lacks the appearances to the women and starts with the appearance to Peter, as proof that stories of the empty tomb, linked to the appearances to women, are late. But the existence of these stories in all four Gospels, as well as in extracanonical gospels, makes it unlikely that such stories of appearances to women as apostolic witnesses were constructed after accounts in which women are absent. It is more reasonable to assume that Paul (or the account Paul is using) dropped the appearances to women because he wished to deny such apostolic authority to women. See Antoinette Wire, *The Corinthian Women Prophets: A Reconstruction through Paul's Rhetoric* (Minneapolis: Fortress, 1990), 162–63; also see Ben Witherington, *Women in the Earliest Church* (Cambridge: Cambridge University Press, 1988), 161–66; and Pheme Perkins, *Resurrection: New Testament Witness and Contemporary Reflection* (New York: Doubleday, 1984), 94, 196.

20. Josephus, *Antiquities* 18.63. See the discussion in the "Slavonic Josephus"

in Alan Watson, The Trial of Jesus (Athens: University of Georgia Press, 1995), 128–36.

21. See Ross Kraemer, *Maenads, Martyrs, Matrons, Monastics: A Source Book on Women's Religions in the Greco-Roman World* (Philadelphia: Fortress, 1988), 218–21. Also see Bernadette Brooten, *Women Leaders in the Ancient Synagogue: Inscriptional Evidence* (Chico, Calif.: Scholars Press, 1982).

22. For reforms in women's legal status under Roman law in the imperial period, see Sarah B. Pomeroy, *Goddesses, Whores, Wives and Slaves: Women in Classical Antiquity* (New York: Schocken, 1975), 149–63.

23. See Sarah B. Pomeroy, *Women in Hellenistic Egypt: From Alexander to Cleopatra* (New York: Schocken, 1984).

24. For the economic status of women slaves and freedwomen in the early Roman period, see Pomeroy, *Goddesses*, 198–202, and *Women in Hellenistic Egypt*, 125–73.

25. Ronald D. Cameron, *The Other Gospels: Non-Canonical Gospel Texts* (Philadelphia: Westminster, 1982), 52.

26. *Second Clement* 12:2–6.

27. *Gospel of Thomas* 22:4–7; in Robert J. Miller, ed., *The Complete Gospels* (Sonoma, Calif.: Polebridge, 1994), 309. See the discussion in Ronald R. MacDonald, *There Is No Male and Female* (Philadelphia: Fortress, 1987), 17–63. Also see Crossan, *Historical Jesus*, 295–98.

28. This term to summarize the understanding of discipleship in the Jesus movement is characteristic of Elisabeth Schüssler Fiorenza; see *In Memory of Her*, 140 and passim.

29. On early Christian social status in Palestine and in the Pauline churches, see Gerd Theissen, *The Sociology of Early Palestinian Christianity* (Philadelphia: Fortress, 1978); also see his *The Social Setting of Pauline Christianity* (Philadelphia: Fortress, 1982); and Wayne A. Meeks, *The First Urban Christians: The Social World of the Apostle Paul* (New Haven: Yale University Press, 1983), 51–74.

30. Meeks, *First Urban Christians*, 75–77.

31. See Phyllis Bird, "'Male and Female He Created Them': Gen. 1:27b in the Context of the Priestly Account of Creation," *Harvard Theological Review* 74 (1981): 129–59; and her expanded version of this article in *Image of God and Gender Models in the Judaeo-Christian Tradition*, Kari Børresen, ed. (Oslo: Solum Verlag, 1991; Minneapolis: Fortress, 1994), 11–34.

32. For a survey of the development of the *imago Dei* text as related to gen-

der, see Børresen, ed., *Image of God*. Ecological theologians have criticized both the dominion concept and the androcentrism of this text; see Rosemary R. Ruether, *Gaia and God: An Ecofeminist Theology of Earth Healing* (San Francisco: Harper, 1992), 19–22.

33. The granting of voting rights for women in modern societies was based on the assumption that married adult women were independent individuals and hence not represented by the male head of family, as had been the traditional political theory. The objection to this change of assumptions was one of the main arguments of those who opposed women's suffrage. See Aileen S. Kraditor, *The Ideas of the Woman Suffrage Movement: 1890–1920* (Garden City, N.Y.: Doubleday, 1971), 16–18.

34. For the understanding of the household, the paterfamilias and his relation to wives, children, slaves, and property (the *familia*) in Roman law, see David Herlihy, "The Household in Late Classical Antiquity" in his *Medieval Households* (Cambridge, Mass.: Harvard University Press, 1985), 1–28.

35. For example, Phyllis Trible's well-known article, "Depatriarchalizing in Biblical Interpretation," *Journal of the American Academy of Religion* 41, no. 1 (March 1973): 30–48.

36. See Anders Hultgard, "God and Image of Woman in Early Jewish Religion," in Børresen, ed., *Image of God*, 35–55. Also see J. Fossum, "Gen 1.26 and 2.7 in Judaism, Samaritanism and Gnosticism," *Journal for the Study of Judaism* (1986) 16: 202–39; J. Jervell, *Imago Dei, Gen 1.26f im Spätjudentum, in der Gnosis und in den paulinischen Briefen* (Göttingen: Vandenhoeck & Ruprecht, 1960); G. W. Nickelsburg, "The Bible Rewritten and Expanded," in *Jewish Writings of the Second Temple Period*, Michael E. Stone, ed. (Philadelphia: Fortress, 1984), 89–156; and Thomas H. Tobin, *The Creation of Man: Philo and the History of Interpretation* (Washington, D.C.: Catholic Biblical Association of America, 1983). For rabbinic commentaries that stress the mutual relation of men and women in creating offspring, superseding the Genesis 2 relation of man to God and woman to man, see Mary Rose D'Angelo, "The Garden: Once and Not Again," in *Genesis 1–3 in the History of Interpretation*, ed. Gregory A. Robbins (Lewiston, Pa.: Edwin Mellen, 1988), 1–42.

37. Ben Sira's *Book of Wisdom* 25:24,26: from *The Apocrypha and Pseudepigrapha of the Old Testament*, R. H. Charles, ed. (Oxford: Clarendon Press, 1913), 1: 402.

38. The *Apocalypse of Moses*, chapters 14–21, hints that the relation of Eve and the devil was a sexual one: see *Apocrypha and Pseudepigrapha*, 2: 145–47. This was widely discussed in rabbinic commentary. See D'Angelo, "The Garden," 19–21 and notes. This view is represented in Louis Ginzberg, *The Legends of the Jews* (Philadelphia: Jewish Publication Society of America, 1913), 1: 103–04, in which the father of Cain is Satan or the fallen angel Samael. This evil ancestry accounts for the evil character of Cain, who is "the ancestor of all the impious generations that were rebellious toward God."

39. For the parallel texts of the *Books of Adam and Eve*, and the *Apocalypse of Moses*, see *Apocrypha and Pseudepigrapha*, 2: 134–54.

40. For the development of the Watcher story in early Judaism, see Bernard P. Prusak, "Woman: Seductive Siren and Source of Sin?" in *Religion and Sexism: Images of Women in the Jewish and Christian Traditions*, Rosemary R. Ruether, ed. (New York: Simon and Schuster, 1974), 89–116.

41. *Testimony of Reuben* 5.1–7: see *Testaments of the Twelve Patriarchs*, in *Apocrypha and Pseudepigrapha*, 2: 299.

42. See Bernadette Brooten, "Jewish Women's History in the Roman Period," in *Christians among Jews and Gentiles*, G. W. E. Nickelsburg and George W. MacRae, eds. (Philadelphia: Fortress, 1986), 22–30. Also see Kraemer, *Her Share*, 93–156.

43. Philo, "On the Creation of the World," 46, 53; See *The Essential Philo*, Nahum Glatzer, ed. (New York: Schocken, 1971), 28, 34. For discussion see MacDonald, *No Male and Female*, 26–30; also see Wayne Meeks, "The Image of the Androgene: Some Uses of a Symbol in Earliest Christianity," *History of Religions* 13 (1974): 165–202.

44. Philo, "The Therapeutae," in *Essential Philo*, 311–30.

45. MacDonald understands the soteriology of Philo as stripping off the body, but Philo suggests an embodied unitary Adam who would have been immortal because the body was held in union with the immortal soul. This view was used by the church fathers to explain both the original immortality of Adam before the fall and the "spiritual" or risen body. Paul's concept of the spiritual or risen body in 1 Corinthians 15 is a form of changed body that is immortal: see *No Male and Female*, 23–63.

46. This view of women becoming spiritually equal by becoming male is evident in sayings such as Logion 114 from the *Gospel of Thomas*: "Simon Peter

said to them, 'Make Mary leave us, for females don't deserve life.' Jesus said, 'Look, I will guide her to make her male, so that she too may become a living spirit resembling you males. For every female who makes herself male will enter the domain of Heaven,'"; in *Complete Gospels*, 322. The *Gospel of Philip* teaches that before the separation of Eve from Adam there would have been no death (and hence no sex). In the ritual of the bridal chamber, the Valentinians symbolized a reunion of the female and the male that restored the original androgynous Adam; see *Gospel of Philip*, in *Nag Hammadi Library*, James M. Robinson, ed. (New York: Harper and Row, 1977), 131–51.

47. In a Hellenistic thanksgiving attributed to Thales (Diogenes Laertius, *Lives of the Philosophers* 1.33) or to Plato (Lactantius, *Divinae Institutiones* 3.19), the Greek male gives thanks that he was born a human being and not an animal, a man and not a woman, a Greek and not a barbarian. A parallel Jewish thanksgiving quoted by Rabbi Judah ben El'ai (150 C.E.) directs the Jewish male to pray daily to God "Blessed (art Thou) who did not make me a gentile; . . . who did not make me a woman, . . . who did not make me a boor." The Hebrew word *bor* (poor and uneducated person) is replaced in a Babylonian version of the prayer with the word *'ebed*, or slave. See MacDonald, *No Male and Female*, 122–23.

48. In addition to Paul's problems with women's social equality seen in 1 Corinthians 11, in 7:21–23 he tells slaves not to be anxious to be freed, spiritualizing slavery as becoming servants of Christ, and thus relativizing the difference between the social and legal conditions of servitude or freedom. For a recent study disputing this reading of Paul in 1 Cor. 7:21–23, see Neil Elliott, *Liberating Paul: The Justice of God and the Politics of the Apostle* (Maryknoll; N.Y.: Orbis, 1994), 32–51. See also Luise Schottroff, *Lydia's Impatient Sisters: A Feminist Social History of Early Christianity* (Louisville: Westminster/John Knox, 1995), 121–35. I find Schottroff's reading of this text more convincing. It would have been a common one in Stoic ethics, with which Paul was probably familiar. See the commentary on this passage in Gordon D. Fee, *The First Epistle to the Corinthians* (Grand Rapids: Eerdmans, 1987), 306–22.

49. Meeks, *First Urban Christians*, 9–50.

50. Several scholars have suggested that Apollos brought this Christian Philonic theology to Corinth. See Crossan, *Historical Jesus*, 298, and MacDonald, *No Male and Female*, 66. Also see Helmut Koester, Birger Pearson, and

Horsley (notes 65–66). While Apollos may have represented such a theology at Corinth, it is so widespread that it must have represented a major school of early Christianity. For the character of early Egyptian Christianity as a community embedded in Alexandrian Judaism and sharing its Platonic biblical exegesis represented by Philo, see Birger A. Pearson, "Early Christianity in Egypt"; A. F. J. Klijn, "Jewish Christianity in Egypt"; and Roelof van den Broek, "Jewish and Platonic Speculations in Early Alexandrian Theology," in *The Roots of Egyptian Christianity*, James E. Goehring, ed., (Philadelphia: Fortress, 1986), 132–75, 190–203. Also see Wire on Apollos, *Corinthian Women*, Appendix 5, 209–11.

51. Prisca or Priscilla, together with her partner Aquila, were well known figures in Roman, Corinthian, and Ephesian Christianity at the time of Paul. They are mentioned in Acts 18:2, 18, and 26 and in 1 Cor. 16:19, Rom. 16:3, and 2 Tim. 4:19. See Meeks, *First Urban Christians*, 26–27, 57, 59.

52. People "of Chloe," i.e., of the household of Chloe, are mentioned in 1. Cor 1:11 as Paul's source concerning quarrels among groups in the church of Corinth. See Meeks, ibid. 57, 59, 75, 118.

53. Phoebe is recommended by Paul in Rom. 16:1 as both a deacon (*diakonos*) of the church at Cenchreae and also as a leader (*prostasis*) whose patronage has extended to many outside this church, including Paul. See Schüssler Fiorenza, *In Memory of Her*, 171–72. Also see Meeks, *First Urban Christians*, 60.

54. Although Paul talks of groups claiming to belong to "Paul," to "Apollos," to "Cephas," and to "Christ" (1 Cor. 1:12), this diffusion of names seems to have been a diversionary strategy concealing the primary rivalry with Apollos, whose partisans were probably the majority. See Wire, *Corinthian Women Prophets*, 39–43.

55. The literature arguing about the meaning of head covering and its ties to a cosmology of subordination of women is extensive. See Wire, *Corinthian Women*, Appendix 8, 220–23. I agree with her that the issue is head covering (not pinned-up versus loose hair), which represents women's social (and, for Paul, cosmological) subordination. See also the discussion of these arguments in MacDonald, *No Male and Female*, 72–91.

56. See Mary Douglas, *Natural Symbols: Explorations in Cosmology* (London: Barrie and Rockcliffe, 1970), and "Introduction to Grid/Group Analysis," in

*Essays in the Sociology of Perception*, Mary Douglas, ed. (London: Routledge and Kegan Paul, 1982). Wire, *Corinthian Women*, 188–95, applies grid/ group analysis to Paul's strictures in 1 Corinthians, and Ross Kraemer applies this analysis to Pauline Christianity in the New Testament generally; *Her Share*, 141–56.

57. Wire suggests that Paul's theology of his own sufferings, as one who has lost worldly status for Christ, reflects his social status as a male Christian Jew, in contrast to the Corinthian women who are economically as well as spiritually "upwardly mobile": 43–71.

58. Paul in 1 Cor. 5:1 says that the case of a man living with his father's wife is the kind of immorality "not found even among pagans." This suggests that his own shocked response reflects Jewish laws on incest. But we are not told whether the man's father was still living or whether the couple was married. Wire suggests that Paul is exaggerating the picture of widespread sexual morality to lead to his main concern, which is to curb female withdrawal from sexual relations based on his assumption that this would cause the males to turn to unlawful sexual relations; *Corinthian Women*, 73–90.

59. Walter Schmithals, *Gnosticism in Corinth* (Nashville: Abingdon, 1971), developed the most extensive argument that Paul's opponents were Gnostics who were *both* ascetics and libertines. See bibliography in Wire, *Corinthian Women*, Appendix 4, 206–8.

60. Jewish society in the Diaspora would have had its own system of law courts for all disputes, and Paul seems to be suggesting that Christians develop a parallel system so they do not need to take disputes before the "unrighteous," i.e., pagans. The rabbis in the Mishnaic tractate *Sanhedrin* forbade Jews to take their cases before gentile courts, i.e., before "heathens"; see Emil Schurer, *The History of the Jewish People in the Age of Jesus* (Edinburgh: Clark, 1979), 2:208–9.

61. Commentators have assumed that the references to fornication and becoming "one body with the prostitute" meant widespread recourse to prostitution among Corinthian Christians. But since the Jewish tradition commonly used prostitution metaphorically to mean any kind of idolatry and forbidden relations with gentiles, Paul's use here may be metaphorical rather than literal. It is striking that Paul has no actual case in mind for which he would presumably have applied the sort of judgment he applies to the man living with his father's wife. See Phyllis Bird, "To Play the Harlot: An Inquiry into an Old Tes-

tament Metaphor," in *Gender and Difference in Ancient Israel,* Peggy L. Day, ed. (Minneapolis: Fortress, 1989), 75–94.

62. Wire points out that Paul's strictures against immorality all have men in mind, while his advice to marry involves women who prefer chastity to marriage: *Corinthian Women,* 73–97.

63. Ibid., 82–83.

64. Ibid., 92.

65. Gerd Theissen suggests that a key issue in eating meat offered to idols and the offensiveness of disorderly eating of the Lord's Supper is social discrimination in which the wealthier can afford meat and furnish it for the socially privileged; Paul wants a Lord's Supper where all are served equally. See *The Social Setting of Pauline Christianity,* 145–68. Wire, by contrast, sees women as providing the common foods, bringing these from their households early. A more symbolic Lord's Supper in which ordinary eating is reserved for the home would deprive women of an important collective role and power; see *Corinthian Women,* 100–10.

66. For Wire's summation of her reconstruction of the Corinthian women prophets' theology of the New Creation, see *Corinthian Women,* 184–88. For a different approach to this same theology in which both Paul's cosmology of subordination in 1 Cor. 11:2–16 and his acceptance of women's baptismal equality in Gal. 3:28 as spiritual masculinity are complementary rather than contradictory, see Lone Fatum, "Image of God and Glory of Man," in *Image of God,* 56–137.

67. Paul's reference to women needing to "have a symbol of authority on [their] head because of the angels" (1 Cor. 11:10) has been the source of extensive exegetical debate. Many suggest that Paul did not spell out this reference to angels because he assumed the Corinthians would understand it. But what did he, and they, understand by it? Does it mean the angels that praise God around the divine throne, in whose company the Corinthian women inappropriately assume themselves to be numbered, as Wire thinks? (*Corinthian Women,* 121–22) Or does it mean fallen angels of the Watcher myth who were seduced by women's wiles, aided by cosmetics and adorned (uncovered) hair, as Prusak ("Women," 98–100) suggests? Perhaps both views of angels are in play here. The Corinthians believe the powers and principalities are already overcome and thus they are praying with a reconciled angelic

company. But Paul, who believes that the fallen angels will not be overcome until Christ "destroys every ruler and every authority and power" in an eschatological future, is warning that the conditions under which women's seductive uncovered hair cause angels to fall are still in place.

68. Wire, *Corinthian Women*, 102–12.

69. Both Schüssler Fiorenza and Wire accept 1 Cor. 14:34–36 as authentic. Schüssler Fiorenza sees it as referring to an uneducated group of wives different from the leaders who are being asked to cover their heads when they pray and prophesy in 11:2–6 (*In Memory of Her*, 232–33). Wire sees this passage as the final goal of Paul's intention in the whole letter to silence women. Both argue that the manuscript tradition in which this text is always present (although in some Latin versions it comes at the end of the chapter) requires one to see it as original. But commentators in the past twenty years have argued that it is a gloss by a later hand, probably by the editor who also created the Pastoral Epistles. The language of the passage is very similar to that found in 1 Tim. 2:11–12. Also Paul could not have silenced all women from speaking when he clearly was affirming women's continued speaking, but with proper attire, in 11:2–6.

I am convinced by the first argument, but I have a different view of the second. My view lies between that of Wire and those who argue that Paul expected women to pray and prophesy. I suggest that Paul did not demand that all women be silent, but the combined effect of veiling in a context of a reasserted cosmology of subordination and the demand for ordered speech would, if accepted, have had the effect of silencing most of the women at Corinth by forbidding the forms and theology that affirmed their speaking. Thus the later editor who added this gloss could have seen himself, not as countering Paul, but simply as explicating Paul's intention. See Wire, *Corinthian Women*, 149–58, 229–31; compare Dennis MacDonald, *The Legend and the Apostle: The Battle for Paul in Story and Canon* (Philadelphia, Westminster, 1983), 87.

70. Mary Rose D'Angelo, "Women's Heads as Sexual Members: Paul and the Unveiled Women of Corinth," unpublished manuscript. Contact D'Angelo at Religious Studies, University of Notre Dame.

71. See Wire, *Corinthian Women*, 159–80.

72. On Paul's dropping of the resurrection appearances to women, see ibid., 161–63.

73. 2 Corinthians 10–13 is generally seen as a fragment of an angry letter, written at a time when Paul was in conflict with most of the Corinthians, following his interventions represented by 1 Corinthians while 2 Corinthians 1–9 is a letter written later when the conflict had been smoothed over. See Dieter Georgi, *The Opponents of Paul in Second Corinthians* (Philadelphia: Fortress, 1986), 10–11.

74. See discussion in Schüssler Fiorenza, *In Memory of Her*, 251–59, 266–70.

75. The concept of "love patriarchalism" (spiritual equality between men and women, master and slaves, combined with continued social hierarchy in the Christianized patriarchal family as model for the church) was first explicated by Adolf von Harnack. It is defended by Theissen (*Social Setting of Pauline Christianity*, 163–68) as already present in Paul's teachings in 1 Corinthians and as representing Christianity's great advance in social relations.

76. See Schüssler Fiorenza on 1 Peter, *In Memory of Her*, 260–65.

77. Ibid.

78. This community of women teachers, classed as "widows," is the basis for Schüssler Fiorenza's claim that there was in the early church something one can call "an ekklesia of women": ibid., 285–315. Recent studies of the *Apocryphal Acts* have collaborated this concept of women teachers, identified particularly with the "widows," as sources of a tradition of "folk stories" that affirm baptism as mandating a radical break with marriage and the subordination to the patriarchal family for women; see Steven L. Davies, *The Revolt of the Widows: The Social World of the Apocryphal Acts* (Carbondale, Ill.: Southern Illinois Press, 1980); MacDonald, *Legend*; and Virginia Burrus, *Chastity as Autonomy: Women in the Stories of Apocryphal Acts* (Lewiston, Pa.: Edwin Mellen, 1987).

79. MacDonald argues that the Thecla legend was already known in oral form and 1 Timothy was written to refute it: *Legend*, 59–65.

80. The English translation of *The Acts of Paul and Thecla* is in the *Acts of Paul, New Testament Apocrypha*, Wilhelm Schneemelcher, trans. vol. 2 (Louisville, Ky.: Westminster/John Knox, 1992).

81. The importance of the story of Thecla for women's claims to ministry is indicated by the fact that, in the earliest reference to it at the end of the second century, the church father Tertullian complains that Christians cite the example of Thecla to justify women's teaching and baptizing; *On Baptism* 1.17. See also Jonette Bussla, "Adam, Eve and the Pastor" in *Genesis 1–3 in the History of Exegesis: Intrigue in the Garden* (Lewistown, N.Y.: Edwin Mellen, 1988), 43–65.

## Chapter Two

1. Helmut Koester, "Gnomai Diaphoroi: The Origin and Nature of Diversification in the History of Early Christianity," in J. M. Robinson and H. Koester, *Trajectories through Early Christianity* (Philadelphia: Fortress, 1971), 114–57.

2. Arthur Voobus, *A History of Asceticism in the Syrian Orient* (Louvain, Belgium: CSCO, 1958), 3–30.

3. See James Robinson, "Very Goddess and Very Man: Jesus' Better Self," in *Images of the Feminine in Gnosticism,* Karen King, ed. (Philadelphia: Fortress, 1988), 113–27; also "Logoi Sophon: On the Gattung of Q," in Robinson and Koester, *Trajectories,* 71–113.

4. Cosmic Christology in the New Testament is found in the Gospel of John 1:1–18, Col. 1:15–20, and Heb. 1:1–4; see Rosemary R. Ruether, *Gaia and God: An Ecofeminist Theology of Earth Healing* (San Francisco: Harper, 1992), 231–34; also see John Ashton, "The Transformation of Wisdom: A Study of the Prologue of John's Gospel," *New Testament Studies* 32 (1986): 161–86.

5. Elisabeth Schüssler Fiorenza, *Revelation: Vision of a Just World* (Philadelphia: Fortress, 1991).

6. *The Gospel of Thomas,* Logion 77b, in *The Complete Gospels,* Robert J. Miller, ed. (Sonoma, Calif.: Polebridge, 1992), 317. For the origins and theology of *The Gospel of Thomas,* see Stevan Davies, *The Gospel of Thomas and Christian Wisdom* (New York: Seabury, 1983), and Stephen J. Patterson, *The Gospel of Thomas and Jesus* (Sonoma, Calif.: Polebridge, 1993).

7. Irenaeus, *Against the Heresies* 1.2–3; 3.3–4. See A. Roberts and W. H. Rambaut, eds., *The Ante-Nicene Library,* vol. 1 (Edinburgh: T. and T. Clark, 1869), 7–15, 260–65; also see Tertullian, *On Prescription of Heretics,* chapters 20–21, 36, in *Ante-Nicene Library,* vol. 15 (1870).

8. See Sheila McGinn-Moorer, *The New Prophecy in Asia Minor and the Rise of Ecclesiastical Patriarchy in Second Century Pauline Traditions* (Ph.D. dissertation: Northwestern University, May 1989), 276–97. Also see T. D. Barnes, "The Chronology of Montanism," *Journal of Theological Studies* (December 1970), 405–6. For a more comprehensive study, see Christine Trevett, *Montanism: Gender, Authority and the New Prophecy* (Cambridge: Cambridge University Press, 1996).

9. Epiphanius, *Panarion* 48.12. See Ronald E. Heine, *The Montanist Oracles and Testimonia* (Macon, Ga.: Mercer University Press, 1989).

10. Ibid., 49.1; see also the *Odes of Solomon* for the female- identified view of

the Holy Spirit in Syriac Christianity: J. H. Charlesworth (Missoula, Mont.: Scholars Press, 1977). Also see Susan A. Harvey, "Women in Early Syriac Christianity," in *Images of Women in Antiquity*, Averil Cameron and Amelie Kuhrt, eds. (Detroit: Wayne State University Press), 288–98.

11. Eusebius, *Ecclesiastical History* 5.18.2–11.

12. Ibid., 5.16.20–22.

13. Epiphanius, *Panarion* 48.2, in Philip Amidon, ed. (New York: Oxford, 1991), 170–72. Also Eusebius, *Ecclesiastical History* 5.4, 14–18 (Cambridge, Mass.: Harvard University Press, Loeb Classical Library, 1926), 443, 471–93.

14. Irenaeus does not mention the Montanists by name but warns against those who oppose the "gift of the Spirit, which in these last days has been poured out on the human race": *Adversus Haereses* 3.2.9, in *Early Christian Fathers*, C. C. Richardson, ed. (Philadelphia: Westminster, 1953), 1:383–84.

15. T. D. Barnes, *Tertullian* (Oxford: Clarendon, 1971), 210–32.

16. *Martyrdom of Saints Perpetua and Felicitas*, H. Musurillo, ed. (Oxford: Clarendon, 1972).

17. Justin Martyr, *Apology* 1.26. R. Joseph Hoffmann, *Marcion: On the Restitution of Christianity: An Essay on the Development of Radical Paulinist Theology in the Second Century* (Chico, Calif.: Scholars Press, 1984), 31–74. Also see Hans J. W. Drijvers, "Marcionism in Syria: Principles, Problems, Polemics," *The Second Century* 6, no. 3 (Fall 1987). Primary sources for Marcion from its opponents are: Tertullian, *Adversus Marcionism*; Irenaeus, *Adversus Haereses* 1.27–28, 4.8.29–30; Clement, *Stromata* 3.3; and Epiphanius, *Panarion* (Amidon edition, 144–60).

18. Adolf von Harnack, *Marcion: Das Evangelium von Fremden Gott* (Leipzig, 1921). Peter Brown, *The Body and Society: Men, Women and Sexual Renunciation in Early Christianity* (New York: Columbia University Press, 1988), 86–90.

19. Arthur Voobus, *Celibacy: A Requirement for Admission to Baptism in the Early Syria Church* (Stockholm: ETSE, 1951).

20. Brown, *Body and Society*, 86–89.

21. Hippolytus, *Refutation of Heresies* 7.17; Tertullian, *De Praescriptione Haereticorum* 6.6; Jerome, Epistle 133.4.

22. Brown, *Body and Society*, 90 and note 28.

23. Ibid., 105–07.

24. Tertullian, *Against the Valentinians* 4; in *Ante-Nicene Christian Library*, vol. 15 (1870).

25. Clement, *Excerpta ex Theodoto*; see also Diedre J. Good, "Sophia in Valentinianism," *Second Century* 4/4 (Winter 1984); and her *Reconstructing the Tradition of Sophia in Gnostic Literature* (Ithaca, N.Y.: Society of Biblical Literature Monograph: 1987); also B. Layton, ed., *The Rediscovery of Gnosticism, Vol. 1: The School of Valentinus* (Leiden: Brill, 1980).

26. "Hypostasis of the Archons," in *The Nag Hammadi Library in English*, James M. Robinson, ed. (New York: Harper and Row, 1977), 152–61.

27. *The Gospel of Philip*, in *The Nag Hammadi Library*, 131–51. See Henry A. Green, "Ritual in Valentinian Gnosticism: A Sociological Interpretation," *Journal of Religious History* 12 (1982): 109–24.

28. *Gospel of Philip*, in *The Nag Hammadi Library*, 131–51.

29. Elaine Pagels, "Pursuing the Spiritual Eve: Imagery and Hermeneutics in the *Hypostasis of the Archons and The Gospel of Philip*," in *Images of the Feminine in Gnosticism*, 187–206.

30. *Gospel of Philip* 72:19–22, in *Nag Hammadi Library*, 143.

31. *The Gospel of Mary*, in *Nag Hammadi Library*, 471–74. Karen King, "The Gospel of Mary Magdalene," in *Searching the Scriptures: A Feminist Commentary*, vol. 2, Elisabeth Schüssler Fiorenza, ed. (New York: Crossroads, 1994), 601–34.

32. Ibid., 472.

33. Ibid., 473–74

34. Gustaf Wingren, *Man and the Incarnation: A Study of the Biblical Theology of Irenaeus* (Philadelphia: Muhlenberg, 1959).

35. Tertullian, *Exhortation to Chastity*, in *Ancient Christian Writers*, vol. 13, William P. Le Saint, ed. (Westminster, Md.: Newman Press, 1951), 42–64; and *On Fasting*, in *Ante-Nicene Christian Library*, vol. 18 (1870), 123–53.

36. Tertullian, *To His Wife* and *On Monogamy*, in *Ancient Christian Writers*, vol. 13, (Westminster, Md.: Newman Press, 1959) 10–36, 70–108.

37. Tertullian, *On the Dress of Women*, 1.1.2., in *Ante-Nicene Christian Library*, vol. 11, Alexander Roberts and James Donaldson, eds. (Edinburgh: T. and T. Clark, 1869), 304–5.

38. Tertullian, *On the Veiling of Virgins*, in *Ante-Nicene Fathers*, vol. 4, A. Cleveland Coxe, ed., (Grand Rapids, Mich.: Eerdmans, 1951), 27–38.

39. Tertullian, *On the Soul* 9, in *Ante-Nicene Fathers*, vol. 3, Coxe, ed., 188–89.

40. Clement, *Strom*. 1.5, in *Ante-Nicene Christian Library*, vol. 4 (1867), 366–70.

41. Clement, *Strom.* 2.23 and 3.17–18, in *Ante-Nicene Christian Library*, vol. 12, 78–83 and 133–38.

42. Clement, *Strom.* 4.19, ibid., 193–96.

43. Clement, *The Instructor*, in *Ante-Nicene Christian Library*, vol. 4, 314–17; also Brown, *Body and Society*, 120–39.

44. Eusebius, *Ecclesiastical History* 6.7 (Loeb Classical Library, 29–31). Chadwick rejects the historicity of this event: *Early Christian Thought and the Classical Tradition* (New York: Oxford University Press, 1966), 67; Peter Brown, however, accepts it: *Body and Society*, 168. See also Aline Rousselle, *Porneia: On Desire and the Body in Antiquity* (New York: Basil Blackwell, 1988), 122–28, for views of castration in antiquity.

45. Brown, *Body and Society*, 168–71.

46. Origen, *On First Principles*, G. W. Butterworth, ed. (New York: Harper and Row, 1966).

47. Origen, *On First Principles* 2.2.2, Butterworth, ed., 81–82.

48. Origen, *Homily on Genesis 1*, in *Fathers of the Church* vol. 7, Ronald E. Heim, trans., (Washington, D. C.: Catholic University of America Press, 1982), 63–66.

49. Origen, *Commentary on Romans* 10.17 (on Phoebe as teaching on women and in private). For his general views on women as forbidden to speak in the public assembly, see "Fragments on 1 Cor," in C. Jenkins, ed., *Journal of Theological Studies* 9 (1907/8):500–14.

50. For fourth-century monasticism, see Derwas Chitty, *The Desert a City* (Oxford: Basil Blackwell, 1966).

51. See Henry Charles Lee, *The History of Sacerdotal Celibacy in the Christian Church* (New York: Russell and Russell, 1957).

52. See Jerome, Epistle 127: also Rosemary Ruether, "Mothers of the Church: Ascetic Women in the Late Patristic Age," in *Women of Spirit: Female Leadership in the Jewish and Christian Traditions*, R. Ruether and E. McLaughlin, eds. (New York: Simon and Schuster, 1979), 71–98. Also see Gillian Clarke, *This Female Man of God: Women and Spiritual Power in the Patristic Age*, A.D. *350–450* (London: Routledge, 1995).

53. Palladius, *Lausiac History*, C. Butler, ed., *Ancient Christian Writers* 34 (Cambridge, 1898): 123ff.; also Paulinus of Nola, Epistle 29. On the dates of Melania the Elder, see F. X. Murphy, "Melania the Elder: A Biographical Note," in *Traditio* 51 (1947): 62–65.

54. Elizabeth A. Clark, *The Life of Melania the Younger: Translation and Commentary* (Toronto: Edwin Mellen, 1983).

55. Jerome, Epistle 108.

56. Gregory of Nyssa, "Life of Macrina," in *Ascetical Works, Fathers of the Church*, vol. 58 (Washington, D.C.: Catholic University of America Press, 1967), 161–94. See also Elizabeth A. Clark, *Women in the Early Church* (Wilmington, Del.: Michael Glazier, 1983), 235–43.

57. Nyssa, "Life of Macrina", in *Ascetical Works*, 172.

58. Ibid., 167–68.

59. Gregory of Nyssa mentions being married in "On Virginity," in *Ascetical Works*, 12–13; see also Peter Brown, *Body and Society*, 292–93.

60. Nyssa, "Life of Macrina," in *Ascetical Works*, 185–91.

61. Gregory of Nyssa, *On the Making of Man*, in *Library of the Nicene and Post-Nicene Fathers*, 2d series, vol. 5, W. Moore and H. A. Wilson, eds. (Grand Rapids, Mich.: Eerdmans, 1954), 387–427.

62. This interpretation of a phrase in Gen. 3:21, "garments of skin," is typical of the Cappadocian fathers, following Origen's view that the created body, originally glorious and immortal, coarsened and became visible and mortal with sin; see Rosemary R. Ruether, *Gregory of Nazianzus: Rhetor and Philosopher* (Oxford: Clarendon, 1969), 135.

63. For Gregory's view (in the persona of Macrina) that the souls do not preexist the bodies but are created as the bodies are conceived, see his "On the Soul and the Resurrection," in *Ascetical Works*, 254–55.

64. "On Virginity," in *Ascetical Works*, 33–34.

65. Ibid., 66–67.

66. "On the Soul and the Resurrection," in *Ascetical Works*, 195– 272.

67. Ibid., 266.

68. Ibid.

69. See Gregory of Nazianzus' letter to Basil (Epistle 40) on his assuming the episcopacy, in which Gregory accuses Basil of deserting their ascetic ideals for worldly power; see also Ruether, *Gregory of Nazianzus*, 34–41.

70. Augustine, *Confessions* 2.3 and 9.9. See also Peter Brown, *Augustine of Hippo* (Berkeley: University of California Press, 1967), 29–31.

71. The Manicheans promoted birth control to prevent souls being born into bodies. Since Augustine had a child in the first year of his relationship with his concubine and no child thereafter, during most of which time he was

a Manichean, it is likely that he practiced such methods of birth control: see Brown, *Body and Society*, 390; for his later denunciation of contraceptive sex in marriage as fornication, see Augustine,"On Marriage and Concupiscence" 1.17, in *Anti-Pelagian Works, Select Library of the Nicene and Post-Nicene Fathers*, 2d series, vol. 5 (New York: Charles Scribners, 1902), 270;"On the Good of Marriage" 10.11;"On Adulterous Marriage" 2.12; in *Treatises on Marriage and Other Subjects, Fathers of the Church*, vol. 27 (New York: Fathers of the Church, Inc. 1955), 23–26 and 115–17.

72. Augustine, *Confessions* 3.10–12; 4.1; 5.10–13. See also Brown, *Augustine of Hippo*, 42–45; S. N. C. Lieu, *Manichaeanism in the Later Roman Empire and Medieval China* (Manchester: Manchester University Press, 1985); and Voobus, *A History of Asceticism*, 109–37.

73. *Confessions* 6,.12–15; see also Brown, *Augustine of Hippo*, 65–72, 88–90.

74. *Confessions*, 8. Also Brown, *Augustine of Hippo*, 107–14.

75. *Confessions*, 9.8–13.; Brown, *Augustine of Hippo*, 129–30.

76. Brown, *Body and Society*, 396.

77. W. H. C. Frend, *The Donatist Church: A Movement of Protest in North Africa* (Oxford: Clarendon, 1952); Brown, *Augustine of Hippo*, 212–25.

78. Augustine, *Two Books on Genesis against the Manichees and On the Literal Interpretation of Genesis: An Unfinished Book*, Roland J. Teske, ed., in *The Fathers of the Church*, vol. 84 (Washington, D.C.: Catholic University of America Press, 1991).

79. Augustine, *The Literal Meaning of Genesis*, in *Ancient Christian Writers*, vols. 41–42, J. H. Taylor, ed. (New York: Newman Press, 1982).

80. Augustine, *Against Julian*, in *The Fathers of the Church*, Matthew A. Schumacher, ed. (New York: Fathers of the Church, 1957).

81. Augustine,"On the Good of Marriage,""On Adulterous Marriages," and "On Holy Virginity," in *Treatises on Marriage and Other Subjects, Fathers of the Church*, 27:3–212; "On Marriage and Concupiscence," in *Anti-Pelagian Works, Select Library of the Nicene and Post–Nicene Fathers*, 5:258–308.

82."Genesis against the Manichees" 1.19, 30; 76–78.

83. Augustine, *The City of God*, trans. Marcus Dods (New York: Western Library, 1950) 12.24–28, and *Literal Meaning of Genesis*, 6.42.

84. Augustine, *Literal Meaning of Genesis*, 9.5.

85. *City of God* 14.22–26

86. *Literal Meaning of Genesis* 11.42, and *City of God* 14.11.

87. Ibid.

88. See, for example, Augustine's view of the human soul as reflection of the Trinity, in which he denies that woman has the image of God in herself when considered as part of the couple: *On the Trinity*, 7.7, 10. See also Augustine's treatise on *The Work of Monks* 40, where he says that women have the image of God but do not symbolize it in their bodies, in which they represent the concupiscent part of the soul: *Nicene and Post-Nicene Fathers* vol. 3 (1956), 524. Also see Rosemary R. Ruether, "Misogynism and Virginal Feminism in the Fathers of the Church," in *Religion and Sexism: Images of Women in the Jewish and Christian Traditions*, R. R. Ruether, ed. (New York: Simon and Schuster, 1974), 156–57.

89. Augustine, "Grace and Free Will," in *Nicene and Post-Nicene Fathers*, 5:436–65.

90. See Elaine Pagels, "Freedom from Necessity: Philosophical and Personal Dimensions of Conversion," in *Genesis 1–3 in the History of Exegesis* (Lewiston, N. Y.: Edwin Mellen Press, 1988), 67–98.

91. Augustine, "On the Grace of Christ" and "On Original Sin," "On the Predestination of the Saints" and "On the Gift of Perseverance," in *Nicene and Post-Nicene Fathers*, 5:214– 255, 497–552.

92. Peter Brown, "Pelagius and His Supporters: Aims and Environment," in *Religion and Society in the Age of Augustine* Brown, (London: Faber, 1977), 183–207; also Pelagius, "Letter to Demetrias," in *Theological Anthropology*, J. Patout Burns, ed. (Philadelphia: Fortress, 1981), 39–55.

93. Augustine, "On Genesis against the Manichaeans" 2.19; and *Literal Meaning of Genesis*, 11.37.

94. *City of God*, 19.14–16.

95. Augustine, Epistle 93; see Peter Brown, "Religious Coercion in the Later Roman Empire: The Case of North Africa," in *History* 48 (1963): 283–305; and "St. Augustine's Attitude to Religious Coercion," *Journal of Roman Studies* 54 (1964): 107–16.

96. Brown, *Augustine of Hippo*, 189–243; and Frend, *Donatist Church*, 227–43.

97. Augustine, *Literal Meaning of Genesis* 9.5

98. Augustine, "On the Good of Marriage," in *Fathers of the Church*, 27: 9–53, and "On Marriage and Concupiscence," *Anti- Pelagian Works, Nicene and Post-Nicene Fathers*, 5: 258– 308.

99. Augustine, "On the Good of Marriage," chapter 10; "The Excellence of Widowhood," in *Fathers of the Church*, vol. 16, chapters 9–11, 23–28.

100. Augustine, "Holy Virginity," in *Fathers of the Church*, vol. 27, chapters 5, 8.

101. Ibid., chapter 9.

102. *City of God* 22.17.

## Chapter Three

1. For example, Jerome, Epistle 48, *Letters of St. Jerome*, trans., C. C. Mierow (Westminster, Md., Newman Press, 1963).

2. See Andrew Kadel, *Matrology: A Bibliography of Writings by Christian Women from the First to the Fifteenth Centuries* (New York: Continuum, 1995), 38–57.

3. One letter preserved as a letter of Jerome urging Marcella to visit the holy land was probably from Paula and Eustochium; ibid. 55.

4. Jerome, Epistle 127.7; see Rosemary R. Ruether, "Misogynism and Virginal Feminism in the Fathers of the Church," in *Religion and Sexism: Images of Women in the Jewish and Christian Traditions*, R. R. Ruether, ed. (New York: Simon and Schuster, 1974), 175.

5. For example, the four prophet daughters of Philip (Acts 21:9). Despite the suppression of the Montanist women prophets in the second century, the Jewish tradition of women prophets, as well as the Pentecostal narrative in which women are included in the prophetic gift (Acts 2:17–18), laid the basis in Christianity for the tradition that women could be prophets.

6. For the literature on the trial of Joan of Arc, see Kadel, *Matrology*, 142–45.

7. See "Declaration," in *Scivias*, Columba Hart and Jane Bishop, translators (New York: Paulist Press, 1990), 59–60; see also the Epilogue of her *Book of Divine Works*, where Hildegard declares that her words came from divine revelation to a "simple and uneducated woman":

> Therefore, let no one be so rash as to alter in any way the content of this book—either by adding to it or by diminishing it by omissions—lest such a person be blotted out of the book of life and out of all good fortune under the sun! There is but one exception to this rule—the editing of words or sentences that have been put down too simply under the inspiration of the Holy Spirit. But anyone who presumed to make changes for other reasons will sin against the Holy Spirit and will not be forgiven in this world or the next

*Hildegard of Bingen's Book of Divine Works with Letters and Songs,* Matthew Fox, ed. (Santa Fe, N.M.: Bear and Co., 1987), 266. For the Latin text of the sections of these two works, see *Patrologia Latina,* J.-P. Migne, ed. (Paris: 1855), vol. 197, column 383–86 and 1037–38. A revised Latin edition of the *Scivias* is available, edited by Adelgundis Fuhrkotter in the *Corpus Christianorum* (Turnholt: Brepols, 1978), vols. 43 and 43A. Hildegard probably had wide reading in the church fathers, but not formal training; see Barbara Newman's introduction to the Hart and Bishop translation of the *Scivias,* 44. For her secret language or *lingua ignota,* see Barbara Newman, *Saint Hildegard of Bingen's Symphonia* (Ithaca, N.Y.: Cornell University Press, 1988), 18.

8. The Latin text of the *Vita* is found in *Patrologia Latina,* vol. 197, columns 93–130, as well as a more recent edition by Monica Klae in *Corpus Christianorum* (Turnholt: Brepols, 1993), vol. 126. There is a German translation by A. Fuhrkotter, *Das Leben der Hl. Hildegard von Bingen* (Dusseldorf, 1968). The only complete English translation is by H. Silvas in the journal *Tjurunga: Australian Benedictine Review* 29 (1985): 4–25; 30 (1986): 63–73; 31 (1986): 31–41 and 32 (1987): 46–59.

9. *Ut mortem inferre minentur*: in letter 103R, 1.76, to Guilbert of Gembloux describing her experiences of revelation and illness. The modern Latin edition of the letters of Hildegard is appearing in *Corpus Christianorum,* L. Van Acker, ed. (Turnholt: Brepols, 1991, 1993). Letter 103R appears in vol. 91A, 258–65. An English translation of the Van Acker edition is being prepared by Joseph L. Baird and Radd K. Ehrman (New York: Oxford University Press, 1994), but this volume only covers the first volume of the Van Acker edition to letter 90. English translations of letter 103R are in Matthew Fox's edition of the *Book of Divine Works with Letters and Songs,* 347–51 (there it is spelled Wibert of Gembloux), and in *Hildegard of Bingen: Mystical Writings,* Fiona Bowie and Oliver Davies, eds. (New York: Crossroads, 1990), 143–46.

10. *Vita;* see excerpt in Bowie and Davies, 64. Hildegard's illnesses probably had a physiological basis, but they also seem closely related to her visions and to the thwarting of her self-expression (Newman, *Saint Hildegard,* 7–11, 129). She continually reports that she became paralyzed by pain when she was blocked from expressing and acting on her visions, but this pain was relieved when she won her way. Unlike later medieval women mystics, Hildegard's health was probably not impaired by severe asceticism. She practiced the Bene-

dictine tradition of moderation, and her works of medicine, *Liber Simplicis Medicinae* and *Causae et Curae*, show a strong respect for the principle of balance in good health. In a letter to the younger woman mystic Elisabeth of Schönau, she warns her against impairing her health by excessive fasting; see *Divine Works*, Fox, ed., 340–42.

11. "Declaration," *Scivias*, see Hart and Bishop translation, 59.

12. The earliest manuscript of the *Scivias* to survive to modern times was prepared about 1165 in the Rupertsberg scriptorium, illuminated with thirty-five miniatures with vivid colors and gold and silver leaf. They were done by artists under Hildegard's personal direction. Unfortunately this original manuscript disappeared during the bombing of Dresden in 1945, but a photocopy was made in 1927 and a hand-painted facsimile was made by the nuns of Eibingen in 1927–33. See Barbara Newman's Introduction to the *Scivias*, 25–26. The Fuhrkotter edition of the *Scivias* in *Corpus Christianorum*, vols. 43–43A has excellent full-color reproductions of these miniatures.

13. For the parallel of Hildegard's *Scivias* with the topics of other twelfth-century summae, such as Hugh of St. Victor's *On the Sacraments of the Christian Church*, see Newman's introduction to the *Scivias*, 23–24.

14. See, for example, letter 77R, probably originally a sermon delivered at Saint Disibod, which Hildegard sent to Abbott Helengerus there about 1170; in this letter she summarizes the whole salvation history in a few pages. Latin: Van Acker, 168– 75; English: Baird and Ehrman, 166–72.

15. The term appears as formulaic in Hildegard's letters to her correspondents as well as her other writings. For discussion, see Barbara Newman, *Sister of Wisdom: St. Hildegard's Theology of the Feminine* (Berkeley: University of California Press, 1987), 1–41.

16. Dean Philip of Cologne (letter 15), in reporting Hildegard's sermon at Cologne, says: "We were greatly astonished that God works through such a fragile vessel, such a fragile sex, to display the great marvels of His secrets, but the 'Spirit breatheth where he will' (John 3:8)." This text is also cited by Arnold, archbishop of Mainz, with 1 Cor. 12:11 (the Spirit allots gifts to each as the Spirit chooses); Amos 7:14 (God made a tiller of fields into a prophet); and Num. 22:28 (God made an ass speak); to explain how God might choose a woman as a prophet (letter 20): in Van Acker, 33, 56; Baird and Ehrman, 54, 71–72.

17. Hildegard uses various terms to refer to the humble matter of the human body, sometimes describing it negatively in a way that suggests its sinful expression ("ashes of ashes and filth of filth": *cinis cineris et putredo putredinis: Scivias, Patrologia Latina*, vol. 197, column 383A); "filthy black mire": *limum nigrum et lutulentum*, column 565A, and sometimes more neutrally as "a little lump of wet clay": *parvam glebam limosae terrae*: columns 441C, 445A.

18. Letter 201R (in Van Acker, vol. 91A, 456–57). See English translation in Bowie and Davies, 130–31.

19. Ibid.

20. In her letter to Guilbert of Gembloux, who asked about the nature of her revelatory experience, Hildegard says that she experiences a light through which she sees the reflection of God, which is known to her as the "reflection of the Living Light," but occasionally she experiences the Living Light directly. When this happens her feelings of sorrow and perplexity drain away and she feels like a young girl and not an old woman (*mores simplicis puelle, et non uetule mulieris habeam*): letter 103R, Van Acker, 262, lines 101–2.

21. *Istus tempus muliebre est, quia iustitia Dei debilis est. Sed fortitudo iustitie Dei exsudet, et bellatrix contra iniustitiam exsistit, quatenus deuicta cadat*: Letter 23, Van Acker, 65–6, lines 158–61. English translation: Baird and Ehrman, 79.

22. Letter 1 and reply: Van Acker, vol. 91, 3–7, and Baird and Ehrman, 28–31.

23. *Vita* 1, 4, in Klaes, *Corpus Christianorum*, vol. 126, 9–10. See also letter 2 to Pope Eugenius (Van Acker, 7–8; Baird and Ehrman, 32–33).

24. The letters of Frederick Barbarossa have not yet appeared in the Van Acker Latin edition. Van Acker follows the traditional ordering of Hildegard's letters in which they appear by rank and then alphabetically by place, starting with ecclesiastical rank and then moving to laypeople by rank, so letters to kings will appear only in section 4, letters 311–31. These letters were published in J.-B. Pitra, *Analecta Sanctae Hildegardis, Analecta Sacra* , vol. 8 (Monte Cassion, 1882). Matthew Fox has two of Hildegard's letters to Frederick (289–92). The German translation by Adelgundis Fuhrkotter, *Hildegard von Bingen, Briefwechsel* (Salzberg: Otto Müller Verlag, 1990) has one letter of Frederick Barbarossa to Hildegard and four letters of Hildegard to Frederick, 81–87.

25. *Vita* (Bowie and Davies, 66).

26. *Tu ergo, o homo, . . . scribe quae uides et audis*: Fuhrkotter, *Corpus Christiano-*

*rum*, 5, lines 75–78 (*Patrologia Latina*, 386). For discussion see Edward Peter Nolan, *Cry Out and Write: A Feminine Poetics of Revelation* (New York: Continuum, 1994), 55–135.

27. For paradise and the fall, see *Scivias*, Book 2, vision 1 (Hart and Bishop, 149–57). For an example of Hildegard's use of the terms "moistness" and "greenness," see section 8 of this vision, where she says that God gave Adam the power of the Holy Spirit to cling to the Word in moist, green fruitfulness: *adhaerentis eidem Verbo in umida uiriditate fructuositatis* (Fuhrkotter, *Corpus Christianorum*, vol. 43, 116, lines 237–38).

28. Letter 23 to the prelates of Mainz (Baird and Ehrman, 76– 79; Van Acker, 61–66). See also Newman, *Symphonia*, 18– 25.

29. See Newman, *Sister of Wisdom*, 111–12.

30. For Lucifer's fall, see *Scivias* 2, vision 2, and 3, vision 1 (Hart and Bishop, 73–76 and 317–21. Also see letter 31R (Baird and Ehrman, 95–99).

31. *Scivias*, 3, vision 1 (Hart and Bishop, 147–48, 153); also see discussion in Newman, *Sister of Wisdom*, 168–69.

32. *Scivias* 2, vision 3 (Hart and Bishop, 177–78).

33. See Pamela Sheingorn, "The Virtues in Hildegard's *Ordo Virtutem*, or, It Was a Woman's World," in *The Ordo Virtutem of Hildegard of Bingen*, Audrey E. Davidson, ed. (Kalamazoo,: Western Michigan University Press, 1992), 43–62.

34. For example, *Scivias* 2, vision 1, where God addresses her in these words: "O diffident mind, who are taught inwardly by mystical inspiration, though because of Eve's transgression you are trodden on by the masculine sex (*quamuis conculcata sis per uirilem formam propter praeuaricationem Euae*), speak of that fiery work this sure vision has shown you" (Hart and Bishop, 150; Fuhrkotter, *Corpus Christianorum*, vol. 43, 112, lines 104–5).

35. *Scivias* 1, vision 2, sections 11–12 (Hart and Bishop, 77–79).

36. *Scivias* 2, vision 6, sections, 76–77 (Hart and Bishop, 276).

37. Letter 52 and reply (Baird and Ehrman, 127–30; Van Acker, 125–30); also *Scivias* 3, vision 6, sections 16–17 (Hart and Bishop, 396).

38. *Book of Divine Works* 1, vision 4, which delineates the microcosm-macrocosm relation between the human body-soul and the dynamic relations of the cosmos. In section 100 we read:

> God gave the first man a helper in the form of woman, who is man's mirror image and in her the whole human race was present in a latent way. . . . Man and woman are in this way so involved with each other that one of them is the work of the othe. . Neither of them could therefore live without the other. Man signifies the divinity, while woman signifies humanity of the Son of God (*Et vir divinitatem, femina vero humanitatem Filii Dei significat*).

*Patrologia Latina*, vol. 197, column 885C.

39. *Book of Divine Works* 1, vision 1 on Wisdom in Creation; 3, vision 8 on Love and Vision 9 on Creation and Wisdom's garment. For discussion, see Newman, *Wisdom's Sister*, 42–88.

40. *Book of Divine Works* 1, vision 1, 17, which parallels the virgin earth and the Virgin Mary.

41. *Scivias* 2, vision 6 (Hart and Bishop, 231–38).

42. *Scivias* 2, visions 4 and 5 (Hart and Bishop, 187–234).

43. *Scivias* 3, vision 11 (Hart and Bishop, 491–511).

44. Letter 52R (Baird and Ehrman, 128–30).

45. Letter 23 (Baird and Ehrman, 79).

46. Ibid.

47. See *Scivias* 2, vision 6, sections 62–70. Hildegard interprets 1 Tim. 3:2, 12 on bishops and deacons having one wife to mean that the church is the wife of the clergy and so to take a human wife would be bigamy: Hart and Bishop, 274. In 2, vision 5, the figure of chastity is pictured as the center of the church's bosom as the key to her ministries (Hart and Bishop, 199–216).

48. *Scivias* 2, vision 5, section 23 on the role of married laypeople in the church who lie in the "clouds" around the church's navel (Hart and Bishop, 214–15).

49. *Scivias*, 3, vision 12, section 8 (Hart and Bishop, 518).

50. See Ida Raming, *The Exclusion of Women from Priesthood: Divine Law or Sex Discrimination?* (Metuchen, N.J.: Scarecrow Press, 1976), 7.

51. See letter 10 to Pope Anthanasius and Hildegard's reply (Baird and Ehrmann, 45–47; Van Acker, 23–25).

52. See letter 15R (Baird and Ehrmann, 54–63; Van Acker, 34–47).

53. *The Letters of Catherine of Siena*, Suzanne Noffke, ed. (Binghamton, N.Y.:

Medieval and Renaissance Texts and Studies, 1988).

54. Mary J. Finnegan, *Women of Helfta: Scholars and Mystics* (Athens: University of Georgia Press, 1991).

55. For a major discussion of Aquinas' theological anthropology, see Kari Børresen, *Subordination and Equivalence: The Nature and Role of Woman in Augustine and Thomas Aquinas* (Washington, D.C.: University Press of America, 1981), 141–334.

56. Aquinas, *Summa Theologica* (hereafter *STh*) 1.75.4–7: *Basic Writings of St. Thomas Aquinas*, Anton C. Pegis, ed. (New York: Random House, 1945), 1:687–94. (hereafter *BW*).

57. *STh* 1.92.1.c, quoting from Augustine, *Genesis ad Litteram* 9.5; BW 1:879–80.

58. *STh* 1.92.1, ad. 1; also 1.99.2, ad. 2: BW 1:880, 936. See Børresen, *Subordination*, 198.

59. Aquinas supposes that women have lesser reason and self- control and so are more governed by emotion in their original created nature, thus in the fall Eve represents "enjoyment in the lower reason," rather than consent in the higher reason, represented by the male: *STh* 2–2.165.2. Women can even be spoken of as incontinent by nature, "because by their frail physique, women seldom get a firm grip on things." Lacking rational judgment, they are swayed by feeling: *STh* 2–2.156.1, ad. 1; *St. Thomas Aquinas: Summa Theologica* (London: Blackfriars, 1964), 44:187 and 21 (hereafter Blackfriars).

60. Børresen, *Subordination*, 236–39.

61. *STh* 1.95.1.c; also *STh* 1–2.82.3.c; BW 1, 911; vol. 2, 676. See Børresen, *Subordination*, 213.

62. *STh* 2–2.163.4.c; Blackfriars 44: 161–63.

63. *STh* 2–2.164.2, ad.1; Blackfriars, 44: 177. See Børresen, *Subordination*, 214–15; for woman's subordination in paradise, see *STh* 1.92.1, ad. 2; BW 1:879.

64. *STh* 1–2.81.4c; BW 2: 670–71. See Børresen, *Subordination*, 203.

65. *STh* 1–2.81, 3, c; BW 2: 669; also 3, 31, 4, ad.1; Blackfriars 52: 23. See Børresen, *Subordination*, 232.

66. *Supplement to the Summa* 39.1, ad. 1; Børresen, *Subordination*, 177.

67. *STh* 2–2.177.2, ad. 3; Blackfriars 45: 133–35. See Børresen, *Subordination*, 239. Aquinas affirms that women were the first witnesses of the resurrec-

tion, but they could not promulgate this themselves publicly but only privately to "the household"; he also sees this role of women as resurrection witnesses as prefiguring their final equality in heaven; see *STh* 3.55.1, ad. 3; Blackfriars 55: 39–41. Also Børresen, *Subordination*, 246.

68. For women's delegated authority as abbesses, see *Supplement to the Summa* 39.1, ad. 2: Børresen, *Subordination*, 239. Canon law denied that women could rule as sovereigns, but feudal custom generally gave women who inherited fiefs the right to rule; see Shulamith Shakar, *The Fourth Estate: A History of Women in the Middle Ages*, (London: Methuen, 1983), 128, 145–49.

69. *Supplement to the Summa* 81.3, ad. 1; see Børresen, *Subordinaton*, 249.

70. Mechthild von Magdeburg, *The Flowing Light of Godhead*, Book 5.24. English edition: translated by Christiane Mesch Galvani; ed. with Introduction by Susan Clark (New York: Garland, 1991), 152–54. German edition: Mechthild von Magdeburg, *Das Fliessende Licht der Gottheit*, Hans Neumann, ed. (Munich and Zurich: Artemis Verlag, 1990), 181–83.

71. Mechthild, book 4.2; Galvani, 96; Neumann, 110.

72. For the general history of the Beguines, see Ernest W. McDonnell, *The Beguines and Beghards in Medieval Culture* (New Brunswick, N.J.: Rutgers University Press, 1954). See also B. Bolton, "Mulieres Sanctae," in *Sanctity and Secularity: The Church and the World*, D. Baker, ed. (Oxford: Blackwell, 1973), 77–95. For Mechthild's life as a Beguine, see Frank Tobin, *Mechthild von Magdeburg: A Medieval Mystic in Modern Eyes* (Columbia, S.C.: Camden House, 1991, 1995), 127–30.

73. The developing belief in purgatory gave women mystics and charismatics a new area of ministry in (1) visions that revealed the fate of souls after death, and (2) influence with God to pray souls out of purgatory into heaven. Hildegard of Bingen was asked about the fate of particular souls on several occasions. Mechthild of Magdeburg not only had visions of the fate of particular souls, but on several occasions intervened with God to pray large groups of souls out of purgatory. See book 2.7, where she influenced God's release of one thousand souls and book 3.15, where she helped release seventy thousand souls. Mechthild did not seem to make a fixed distinction between hell and purgatory, but assumed gradations of suffering that ran from purgatory to hell and saw God as reaching down even into hell to have mercy on souls. For her such suffering after death reflects the soul's own chosen spiritual state, espe-

cially its failure to "sigh" (i.e. to repent); while God for her is utterly compassionate rather than punitive: See book 7.41. For a discussion, see Barbara Newman, "On the Threshold of Dead: Purgatory, Hell and Religious Women," in her *From Virile Woman to WomanChrist: Studies in Medieval Religion and Literature* (Philadelphia: University of Pennsylvania Press, 1995), 108–36.

74. Books 2.24; 4.2, 5.11, and 7.28: Galvani, 50, 96, 138, and 195.

75. See Prologue and book 1,1 of *The Flowing Light of Godhead.*

76. The Low German original of Mechthild's book has not been found. Around 1290 Heinrich of Halle, who collected and organized the original Low German version, translated it into Latin as *Lux Divinitatis fluens in corda veritatis*. This version, on parchment, is in the university library of Basel. About 1344–45 Heinrich of Nordlingen and the Friends of God in Basle made a translation of the Low German text into Middle High German, the only copy of which is in the library of the Benedictine Monastery of Einsiedeln. This text, plus a free translation into modern German, was published by Morel Gall in 1869. The best modern version of the fourteenth-century text is edited by Hans Neumann, published in 1990 (see note 70 above).

77. Book 2.26:

> *Das buch ist drivaltig und bezeichent alleine mich. Dis bermit, das hie umbe gat, bezeichent min reine, wisse, gerehte menscheit, die dur dich den tot leit. Du wort bezeichent mine wunderliche gotheit; du vliessent von* stunde *ze stunde in dine sele us von minem gotlichen munde. Du stimme der worten* bezeichtenet *minen lebendigen geist und vollebringet mit im selben die rehten warheit Neumann, 68.*

78. Book 2.26: Galvani, 56–57; Neumann, 68–69.

79. Galvani, 50; Neumann, 59.

80. For Mechthild's picture of the coming of the Antichrist and the sufferings that will befall the saints at that time, see particularly book 6.15 (Galvani, 182–86).

81. Barbara Newman, *From Virile Woman to WomanChrist*, 137–67.

82. Book 3.9: Galvani, 74.

83. Ibid.

84. Book 5.9: Galvani, 137. Mechthild is speaking here of the resurrection from the dead when the souls receive back their original unfallen bodies, without those qualities of "sinful human sap," which came to humans in general,

and "cursed blood," which came to women, from eating the apple: *"Aber das sundige menschliche saf, das Adam us oppfel beis, das noch naturlich allu unsru lider durgat, und dar zu das verfluchte blut, das Even und allen wiben von dem oppfel entstunt, das wart inen nit wider gegeben"*: Neumann, 163. For the symbolism of liquids in Mechthild—water, blood, milk, and wine—and their relation to this particular passage, see James C. Franklin, *Mystical Transformations: The Imagery of Liquids in the Work of Mechthild of Magdeburg* (London: Associated University Presses, 1978).

85. Galvani, 15–16.

86. Book 1.3: Galvani, 8–9.

87. Book 1.4: Galvani, 9.

88. For example, book 2.2: "When the maiden pursues the youth eagerly, His noble nature is so willing that He receives her and she gladly leads Him as her heart desires" (Galvani, 29); book 2.22: "The worthiest angel, Jesus Christ, who soars above the Seraphim, who must be God undivided with His Father, that is whom I must take into my arms, to eat and drink Him and do with as I please" (Galvani, 47); book 2.25: Christ speaking to the soul, "And you shall have power over Me Myself. I am lovingly inclined to you" (Galvani, 54); book 4.15: Speaking of the highest state of love of God, "This state can only be attained when a complete exchange occurs with God, namely that you give God all that is yours, inwardly and outwardly, then will He truly give you what is His, inwardly and outwardly" (Galvani, 113); book 7.16: On the longing of the soul to be with God, God replies to the soul, "Our Lord spoke: I have longed for you since the world began. I long for you, and you long for Me. When two fervent desires come together, love is perfected" (Galvani, 221).

89. Book 1.4: Galvani, 9

90. Book 4.12 Galvani, 108–11.

91. Book 3.10 Galvani, 76–78.

92. Book 4.2 Galvani, 99. There are different views of the severity of the ascetic practices of bodily self-punishment. In this passage Mechthild clearly speaks of flagellation, as well as fasting and vigils, and says, "These were the weapons of my soul with which I conquered my body so successfully that for twenty years there was never a time when I was not tired, sick and weak." There is a suggestion that in her later years she was easier on her body and the sickness of older years was enough bodily suffering without special efforts to increase it.

See Carolyn Bynum, *Jesus as Mother: Studies in the Spirituality of the High Middle Ages* (Berkeley: University of California Press, 1982), 231.

93. Book 1.29: Galvani, 18.

94. Book 2.19: Galvani, 41.

95. Book 5.12: "Meister Heinrich, uch wundert *sumenlicher* worten, die in diesem buche gescriben sint": Neumann, 166.

96. Book 7.37: Galvani, 242–43.

97. It was customary for an anchoress to adopt the name of the church to which she was attached. For the church of Saint Julian at Conisford, see Michael McLean, *Guide Book to St. Julian's Church and Lady Julian's Cell* (Norwich, 1979). There is no record of Julian's original family and given names.

98. Julian's literacy, as well as the financial support necessary to support an anchoress, suggests both a prosperous family and good social connections. See Joan M. Nuth, *Wisdom's Daughter: The Theology of Julian of Norwich* (New York: Crossroads, 1991), p.10.

99. Chapter 1, short text. For the Middle English text of the short and long texts, see *The Book of Showings to the Anchoress Julian of Norwich*, parts 1and 2, Edmund Colledge, O.S.A., and James Walsh, S.J., eds. (Toronto: Pontifical Institute of Mediaeval Studies, 1978) (hereafter Colledge and Walsh). There are many modern English translations; I refer here primarily to *Julian of Norwich, Showings*, Edmund Colledge, O.S.A., and James Walsh, S.J. (New York: Paulist Press, 1979) (hereafter Colledge and Walsh, Paulist edition).

100. For an insightful interpretation of the three prayers, see Grace M. Jantzen, *Julian of Norwich, Mystic and Theologian* (London: SPCK, 1987).

101. Chapter 2, short text: Colledge and Walsh, part 1, 207–9.

102. The sixteen showings described in the short text are summarized in the first chapter of the long text: Colledge and Walsh, Paulist edition, 175–77.

103. Chapters 2 and 10–12; short text: Colledge and Walsh, Paulist edition, 128–29 and 141–44.

104. In chapter 86 of the long text, Julian speaks of meditating on the visions for "fifteen years after and more"; in chapter 51 of the long text she speaks of receiving specific instruction on how to interpret the parable of the servant: "Twenty years after the time of the revelation except three months" (i.e., c. February 1393). This statement indicates that the parable of the servant was part of the original revelation, but Julian did not include it in the short text because

she was puzzled by its apparent contradiction of church teaching. This suggests a process of writing the long text beginning around 1388, but completing it only after February 1393, when she received the instruction on the meaning of the servant parable. See Colledge and Walsh, part 1, 18–25.

105. There is no evidence when Julian entered the anchorhold. It was at least by 1393, when the first will given to support her in the anchorhold is dated. But most scholars think she probably entered it earlier, perhaps shortly after the visions of 1373, in order to meditate on them. See Colledge and Walsh, part 1, 33–35; also Jantzen, *Julian of Norwich*, 21–25.

106. *The Book of Margery of Kempe*, B. A. Windeatt (Harmondsworth, England: Penguin, 1985), 42.

107. The rule for the life of an anchorite is laid out in Ancrene Riwle, see E. J. Dobson, *The Origin of the Ancrene Wisse* (Oxford: Clarendon, 1976). For other rules see also Aelred Rievaulx, *Regula ad Sororem*, in *Treatises and Pastoral Prayers* (Kalamazoo, Mich.: Cistercian Publications, 1971). Also see discussion in Jantzen, *Julian of Norwich*, 28–48.

108. Colledge and Walsh suggest that Julian may have been a nun at the Benedictine community at Carrow before becoming an anchorite and so got a solid education there. They believe she knew Latin and had a good grounding in Latin Scripture, the Latin church fathers and liberal arts, as well as vernacular classics: see part 1, 43–59. Others, such as Jantzen, see her as more self-educated on the basis of her own reading; *Julian of Norwich*, 15–20.

109. The time when Julian lived in Norwich saw the ravages of the Black Plague, several major famines, the beginnings of the Hundred Years War, peasant revolts that sacked churches and monasteries, and the persecution and martyrdom of the Lollards: see Jantzen, *Julian of Norwich*, 3–12. For the location of Saint Julian's Church in Conisford, see Norman P. Tanner, *The Church in Late Medieval Norwich*, 1370–1532 (Toronto: Pontifical Institute of Mediaeval Studies, 1984), xii.

110 Chapter 6, short text.

111. Colledge and Walsh, part 1, 222.41–42 and part 2, 285.2.

112. On Julian's education, see note 108 above. Also see Nuth, *Wisdom's Daughter*, 8–10.

113. For example, chapter 43, long text: "as to my syghte": Colledge and Walsh, part 2, 477.22; also chapter 65, long text: 627.2; chapter 73, long text: 666.2–8.

114. Chapter 80, long text: see discussion in Jantzen, *Julian of Norwich*, 95–106.

115. Versions of this phrase appear throughout the short and long texts; for example, chapter 15, short text: "I wille make alle thynge wele, I schalle make alle thynge wele, I maye make alle thynge wele and I can make alle thynge wele and powe schalle se pat thy selfe, that alle thynge schalle be wele": Colledge and Walsh, part 1, 249.2–5; also chapter 16, short text: part 1, 252.11–12 and chapter 27, long text: part 2, 405.13–14.

116. For the theodicy of Julian, see Denise N. Baker, *Julian of Norwich's Showings: From Vision to Book* (Princeton, N.J.: Princeton University Press, 1994), 63–82.

117. See chapter 23, short text, and chapters 11 and 27, long text.

118. Julian is not a precise philosophical thinker and so her discussion of the dualism between soul and body, interior and exterior, the godly and the beastly wills, and substance and sensuality do not always seem consistent. See chapters 19, 45, 55 and 64, long text. Jantzen sees Julian's distinction of substance and sensuality as best translated to mean essence and existence, rather than soul and body: see her *Julian of Norwich*, 127–61.

119. In chapter 14, short text and chapter 29, long text, Adam's fall is discussed in terms of our assurance that God can forgive even the greatest sin, since God has already remedied the greatest sin possible: namely, Adam's fall.

120. In chapter 47, long text, Julian sees our inability to remain focused in blissful union with God in this present life, without falling back into feelings of separation, as the foundational expression of our fallen state, "the opposition that is in ourselves and that comes from the old root of our first sin"; Colledge and Walsh, Paulist edition, 261.

121. "But I did not see sin, for I believe that it has no kind of substance, no share in being, nor can it be recognized except by the pain caused by it": chapter 27, long text: Colledge and Walsh, Paulist edition, 225; also Colledge and Walsh, part 2, 406.26–28.

122. Thus chapter 27, long text: "Sin is necessary, but all will be well"; also chapters 35 and 61, long text; see discussion in Margaret Ann Palliser, O.P., *Christ, Our Mother of Mercy: Divine Mercy and Compassion in the Theology of the Showings of Julian of Norwich* (New York: Walter de Gruyter, 1992), 102–6.

123. Chapter 51, long text; Julian says that it was twenty years, less three months, after the parable of the servant was revealed to her that she received

the explanation of it. The interpretation of this parable is central to Julian's exploration of the problem of evil in relation to divine goodness: see Jantzen, *Julian of Norwich*, 190–96; also Nuth, *Wisdom's Daughter*, 44–54, and Baker, *Julian of Norwich's Showings*, 83–106.

124. See chapter 39, long text where she speaks of the sinful soul being healed by the medicines of contrition, compassion, and longing for God, so that the wounds of sin are not seen by God as wounds but as honors; also chapter 56, long text, where she says that the pains caused by sin will themselves be redemptive: "When our sensuality by the power of Christ's passion can be brought up into the substance, with all the profits of our tribulation which our Lord can make us obtain through mercy and grace"; Colledge and Walsh, Paulist edition, 289.

125. Thus chapter 43, long text: "For he (God) beholds us in love and wants to make us partners in his good will and work": Colledge and Walsh, Paulist edition, 253.

126. Julian has a strong sense of solidarity with the human community, for whom we should seek to do good but not spend our time in judgmental scrutiny of other's sins: i.e. chapter 79, long text: "I was taught that I ought to see my own sin and not other men's, unless it may be for the comfort and help of my fellow Christians" (Colledge and Walsh, Paulist edition, 334).

127. Chapter 32, long text; also chapter 46, long text.

128. Chapter 27, long text.

129. See Baker, *Julian of Norwich's Showings*, 107–34; also Bynum, *Jesus as Mother*; Ritamary Bradley, "Patristic Background of the Motherhood Similitude in Julian of Norwich," *Christian Scholar's Review* 8 (1978): 101–13; Jennifer Heimmel, "God Is Our Mother: Julian of Norwich and the Medieval Image of Christian Feminine Divinity," *Elizabethan and Renaissance Studies* 92:5 (Salzburg: Institute für Anglistik und Amerikanistik, Universität Salzburg, 1982).

130. Chapters 52–62, long text.

131. Chapters 58, 59, long text: translation from James Walsh (New York, Harper and Row, 1961), 159–61.

132. See Baker, *Julian of Norwich's Showings*, 122–23.

133. Chapter 60, long text.

134. Ibid.

135. Chapter 25, short text: Colledge and Walsh, Paulist edition, 170.

## Chapter Four

1. See Paula Datsko Barker, *A Mirror of Piety and Learning: Caritas Perckheimer Against the Reformation*, (Ph.D. diss, Divinity School, University of Chicago, December 1990); see also her "Caritas Perckheimer: A Female Humanist Confronts the Reformation," *Sixteenth Century Journal*, 26/2 (Summer 1995): 259–72.

2. For Catherine Schutz Zell's tract in defense of her marriage, see Paul A. Russell, *Lay Theology in the Reformation: Popular Pamphleteers in South–West Germany, 1521–1525* (Cambridge University Press, 1986), 204–05; also Mariam U. Chrisman, "Women and the Reformation in Strasbourg, 1490–1530," *Archiv fur Reformation Geschichte* 63 (1972), 150–54.

3. See Merry E. Wiesner, *Women and Gender in Early Modern Europe* (Cambridge University Press, 1993), 30–34. Also Thomas Kuehn, *Law, Family and Women: Toward a Legal Anthropology of Renaissance Italy* (Chicago: University of Chicago Press, 1991).

4. Lisa Hopkins, *Women Who Would Be Kings: Female Rulers of the Sixteenth Century* (New York: St. Martins Press, 1991).

5. Wiesner, *Women and Gender*, 239–58.

6. The pioneering study on women and work in early modern Europe, although limited to England, is Alice Clark, *The Working Life of Women in the Seventeenth Century* (London: Routledge and Kegan Paul, 1911). See also Merry E. Wiesner, *Working Women in Renaissance Germany* (New Brunswick, N.J.: Rutgers University Press, 1986). And her "Making Ends Meet: The Working Poor in Early Modern Europe," in *Pietas et Societas: New Trends in Reformation Social History*, Kyle C. Sessions and Philip N. Bebb, eds. (Kirksville, Mo.: Sixteenth Century Journal Publishers, 1985), 79–88. See also Barbara Hanawalt, ed., *Women and Work in Preindustrial Europe* (Bloomington: Indiana University Press, 1986), and David Herlihy, *Opera Mulieribus: Women and Work in Medieval Europe* (New York: McGraw-Hill, 1990). For the effects of the Protestant redefinition of vocation, liturgy, and the elimination of veneration of Mary and the saints on women's work, see Merry Wiesner, "Women's Response to the Reformation," in R. Po-Chia Hsia, ed., *The German People and the Reformation* (Ithaca, N.Y.: Cornell University Press, 1988), 148–71.

7. There are numerous references to women as students or teachers in Spanish and Italian universities from the thirteenth into the sixteenth centuries, but these seem to have been occasional attendance at or giving of lec-

tures, not a regular opportunity to gain a degree or a full appointment. For example, in the early sixteenth century, Olympia Morata, sixteen-year-old daughter of a classics professor, was exhibited as a kind of child prodigy of her father in a lecture on Cicero's philosophy at the University of Ferrara. Of greater importance, she was appointed tutor for the daughter of Rene of France, when such tutors were usually male, see Phyllis Stock-Morton, *Better Than Rubies: A History of Women's Education* (New York: Putnam, 1970), 24, 40, 51. In the early seventeenth century the educated Dutch woman Anna Maria Shurman was allowed to attend some lectures at the University of Utrecht, but had to stand behind a curtain; See Wiesner, *Women and Gender*, 133–35. Southern universities were lay, while northern universities were clerical, and this was an additional impediment for women attending the latter.

8. Wiesner, *Women and Gender*, 126–43; see also Caroline Lougee, *Les Paradise des Femmes: Women, Salons and Social Stratification in Seventeenth Century France* (Princeton, N.J.: Princeton University Press, 1976).

9. "Sermon on the Estate of Marriage" (1519), in *Luther's Works*, vol. 44, James Atkinson, ed. (Fortress, 1966), 8 (hereafter *LW*).

10. In his 1519 "Sermon on the Estate of Marriage" (ibid., 9), Luther says, "If Adam had not fallen, the love of bride and groom would have been the loveliest thing." For Luther's metaphors on fallen sex as like an epileptic or apoplectic fit, see his "Lectures on Genesis," chapters 1–5, *LW* vol. 1, section 2:18, 119, and section 2:22, 134. For an overview of Luther's understanding of gender and the image of God, see the essay by Jane Dempsey Douglas in *The Image of God: Gender Models in the Judaeo-Christian Tradition*, Kari E. Børresen, ed. (Minneapolis: Fortress, 1995), 238–51.

11. *LW*, vol. 1, 2:27, 69.

12. Ibid., 68–69; also in his commentary on 1 Corinthians, *LW* vol. 28, 16, Luther says, "A man is nobler than a woman, yet woman is just as much a creation of God as is man. For God all things are equal which yet among themselves are unequal." Also in Luther's Commentary on 1 Timothy, *LW* vol. 28, Luther says: "God himself has so ordained that man be created first — first in time and first in authority. His first place is preserved in the Law. Whatever occurs first is called most preferable. Because of God's work, Adam is approved as superior to Eve because he has the right of primogeniture." Luther goes on to claim that this primacy also meant that Adam was not deceived by the serpent

because he was superior in wisdom: "Adam was wiser than Eve. . . . Paul has thus proved that by divine and human right Adam is the master of the woman," 278–79.

13. *LW* vol. 1, 2:17, 104; 2:22, 133.

14. Ibid., 1:25, 72.

15. Ibid., 2:16–17.

16. Ibid., 2:12, 100; 2:21, 130.

17. Ibid., 2:3, 81–82; 3:1, 151; and 3:6, 162.

18. Ibid., 3:13, 182; see also Luther's Commentary on 1 Timothy, *LW* vol. 28, 278.

19. Ibid., 3:16, 202–03.

20. Ibid., 198–99: also in his 1522 "Treatise on the Estate of Marriage," Luther says that a woman in the throes of childbirth should not be comforted with miraculous saints' tales but with forthright advice to do her duty, saying "Dear Grete, remember that you are a woman, and that the work of God in you is pleasing to Him . . . Work with all your might to bring forth the child. Should it mean your death, then depart happy for you will die a noble death in submission to God." *LW* vol. 45, 40.

21. "Lectures on Genesis," chapters 1–5, *LW* vol. 1, 1:28, 71

22. Ibid., 2:18, 116.

23. "Commentary on 1 Timothy," *LW* vol. 28, 279.

24. "Treatise on the Estate of Marriage," *LW* vol. 45, 40–41.

25. "Commentary on 1 Timothy," *LW* vol. 28, 276–77.

26. Ibid., 276–77.

27. John Calvin, *Institutes of the Christian Religion*, 2.13.3, John T. McNeil, ed. (Philadelphia: Westminster, 1960), 479 (hereafter *Inst.*)

28. John Calvin, *Commentaries on the Book of Genesis*, vol. 1, John King, ed. (Edinburgh: Calvin Translation Society, 1847), 95 (hereafter *Comm. Gen.*).

29. Ibid., 94.

30. Ibid., 96, 129.

31. Ibid., 129–30.

32. Ibid., 130.

33. *Inst.*, 146.

34. *Comm. Gen.*, 146.

35. Ibid., 152.

36. Ibid., 172.

37. John Calvin, *Commentary on the Epistle of Paul the Apostle to the Corinthians*, John Pringle, ed. (Edinburgh: Calvin Translation Society, 1848), 354 (hereafter *Comm. Cor.*).

38. John Calvin, *Commentaries on the Epistles to Timothy, Titus and Philemon*, William Pringle, ed. (Edinburgh: Calvin Translation Society, 1856), 68 (hereafter *Comm. 1 Tim.*).

39. *Inst.* 4.10.31, 1208–9; also *Comm. Cor.* 14:34, where Calvin says that the things that Paul is treating of here (i.e. women asking their husbands at home, if they want to learn anything) are "intermediate and indifferent, in which there is nothing unlawful, but what is at variance with propriety and edification," 469. Since Calvin has just before strongly endorsed the statement in 1 Cor. 14:34, "Let them be in subjection, even as the law says," to deny women the office of teaching on the ground that women are in subjection and "she is consequently, prohibited to teach in public," it does not seem that Calvin is defining this prohibition as "indifferent." What is "indifferent" is whether women are to learn only at home from husbands, or whether they "consult the prophets themselves"; i.e., study the Scripture themselves, since, as Calvin notes, not all husbands are competent to teach their wives.

40. *Comm. 1 Tim.*, 67. Calvin seems to be drawing on the late medieval nominalist distinction between God's *potentia ordinata* and *potentia absoluta*, by which God establishes ordinary laws of creation, but these laws do not exhaust God's potential nature and will, and so God can at times suspend such laws. See Heiko Oberman, *The Harvest of Medieval Theology: Gabriel Biel and Late Medieval Nominalism* (Cambridge: Harvard University Press, 1963).

41. *Comm. 1 Tim.*, 68. See also John L. Thompson, "*Creata Ad Imaginem Dei, Licet Secundo Gradu*: Women as the Image of God According to John Calvin," *Harvard Theological Review* 81, no. 2 (1988): 137–38 and notes, where he cites Calvin's 1554 letter to Bullinger and 1559 letter to William Cecil on obedience to female rulers.

42. *Inst.* 4.10.31, 1208–9. Jane Dempsey Douglas construes Calvin's discussion of speaking in public in this text, as well as his language about matters that are "indifferent" (note 39, above) to mean that the prohibition of women's teaching and hence ordination can be regarded as changeable human arrangements. I disagree that Calvin can be interpreted as intending this in these pas-

sages. In the *Institutes* he speaks of a suspension of the laws of women covering their head and speaking in public not only as an emergency situation where concern for the neighbor is at stake, but in language that has to do with the public sphere outside the house; i.e., the streets or perhaps a public forum, not especially with the church. His continuous prohibition of the office of teaching to women as rooted in the ordinance of creation, reinforced in sin, precludes the possibility that he regards these matters as "indifferent." See Douglas's essay in *Image of God*, Kari Børresen, ed., 251–61; also see John L. Thompson (note 41 above) who disputes this aspect of Douglas's interpretation of Calvin in her article, as well as in her book *Women, Freedom and Calvin* (Philadelphia: Westminster, 1985).

43. For misogynist popular fabliaux and sermons and their relation to wife-beating, see Mary Potter Engel, "Historical Theology and Violence against Women: Unearthing a Popular Tradition of Just Battery" in *Revisioning the Past: Prospects in Historical Theology*, Mary Potter Engel and Walter E. Wyman, eds. (Minneapolis: Fortress, 1992), 51–76.

44. Christine de Pizan, *The Book of the City of Ladies* (New York: Persea, 1982); also her *Treasure of the City of Ladies or Book of the Three Virtues* (New York: Penguin, 1985). For a biography see Charity Cannon Willard, *Christine de Pizan: Her Life and World* (New York: Persea, 1984).

45. For a good collection of the imagery of witchcraft persecution, often featuring nude women as witches, see Grillot de Givry, *Witchcraft, Magic and Alchemy* (1931), republication New York: Dover, 1971.

46. *Malleus Maleficarum*, trans. Montague Summers (New York: Dover, 1971), part 1, section 6. For a collection of primary documents on witch-hunting, see Alan C. Kors and Edward Peters, eds., *Witchcraft in Europe 1100–1700: A Documentary History* (Philadelphia: University of Pennsylvania Press, 1972). For major studies of witch-hunting in Europe, see H. C. Midelfort, *Witchhunting in Southwestern Germany, 1562–1684: The Social and Intellectual Foundations* (Stanford, Calif.: Stanford University Press, 1972), and E. William Monter, *Witchcraft in France and Switzerland: The Borderlands During the Reformation* (Ithaca, N.Y.; Cornell University Press, 1976). Merry Wiesner's chapter on witchcraft in *Women and Gender* has an excellent bibliography, 235–38.

47. See Sigrid Brauner, "Martin Luther on Witchcraft: A True Reformer?" in *The Politics of Gender in Early Modern Europe*, Jean R. Brink, Allison P. Coudert,

and Maryanne C. Horowitz, eds. (Kirksville, Mo.: Sixteenth Century Journal Publishers, 1989), 29–42; also see Allison P. Coudert, "The Myth of the Improved Status of Protestant Women: The Case of the Witchcraze," ibid., 61–89.

48. William Perkins, *Christian Oeconomie* (1590). See *The Work of William Perkins* (Appleford, England: Sutton Courtenay, 1970), 429. See also Edmund Morgan, *The Puritan Family* (New York: Harper and Row, 1966), and John Demos, *A Little Commonwealth* (New York: Oxford University Press, 1970).

49. Perkins, *Christian Oeconomie*, in *Work*, 429.

50. Perkins, *The Damned Art of Witchcraft*, in *Work*, 596.

51. Reginald Scot, *The Discoverie of Witchcraft* (1589) (New York: Dover, 1972), 30–31 and passim.

52. Heinrich Cornelius Agrippa von Nettesheim, *De nobilitate et praecellentia foeminei Sexus*, Charles Bene, ed. (Geneva: Droz, 1990). Early English translations: Edward Fleetwood, *The Glory of Woman or a Treatise Declaring the Excellency and Preheminence of Women above Men* (London: R. Ibbitson, 1651); Henry Care, *Female Pre-eminence or the Dignity and Excellency of That Sex, above the Male* (London: 1670). For Agrippa's life and thought, see Charles G. Nauert, *Agrippa and the Crisis of Renaissance Thought* (Urbana: University of Illinois Press, 1965). Agrippa was a maverick scholar who studied hermetic and kabbalistic writings, belonged to an occult brotherhood, traveled and taught in many areas of Europe. Although he was friendly with some Reformers, he remained a Catholic.

53. See Barbara Newman, "Renaissance Feminism and Esoteric Theology: The Case of Cornelius Agrippa," in her *From Virile Woman to WomanChrist: Studies in Medieval Religion and Literature* (Philadelphia,: University of Pennsylvania Press, 1995), 230–31.

54. Barbara Newman's translation, ibid., 239. There has been a dispute over whether Agrippa's treatise was serious or intended as a satire. Newman sees it as having elements of several genres, combining a rhetorical display of arguments that reverse tradition, with speculative themes from Kabbalism on feminine aspects of the divine and serious evangelical protests against tyrannical authority.

55. Ibid., 241.

56. Henry Care's translation (1670), 78.

57. See Katherine Usher Henderson and Barbara F. McManus, *Half-*

*Humankind: Contexts and Texts of the Controversy about Woman in England, 1540–1640* (Urbana: University of Illinois Press, 1985), 189–216.

58. Ibid., 217–63.

59. Rachel Speght, *A Mousell for Melastomus, The Cynicall Bayter of, and foule-mouthed Barker against Evahs Sex* (London: N. Oakes for T. Archer, 1617).

60. In Henderson and McManus, *Half-Humankind*, 227.

61. See Hilda L. Smith, *Reason's Disciples: Seventeenth Century English Feminists* (Chicago: University of Illinois Press, 1982), 76–95; also Moira Ferguson, *First Feminists: British Women Writers, 1578–1799* (Bloomington: Indiana University Press, 1985), 84–101.

62. "Letters Concerning the Love of God," in *The First English Feminist*, edited and Introduction by Bridget Hill (New York: St. Martin, 1986), 19ff.

63. For Astell's life see Ruth Perry, *The Celebrated Mary Astell: An Early English Feminist* (Chicago: University of Chicago Press, 1986).

64. Mary Astell, *A Serious Proposal to the Ladies . . . by a Lover of Her Sex* (1694), unabridged republication of the 1701 London edition (New York: Source Book Press, 1970).

65. Mary Astell, *Some Reflections upon Marriage* (with additions), 4th ed., 1730 (New York: Source Book Press, 1970).

66. The major Cambridge Platonists were Benjamin Whichcote, John Smith, Henry More, and Ralph Cudworth, all born between 1609 and 1618 and working into the 1680s. John Norris, 1657–1711, is seen as the last of the Cambridge Platonists. See C. A. Patrides, ed., *The Cambridge Platonists* (Cambridge, Mass.: Harvard University Press, 1970).).

67. Astell's major work on Christianity against John Locke was *The Christian Religion as Profess'd by a Daughter of the Church of England* (1705).

68. Astell, *A Serious Proposal*, 64–67.

69. Elizabeth Poole was a seamstress, Elizabeth Warren a teacher, Katherine Chidley a businesswoman dealing in textiles, and Mary Pope inherited a salting business; see Phyllis Mack, *Visionary Women: Ecstatic Prophecy in Seventeenth Century England* (Berkeley: University of California Press, 1992), 96.

70. Ibid., 413–14.

71. Mary Cary, "A Word in Season to the Kingdom of England" (1647). Cary's tracts are found on microfilm in the Thomason Tracts, British Museum. For Cary's activities during the English Civil War, see Christopher Hill, *The World Turned Upside Down: Radical Ideas during the English Revolution* (London:

Penguin, 1975), 321–23, 340.

72. Mary Cary, "The Little Horns Doom: A New and More Exact Mappe of New Jerusalem's Glory" (1651), introductory preface. See also Rosemary R. Ruether, "Prophets and Humanists: Types of Religious Feminism in Stuart England," *Journal of Religion* 70, No. 1 (January 1990): 7–8.

73. See William C. Braithwaite, *The Beginning of Quakerism*, 2d ed. (Cambridge University Press, 1955).

74. Fell wrote an account of her own life, "A Relation of Margaret Fell, her Birth, Life, Testimony and Suffering" (1690); see Mary Garman, Judith Applegate, Margaret Benefiel, and Dortha Meredith, eds., *Hidden in Plain Sight: Quaker Women's Writings 1650–1700*, (Wallingford, Pa.: Pendle Hill, 1996), 244–54. When George Fox married Margaret Fell in 1669 he signed a contract waiving his legal claim to her property: see Mack, *Visionary Women*, 226–27. For a recent life of Fell, see Bonnelyn Young Kunze, *The Family, Social and Religious Life of Margaret Fell* (Ph.D. diss: University of Rochester, 1986).

75. See Mack, *Visionary Women*, 171, note 20. A partial list of Quaker women's writings in the seventeenth century is found in Mack, 428–32. See also the titles under the names of these Quaker women in the checklist of women's published writings in the seventeenth century in Mary Prior, *Women in English Society, 1500–1800* (London: Methuen, 1985), 242ff.

76. For Dorothy White's life and several of her writings, see *Hidden in Plain Sight*, 28–30 and 137–48.

77. Ibid., 309–440.

78. Mack, *Visionary Women*, 242, note 10.

79. Margaret Fell, *Women's Speaking Justified and Other Seventeenth Century Quaker Writings about Women*, Christine Trevett, ed. (London: Quaker Home Service, 1989), 5.

80. Ibid. For the imagery of the two seeds, see also Sarah Blackborow's 1658 tract and the petition of the "7000 Handmaidens of the Lord" to Parliament (1659), in *Hidden in Plain Sight*, 56 and 64.

81. Fell, *Women's Speaking*, 6–8, 13–16.

82. Ibid., 8, 12.

83. Ibid., 8–10.

84. This tract by Cole and Cotton and the Quaker catechism are found in the Friends Library, London.

85. Mack, *Visionary Women*, 140 and passim.

86. *Women's Speaking Justified*, 5–6.

87. For an account of a Quaker woman's dream in which Christ and his bride, the church, are depicted as a Quaker couple, both in plain garb, see Mary Pennington's journal, in *Hidden in Plain Sight*, 225.

88. John Perrot signed his letter to Friends,"I am your sister in our Spouse, John"; Mack, *Visionary Women*, 154–57.

89. *Women's Speaking Justified*, 11.

90. Mack, *Visionary Women*, 172–78.

91. For a discussion of the Quaker view of the self, see ibid, 135–37.

92. See *Hidden in Plain Sight*, 35–37.

93. Mack, *Visionary Women*, 137.

94. Ibid., 136.

95. The residual presence among Quakers of the Christian tradition that those transformed in Christ should be celibate is shown by the fact that two Quaker women prophets, Dorothy Waugh and Mary Clark, advocated marital sexual abstinence: ibid, 227, note 45.

96. Jane Ashburner, an early Quaker convert from Lancashire, thus addressed the rector of Aldingham in 1655:"I am come to bid thee come down, thou painted beast": ibid., 1–2, 421.

97. Ibid., 249–50. Mary Fisher, a Quaker missionary to the Middle East and the Americas, was stripped and pricked as a witch by Boston Puritans in 1656: see Rosemary R. Ruether and Catherine Prellinger,"Women in Sectarian and Utopian Groups," in *Women and Religion in America: The Colonial and Revolutionary War Periods*, Rosemary R. Ruether and Rosemary S. Keller, eds. (San Francisco: Harper and Row, 1983), 279.

98."A Seventeenth Century Quaker Women's Declaration," transcribed and with headnote by Milton D. Speizman and Jane C. Kronich, in *Signs: Journal of Women in Culture and Society*1, no. 1 (Autumn 1975), 231–45.

99. Some Quaker women, like Susannah Blanford, rejected women's meetings as against biblical authority, while others appealed to their sisters to keep up their meetings: see *Hidden in Plain Sight*, 294, and 519–33.

## Chapter 5

1. Clarke Garrett doubts that the Wardleys actually were Quakers, since the Quakers themselves do not record this fact; see his *Spirit Possession and Popular Religion: From the Camisards to the Shakers* (Baltimore: Johns Hopkins University

Press, 1987), 141–42. But the Shakers themselves claim a relation to the Quakers, although one altered by the influence of the Camisards. See Edward Deming Andrews, *The People Called Shakers: A Search for the Perfect Society* (New York: Dover, 1963), 5.

2. See Hillel Schwartz, *The French Prophets: The History of a Millenarian Group in Eighteenth Century England* (Berkeley: University of California Press, 1980).

3. See Catherine F. Smith, "Jane Lead: The Feminist Mind and Art of a Seventeenth Century Protestant Mystic," in *Women of Spirit: Female Leadership in the Jewish and Christian Traditions*, Rosemary Ruether and Eleanor McLaughlin, eds. (New York: Simon and Schuster, 1979), 183–203. Also see Nils, B. Thune, *Behemists and Philadelphians: A Contribution to the Study of English Mysticism in the 17th and 18th Centuries* (Uppsala, Sweden: Almgvist and Wikselts, 1948).

4. See Earl Kent Brown, "Women of the Word: Selected Leadership Roles of Women in Mrs. Wesley's Methodism," in *Women in New Worlds*, Hilah Thomas and Rosemary S. Keller, eds., vol. 1 (Nashville: Abingdon, 1991), 69–87.

5. The fact that Lee's marriage banns were announced in the Manchester cathedral in the successive weeks of December 20 and 27, 1761, and January 6, 1762, indicates that she had not formally rejected a relation to the established church; see Andrews, *The People Called Shakers*, 7.

6. *Testimonies of the Life, Character, Revelation and Doctrine of our Ever Blessed of Mother Ann Lee* (Hancock, Mass.: J. Tallcott and J. Deming, 1816).

7. Ibid., 55–64.

8. Ibid.; see also Fredrick W. Evans, *Compendium of the Origin, History, Principles, Rules and Regulations, Government and Doctrines of the United Society of Believers in Christ's Second Appearing, With Biographies of Ann Lee, William Lee, James Whittaker, J. Hockness, James Meacham and Lucy Wright* (New Albany, N.Y.: Charles Van Benthuysen and Sons, 1867), 160–80.

9. Ibid., 183–86; also Calvin Green, *Biographical Account of the Life, Character and Ministry of Father Joseph Meacham* (Sabbathday Lake Manuscript), 1827). See Kathleen Deignan, *Christ Spirit: The Eschatology of Shaker Christianity* (Metuchen, N.J.: Scarecrow Press, 1992), 67 and 187, note 2.

10. Stephen A. Marini, *Radical Sects of Revolutionary New England* (Cambridge, Mass.: Harvard University Press, 1982), 130ff. Also Andrews, *The People Called Shakers*, 56–57.

11. On the life and writings of Lucy Wright, see *Mother's First– Born Daughters: Early Shaker Writings on Women and Religion*, Jean M. Humez, ed. (Bloom-

ington: Indiana University Press, 1993), 64–132.

12. See Edward Deming Andrews, *The Gift to Be Simple: Songs, Dances and Rituals of the American Shakers* (New York: Dover, 1962).

13. See Joseph Meacham, *A Concise Statement of the Principles of the Only True Church, according to the Gospel of the Present Appearance of Christ: as Held to and Practiced upon by the True Followers of the Living Savior, at New Lebanon, & Together with a Letter from James Whittaker, Minister of the Gospel in this Day of Christ's Second Appearing—to his Natural Relations in England.*, October 9, 1785 (Bennington, Vt.: Haswell and Russell, 1790).

14. John Dunlavy was a New Light Presbyterian preacher converted in the Kentucky revival of 1799–1800. His major writing is *The Manifesto; or, A Declaration of the Doctrines and Practice of the Church of Christ* (Pleasant Hill, Ky.: P. Bertrand, 1818). See also Deignan, *Christ Spirit*, 125–56.

15. Green was born a Shaker when his mother joined the sect in 1780. One of his major works is *A Summary View of the Millennial Church, or United Society of Believers (Commonly called Shakers), Comprising the Rise, Progress and Practical Order of the Society, Together with General Principles of their Faith and Testimony, Published by the Order of the Ministry, in Union with the Church* (Albany, N.Y.: Packard and Van Benthuysen, 1823, 1848). Green also edited the later editions of the *Testimony* with Youngs.

16. References will be taken from the fourth edition of the *Testimony of Christ's Second Appearing*, Benjamin S. Youngs and Calvin Green, eds. (Albany, N.Y.: Van Benthuysen, 1856).

17. There is also a literature of detractors from Shakerism, some of them ex-members, but their writings obviously have to be considered with caution equal to that applied to the literature of believers. Examples are: Reuben Rathburn, *Reasons Offered for Leaving the Shakers* (Pittsfield, Mass.: Chester Smith, 1800), and Amos Taylor, *A Narrative of the Strange Principles, Conduct and Character of the People Known by the Name of Shakers; Whose Errors have Spread in several Parts of North-America* (Worcester, Mass.: privately printed, 1782).

18. For a reconstruction of Lee's own self-understanding, as distinct from later Shaker development, see Deignan, *Christ Spirit*, 29–39.

19. Ibid., 40–64.

20. This and the following extract are from *Testimonies*, chapter 4, sections 3–5.

21. See *Women in American Law*, vol. 1, *From Colonial Times to the New Deal*,

Marlene Stein Wortman, ed. (New York: Holmes and Meier Publishers, 1985), 13–19, 95–96.

22. The concept of Mary as New Eve and representative of the church, parallel to Christ as New Adam, is suggested by the Lucan annunciation story (1:38) and was developed by the second-century church fathers Irenaeus and Tertullian.

23. The notion that Christ's passion on the cross was also an ecstatic "ejaculation" whereby he fructified Mother Church was developed by fourth-century church fathers and became a favorite motif in medieval symbolism. For this idea in patristic thought, see Methodius, *Symposium*, Logos 3.8.

24. The image of Christ-church as bridegroom-bride is rooted especially in Ephesians 5.

25. See Rosemary Ruether, *Mary: The Feminine Face of the Church* (Philadelphia: Westminster, 1977).

26. For example, Linda A. Mercadante, *Gender, Doctrine and God: The Shakers and Contemporary Theology* (Nashville: Abingdon, 1990).

27. Testimony (1856), Book 1: chapters 1–4, 1–23.

28. Ibid., chapter 3, 11–14.

29. Ibid., chapter 4, 28–29, 32.

30. Ibid., chapter 7, sections 25, 30, 34–5, 36.

31. Ibid., chapter 2, section 18, 7, and chapter 9, sections 7–8, 42–43.

32. Ibid., Book 3, chapter 2, 78–79.

33. Ibid., chapter 2, section 33, 82.

34. Ibid., chapter 4, section 12, 90–91.

35. Ibid., chapter 4, sections. 36–46, 93–95.

36. Ibid., Books 5, 6, 119–316.

37. Ibid., Book 6, chapters 4–5, 253–65.

38. Ibid., chapter 7, 170–74.

39. Ibid., Book 7, chapter 1, section 13, 319, and chapter 5, section 6, 342.

40. Ibid., chapter 2, sections 33–38, 327–28; chapter 3, sections 31–36, 333–34; chapter 5, sections 25–42, 345–57.

41. Ibid., Book 8, chapter 1 section 1–6, 359–60.

42. Ibid., chapter 5, sections 7–12, 380–81.

43. Ibid., chapter 9, section 4, 408.

44. Ibid., chapters 7–10, 390–414.

45. Ibid., chapter 5, section 13, 381, sections 26–27, 383.

46. Ibid., Book 9, part 2, chapter 1, 503–11.

47. Ibid., chapter 4, 528–33; see also Frederick W. Evans, *A Short Treatise on the Second Appearing of Christ in and Through the Order of the Female* (Boston: Bazin and Chandler, 1853), 12.

48. *Testimony* (1856), Book 9, chapter 3, sections 1–3, 521; section 31, 526; chapter 4, sections 14–15, 531. See also Evans, *Short Treatise*, 14 where he says that the "necessary consequence of sinning against and hating Wisdom, The Mother Spirit in the Godhead, is the degradation and oppression of woman." In his *Shaker Communism* (London: J. Burns, 1871), Evans interprets the fall of humanity as creating a disordered relation between male and female, resulting in male dominance and the oppression of woman, an oppression overcome in Shakerism.

49. See Deignan, *Christ Spirit*, 165–77

50. Ibid., 216–33.

51. See Wendy Chmielewski, et al, *Women in Spiritual and Communitarian Societies in the United States* (Syracuse, N.Y.: Syracuse University Press, 1993), 119–31.

52. Deignan, *Christ Spirit*, 216–17.

53. Anna White and Leila S. Taylor, *Shakerism: Its Meaning and Message* (Columbus, Ohio: Frederick J. Heer Press, 1904), 215–18.

54. Ibid., 256.

55. The Marquis de Condorcet defended women's equality as humans and hence right to equal citizenship before the French Revolutionary Assembly, but lost. His address can be found in *Journal de la Societé de 1789*, 3 July, 1790; English: *The Fortnightly Review 13*, no. 42 (June 1870): 719–20; see also Edward Goodell, *The Noble Philosopher: Condorcet and the Enlightenment* (Buffalo, N.Y.: Prometheus, 1994).

56. Abigail Adams and John Adams, *Familiar Letters of John Adams and His Wife, Abigail Adams, during the Revolution*, Charles Frances Adams, ed. (New York: Hurd and Houghton, 1876). See also Rosemary S. Keller, *Abigail Adams and the American Revolution* (New York: Arno, 1982), 154–80.

57. See Celia Morris Eckhardt, *Fanny Wright: Rebel in America* (Cambridge, Mass.: Harvard University Press, 1984).

58. Gerda Lerner, *The Grimké Sisters from South Carolina: Rebels against Slavery* (Boston: Houghton Mifflin, 1967).

59. See Robert W. Doherty, *The Hicksite Separation: A Sociological Analysis of*

*Religious Schism in Early Nineteenth Century America* (New Brunswick, N.J.: Rutgers University Press, 1967); see Thomas D. Hamm, *The Transformation of American Quakerism: Orthodox Friends, 1800–1907* (Bloomington: Indiana University Press, 1988).

60. Although Angelina Grimké and Sarah Grimké were often threatened with disownment for their antislavery activism outside approved orthodox Quaker circles, they were both actually disowned with Angelina's marriage—Angelina for marrying out of meeting and Sarah for attending the wedding. See Lerner, *The Grimké Sisters*, 132–33, 255–56.

61. See Larry Ceplair, *The Public Years of Sarah and Angelina Grimké: Selected Writings, 1835–1839* (New York: Columbia University Press, 1989), 36–79.

62. Sarah Grimké, "An Epistle to the Clergy of the South" and "Address to the Free Colored People of the United States"; Angelina Grimké, "An Appeal to the Women of the Nominally Free States" and Angelina and Sarah Grimké, "To Clarkson," in Ceplair, *The Public Years*, 90–115, 119–25, 131–32, 132–33,

63. In addition to African American friends, the Grimké sisters discovered after the Civil War that they had black nephews, the children of a brother and a slave woman. The sisters took these nephews under their wing and raised money for their education, despite their own impoverished circumstances. Two of the nephews became notable leaders. Francis James Grimké graduated from Princeton Theological Seminary and was a leading pastor in Washington, D.C., for many years, while Archibald Henry Grimké graduated from Harvard Law School and was a political leader in the African American community. See Lerner, *The Grimké Sisters*, 362–65.

64. See Ceplair, *The Public Years*, 139; also Kathryn Kish Sklar, *Catherine Beecher: A Study in American Domesticity* (New Haven: Yale University Press, 1973).

65. Angelina Grimké, "Letters to Catherine E. Beecher in Reply to an Essay on Slavery and Abolitionism, addressed to A. S. Grimké," ibid., 146–203.

66. Ibid., 204–72.

67. Robert H. Abzug, *Passionate Liberator: Theodore Dwight Weld and the Dilemma of Reform* (New York: Oxford University Press, 1980).

68. For this argument in Angelina Grimké's "Appeal to Christian Women of the South," see Ceplair, *The Public Years*, 30–39.

69. Ibid., 205.

70. Ibid., 209.

71. Ibid., 208.

72. Ibid., 241–45.

73. Ibid., 245.

74. Ibid., 269.

75. See the interchange of letters in August and September 1837 between the Grimké sisters and Theodore Weld, Henry Wright, and Amos Phelps, defending their speeches and writings on women's rights: ibid., 277–94.

76. There was conflict between abolitionist men and Elizabeth Cady Stanton and Susan B. Anthony over the question of supporting the Fourteenth Amendment, which gave the vote to black men while explicitly excluding women, or withholding support until an amendment was proposed that included both. This disagreement caused an split in the women's suffrage movement that was not healed until the 1890s with the amalgamation of the American and National Women's Rights Association (significantly, at a time when black rights had been shelved by reformers and suffrage leaders). See Kathleen Barry, *Susan B. Anthony: Biography of a Singular Feminist* (New York: Ballantine, 1988), chs. 6–7.

77. The marriage of Angelina Grimké and Theodore Weld took place in a home rather than a church. An African American confectioner was employed to make the cake, using only free (not slave-grown) sugar, black and white friends attended; and the blessing was offered by a black and then a white minister. Weld's vows included his repudiation of unjust dominance over his wife found in current laws. See Lerner, *The Grimké Sisters*, 238–42.

78. Angelina bore three children between her thirty-fourth and fortieth years, a late childbearing that significantly impaired her health. In later years Weld and the sisters founded and ran several model schools and were involved in an experiment with a utopian community, the Raitain Bay Union. See ibid., 269–368.

79. See Margaret Hope Bacon, *Valiant Friend: The Life of Lucretia Mott* (New York: Walker and Company, 1980), 25–26, 39.

80. Ibid., 43–52.

81. Ibid., 41–42. Lucretia Mott initiated the insistence that the household use only free produce, and James Mott helped found the Free Produce Society in 1826. He reorganized his business in 1830 to use wool rather than cotton, since virtually all cotton was slave-produced.

82. Ibid., 59–61.

83. Ibid., 77.

84. Ibid., 86–99.

85. For the complete text of the Declaration of Sentiments and Resolutions of the 1848 Seneca Falls meeting, see Elizabeth Cady Stanton, Susan B. Anthony and Matilda Joselyn Gage, *The History of Woman Suffrage*, vol. 1.

86. *Lucretia Mott: Her Complete Speeches and Sermons*, Dana Green, ed. (New York: Edwin Mellen, 1980), 393–94.

87. A photo of this sculpture is in Bacon, *Valiant Friend*, facing 207.

88. See, for example, her sermons and speech, "The Truth of God" (September 23, 1841); "The Religious Instinct in the Constitution of Man" (September 26, 1858); "One Standard of Goodness and Truth" (June 6, 1860); "When the Heart Is Atuned to Prayer" (November 24, 1867); "Religious Aspects of the Age" (January 3, 1869); and "There Is a Principle in the Human Mind," (March 14, 1869), in *Lucretia Mott*, Green, ed., 25–34, 235–60, 299–310 and 315–42.

89. See, for example, her speech to the medical students of Philadelphia on February 11, 1849; ibid., 83–85.

90. See her sermon, "Likeness to Christ" (September 30, 1849), ibid., 107–14; also her remarks on the divinity of Christ in her speech "A Faithful Testimony against Bearing Arms" (September 19, 1875), ibid., 378.

91. See "Abuses and Uses of the Bible" (November 4, 1849), ibid., 123–34.

92. See particularly her "Discourse on Women" (December 17, 1849), ibid., 143–62.

93. See her "The Principles of Co-Equality of Woman with Man" (September 6, 1853), ibid., 203–10.

94. See her "Religious Aspects of the Age," ibid., 315–26.

95. See her remarks in "The Truth of God," ibid., 30, and also in the "Discourse on Woman," 162.

96. See her "The Argument That Women Do Not Want to Vote" (May 9, 1867), ibid., 287–90.

97. See her "The Laws in Relation to Women" (October 5, 1853), ibid., 218.

98. See her "I Am Not Here as a Representative of Any Sect" (May 30, 1867), and also "Laboring to Obtain the Divine Kingdom" (November 27, 1877), ibid., 291–98 and 391–92.

99. See her "The Necessity of Our Cause" (November 22, 1866), ibid., 283–86.

100. See, for example, her speeches and sermons "Going to the Root of the Matter" (November 19, 1868); "The Subject of Peace Is taking a Deep Hold" (September 19, 1869); "To Carry Out Our Convictions for Peace" (May 6, 1877); "There Was No Man That Did Not Know War Was Wrong" (May 20, 1877); and "The Natural Instincts of Man are for Peace" (September 16, 1877); ibid., 311–14, 343–48, 385–90.

101. Aileen S. Kraditor, *The Ideas of the Woman's Suffrage Movement, 1890–1920* (Garden City, N.Y.: Anchor, 1971), 38-63, 105-84, and passim.

102. See Anna Howard Shaw, *Speeches*, Wilmer A. Linkugel, ed. (Ph.D. diss., University of Wisconsin, 1960, 3. vols.); also see Mary D. Pellauer, *Toward a Tradition of Feminist Theology* (New York: Carlson, 1991), 219–84. For Frances Willard's response to this challenge to biblical authority, see her letter to Elizabeth Cady Stanton reprinted in the *Original Feminist Attack on the Bible (The Women's Bible)* (New York: Arno, 1974), 200–201. A new biography of Willard draws on her recently discovered diaries: Carolyn De Swarte Gifford, *Writing Out My Heart* (Chicago: University of Illinois Press, 1995).

103. For Anthony's personal views on religion and its relation to public policy, see Pellauer, *Toward a Tradition*, 153–218.

104. See Elizabeth Griffith, *In Her Own Right: The Life of Elizabeth Cady Stanton* (New York: Oxford University Press, 1989), 19–22.

105. *The Women's Bible*, Parts 1 and 2 (New York: European Publishing Company, 1895, 1898).

106. The NAWSA debate, including Anthony's intervention and the final vote, was included in the 1898 edition of *The Women's Bible*; see the 1974 Arno Press edition, 215–17. Stanton clearly saw this debate and vote as discrediting NAWSA, rather than the *Women's Bible*, appending to the report of the vote a quote from John 8:31, "The truth shall make you free."

107. *The Women's Bible* (1974 Arno Press ed.), 15.

108. Ibid., 14–15. Although the Shakers were major promoters of the view that Genesis 1:27 proved divine androgyny, the belief that God could be called Mother as much as Father had become widespread in progressive American culture in the 1890s, expressing a rejection of the Calvinis "angry God" for a kindly and nurturing view of God's nature and relation to us. In 1875 with the publication of the first edition of Mary Baker Eddy's *Science and Health with a Key to the Scriptures*, Christian Science adopted a revived version of the Lord's Prayer that addressed God as "Father-Mother God." Stanton probably heard

this term for God from Unitarian preacher Theodore Parker; see Pellauer, *Toward a Tradition*, 208.

109. *The Women's Bible*, 1974 ed. 21.

110. Ibid., 23–27.

111. Ibid., 25. This thesis was fully developed in Joselyn Matilda Gage, *Women, Church and State*, 1893 (reprint, Watertown, Mass.: Persephone Press, 1980).

112. *The Women's Bible* (1974 Arno Press ed.), 136, 152–75.

113. See Stanton's Introduction to the *Women's Bible*, ibid., 7–13.

114. See Stanton's address on "Womanliness," reprinted in *The History of Woman Suffrage*, vol. 4 . At Stanton's urging the National Women's Suffrage Association passed a resolution in 1878 that proclaimed that woman's duty to herself is self-development, not self-sacrifice, and that the Christian church has done untold harm to women and to the human race by promoting the ideal of self-sacrifice for women; see Pellauer, *Toward a Tradition*, 40 and 328, note 91.

115. Elizabeth Cady Stanton, "The Solitude of the Self," reprinted in *The History of Woman Suffrage*, vol. 1. For Stanton's theology of the solitary self, see Pellauer, *Toward a Tradition*, 118–40.

116. Gage herself broke with the National American Women's Suffrage Association because of its amalgamation of radical and evangelical feminists and founded her own organization, the Women's National Liberal Union. For a sympathetic account of Gage's participation in the women's suffrage struggle from 1870 to 1900, see Sally Roesch Wagner's Introduction to Gage's *Woman Church and State* (1980 Persephone Press ed.), xv–xxxix.

117. Horace Bushnell, *Women's Suffrage: The Reform Against Nature* (New York: Charles Scribners and Company, 1869).

## Chapter Six

1. Elizabeth Grossman had a chapter on "Mann und Frau" in her *Habilitation* on Alexander Hales in 1964. She was unable to obtain a professorship in Germany and so taught for years in Japan, but has continued to write on women Medieval and Renaissance writers. See Helen Schweigen-Straumann, "Zum Werdegang von Elisabeth Gossmann, " in *Theologie zwischen Zeiten und Kontinenten*, Theodor Schneider and Helen Scweigen-Straumann, eds. (Basel: Herder Verlag, 1993), 483–88.

2. Charles Porterfield Krauth, *The Conservative Reformation and Its Theology* (Philadelphia: Lippincott, 1971).

3. Herman S. Reimarus, *The Goal of Jesus and His Disciples,* trans. George Wesley Buchanan (Leiden: Brill, 1970): and *Fragments,* trans. Ralph S. Fraser (Philadelphia: Fortress, 1970).

4. See Friedrich Schleiermacher, *On Religion: Speeches to Its Cultured Despisers* (New York: Cambridge University Press, 1988).

5. Karl Barth, *The Epistle to the Romans* (London: Oxford, 1933).

6. Shelley Baranowske, *The Confessing Church, Conservative Elites and the Nazi State* (Lewistown, N.Y.: Edwin Mellen Press, 1986): and Larry Rasmussen, *Dietrich Bonhoeffer, Reality and Resistance* (Nashville: Abingdon, 1972).

7. Schleiermacher, *On Religion,* 37, 47; also *The Christian Household,* trans. Dietrich Seidel and Terence N. Tice (Lewistown, N.Y.: Edwin Mellen Press, 1991).

8. Karl Barth, *Church Dogmatics: The Doctrine of Creation* 3.1, G. W. Bromiley and T. F. Torrance, eds. (Edinburgh: T. and T. Clark, 1958), 288–301.

9. Barth, *Church Dogmatics* 3.4 (1961), 169–70.

10. Ibid., 155ff.

11. *European Women on the Left* (Westport, Conn.: Greenwood Press, 1981); see also Margaret Randall, *Gathering Rage: The Failure of Twentieth Century Revolutions to Develop a Feminist Agenda* (New York: Monthly Review Press, 1992).

12. Dorothee Soelle, *The Strength of the Weak: Toward a Christian Feminist Identity* (Philadelphia: Westminster, 1984), 96–117; also her *The Window of Vulnerability: A Political Spirituality* (Minneapolis: Fortress, 1990), 61–74; and *Thinking about God: An Introduction to Theology* (London: SCM, 1990), 68–76; and her new preface to *Creative Disobedience* (Cleveland: Pilgrim, 1995), xvi-xxi.

13. See *Creative Disobedience,* ix.

14. Ibid., x.

15. Soelle explores the systems of militarism and global poverty in several books; see particularly *Of War and Love* (Maryknoll, N.Y.: Orbis, 1983); *Window of Vulnerability,* ix–xii, 3–11, and 42–49. Also see her *Stations of the Cross: A Latin American Pilgrimage* (Minneapolis: Fortress, 1993) and *The Arms Race Kills Even Without War* (Philadelphia: Fortress, 1983).

16. Soelle, *Political Theology* (Philadelphia; Fortress Press, 1974), vii–viii, xx.

17. For Soelle's evaluation of Bultmann, including her report of his letter to

her in response to her writings on political theology repudiating the idea of corporate sin, see *Window of Vulnerability*, 122–32.

18. Soelle, *Political Theology*, 83–107.

19. Soelle, *Thinking about God*, especially 7–41; also *Window of Vulnerability*, 105–16.

20. See Soelle's *Strength of the Weak*, 96-97, and *Window of Vulnerability*, 85-92; also *Thinking about God*, 171–95.

21. Soelle's first book, *Christ the Representative* (German, 1965; English, Philadelphia: Fortress, 1967), developed her Christology based on Bonhoeffer's view of Christ as the powerless one in whom we encounter the powerless God against oppressive power. For additional reflections on Christ, see *Thinking about God*, 102–19, and *Theology for Skeptics: Reflections on God* (Minneapolis: Fortress, 1995), 85–98.

22. Soelle refers often to the mystical tradition as one from which we can draw an alternative understanding of God and the human person in relation; see her *Strength of the Weak*, 86–90, 103–5. She is currently (1997) working on a new book on mysticism.

23. For example, Harvey Cox, *The Secular City*; see also Dorothee Soelle, *Truth Is Concrete* (London: burns and Oates, 1969), 14.

24. Soelle's major book on creation is *To Work and to Love: A Theology of Creation*, with Shirley A. Cloyes (Philadelphia: Fortress, 1984).

25. Soelle's protests against the belittlement of the human in Protestant theology are found scattered in many of her writings. See, for example, *Creative Disobedience*, 30–40, and *To Work and to Love*, 7–8, 43–46.

26. Soelle's protests against both the religious and secular forms of a psychology of helplessness before power are found in many places in her writing. See *Strength of the Weak*, 95–96, *Of War and Love*, 97–98, and *Political Theology*, 89–91.

27. Soelle's major essay on Christofascism is in *Window of Vulnerability*, 133–41. See Also *Thinking about God*, 165–67.

28. See *To Work and to Love*, 46–47.

29. Soelle often analyzes what she sees as the "bourgeois personality" closed to real relationships; see *Strength of the Weak*, 24–30, and *To Work and To Love*, 31–32.

30. *Creative Disobedience*, 7–22.

31. The slogan over the gates of Auschwitz. For Soelle's image of the world

power system as that of a "man-eating ogre," see *Of War and Love*, 3–4.

32. See Soelle's book *Suffering* (Philadelphia: Fortress, 1975), 61-86, 121-150; also *Strength of the Weak*, 90–92, and *Thinking about God*, 54–67.

33. See *Strength of the Weak*, 118–131.

34. Soelle develops her theology of the church in *Thinking about God*, 136–54, in terms of word, service, and community, but suggests that one can often better find the reality of the church outside the institutional church, among the peace and justice movements; see, for example, *Truth Is Concrete*, 101–9.

35. *Theology for Skeptics*, 85–98.

36. On Soelle's theology of the cross, see *Suffering*, 9–32; also *Thinking about God*, 120–21, and *Theology for Skeptics*, 99–108.

37. For Soelle's theology of the resurrection, see *Thinking about God*, 132–36; also *Truth Is Concrete*, 43–60, and *Strength of the Weak*, 71–76.

38. On the cross and the mandate for Christians to suffer, see *Suffering*, 145–50 and 162–74.

39. On Soelle's critique of the immanence/transcendence dualism, see *Theology for Skeptics*, 37–50; *Thinking about God*, 189–95; and *To Work and to Love*, 13–14.

40. For Soelle's theology of redemption as fulfillment, see *Creative Disobedience*, 41–48, and *Window of Vulnerability*, 12–22.

41. Soelle celebrates holistic sex as a part of redemption in *To Work and to Love*, 115–40.

42. In her recent book, *Den Himmel Erden* (Eng. *On Earth as in Heaven*, Louisville, Ky.: Westminster/John Knox Press, 1996), on ecofeminist reflections on the Bible, Soelle draws out the connection of feminism and ecology that had been latent in her earlier thought on defense of creation.

43. Andrea M. Johnson, national coordinator of the Women's Ordination Conference of the United States, and Maureen Fiedler of the Quixote Center confirmed that they have heard from sources close to bishops that opposition to women's ordination and to abortion are the litmus tests for appointment of new bishops, but whatever directives sent from the Vatican to enforce this have not been made public; phone conversation with Maureen Fielder and Andrea Johnson, December 20, 1996.

44. See Marie-Therese van Lunen-Chenu, "New Catholic Women in France," in *The Voice of the Turtledove: New Catholic Women in Europe*, Anne

Brotherton, ed. (New York: Paulist Press, 1992), 61–84.

45. Guilia P. Di Nicola," New Catholic Women in Italy," in *Voice of the Turtledove*, 127–48. See particularly Kari Elisabeth Børresen, "Italian Research on Women in Christian Antiquity," *Augustinian Studies* 25 (Philadelphia, 1994): 137–52.

46. This thesis was published in French by the University of Oslo Press in 1968. It was translated and published in English in 1981 by the University Press of America. The English edition has been reprinted with a new promotion by Kok Pharos Publishing House in 1995.

47. Kari E. Børresen, "God's Image, Man's Image? Patristic Interpretation of Gen. 1, 27 and 1 Cor. 11,7" in *Image of God and Gender Models in the Judaeo-Christian Tradition* (Oslo: Solum Forlag, 1991; reprint Minneapolis: Fortress, 1995), 188–207.

48. Børresen, "God's Image, Is Woman Included? Medieval Interpretation of Gen. 1,27 and 1 Cor. 11,7," ibid., 208–27. Also see Kari E. Børresen and Kari Vogt, *Women's Studies of the Christian and Islamic Traditions: Ancient, Medieval and Renaissance Foremothers* (Dordrecht/Boston/London: Kluwer Academic Publisher, 1993), 13–57.

49. See Børresen, "The Ordination of Women: Nurture Tradition by Continuing Inculturation," *Studia Theologica* 46 (1992): 3–13. For Børresen's critique of mariological anthropology, see her *Anthropologie Medievale Et theologie Mariale* (Oslo: Solem Verlag, 1971).

50. Børresen, *Women's Studies*, 295–314.

51. See the foreword to the 1995 Kok Pharos edition of *Subordination and Equivalence*, and the interview with Christine Amadou in the same volume, xix and xxiii–xix.

52. Sieth Delhaas, *Catharina J. M. Halkes: A Modern Church Mother* (n. p., 1982).

53. See Catharina J. M. Halkes and Annelies van Heijst, "New Catholic Women in the Netherlands," in *Voice of the Turtledove*, 149–70; also Halkes, *Storm after Silence* (1964).

54. *Voice of the Turtledove*, 153–55; also see Walter Goddijn, "Toward a Democratic Ideal of Church Government in the Netherlands, 1966-1970," in *A Democratic Catholic Church: The Reconstruction of Roman Catholicism*, Eugene Bianchi and Rosemary Ruether, eds. (New York: Crossroads, 1992), 156–71.

55. Catharina Halkes, *Met Miriam is het Begonnen* (Kampen: Kok, 1980).

56. *Voice of the Turtledove*, 156–57; also her "History of Feminist Theology in Europe," in *Yearbook of the European Society of Women for Theological Research*, 1993.

57. Published in English as *New Creation: Christian Feminism and the Renewal of the Earth* (London: SPCK, 1989).

58. Halkes, "Humanity Re-imagined: New Directions in Feminist Theological Anthropology," in *Liberating Women: New Theological Directions*, reader for the 1991 Conference of the European Society of Women for Theological Research (University of Bristol, 1991), 75–93. This address by Halkes was less a new direction than a densely packed defense and mini-systematics of her theological keynotes.

59. See her *New Creation*, 141–42; also "Humanity Re-imagined," 85.

60. "Humanity Re-imagined," 88

61. Ibid., 83.

62. See Halkes, *New Creation*, 142–50; also "humanity Re-imagined," 86–88.

63. "Humanity Re-imagined," 90–93.

64. *New Creation*, 10–18.

65. *New Creation*, 162, and "Humanity Re-imagined," 93.

66. The European Society of Women for Theological Research was founded in 1985 in Boldern, Switzerland. It held its inaugural conference at Magliaso in 1986 and has held all-European gatherings of feminist theologians approximately every two years.

67. The public name of Wells for India is Third World Link. For further information, contact Nicolas and Mary Grey, Westmill, Fullerton Road, Whirwell, Hampshire, SP11 7JS, UK.

68. Mary Grey, *The Wisdom of Fools: Seeking Revelation for Today* (London: SPCK, 1993), 1–13.

69. Mary Grey, *Redeeming the Dream: Feminism, Redemption and Christian Tradition* (London: SPCK, 1989), 24–27.

70. Ibid., 63–82.

71. Ibid.,82–83.

72. Ibid.,88–93.

73. Ibid.,128.

74. *Wisdom of Fools*, 81–92.

75. *Redeeming the Dream*, 95–103.

76. Ibid., 118–25.

77. *Wisdom of Fools*, 120–36.

78. *Redeeming the Dream*, 87–93.

79. *Wisdom of Fools*, 67–80.

80. See the handbooks for the biennial meetings of the European Society of Women for Theological Research, which show the range of feminist theological work being done by European women through reprints of the major addresses and reports of the research of those attending. For information on how to obtain copies of these handbooks, contact Dr. Ursula King, Department of Theology and Religious Studies, University of Bristol, Bristol, UK.

81. I base my remarks here on the panel discussion led by Eastern European women at the meeting of the European Society for Women in Theological Research, Bristol, England, September 2–6, 1991.

82. This was a major source of tension between the delegation of Western European women and Third World women at the meeting of the First-Third World feminist theological dialogue in Cost Rica in December 1994. The papers from this conference, edited by Mary John Mananzan et al., are found in *Women Resisting Violence: Spirituality for Life* (Maryknoll, N.Y.: Orbis, 1996).

83. These remarks on the role of the state in forcing the churches of Scandinavia and Germany to accept an open policy on women and gays in ministry are based on personal statements to me by lesbian women in ministry in Sweden during my stay there as a Fullbright scholar in 1985, as well as my visits with German feminists in April of 1996.

84. My knowledge of the Frauenstudien und Bildungszentrum is based on my visits from 1988 to 1996 in Germany with women who work there, as well as a study trip undertaken by leaders of this group to study Womenchurch in the United States in the summer of 1995.

85. See, for example, Andy Smith, "For All Those Who Were Indian in a Former Life," in *Ecofeminism and the Sacred*, Carol J. Adams, ed. (New York: Continuum, 1993), 168–71.

86. One of the leading figures in the German goddess spirituality movement is Heide Gottner-Abendroth. See her *Die Tanzende Göttin: Prinzipien einer Matriarchale Asthetik* (Münich: Frauenoffensive, 1984); in English: *The Dancing Goddess: Principles of a Matriarchal Aesthetic* (Boston: Beacon, 1987); see also her incomplete four-volume study, *Das Matriarchat* (Stuttgart: Kohlhammer, 1988– ), vol. 1: *Geschichte seiner Erforschung* (1988).

87. See for example, Mary Condren, *The Serpent and the Goddess: Women,*

*Religion and Power in Celtic Ireland* (San Francisco: Harper and Row, 1989). The Irish feminists also have a journal, *Womanspirit: The Irish Journal of Feminist Spirituality,* which reflects this spectrum of views (address: c/o 52 Rosemount Court, Booterstown, C. Dublin, Ireland).

88. See Mary Daly, *Outercourse: The Be-Dazzling Voyage* (San Francisco: HarperSanFrancisco, 1992).

89. *Statement of the European Women's Synod* (unpublished, distributed at the end of the conference).

90. Ibid.

## Chapter Seven

1. Michael Kilian, "Suffragists; Statue Remains Banned in Capitol Rotunda," in *The Chicago Tribune,* August 9, 1996, section 1, 1.

2. See Rosemary Ruether, "Christianity and Women in the Modern World," in *Today's Women in World Religions,* Arvind Sharma, ed. (Albany: SUNY Press, 1994), 269–76.

3. Letty Russell, *Household of Freedom: Authority in Feminist Theology* (Philadelphia: Westminster, 1987), 12.

4. Ruether, "Christianity and Women in the Modern World," 276–84.

5. Sallie McFague, professor of theology at Vanderbilt Divinity School, is the author of an important trilogy of feminist theology: *Metaphorical Theology: Models of God in Religious Language* (Philadelphia: Fortress, 1982); *Models of God: Theology for an Ecological, Nuclear Age* (Philadelphia: Fortress, 1987); and *The Body of God: An Ecological Theology* (Minneapolis: Fortress, 1993).

6. Russell, *Household of Freedom,* 88.

7. Letty Russell, *Christian Education in Mission* (Philadelphia: Westminster, 1967).

8. Philadelphia: Westminster, 1974. She is also co-editor of *Inheriting Our Mother's Gardens* (Philadelphia: Westminster, 1988), and *Dictionary of Feminist Theologies* (Louisville: Westminster, 1996).

9. Letty Russell, *The Future of Partnership* (Philadelphia: Westminster, 1979); *Growth in Partnership* (Philadelphia: Westminster, 1985); *The Household of Freedom: Authority in Feminist Theology* (Philadelphia: Westminster, 1987); and *The Church in the Round: Feminist Interpretation of the Church* (Philadelphia: Westminster, 1993).

10. The various activities of Letty Russell in enabling other women to do

feminist work are only partially known to me. Among the activities where I have witnessed her work firsthand are: her support from 1983 to the present for the Women's Commission of the Ecumenical Association of Third World Theologians; the sessions of the Society of Biblical Literature on Feminist Interpretation of the Bible, from which flowed publications that she edited, such as *Feminist Interpretation of the Bible*; the organizing and editing with Shannon Clarkson of the *Dictionary of Feminist Theologies* (Louisville; Westminster/John Knox 1996); the enablement of many Third World women to study theology, including the organizing of the Doctor of Ministry program in feminist theology at San Francisco Theological Seminary for those women who are unable to study full-time away from their countries; and her many trips to lecture and bring students to study abroad with Third World women. This work of solidarity with Third World women is rooted in Russell's thirty-five years of work in key commissions with the World Council of Churches.

11. This motif is found throughout Russell's writings; for example, *Human Liberation in a Feminist Perspective*, 27–28; *Becoming Human* (Philadelphia: Westminster, 1982), 39–41; *The Future of Partnership*, 51–53. See also her "Authority and the Challenge of Feminist Interpretation," in *Feminist Interpretation of the Bible*, 137–46.

12. See Russell's *Human Liberation in a Feminist Perspective*, 20. This book also has a preface by Elizabeth Moltmann-Wendel and Jürgen Moltmann, 11-15.

13. Ibid., 183; also *The Future of Partnership*, 14, 160–63.

14. On vertical violence between the oppressed, see *Human Liberation in Feminist Perspective*, 68–69 and 118–21.

15. See her remarks on status inconsistency as a white middle-class female: *Household of Freedom*, 76–77.

16. *Human Liberation in a Feminist Perspective*, 25–26.

17. For some examples on the role of Christ, see *Human Liberation in a Feminist Perspective*, 65–66, 135–40. On 161 of this book she says, "The church is one of the signs of cosmic salvation and not the exclusive mediator of that salvation"; see also *Household of Freedom*, 73–76.

18. *Human Liberation in a Feminist Perspective*, 41; *Future of Partnership*, 44–45.

19. *Future of Partnership*, 49–51.

20. *Human Liberation in a Feminist Perspective*, 122–25.

21. *Future of Partnership*, 126–31.

22. Mary Daly, *Outercourse: The De-Dazzling Voyage* (San Francisco: HarperSanFrancisco: 1992), 22–76.

23. Ibid., 76–78, 87–114.

24. Ibid., 134–40.

25. This shift in Daly's thinking in the midst of writing *Beyond God the Father* was made evident to me in the winter of 1973. I was editing a book on views of women in the Jewish and Christian traditions from biblical times to the present, published by Simon and Schuster in 1974 as *Religion and Sexism*. I had asked Daly to contribute the final chapter. She had sent me a rough draft of a chapter and then later asked me to edit it to change the terms "sisterhood" and "the women's movement" as "church" and as "Christ" to "anti-church" and "anti-Christ" in accordance with changes she was making in the language of her book, *Beyond God the Father*, which she was writing at that time. She later withdrew the chapter from my book altogether.

26. Mary Daly, *Gyn/ecology: The Metaethics of Radical Feminism* (Boston: Beacon, 1978); *Pure Lust: Elemental Feminist Philosophy* (Boston: Beacon, 1984); *Outercourse*, 200–291.

27. Daly describes some revelatory encounters with plants in her childhood and young adult life. As she developed her mature philosophy after 1980, she moved to a country house where she enjoys communication with her cat "familiar" and with cows and spiders. Her "pirate cove" on the other side of the moon is occupied by herself, her cat, and a cow. She also explores archaic sites in New England, Ireland, and Crete and records mysterious experiences with bees: see *Outercourse*, 23, 51–52, 218–20, 254–56, 303–5, 342–43, 346–47, 349, 364–66. On familiars, see also Daly, *Webster's First Intergalactic Wickedary of the English Language*, with Jane Capute (Boston: Beacon, 1987), 50–51.

28. *Wickedary*; see *Outercourse*, 292–406.

29. See Daly's description of the importance of the ontological truth quest in her scholastic studies; also "The Women's Movements as an Ontological Movement," in *Outercourse*, 59, 69, 74, and 159–60.

30. Daly's radicalized ontological, moral, and epistemological dualism results in a worldview strikingly similar to Gnosticism. As in Gnosticism, Daly sees the "visible" world as completely demonic, created by demonic rulers. A small elite who have "sparks" of true being are engaged in disenchanting the mystifications of the demonic world and escaping back to their true home in

the realm of authentic being . The difference from ancient Gnosticism is that Daly sees the demonic world as a false construction by male humans against women, while the cognitive elite are female. Also unlike ancient Gnosticism, the physical world of female embodiedness, earth, and the planets are the realm of true being against an antiworld of patriarchal lies. Yet some scholars have suggested that the spirit-matter dualism in Gnosticism was itself a symbolic language for an existential repudiation of an evil cultural-political system; see, for example, Hans Jonas, *The Gnostic Gospel: The Message of the Alien God and the Beginnings of Christianity* (Boston: Beacon, 1958), 29–100. Some ancient Gnostics also identified the evil world with patriarchal power against a redeemed world that included women; see chapter 1 of this book.

31. See *Gyn/ecology*, 81–81; also *Wickedary*, 232–33.

32. For archaic time, also gynocentric memory, see *Wickedary*, 79, 136.

33. For boro-cracy, stag-nation, snools and henchwomen or token erasers, token torturers, see *Pure Lust*, 20; *Wickedary*, 186, 227, 229, 231.

34. See *Outercourse*, 110, 129–33, 151–52, 157–58.

35. For "tribes" of Hag and Nag words, witch, bitch, and lunatic fringe, see *Wickedary*, 137–38, 147–78, 180–81, 108–9, 143.

36. *Outercourse*, 346–47, 357–58, 366–67.

37. See Daly's remarks about Chernobyl and the December 6, 1989, Montreal massacre in *Outercourse*, 306–9, 400–401.

38. See Daly's description of the May 14, 1989, event in Cambridge, Massachusetts, "The Witches Return," in *Outercourse*, 394–99.

39. For Daly's use of Susan B. Anthony's "famous last words," see *Outercourse*, 411–12.

40. The term "sectarian closure" is, as far as I know, my own coinage. It expresses an exclusivist view of truth and a favored elect who possess the truth. It has been common in Christianity in both an establishmentarian and a radical form. In the former it assumes an institutionalized possession of truth by a divinely ordained teaching authority that cannot err (e.g., Roman Catholicism), while its radical form arises with a group that claim they have rediscovered the truth against a corrupt and demonic establishment and call for their followers to cut off all connection with those persons who remain in these "bad old" churches. Quakerism reflected this left sectarianism in the nineteenth century. Left sectarianism has also been common in secular form among ideological revolutionary parties.

41. Russell, *Human Liberation in Feminist Perspective*, 167–68.

42. For Daly's appreciative relations with her father, male teachers, and friends, see *Outercourse*, 29, 76, 91. It has been widely reported that Daly refuses to teach males, but she denies this. The Boston College administration has tried over many years to make a case against Daly as excluding men and those of different ideologies by sending "plants" and observers into her classes, but have failed to make their case. See *Outercourse*, 225–29.

43. This statement is based on some personal experiences that I have witnessed or that were told to me, in which Mary Daly urged women to cut off relations with sons.

44. Some of my writings that discuss my family and early education are "Beginnings: An Intellectual Autobiography," in *Journeys: Theological Autobiographies*, Gregory Baum, ed. (New York: Paulist Press, 1975), 34–56; *Disputed Questions: On Being a Christian* (Nashville: Abingdon, 1982); "Robert Palmer: First the God, Then the Dance," *Christian Century* (February 7, 1990): 125–26; "A Wise Woman," *Christian Century* (February 17, 1993): 164–65; and "Solidly Rooted: Ready to Fly," in *The Witness* (December 1994): 8–10.

45. Some of my work in helping to organize and publish work of Third World women is reflected in books I edited: *Faith and the Intifada: Palestinian Christian Voices* (Maryknoll, N.Y.: Orbis, 1992); and *Women Healing Earth: Third World Women on Ecology, Feminism and Religion* (Maryknoll, N.Y.: Orbis, 1996).

46. Archaeological work in Peru has uncovered evidence of human sacrifice in which great chiefs were buried with wives, concubines, and servants; for example, the burial of the chief called the "Lord of Sepan," on view at the National Archaeological Museum in Lima, Peru.

47. See my *Gaia and God: An Ecofeminist Theology of Earth Healing* (San Francisco: HarperSanFrancisco, 1992), especially 143–201.

48. The categories of greed, hatred, and delusion are key for the social justice thought of an "engaged Buddhism." I owe my insight into engaged Buddhism to Sulak Sivaraksa; see his *Seeds of Peace: A Buddhist Vision for Renewing Society* (Berkeley, Calif.: Parallax, 1992).

49. For process theology, see especially Marjorie Suchocki, *The End of Evil: Process Eschatology in Historical Context* (Albany: SUNY Press, 1988).

50. No one book or article of mine is the source for these remarks, although much of these ideas are developed in *Gaia and God*; see also my essay, "Ecological Crisis: God's Presence in Nature," in Rosemary R. Ruether and Douglas

John Hall, *God and the Nations* (Minneapolis: Fortress, 1995) 81–92.

51. Carter Heyward, *A Priest Forever* (New York: Harper and Row, 1976).

52. Ibid.

53. Washington, D.C.: University Press of America, 1982.

54. See particularly Heyward's contribution in *God's Fierce Whimsey: Christian Feminism and Theological Education*, written by a multiracial group of women theological educators who called themselves the Mudflower Collective (New York: Pilgrim, 1985).

55. Carter Heyward et al., *Feminist Reflections on Nicaragua* (Maryknoll, N.Y.: Orbis, 1987).

56. *The Redemption of God*, especially 149–78.

57. See Heyward's article on coming out that appeared in *Christianity and Crisis* (June 11, 1979): 153–56; reprinted in *Our Passion for Justice: Images of Power, Sexuality and Liberation* (Cleveland: Pilgrim, 1984), 75–82.

58. See her "Coming Out: Coming into Our Yes," in *Touching Our Strength: The Erotic as Power and the Love of God* (San Francisco: Harper and Row, 1989), 20–36; also her *Coming Out and Relational Empowerment: A Lesbian Feminist Theological Perspective* (Wellesley, Mass.: Stone Center, no. 38, 1989).

59. "Coming Out," in *Touching Our Strength.*

60. Published by HarperSanFrancisco, 1993.

61. See, for example, Sheila Beinenfeld, "Look Back in Anger," in the *Women's Review of Books* (April 11, 1994): 7–8. See also the reviews in *Princeton Seminary Bulletin* 16, no. 3 (1995): 38–40, and in the *Journal of Pastoral Theology* 4 (Summer 1994): 121–23. For a feminist critique based on an analysis of personal relations, see the review by K. Roberts Skerrett, "When No Means Yes: The Passion of Carter Heyward," in *Journal of Feminist Studies in Religion*, 12, no. 1 (Spring 1996): 71–92.

62. For more sympathetic responses, see Katherine Hancock Ragdale, *Boundary Wars* (New York: Pilgrim, 1996); and Karen Lebacqz and Ron Barton, *Boundaries, Mutuality and Professional Ethics* (New York: Pilgrim, forthcoming).

63. Feminist and liberation theologians emphasize unity of theory and practice. Any feminist or liberation theology in which personal practice is in wide discrepancy with one's theory would be thrown in question. Heyward is vulnerable to this question because she has been so autobiographical in her writ-

ing, revealing intimate details of experiences of sexual relations and struggles with bulimia and alcoholism.

64. A growing group of womanist theologians and ethicists are teaching and publishing in the academy of religious studies. The best known figures are Katie G. Cannon, Toinette Eugene, Jacquelyn Grant, Emilie Townes, and Delores Williams.

65. The term "womanist" is drawn from Alice Walker's *In Search of Our Mother's Gardens*, where "acting womanish" means "wanting to know more than is good for one. . . outrageous, audacious, courageous, and willful behavior." See Delores Williams, "Womanist Theology: Black Women's Voices," in *Learning to Breathe Free: Liberation Theologies in the United States*, Mar Peter-Raoul, Linda Rennie Forcey, and Robert Frederick Hunters, eds. (Maryknoll, N.Y.: Orbis, 1990), 62.

66. Ibid., 62–69.

67. See Williams's introduction to her *Sisters in the Wilderness: The Challenge of Womanist God-Talk* (Maryknoll, N.Y.: Orbis, 1993), 1–14; also her "A Womanist Perspective on Sin," in *A Troubling in My Soul: Womanist Perspectives on Evil*, Emilie Townes, ed. (Maryknoll, N.Y.: Orbis, 1993), 130–49.

68. See Williams, "Sin, Nature and Black Women's Bodies," in *Ecofeminism and the Sacred*.

69. See *Sisters in the Wilderness*, 90–91, 179–84.

70. Ibid., 40–49.

71. See her "A Womanist Perspective on Sin," 144.

72. *Sisters in the Wilderness*, 143–53.

73. Ibid., 149, 268–69, note 9.

74. Ibid., 15–33.

75. Ibid., 23–26.

76. Ibid., 60–83; see also her "Black Women's Surrogacy Experience and the Christian Notion of Redemption," in *After Patriarchy: Feminist Transformations of the World Religions*, Paul M. Cooey, William R. Eakin, and Jay B. McDaniel, eds. (Maryknoll, N.Y.: Orbis, 1991) 1–14.

77. Ibid., 175.

78. Ibid., 161–66. Williams was particularly attacked after the 1993 Women's Conference on "Reimagining God," for her critique of the traditional Christian concept of atonement through vicarious suffering. See her columns

in the magazine *The Other Side*: "Christian Scapegoating" (May–June 1993): 43–44; "The Crucifixion Double-Cross" (September–October 1993): 25–27; and "reimagining the Truth" (May–June 1994): 53.

79. *Sisters in the Wilderness*, 204–19.

80. See Ada María Isasi-Díaz, *Mujerista Theology* (Maryknoll, N.Y.: Orbis, 1996), 13–34.

81. San Francisco: Harper and Row, 1988; reprint, Minneapolis: Fortress, 1992).

82. Ibid., 12–56, and *En la Lucha: Elaborating a Mujerista Theology* (Minneapolis: Fortress, 1993), 62–79.

83. *Mujerista Theology*, 204.

84. *Hispanic Women*, 94–104.

85. Ibid., 100. Also see *Mujerista Theology*, 170–202.

86. *En la Lucha*, 11–14.

87. Ibid., 14–16.

88. Ibid., 186–204.

89. Ibid., 166–184.

90. *Mujerista Theology*, 148–169.

91. *En la Lucha*, 45–52.

92. The Hispanic women's movement Las Hermanas has been one model for such a new community of faith; see ibid., 39–41, and *Mujerista Theology*, 170–72.

93. *Mujerista Theology*, 105–27 and 304–5.

## Chapter Eight

1. Gustavo Gutiérrez, *Liberation Theology*, 15th anniversary ed. (Maryknoll, N.Y.: Orbis, 1988).

2. See Prologue by Mary John Mananzan, in *Women Resisting Violence: Spirituality for Life*, Mary John Mananzan et al., eds. (Maryknoll, N.Y.: Orbis, 1996), 1.

3. This account is taken from my personal remembrance of these events as a delegate to this conference.

4. For this history of the EATWOT process and the emergence of Third World feminist theology within it to 1993 from her experience, see Virginia Fabella, *Beyond Bonding: A Third World Women's Theological Journey* (Manila:

Institute of Women's Studies, 1993).

5. Major papers and statements from the intercontinental conference, as well as continental conferences, are found in *With Passion and Compassion: Third World Women Doing Theology*, Virginia Fabella and Mercy Amba Oduyoye, eds. (Maryknoll, N.Y.: Orbis, 1988).

6. Major papers that emerged from this conference are found in *Women Resisting Violence*.

7. White Western people tend to assume the term "Third World" is a put-down that implies a "third-down" on some hierarchical scale. In her book *Beyond Bonding*, however, Virginia Fabella recalls that this term had a different meaning for the EATWOT movement. She suggests a parallel to the French revolutionary term "third estate," meaning a whole new group that is emerging beyond the dominant hierarchy and reshaping a new majority; se 3–4.

8. See issues of the Indian women's journal, *Manushi*; address: C1 1202, Lajpat Nagar, New Delhi, 110024.

9. These remarks about the relation of Aruna Gnandason and Mary John Mananzan to the women's movements of their countries are drawn from personal conversations and experiences with them. See Gabriele Dietrich, "South Asian Feminist Theory and its Significance for Feminist Theology," in *The Power of Naming: Concilium Reader in Feminist Theology*, Elisabeth Schüssler Fiorenza, ed. (Maryknoll, N.Y.: Orbis, 1996), 45–59.

10. These remarks are drawn from my personal experience during a 1994 lecture trip to Brazil, Argentina, and Chile. My agenda was to interconnect the secular women's movement in those countries and feminist theologians, particularly in relation to issues of reproductive rights. Catholic feminist theologians were very concerned about censure from the church if they ventured into those topics. See María José F. Rosado Nunes, "Women's Voices in Latin American Theology," in *The Power of Naming*, 14–26.

11. María Clara Bingemer, Tereza Cavalcanti, and Ana María Tepedino are Catholic laywomen who teach at the Catholic University of Rio de Janeiro. In São Paulo the Methodist College has a lively program of graduate women's studies that includes religious issues affecting women. This information comes from my own trips and personal experience giving lectures at these universities.

12. Information comes from personal trips to Santiago, Chile, and Lima, Peru, and extended association with leaders of these two groups. The Con-spi-

rando collective and its publications can be contacted through Judy Ress, Casilla 371–11, Correo Nuñoa, Santiago, Chile; and Talitha Cumi through Rosa Dominga Trapasso, Republica de Portugal 492, Lima 5, Peru.

13. The Maryknoll sisters and lay missionaries have played a key role in these Catholic feminist networks.

14. "Ecofeminism and Panentheism," interview by Mary Judy Ress, *Creation Spirituality* (November/December 1993): 9–11.

15. Ibid.

16. The major publication of liberation theology, edited by Ignacio Ellacuria and John Sobrino, *Mysterium Liberationis: Conceptos fundamentales de las teología de la liberación* (Madrid: Editorial Trotta, 1990), 2 vols., contains two essays by women, both with explicitly female themes: "Teologîa de la Mujer," by Ana María Tepedino and Margarida L. Ribeiro Brandao; and "María," by Ivone Gebara and María Clara Bingemer. These two essays total 30 pages out of 622 pages (287–98 and 601–18). In the English abridged edition, published by Orbis, 1993, these essays are 222–31 and 482–95.

17. See especially Franz Hinkelkammert, *The Ideological Weapons of Death: A Theological Critique of Capitalism* (Maryknoll, N.Y.: Orbis, 1986).

18. See Leonardo Boff, *Ecology and Liberation: A New Paradigm* (Maryknoll, N.Y.: Orbis, 1995). Also the interview of Pablo Richard in Elsa Tamez, *Against Machismo* (Oak Park, Ill.: Meyer-Stone Books, 1987).

19. Numerous publications erupted from the observances of the Five Hundred Years of Resistance in the Americas. See, for example, Michael McConnell, et al., *Dangerous Memories: Invasion and Resistance since 1492* (Chicago: Chicago Religious Taskforce on Central America, 1991). Regina de Silva completed her thesis for the *Licenciatura* in theology at the Seminário Bíblico in San José, Costa Rica, on the theme of *Mulher Negra e Jubileu: Desafios á Teología Latino Americana.*

20. Boff, *Ecology and Liberation*, 123–30.

21. Elsa Tamez, "Quetzalcóatl y El Dios Cristiano," in *Cuadernos de Teología y Cultura*, no. 6 (1992): San José, Costa Rica.

22. Pablo Richard, ed., *The Idols of Death and the God of Life* (Maryknoll, N.Y.: Orbis, 1983).

23. Tamez, "Quetzalcóatl," 24–25.

24. In *Women Resisting Violence*, 11–19.

25. *Nuestro Clamor por la Vida: Teología latinoamericana desde la perspectiva de la mujer* (San José, Costa Rica: DEI, 1992); English: *Our Cry for Life* (Maryknoll, N.Y.: Orbis, 1993).

26. See Aquino's "Perspectives on a Latina's Feminist Liberation Theology," in *Frontiers of Hispanic Theology in the U.S.*, Allan F. Deck, ed. (Maryknoll, N.Y.: Orbis, 1992), 24.

27. *Our Cry for Life*, 178–90.

28. See her "Directions and Foundations of Hispanic/Latino Theology: Toward a Mestiza Theology of Liberation," in *Mestizo Christianity: Theology from the Latina Perspective*, Arturo J. Banvelas ed. (Maryknoll, N.Y.: Orbis, 1995), 192–208.

29. *Women Resisting Violence*, 100–108.

30. Ivone Gebara, "Women Doing Theology in Latin America," in Through Her Eyes: Women's Theology from Latin America, Else Tamez, ed. (Maryknoll, N.Y.: Orbis, 1987), 38; see also her book Teología a Ritmo de Mujer (Madrid: San Pablo, 1995), 12.

31. Gebara, "A Cry for Life from Latin America," in *Spirituality of the Third World: A Cry for Life*, K. C. Abraham and Bernadetee Mbuy-beya, eds. (Maryknoll, N.Y.: Orbis, 1994), 109–18.

32. See her chapter "La Bíblia y la Mujer: una hermenéutica feminista," in *Teología a Ritmo de Mujer*, 27–38.

33. Ibid., 109-56; see the condensed English translation in Rosemary R. Ruether, *Women Healing Earth: Third World Women on Ecology, Feminism and Religion* (Maryknoll, N.Y.: Orbis, 1996), 13–23.

34. See her "En los Orígenes del Mal," and "Cuerpo de Mujer," in *Teología a Ritmo de Mujer*, 39–52 and 71–88.

35. Ibid., 146–56.

36. See her chapter, "Cristología fundamental," in *Teología a Ritmo de Mujer*, 53–70.

37. See her " The Face of Transcendence as a Challenge to Reading the Bible in Latin America," in *Searching the Scriptures*, vol. 1, Elisabeth Schüssler Fiorenza, ed. (New York: Crossroads, 1993) 178.

38. The volume, *The Will to Arise: Women, Tradition and the Church in Africa*, Mercy Amba Oduyoye and Musimbi Kanyoro, eds. (Maryknoll, N.Y.: Orbis, 1992), is the first input of the Biennial Institutes of African Women in Reli-

gion and Culture, a project of the Circle of Concerned African Women Theologians. See Teresia M. Hinga, "Between Colonialism and Inculturation: Feminist Theologies in Africa," in *The Power of Naming*, 36–44.

39. In 1996, orthodox (mostly Coptic) Christians in Africa numbered 30 million out of a total number of Christians of 351.8 million: *World Almanac* (Mahwah, N.J.: Funk and Wagnalls, 1996), 646.

40. See Tumani Mutasa Nyajeka, *The Meeting of Two Female Worlds: American Women Missionaries and Shona Women at Old Mutare and the Founding of Rukwadzano* (Ph.D. diss., Northwestern University, 1996).

41. Family breakup was particularly bad in South Africa. See Jacklyn Cock, *Madams and Maids: Domestic Workers under Apartheid* (London: Women's Press, 1989). For general economic distortion due to colonization, see Walter Rodney, *How Europe Underdeveloped Africa* (Nairobi: Heinemann, 1972).

42. See Adrian Hastings, *A History of African Christianity, 1950–1975* (Cambridge: Cambridge University Press, 1979), 67–85.

43. See H. W. Turner, *African Independent Church* (Oxford: Oxford University Press, 1967), 2 vols. Also J. Akinyele Omoyajowo, *Cherubim and Seraphim: The History of an African Independent Church* (New York: NOK, 1982).

44. See Rosalind Hackett, "Women as Leaders and Participants in Spiritual Churches," in *New Religious Movements in Nigeria*, R. Hackett, ed. (Lewiston, N.Y.: Edwin Mellen Press, 1987), 191–208; also Helen Callaway, "Women in Yoruba Tradition and in the Cherubim and Seraphim Society," in O. U. Kalu, *The History of Christianity in West Africa* (London: Longmans, 1980), 321–32; and Cynthia Hoehler-Fatton, *Women of Fire and Spirit: History, Faith and Gender in Roho Religion in West Kenya* (New York: Oxford University Press, 1996).

45. J. Akinyele Omoyajowo, *The Cherubim and Seraphim in Relation to Church and State* (Ibadan, Nigeria: Claveriarum Press, 1975).

46. See Mercy Amba Oduyoye, *Daughters of Anowa: African Women and Patriarchy* (Maryknoll, N.Y.: Orbis, 1995), 123–30. Also see Brigid Maa Sackey, *Women, Spiritual Churches and Politics in Ghana* (Ph.D. diss., Temple University, 1996).

47. David Birmingham, *The Decolonization of Africa* (Athens: Ohio University Press, 1995).

48. John Mbiti, *African Religion and Philosophy* (London: Heinemann, 1969).

49. E. Bojaji Idowu, *Olodumare: God in Yoruba Belief* (London: Longmanns, 1962).

50. Emmanuel Martey, *African Theology: Inculturation and Liberation* (Maryknoll, N.Y.: Orbis, 1993), 63–85.

51. Ibid., 95–114.

52. Allan Boesak, *Farewell to Innocence: A Socio-Ethical Study of Black Theology and Power* (Maryknoll, N.Y.: Orbis, 1986).

53. See John Mbiti, "An African Views American Black Theology," also Desmond M. Tutu, "Black Theology/African Theology: Soul Mates or Antagonists?" in James H. Cone and Gayraud S. Wilmore, Eds., *Black Theology: A Documentary History, vol. 1: 1966–79*, (Maryknoll, N.Y.: Orbis, 1993) 379–92.

54. For an example of a paternalistic view of African women in traditional religion, see John Mbiti, "Flowers in the Garden: Women in African Religion," in Jacob K. Olupona, *African Traditional Religion in Contemporary Society* (New York: Paragon House, 1991), 59–71. See the critique of Mbiti by Mercy Amba Oduyoye in *Religious Plurality in Africa*, Jacob K. Olupona and Sulayman S. Nyanga, eds. (New York: Mouten de Gruyter, 1993), 341–65.

55. See Martey, *African Theology*, 121–36.

56. The writings of these African women theologians are found particularly in the book *The Will to Arise*; also see the section on Africa in *With Passion and Compassion*, as well as collections of African theology, Third World theology, and Third World women's theology; see, for example, Mercy Amba Oduyoye's article "Liberation and Development of Theology in Africa," in Marc Reuver, et al., ed., *The Ecumenical Movement Tomorrow* (Kampen, Netherlands: Kok, 1993), 203–210.

57. See notes 38 and 46 of this chapter.

58. This principle is stated or assumed throughout *The Will to Arise*; see also Mercy Amba Oduyoye, "The Spirituality of Resistance and Reconstruction," in *Women Resisting Violence*, 166–70.

59. Oduyoye, *Daughters of Anowa*, 40–42, 120–23; also Elizabeth Amoah, "Femaleness: Akan Concepts and Practices," in Jeanne Becker, *Women, Religion and Sexuality: The Impact of Religious Teachings on Women* (Geneva: World Council of Churches, 1990), 129–53.

60. Mercy Amba Oduyoye, "Women and Ritual in Africa," in *The Will to Arise*, 14.

61. See Rosemary Edet, "Christianity and African Women's Rituals," in *The Will to Arise*, 31–32.

62. Oduyoye, "The Spirituality of Resistance and Reconstruction," in

*Women Resisting Violence*, 167.

63. See, for example, Anne Nachisale Musople's article, "Sexuality and Religion in a Matriarchal Society," in *The Will to Arise*, where Malawian matrilinial societies are described as both empowering and overworking women:

> In the villages, both men and women wake up early in the morning and go to the farm to till the ground. At daybreak both men and women come home, but the woman carries a bundle of firewood on her head. She carries two hoes in her hand and a baby at hr back. The man just walks home with nothing in his hands. When they reach home, the man sits down to rest, while the woman makes fire and cooks food for the day. After eating, the man either sleeps or goes to drink beer at the nearby village. The woman never rests, but looks for food for the rest of the day. The men do not give the women money to buy the food. The woman is the primary source of nourishment and nurture. (p.106)

64. Oduyoye, *Daughters of Anowa*, 183.

65. Ephraim Mosothoane of the Department of Religion and Biblical Studies of the University of the Transkei (UNITA), Umtata, South Africa, told me when I visited there in 1990 that the African traditional initiation rites taught girls how to do sexual play without penetration and impregnation. The missionaries repressed these initiation rites, with the result that teenage pregnancy became common.

66. Oduyoye, "Spirituality of Resistance and Reconstruction," in *Women Resisting Violence*, 167–68.

67. Ibid., 170.

68. See Therese Souga, "The Christ Event from the Viewpoint of African Women: A Catholic Perspective," and Louise Tappa, "A Protestant Perspective," in *With Passion and Compassion*, 22–46.

69. See Elizabeth Amoah and Mercy Oduyoye, "The Christ for African Women," ibid., 47–59; and Teresia Hinga, "Jesus Christ and the Liberation of Women in Africa," in *The Will to Arise*, 183–94.

70. According to the 1996 *World Almanac*, the population of Asia is 3.247 billion, or about 56 percent of the population of the world. The seven major linguistic zones of Asia are Semitic, Ural–Altaic, Indo–Iranian, Dravidian, Sino-Tibetan, Malayo-Polynesian, and Japanese. This does not include hundreds of tribal languages spoken in the region.

71. The Christian population is about 95 percent of the Filipino population. Another 5 percent is Muslim. South Korea is about 40 percent Christian, including Protestants and Catholics.

72. The feminist theologians at Madras, India (December 14–21, 1990), were from the Philippines, Korea, India, Hong Kong, Taiwan, Malaysia, Indonesia, and Sri Lanka. Only the Filipino paper has been published: "Toward and Asian Principle of Interpretation: A Filipina Women's Experience" (Manila: Women's Institute Press, 1991), authored collectively by Rosario Battung, Virginia Fabella, Arche Ligo, Mary John Mananzan, and Elizabeth Tapia. I have unfinished typescripts of two other papers: "The Critical Hermeneutical Principles of Korean Women Theologians," by Yang, Mi Gang and Kim, Jeang Soo, Chung Hyun Kyung and Lee-Park, Sun Ai; and "Breaking the Silence: Indian Women in Search of Hermeneutical Principles," authors not identified.

73. See Feliciano V. Carino, *Religion and Society: Towards a Theology of Struggle* (Manila: Forum for Inter-disciplinary Endeavors and Studies, 1988).

74. See Commission on Theological Concerns: Christian Conference of Asia, ed., *Minjung Theology: People as the Subjects of History* (Maryknoll, N.Y.: Orbis, 1983).

75. The leading Indian liberation theologian is Samuel Ryan, S.J. Aloysius Pieris of Sri Lanka has done the major work on inculturation and liberation theology in a Buddhist worldview: see his *An Asian Theology of Liberation* (Maryknoll, N.Y.: Orbis, 1988).

76. See J. S. Woodroffe, *Sakti and Shakta* (Madras: Vedanta Press, 1951). The Indian women's hermeneutical paper makes Shakti the key symbol for women's empowerment in the Indian culture.

77. Korean feminist theologian Chung Hyun Kyung has particularly drawn on shamanism for her feminist theology: see her "Han-pu-re: Doing Theology from Korean Woman's Perspective," in *We Dare to Dream: Doing Theology as Asian Women,* Virginia Fabella and Sun Ai Lee-Park, eds. (Maryknoll, N.Y.: Orbis, 1990), 135–46.

78. See V. Devashayam, ed., *Dalits and Women: Quest for Humanity* (Madras: Gurukul Lutheran Theological College, 1992).

79. From the Indian paper "Breaking Silence," 5–6.

80. The 1990 issue of the Asian women's theological journal *In God's Image* was devoted to the theme of reunification.

81. See Chung Hyun Kyung, "Your Comfort vs. My Death," in *Women Resist-*

*ing Violence*, 129–40.

82. See Rita Nakashima Brock and Susan Brooks Thistlethwaite, *Casting Stones: Prostitution and Liberation in Asia and the United States* (Minneapolis: Fortress, 1996), 191–201.

83. See "Toward an Asian Principle of Interpretation," 17.

84. Ibid., 18–20.

85. See Kwok Pui-Lan, "Chinese Non-Christian Perceptions of Christ," in *Any Room for Christ in Asia?* Leonardo Boff and Virgil Elizaondo, eds. (Maryknoll, N.Y.: Orbis, 1993), 25–26.

86. This Asian perception of Jesus as one suffering from bad karma comes from a discussion with Chung Hyun Kyung at Union Theological Seminary in New York City, November 13, 1996.

87. Kwok Pui-Lan, "Chinese Non-Christian Perceptions of Christ," 26–27.

88. Ibid., 30–31.

89. See Aloysius Pieris, "Does Christ Have Any Place in Asia? A Panoramic View," in *Any Room for Christ in Asia/*, 37–42.

90. See Virginia Fabella, "Christology from an Asian Women's Perspective," in *We Dare to Dream: Doing Theology as Asian Women* (Maryknoll, N.Y.: Orbis, 1990), 3–14.

91. London: Zed, 1989.

92. See Aruna Gnanadason, "Toward a Feminist Eco-Theology for India," in *Women Healing Earth*, Rosemary R. Ruether, 75–76.

93. Rita Shema, *The Reenvisioning of Shakta-Tantra as a Foundation for a Hindu Ecofeminist Philosophy* (Master's thesis; Women and Religion Program of the Claremont Graduate School, Claremont, Calif.; June, 1997).

94. *Minjung Theology*, 55–69.

95. Ibid.

96. Chung Hyun Kyung, "Han-pu-re: Doing Theology from Korean Women's Perspective," 139–42.

97. Ibid., 143.

98. Ibid., 143-44.

99. Ibid., 144.

100. Chung Hyun Kyung, *Struggle to Be the Sun Again: Introducing Asian Women's Theology* (Maryknoll, N.Y.: Orbis, 1990) 111–13.

101. Chung Hyun Kyung, "Come Holy Spirit: Renew the Whole Creation:

An Introduction to the Theological Theme," at Seventh Assembly of World Council of Churches, Canberra, Australia, February 8, 1991; from a typescript of the talk.

102. The video of Chung Hyun Kyung's presentation at the Seventh Assembly of the World Council of Churches in Canberra is available from Lou Niznik, 15726 Ashland Drive, Laurel, MD 20707.

## Conclusions

1. Elisabeth Schüssler Fiorenza, "Ties That Bind: Domestic Violence against Women," in *Women Resisting Violence: Spirituality for Life,* Mary John Mananzan et al., eds. (Maryknoll, N.Y.: Orbis, 1996), 43.

2. Mary Daly, *Beyond God the Father: Toward a Philosophy of Women's Liberation* (Boston: Beacon, 1973), 73.

3. Rosemary R. Ruether, "Can Christology Be Liberated from Patriarchy?" in *Reconstructing the Christ Symbol: Essays in Feminist Christology,* Maryanne Stevens, ed. (New York: Paulist Press, 1993), 7–29.

4. Elizabeth Amoah and Mercy Amba Oduyoye, "The Christ for African Women," in *With Passion and Compassion: Third World Women Doing Theology,* Virginia Fabella and Mercy Amba Oduyoye, eds. (Maryknoll, N.Y.: Orbis, 1988), 35–36.

5. The theory of development of doctrine was proposed particularly by Cardinal John Henry Newman. It is the key theme for the relation of Scripture and tradition for Catholic feminist theologian Kari Elisabeth Børresen, who sets this view over against the Protestant view of return to the Bible: see chapter 6 above.

# Index


Abel, 27, 85, 89, 99, 155
abolitionist feminists, 160–77
abortion, 190, 236, 238
Abraham, 83, 155, 232
abstinence from sex. *See* Celibacy
Adam, 24–29, 46, 56, 57, 72–73, 74, 83, 88, 89, 91, 95, 99, 100, 103, 107, 108, 117, 118, 119, 121, 122, 123, 124, 129, 131, 132, 137, 138, 149, 150, 153, 154, 155, 156, 169, 170, 175, 181, 186
Adams, Abigail, 160
Adams, John, 160
African liberation theology, 258, 259
African American denominational churches, 234
Agrippa, Cornelius, 129, 130, 131, 132, 133
Albigensians, 156
Alethians, 159
Alexander, 42
Allende, Salvador, 241
Alliance of Women for Peace, 159
Ambroasiaster, 191
Ambrose, 70
American Anti-Slavery Society, 162
Amoah, Elizabeth, 259, 278
Anabaptists, 156
angels, 27, 28, 33, 34, 36, 49, 61, 89, 90, 91
Anna, 129
Anthony, Saint, 63
Anthony, Susan B., 7, 166, 168, 169, 173, 174, 209, 220
anthropology of gender, 9–10, 24, 88
of Luther and Calvin, 117–26
Antichrist, 83, 91, 99, 156
apartheid, 254, 257, 258
Apollos, 31–32, 33
Aquila, 32
Aquino, María Pilar, 248–49, 250
Arch Street Society, 161
Aristotle, 92, 94
asceticism, 62, 63, 64, 65, 66, 67, 69, 70, 79, 102
Astell, Mary, 134–35
Athanasius, 63
Augustine, 4, 5, 51, 62, 69–76, 94, 95, 100, 191

Bahemuka, Judith Mbula, 259
baptism, 14, 16, 47, 48, 54, 56, 70, 169
theology of, 2–3, 29–30, 31, 36, 37, 39
Barbarossa, Frederick, 87
Barth, Karl, 179, 180, 181, 182, 183, 184
Basil, 191
Basil the Great, 62, 65, 66
Bathhurst, Elizabeth, 137
Beecher, Catherine, 162, 165
Beelzebul, 18. *See also* Satan
Beguines, 98, 100
Bernard of Clairvaux, 87
Beya, Bernadette Mbuy, 259
Bird, Phyllis, 25
birth, 66, 67, 73, 260. *See also* Childbear-

ing; Sex and procreation
birth control. *See* Contraception
Black Consciousness Movement, 258
black theology, 231, 232, 233, 258
blacks, 162, 232, 233, 234
equal rights for, 163
slavery of, 7, 160–77, 231. *See also* Abolitionist feminists
Boehme, Jacob, 148
Boesak, Allan, 258
Boff, Leonardo, 246
Bonhoeffer, Dietrich, 180
Børresen, Kari Elisabeth, 190–93
bride of Christ, 140, 141, 153
Brock, Rita Nakashima, 211
Buber, Martin, 181
Bultmann, Rudolf, 179, 180, 183, 184
Bushnell, Horace, 176

Caesar, 22
Cain, 27
Calvin, John, 4, 122–26
Camisards, 148
Cary, Mary, 136
Catherine de Medici, 114
Catherine of Siena, 93
Catholicism, 75, 190, 194, 216, 221, 235, 238, 244
*See also* Feminist theologies, and Catholicism
Cavendish, Margaret, 133
celibacy, 4, 5, 22, 29, 30, 31, 32, 34–35, 39, 41, 54, 56, 62, 64, 67, 71, 92, 113, 117, 120, 149, 150, 151, 156, 158
Charles, King of England, 136
Charles IX, 114
chastity, 67, 92, 98. *See also* Celibacy
Chenu, Marie-Dominique, 190
Chevers, Sarah, 142
child brides, 264
childbearing, 40, 68, 79, 96, 118, 119, 120, 121, 261. *See also* Birth; Sex and procreation
Chloe, 32
Chrysostom, John, 122, 191
Chung Hyun Kyung, 269, 270, 271, 272, 280
Circle of Concerned African Women Theologians, 254
Clement, 58, 59–60, 66, 74, 191
clitoridectomy, 255
Cole, Mary, 140
colonialism, 249, 251, 255, 261
comfort women. *See* Prostitution
Confucianism, 270
Congar, Yves, 190
continence, 59, 60, 70, 76. *See also* Celibacy
contraception, 190, 236, 238
Copernicus, 193
Corinth, Corinthians, 31–38
Cotton, Priscilla, 140
creation of humans, 2, 3, 24–29, 117, 131, 132, 137–38, 156
*See also* Adam; Eve

Dalits, 266
Daly, Mary, 205, 210, 211, 215–21, 222, 223, 224, 276
Darwin, Charles, 193
Davies, Lady Eleanor, 135
De Meung, Jean, 127
De Pizan, Christine, 127
Declaration of Sentiments, 168
Declaration of Independence, 160
Demiurgos, 55
demonarchy, 234
devil. *See* Satan
divorce, 238
Donatism, Donatists, 71, 75
Douglas, Mary, 33
Douglass, Sarah, 167
dowry deaths, 265
Dunlavy, John, 150–51

Ecclesia, 91, 92

ecofeminism, 267
Ecumenical Association of Third World Theologians (EATWOT), 241, 242, 243
Edet, Rosemary, 259
Egeria, 79
Ekeya, Bette, 259
Eku, 278–79
Elizabeth of Schönau, 84, 85
Emmelda, 64
English Civil War, 135, 136
Erasmus, 116
Essenes, 15, 46
Esther, 139
Eudocia, 79
Eugenius III, 87
Eustochium, 64
Eve, 26–29, 55, 56, 57, 72–73, 77, 83, 88, 89, 90, 91, 92, 95, 99, 100–101, 103, 107, 117, 118, 119, 120, 121, 122, 123, 124, 128, 129, 130, 131, 132, 137, 138, 149, 150, 153, 154, 155, 156, 169, 170, 186, 187

Fabella, Virginia, 241
fall, the, 3, 4, 26–29, 66, 68, 72, 74, 75, 83, 84, 91, 95, 96, 99, 101, 108, 117, 119, 120, 122,123, 124, 129, 131, 138, 154, 155, 156, 157, 164, 169, 170, 175
fasting. *See* Asceticism
Felicitas, 53
Fell, Margaret, 137, 138, 139, 140, 141, 143
Fell, Sarah, 143
Fell, Thomas, 137
female feticide, 265
female metaphors for God. *See* God, gender symbolism for
female silencing. *See* Women, and speaking in the church
feminist theologies
  and Catholicism, 190–202
  and German Protestantism, 179–89
  contemporary Christian, 7
  ecological liberation theology, 224
  European in the 1990s, 202–7
  in Africa, 254–62
  in Asia, 262–72
  in Latin America, 245–54
  Korean, 270
  liberation, 214, 225, 239, 247, 250, 253
  Renaissance, 127
  Third World, 242, 243
Filipino Theology of Struggle, 263
Finney, Charles Grandison, 174
Fiorenza, Elisabeth Schüssler, 211, 274
First World–Third World issues, 198, 242
Fox, George, 136, 137

Gabriela, 244
Gage, Matilda Joslyn, 173, 176
Garrison, William Lloyd, 161, 167
Gebara, Ivone, 242, 245, 250–54, 274
gender and redemption
  in second-century Christianities, 51–62
  in the first Jesus movement, 14–21
  in the Hellenistic world, 21–24
  in the patristic era, 45–77
  *See also* Gender hierarchy
gender anthropology. *See* Anthropology of gender
gender hierarchy
  in creation, 36, 72
  in the church, 9, 30–43, 90
  in the family, 25, 39, 40, 41, 90, 117
  in heaven, 77
  in society, 8
gender identities, 228
Genesis, Jewish and early Christian readings of, 24–30
Gnanadason, Aruna, 243, 268
gnosticism, 49
God, gender symbolism for, 5, 152

Gospel Order of the Millennial Church of Christ's Kingdom, 150
Gossman, Elizabeth, 179
Green, Calvin, 151
Green Revolution, 267
Gregory Nazianzus, 191
Gregory of Nyssa, 3, 51, 64, 65–69, 71, 74, 79, 80, 62
Grey, Mary, 190, 198–202
Grimké, Angelina, 6, 7, 160, 161, 162, 163, 165, 166, 167, 171, 173, 174
Grimké, Sarah, 6, 7, 160, 161, 162, 163, 164, 165, 166, 167, 171, 173, 174
Gutiérrez, Gustavo, 241

Hagar, 232, 233
Halkes, Catharina, 190, 193–98, 202
han, 269–70
*han-pu-re*, 270, 271
Hannah, 139
Hapsburgs, 114
head coverings. *See* Women, and head coverings
heavenly state, 5
Heinrich of Halle, 98, 103
Heinrich, archbishop of Mainz, 87
Heracleon, 55
Heyward, Carter, 210, 224–29, 239
Hicksites, 161, 167
Hildegard of Bingen, 81–92, 97, 98, 99, 105, 192
Hindu castims, 264
Hinga, Teresia, 259
Holocaust, 182, 184
homosexuals, 203
Hrotsvit, 80
Hulda, 139

Idowu, E. Bojaji, 257
image of God, 24–25, 26, 27, 28, 61, 66, 72, 77, 79, 97, 104, 109, 118, 121, 122, 126, 129, 132, 138, 141, 157, 163, 169, 174, 175, 192, 193, 196, 197, 238 , 275
    *See also* Creation of humans
incest, 265
Irenaeus, 50, 53, 58, 59, 74
Irigaray, Luce, 202
Isabella Clara Eugenia, 114
Isabella of Castile, 114
Isasi-Díaz, Ada María, 210, 234–39

James, 45
Jeremiah, 140
Jerome, 63, 64, 71
Jesus
    Asians' perception of, 266–67
    crucifixion of, 20, 102, 105, 234
    identified with Wisdom or Logos, 46, 47, 58, 59, 60, 61, 66, 111, 129, 157, 199
    maternal aspects of, 110
    metaphors for, 152, 278
    resurrection of, 129
    story, 276, 277, 278
Jesus movement, the first, 14–21
Joan of Arc, 81
Joanna, 139
John the Baptist, 14, 15, 16, 32
Johnson, Adelaide, 209
Jones, Sarah, 141
Judaism. *See* Temple Judaism
Judas the Galilean, 15
Judith, 139
Julian of Norwich, 5, 104–11, 192, 193
Julian of Eclanum, 72
Justin, 54
Jutta of Sponheim, 81, 82, 87

Kanyoro, Musimbi, 259
Katoppo, Marianne, 241, 242
Killam, Margaret, 142
kingdom of God. *See* Reign of God
Knox, John, 114
Kraemer, Heinrich, 127
Kuno, 87
Kwan In, 272

Lead, Jane, 148
Lee, Ann, 148, 149, 150, 151, 152, 153, 154, 156, 157, 158, 159
Lee, William, 149
lesbians, 203, 206, 227–28, 239
Levi, 57
liberation, total, 212, 213
liturgizing, 235
Logos. *See* Jesus, identified with Wisdom or Logos
Lord's Supper, 36–37
Love, 90, 92
Lucifer, 83, 88, 89. *See also* Satan
lust, 28, 35, 66, 67, 71, 73, 88, 89, 95, 96, 117, 118, 120, 123, 149, 151, 154, 155
Luther, Martin, 4, 116, 117–22, 124, 127, 180

Mack, Phyllis, 136, 141
Macrina, 64–65, 68, 69, 71, 79
male liberation theologians, 245, 246, 263
Mananzan, Mary John, 241, 244
Manicheanism, Manicheans, 70, 71, 72, 75
Marcella, 63, 64, 71, 79
Marcion, Marcionism, 54–55, 58, 156
Marcus, 55
Margaret of Austria, 114
Margaret of Parma, 114
Margery of Kempe, 105
Mariology, 192
marriage, 2, 3, 32, 35, 40, 42, 57, 59, 60, 62, 63, 66, 67, 72, 75, 76, 117, 120, 123, 144, 172, 236, 238
Martha, 139
Mary, mother of Jesus, 16, 57, 83, 89, 90, 91, 92, 96, 99, 100, 116, 129, 153, 159, 245
Mary, sister of Martha, 139
Mary Magdalene, 57–58, 139, 245
Mary of Hungary, 114
Mary Queen of Scots, 114, 115
Maximilla, 52, 53
Mbiti, John, 257, 258
McFague, Sallie, 210
Meacham, Joseph, 150, 152, 153, 158
Mechthild of Magdeburg, 93, 97–104, 105
Melania the Elder, 63, 71, 79
Melania the Younger, 63, 71, 79
menstruation, 101
  taboos, 260
*mestizaje/mulatex*, 237, 238
metanoia, 271
Methodist revival movement, 148, 149
minjung theology, 244, 263, 264, 266, 269, 270
*minnesinger* poetry, 100, 101
Miriam, 139
misogyny, 127, 128, 133
missionaries, 256, 257
Moltmann, Jürgen, 212
monasticism, 62–66
Monica, 71
Montanism, Montanists, 51–53, 62, 278
Montanus, 52, 53
More, Thomas, 116
Mosala, Itumeleng, 258
Moses, 83, 155
Mott, James, 167
Mott, Lucretia, 6, 7, 161, 166, 166–73, 175, 209
*mujerista* theology, 235, 236, 237, 238, 239, 276
Munda, Constantia, 131
music, 91
Musopole, Anne Nachisale, 259
mutuality, 214, 215, 223, 224, 225, 226, 227
mysticism. *See* Sapiental mysticism

Nasimuyu-Waskike, Anne, 259
National-American Women's Suffrage Association, 174
Naucratius, 65

Nazism, 180, 182, 186, 205
Negroes. *See* Blacks
Nephilim, 27–28
New Creation, 212, 213, 215, 223
New Light Baptists, 149, 150
New Prophecy, 51–52
Newman, Barbara, 100
Noah, 83, 89, 155
Norris, John, 134
nuns, 92, 93, 98, 116
Nwachuku, Daisy, 259

Oduyoye, Mercy Amba, 241, 259, 278, 279, 281
Okure, Teresa, 259
Origen, 58, 60–62, 63, 66, 74, 100
Owanikin, R. Modupe, 259

Park, Sun Ai, 241, 244
partnership, 214
patriarchy. *See* Gender hierarchy
Paul, 2, 3, 13, 22, 23, 30–43, 54, 73, 85, 99, 122, 124, 126, 130, 140, 157, 164, 165, 175
  teaching on gender roles, 30–43
Paula, granddaughter of Paula, daughter of Toxotius, 64, 79
Paula, mother of Eustochium and Toxotius, 64, 71, 79
Pelagianism, Pelagians, 71
Pelagius, 75
Perkins, William, 128
Perpetua, 53, 79
Peter, 57, 130, 153
Peter, brother of Macrina, 64
Philadelphia Female Anti-Slavery Society, 167
Philadelphians, 148
Philip, 121, 129
Philip, Dean, 93
Philo, 29, 31, 66
Phiri, Isabel, 259
Phoebe, 32
Pinian, 64, 71
Pirckheimer, Caritas, 113
Plato, 66
Pleroma, 55, 69
polygamy, 255, 257, 260
poor, the, 47, 144, 222, 251
  Jesus and, 18
Priscilla, 32, 52, 129
Priscillian, 156
Proba, 79
procreation. *See* Sex and procreation
prostitution, 238, 265
Ptolemaeus, 55

Quakers, 5, 6, 134–45, 148, 160, 161, 167, 169, 172, 273

rape, 265
reign of God, Jesus' teaching on, 19–20, 21
Reimarus, Herman, 180
religious laws, 17–18
  *See also* Paul, teaching on gender roles; Temple Judaism
resurrection, theology of, 38, 68, 76
Richard, Pablo, 246, 247
Ruether, Rosemary Radford, 221–24
Rufinus, 63, 71
Russell, Letty, 210, 211–15, 220, 222, 223
Ruth, 139

Saint, Disibod, 81, 82, 87, 93
Salic Law, 114
Salome, 23
salvation, 47, 48, 77
Sancroft, William, 134
sapiental mysticism, 46, 47
Sarai, 232, 233
Satan, 15, 16, 18, 41, 46, 52, 83, 89, 91, 99, 119, 128, 138, 156, 187
  *See also* Antichrist, Beelzebul, Lucifer, Serpent

Schleiermacher, Friedrich, 180, 181, 184
*Scivias*, 82, 83
Scot, Reginald, 128
serpent, 26, 56, 138–39, 154, 254
*See also* Satan
sex and procreation, 4, 66, 67, 73, 76, 117, 119, 141, 155
sex tourism, 265
sexual continence. *See* Continence
sexual initiation practices, 261
Shaker Bible. *See The Testimony of Christ's Second Appearing*
Shakers, 147–59, 278
Shakti, 264, 267, 268
shamanism, 257, 264, 270
Sharpe, Joane, 131
Shaw, Anna Howard, 173, 176
Shema, Rita, 268
Shiva, Vandana, 267, 268
Silva, Silvia Regina, 246
slaves, slavery, 7, 30, 31, 38, 39, 40, 49, 57, 75, 145, 160, 231
abolition of, 160–77
in the Hellenistic world, 22
*See also* Abolitionist feminists; Blacks
snools, 218, 219, 220
Society of Friends. *See* Quakers
Society of New Lebanon, 150, 159
Soelle, Dorothee, 182–89
Sophia (Wisdom), 55, 57, 199, 200, 201, 202
Sowernam, Ester, 131, 132, 133, 138
speaking in tongues, 37
Speght, Rachel, 131, 138
Spirit Churches, 261
Sprenger, Jacob, 127
Stanley, Abraham, 149
Stanton, Elizabeth Cady, 7, 166, 168, 169, 173, 174, 175, 176, 209, 210
storytelling, 235
suffrage, 173, 174, 175, 209
Swetnam, Joseph, 131, 132
Tamez, Elsa, 242, 246, 247, 248, 250, 280
Tarango, Yolanda, 235
temple Judaism, 15–18
Tertullian, 50, 53, 58, 59
*Testimony of Christ's Second Appearing, The*, 151, 153, 154, 156
Thamyris, 42
Thecla, 42, 64
Theocleia, 42
theodicy, 107. *See also* Fall, the
Theodotus, 55
Theosebia, 67
Thomas Aquinas, 4, 5, 92–97, 191
Thompson, George, 161
Tillich, Paul, 179, 180
tongues, speaking in. *See* Speaking in tongues
Torah, 15, 16
*See also* Temple Judaism
Torres, Sergio, 241
Toxotius, 64
Travers, Rebecca, 137
Trible, Phyllis, 211
Tryphaena, Queen, 42
Tudor, Elizabeth, 114, 115
Tudor, Mary, 114, 115
Tutu, Desmond, 258

Universal Peace Union, 159

Valentinianism, 55–58
Valentinius, 55, 58
Virgil, 79
virginity, 3, 4, 29, 67, 72, 76, 92
Volmar, 82, 87
Von Nettesheim, Agrippa, 5, 6, 122, 273
Von Stade, Richardis, 82

Waldensians, 156
Wardley, James, 148
Wardley, Jane, 148
Wardley Society, 148, 149

Weld, Theodore, 162, 163, 166
White, Anna, 159
White, Dorothy, 137
Whitefield, George, 148
Whittaker, James, 150
Whore of Babylon, 140, 141
widow burning, 264, 265
widowhood rituals, 260
wife battering, 265
Wilkins, Rich, 134
Willard, Frances, 173, 176
Williams, Delores, 210, 229–34, 239, 279
Wisdom, 90, 92. *See also* Jesus, identified with Wisdom or Logos; Sophia
witch hunting, 127, 133, 143
witchcraft, 127, 128
Wollstonecraft, Mary, 6, 167
womanism, 230
women,
  African American, 230, 233, 234. *See also* Blacks
  and head coverings, 36, 37
  and leadership in the church, 6, 125
  and speaking in the church, 7, 125, 126, 136, 139, 140, 172, 175
  Hispanic, 235, 236, 237, 238, 239
  ordination of, 190, 202, 210
  publishing by, 116
  support of themselves, 115
  Third World, 212
  visionaries, 136
*Women's Bible, The*, 174, 175
women's rights, 173
Womenchurch, 201, 204
Woolman, John, 161
World Anti-Slavery Convention, 168
Wright, Frances, 160
Wright, Lucy, 150

Youngs, Benjamin Seth, 151, 155, 157

Zell, Catherine, 113
Zell, Matthew, 113